WAR and DEFEAT

– The Jesus Army and Fellowship Revisited

By John Everett

Grosvenor House
Publishing Limited

The right of John Everett to be identified as the author of this
work has been asserted in accordance with Section 78
of the Copyright, Designs and Patents Act 1988

The book cover is copyright to John Everett

This book is published by
Grosvenor House Publishing Ltd
Link House
140 The Broadway, Tolworth, Surrey, KT6 7HT.
www.grosvenorhousepublishing.co.uk

A CIP record for this book
is available from the British Library

Paperback ISBN 978-1-80381-987-7
Hardback ISBN 978-1-80381-988-4

Contents

Foreword

Anyone who looks into the story of the Jesus Army and its eventual collapse will be struck by the immense courage of former members such as John and the efforts they have gone to in order to expose the truth of what was happening within the organisation. It takes great strength of character to take a stand against a much more powerful adversary, and it often comes at great personal cost.

Many people will have heard of the Jesus Army and may be dimly aware that it collapsed following an abuse scandal. From the late 1970s to the early 1990s accusations swirled around about the Jesus Fellowship being a cult. Thanks in part to John's efforts at documenting his own experiences within the Fellowship, concerns about some of the practices, such as the corporal punishment of children and an excessive emphasis on celibacy, led to their exclusion from the Evangelical Alliance in 1986. However, far from dying away the Jesus Fellowship went on to become the Jesus Army and continued its exponential growth curve.

Maybe society preferred to believe the Holy Spirit really was at work in Bugbrooke? Or perhaps that it was convenient not to question it too much knowing that the Jesus Army provided help for the vulnerable in society? Or perhaps there was an assumption they were an essentially harmless, if eccentric, religious sect – a familiar sight on the streets of 80's Britain with their Jesus Army buses, the unwitting butt of jokes on late-night talk shows?

But the truth of what was happening to women and children in their community homes is now unquestionable. Figures from the recent redress scheme paint a stark story. Over 800 applications for compensation have been received. One in six children brought up in its community homes are thought to have been sexually abused. Over 500 alleged perpetrators of physical, sexual and emotional abuse have been identified, 162 of them elders within the community. These include the Jesus Army's controversial leader, Noel Stanton, who died in 2009; but who, following recent and historic allegations, has now been accused of the sexual abuse of children. But this is more than just an abuse story. Whether or not you call them a cult, the Jesus Fellowship was undoubtedly under the sway of Noel Stanton and used coercive control in order to keep its members in thrall. People who stood up to Noel would be excommunicated (as John was).

Women who complained about abuse were branded Jezebels. Members were terrified into silence by the fear of damnation.

But it is important to remember too that many good people joined the Jesus Army; that within its ranks there were men and women like John, devoted to helping their fellow man; that it wasn't all black and white — the good was mixed in with the bad.

Some of the many documentaries made about the Jesus Army show the heady early days, the fervour of the evangelical worship, the inspiring vision of trying to live like the early Christians, growing food and sharing everything in common — something which was guaranteed to appeal to the 'good life' generation of the 1970s. One can see how timely were moves to tackle homelessness and help the vulnerable as the Jesus Army took to the streets in the 1980s. One can even admire the audacity of trying to appeal to disaffected youth in the 1990s and 2000s using rave culture to spread their message.

Perhaps, ultimately, this was the reason the Jesus Army existed for 50 years: because society wanted to believe the Holy Spirit really was at work; because the gloss of evangelical enthusiasm and doing good work blinded everyone to the reality of what was going on. And it is thanks to the unstinting efforts of survivors, people like John, who have doggedly, determinedly continued their attempts to get their stories heard and achieve justice, that it can now harm people no longer. Society owes John and other survivors a big debt.

Katie Buchanan. Co-founder and director, Big Sister Films

Glossary

Abbreviations and names associated with or sometimes
used as alternatives for "Jesus Army"

Bugbrooke – a village about 5 miles from Northampton. The location of the Baptist chapel where the Jesus Fellowship movement began; also the home to quite a number of the New Creation Christian Community households.

Quite often the single word "Bugbrooke" has been used as short-hand – a kind of commonly used name – for the whole organization.

JFC: Jesus Fellowship Church – the inclusive official (legal) name for the whole church with its different levels of membership. Originally, it was Jesus Fellowship Church (Baptist).

The Bugbrooke Church – a colloquial reference to the JFC above.

NCCC: The New Creation Christian Community – The official collective name for all the different households which operate within the community structure of the church.

JA: The Jesus Army – the name chosen in 1987 by the JFC to represent its outward-looking, outreach/evangelistic face. "The JA" has often been used by many since then as a shorthand name for the whole of the JFC.

The Modern Jesus Army – the rebranded name of the Jesus Army.

Jesus People – an adopted name used in outreach/evangelism by the JA.

The Multiply Christian Network – then name chosen by the JFC for loose affiliations established with other Christian fellowships "of like mind".

JFC Trusts, Charities and Businesses

JACT: The Jesus Army Charitable Trust – The main registered charity.

Heartcry – working name for JACT.

Jesus Fellowship Life Trust – a smaller registered charity.

Jesus Fellowship Community Trust – the main "umbrella" members' trust responsible for holding and administrating the collective wealth of the JFC.

Jesus Fellowship Housing Association Ltd. – the association responsible for tenancy arrangements within the NCCC households.

HOG or HOG Ltd: House of Goodness Ltd. – the holding company for the other JFC businesses. These include:

Skaino Services – a building firm.

Goodness Foods – a chain of health-food shops.

TBS: Towcester Building Supplies – Builders Merchants located in various towns.

Heritage Design – an architectural firm.

Community Precepts – an "antescript" postscript.

I must have been about three-quarters of my way through writing this book before I was given a document called "New Creation Christian Community Precepts". It had been issued by "Noel and Mike" – Noel Stanton and, presumably, Mick Haines, his successor – in November 1991. This was the first time I'd even heard of such a document, let alone seen it. These precepts are of immense significance: they set out in black and white many of the strictures and prohibitions which Community leaders have frequently dismissed – to "outsiders" – as fabrications and lies.

I have chosen not to try and incorporate these precepts before chapter twenty-eight of the book and have therefore left the preceding chapters exactly as written before the precepts came to my attention. I think this will have a more powerful impression on my readers as they evaluate my testimony against the content of the indisputable evidence reproduced below. It's possible, I suppose, that some may imagine I've just made up the following "rules". So be it. I cannot, unfortunately, show them to you in person; but there will now be hundreds of ex-members who will, with something of a shudder, corroborate their authenticity.

Please take just a few moments to read through these precepts before heading off to Chapter One. You will find them revelatory, and they will remain with you as a frame of reference throughout the rest of the book.

Precepts Page One:

FROM: MIKE AND NOEL TO: HOUSEHOLD LEADERS   DATE: 28-11-91

NEW CREATION CHRISTIAN COMMUNITY PRECEPTS

(For style 3 Covenant Members of the Church)

As a people of "New Creation" committed to developing a kingdom of God culture, we have taken a stand against the spirit of the world in many aspects of our life together. This is particularly true of our community houses, where over the years we have established a number of "precepts" to guide our practice and act as benchmarks for our radical commitment. It does seem that in recent years some of our distinctiveness from the culture of the world around us has been lost. We are therefore listing below a number of precepts covering what seem to have become "grey areas" in our community life. Please consider before God whether they highlight a loss of radicality in your community house life, and if so take appropriate action.

We do not listen to secular music, watch secular TV/video or read secular books.

We only listen to Christian music, watch Christian videos and read Christian literature recommended by the Church.

All tape recorders, walkmen, video players, etc. are kept under central household or Church control.

We do not have TV's, radios, stereos or CD players in our houses or vehicles.

We do not use telephone services to listen to music, sports reports or any other entertainment services.

We do not go to cinemas, theatres, sporting events, concerts or other places of entertainment.

We do not visit public houses or clubs except for evangelistic purposes.

We neither hold nor attend parties, barbeques, buffets etc. except for evangelistic purposes.

We do not go swimming for exercise or pleasure, neither do we sunbathe.

x

We do not go on holidays, nor on recreational outings to seaside resorts, zoos, museums, etc.

We take no part in the celebration of Christmas, Easter or other worldly festivals.

All cameras are kept under central household or Church control and not used personally.

We do not engage in competitive sports or games, neither do we allow them on our premises.

We do not have hobbies or amusements; we develop skills only as recommended by the Church.

We do not smoke tobacco, drink alcohol or take unprescribed drugs, neither do we allow them on our premises.

We furnish and equip our houses simply, without the trappings of middle-class ostentation.

We dress simply and modestly, avoiding clothing which is suggestive, or fashionable for fashion's sake.

Precepts Page Two:

We do not wear cosmetics, jewellery, earrings or other forms of outward adornment.

We purchase food, clothing and other personal and household items only from the FDC [Food Distribution Centre – i.e. central supply centre] or under its covering.

Our clothing reflects the difference between the sexes; in particular, sisters do not wear trousers.

Our hairstyles reflect the difference between the sexes; we cut one another's hair if at all possible.

We do not purchase sweets, drinks or other snack refreshments.

We do not have special diets unless recommended by our doctors and the Church.

We accept the food provided for us with thanksgiving; and eat what is set before us.

We do not purchase take-away foods nor eat out unless recommended to do so by the Church.

We accept as self-denials not drinking coffee, and not having sugar in our drinks or on our cereals.

We do not have private medical treatment unless recommended by our doctors and the Church.

We do not engage in weight training, workouts or other keep-fit techniques.

We maintain a holy segregation between the sexes and do not allow flirtation.

We accept that all equipment in the community house is communal rather than personal.

We pay all our income, including gift money and tips, into the common purse.

We do not have personal bank or savings accounts.

We see our jobs as "Unto the Lord" and do not allow secular employment to override Church interests.

We accept that all vehicles and transport in the community house are communal rather than personal.

We drive sensibly, non-competitively and within the law, safeguarding our passengers.

We attend all meetings in the Church programme, arriving punctually and staying to the end.

We maintain a full involvement in meetings, respecting the word of God in them.

We mix with the people of the world only to befriend them and win them for Christ.

Our families accept that all our precepts apply to children in community as well as adults.

We avoid the unholiness and indulgence of the world in the conception, birth and upbringing of children.

Husbands in community are subject to the authority of the Church.

Wives in community are subject to their believing husbands.

Children in community are subject to their parents, and adults generally.

Our children take no part in extra-curricular school activities.

Our children are withdrawn from any school activities which would compromise our principles.

Precepts Page Three:

Our children have only educational toys; not cuddlies, gadgets or competitive games.

We do not have pets and keep no animals on our premises except working cats and dogs.

We uphold the practice of our precepts when visiting friends and relatives.

Author's introductory Comments

I dedicate this book to my wonderful wife, Jeanne, who has lovingly supported me ever since I left the New Creation Christian Community. This has included many tempestuous years and we have endured significant challenges. But our love is far stronger for it all as we head off – hopefully – into the golden years of our life together.

In 2014 the Jesus Fellowship Church (JFC) and its outreach arm, the Jesus Army (JA), initiated a process of internal disclosure which afforded its members the opportunity to report any recent or historic incidents of physical, emotional, financial or sexual abuse. This came in response to increasing awareness of evidence to support the plausibility of abuse allegations, including those made against the late founder and leader, Noel Stanton. Northamptonshire Police took possession of the disclosed information during the course of a wide-ranging investigation into abuse allegations which was codenamed "Operation Lifeboat". The investigation led to a number of successful criminal prosecutions, including convictions for sexual abuse.[a] In 2015 an independent church-based advisory service began an investigation into safeguarding procedures within the JFC; several leaders were subsequently dismissed from their positions, others resigned. Recognizing the dreadful significance and weight of what had already come to light and the failings identified, the JFC's five senior "apostolic" leaders chose to step down in 2017 whilst further independent and police investigations continued. Mick Haines, who replaced Noel Stanton as senior pastor, was one of these men. The "National Leadership Team" (NLT) was left with interim responsibility for management of the JFC affairs.

Ultimately, however, the NLT concluded it would be impossible for the church to continue under the shadow of all the abuses and problems which had been revealed. They issued a statement explaining that they no longer had either the desire or the capability of leading the JFC, and nor did they feel that anyone else could, or should, try to. Instead, they recommended to the JFC members that the church be dissolved, and on Sunday 26th May 2019 the members of the Jesus Fellowship Church voted to revoke its constitution. Fifty years' on from its origin in Bugbrooke village, Northants, the Jesus Fellowship – more commonly known since 1987 as the Jesus Army – had run its course.

Since leaving JFC membership in 1982 and up until their 2019 demise, I had been episodically engaged in trying to expose what I believed to be the dangers of their teaching and lifestyle, a campaign I pursued with conviction right to the very end despite the toll it took on me and the many times I felt extremely feeble ranged against their apparent might. I sometimes felt my

---

[a] Please see the Appendix for further information concerning Operation Lifeboat and the convictions which it led to.

efforts were naïve and foolish, or even pointless; but they were the best I could muster within the limitations of my personal resources and abilities. In line with the military associations derived from the "Jesus Army" branding and uniform, I've called the story of my near-lifetime opposition one of war and defeat: a war which ended when the Jesus Army faced defeat. But it wasn't an ending with any corresponding sense of victory to which I can personally lay claim. Some of the battles and skirmishes I took part in had an element of triumph; but many didn't. The war was ultimately won on a number of fronts, some of them opening up when internal abuse and negligence left the JFC dangerously exposed. The "advantage" – if I may be allowed to call it that – was pressed home by others, and I hope I've given them the acknowledgement they deserve throughout my story.

What follows is in no way intended to be a comprehensive history of the JFC: such a book would require and merit a far greater amount of research than I've yet been able to attempt – but may possibly undertake as a future project. Even so, within the pages of "War and Defeat" many of those who have been involved with the JFC or the JA will find people they know as well as places, experiences and events they recognize and can immediately relate to. The book itself might best be summarised as the collective account of all my personal encounters with the JFC. Taken together, these interactions can justifiably be called "a lifetime's battle" and form a substantive body of experience which is undoubtedly unique. As such, it is something I can now look back on with a certain pride, even if it amounts to no more than knowing I stuck to my guns until the war was over.

In a formal letter received from Noel Stanton in January 1982 I was explicitly told that, unless I returned to the Jesus Fellowship Church as a member, I would face God's judgement and be treated as an outcast. I refused to return and my punishment was invoked.

What follows throughout the following eight parts – thirty-nine chapters – is a story covering the circumstances and consequences of my involvement with the JFC up to 2023, the year when the Jesus Fellowship Charitable Trust began to issue apologies and redress payments to those who had been adversely affected through membership of the NCCC or damaged in consequence of mistreatment or assault by JFC brothers or sisters. Within the story, I have included everything which I believe is of relevance to my becoming a member in the first place, my reasons for leaving, the consequences of my leaving, and the efforts I've made to speak the truth openly as both a warning to those thinking about involvement and also an encouragement for those thinking about leaving.

Most names used in the book are genuine. A few people have been given an alias, however, in the interests of identity protection, confidentiality and privacy.

1926 to 1988

(1926 being the year when Noel Stanton was born)

PART ONE

A bruised reed

Editorial aside about "ise" and "ize"

I've only recently realised that, according to most UK English dictionaries, the preferred way of spelling "realise" is actually "realize". I suspect there are many, like myself, who have passed over the word thousands of times in a kind of dyslexic haze without caring too much about the exact spelling.

I think I first became aware of the heated distinction between the "ise" and "ize" spelling whilst watching an episode of "Inspector Morse". Morse, in his typically high-handed erudite way berates his sidekick, Lewis, for using the "ise" spelling: he insists that the "eyes" sound should be spelt "ize" in what he calls "proper English". But when I decided to check for myself, it didn't appear to be quite so simple as Morse would have had us believe. Truth be told, I've floundered around for a long time before finding any foolproof system to guide me in this hot potato of linguistic accuracy. One piece of grammatical advice that has been of enormous help to me is simply that of consulting a good English dictionary – which is also especially useful when deciding whether or not a word should be capitalised; or should that be capitalized? But, confusingly, most dictionaries often give the "ize" spelling as their *main* entry whilst adding in parenthesis that "ise" is acceptable as an *alternative*. Help!

Rescue from complete bewilderment came after I'd read Gyles Brandreth's wonderful book "Have You Eaten Grandma?". On pages 149 and 150 he lists twenty-eight words which absolutely *must* be spelt with the "ise" ending. These include chastise, demise, disguise, enterprise, merchandise, reprise, revise and televise. To this list I've added "baptise" – I just cannot bring myself to spell it with an ize.

These words aside, Brandreth advises that the "ize" spelling is "*more up-to-speed with current practice than I am*". Like him, I'm not altogether comfortable with this practice and my natural instinct cries out to spell "finalize" as "finalise". In the interests of consistency, however, I've fallen into line and have used "ize" for all the words where such a spelling is given as the main listing in my old-faithful dictionary.[a]

---

[a] The Oxford Dictionary and Thesaurus. 1997.

1

CHAPTER ONE: The Judgement of Matthew Eighteen

Summer 1975

I used to shudder at the thought of being interred in one of those huge, institutional, dreary, and often smelly, Victorian–era psychiatric hospitals – more commonly and unkindly known as "loony bins" back in the day. We had one of these dreadful places in a village called Arlesley, not many miles from where I grew up. The village name became synonymous with the hospital itself.

'*You'll end up in Arlesley*,' people would say when they wanted to scare the living daylights out of you. It certainly worked with me! So I can't pretend to have been anxiety-free when, as an eighteen-year-old volunteer, I got off the bus to begin the long walk up the tree-lined drive leading to the hospital buildings. I'd never actually *seen* the place before, even from a distance, let alone *visited* it. At least there were no entry guards or security fences as in my wild, childish imaginings. A few people were walking around within the beautifully kept grounds, some of them – somehow or another – instantly recognizable as "residents"; and it was quite evident that they were free to wander off into the nearby village if they so wished. Illusions of Bedlam-style pandemonium were finally laid to rest as I took it all in and allowed the reality of experience to replace the fantasy of imagination.

Even so, it was impossible not to be depressed by the internal condition of the hospital wards, which were predominantly gloomy and intimidating. In places, I was very nearly sickened by the unpleasant smells. I came to learn that the hospital was amongst the more depressing of mental institutions. It was, put crudely, a huge dumping ground for the county, where long-term patients who couldn't be treated elsewhere – or who weren't *wanted* elsewhere – were accommodated. Worst of all was the geriatric ward. It was located in a long, shed-like structure which had been built with cheap, functional materials and was detached from the main hospital building itself. The poor souls who were interned there really were the pathetic dross of the system, and I certainly don't mean to use the words unkindly. Most of them were sat completely motionless around the perimeter of the ward and, from what *I* observed while there, the only time they seemed to take any genuine notice of what was going on round about them was when they had their mid-day meal brought to them.

Having seen enough for my first day as a hospital volunteer, I was more than glad to find myself walking back down the long drive, unchecked, and out through the open gates into the village. Although *some* of my fanciful, bleak impressions had been confirmed by the more depressing features of the hospital, *many* of them had been dispelled. I grew to enjoy and look forward to my weekly visits to the hospital; and this wasn't *only* on account of the friendships I struck with some of the young and flighty nurses. I also formed meaningful relationships with many

3

of the patients, some of whom, I felt, had no business to be there: they seemed perfectly "normal" in my inexperienced assessment.

My regular visits to Arlesley were left behind when I went off to university. I would never again walk up that long drive whose canopy of trees had watched over me to witness a young man anxiously crossing the threshold separating fact and fantasy. Twelve years on, however, as part of my training to become a vicar in the Church of England, I began to visit another large Victorian-era asylum: Winterton, not far from Durham. If *this* hospital was typical of others around the country, then it was evident that enormous changes had taken place, even in such a comparatively short time. The building was bright, well decorated, and there were only a few wards where the smell came anywhere near to being that which could be described as odious.

Regardless of such improvements, there was still something about these places which seemed to me to be so numbingly institutional that even the *thought* of being interred as a patient in one of them was enough to give me a severe attack of the heebie-jeebies. On the other hand, the hypothetical prospect of my becoming a patient in one of the smaller hospitals which offered "acute" short-term treatment didn't seem *quite* so alarming. I sometimes couldn't help but feel pretty certain that, if it were ever to actually happen, not only would I make the most of the opportunity to have a bloody good rest but I would also make damn certain I *enjoyed* the experience. What could be so awful, I wondered, about being able to spend a few days or weeks attending craft workshops, joining in group discussions, watching TV, listening to my favourite music, playing chess, and relaxing in the evening over a jigsaw puzzle and cup of hot cocoa? I could almost have envied those who were so fortunate.

February 1988

'Don't jump! Think of your family!' he quipped jokingly with a relaxed laugh. He was speaking to a friend who was stood looking out of a metal-framed window onto a drop of some thirty feet or so below. I'd never seen him before; he was a visitor to the hospital. But I instantly disliked him. I glared at him as I walked past, despising the intrusion of unwelcome humour into my miserable world; especially such grossly insensitive humour, which reverberated through my head with cruel pain.

How can he be allowed to say such a thing in a place like this? Doesn't he know why some of us are here? Oh my God, help me! Help me, please! Please help me!

It had become virtually impossible, even for a few seconds, to tear my thoughts away from the relentless mental invitation to hurl myself from some great height.

Surely I will then be relieved of this deep inner-torment. But how can I know? If only, somehow, I could give it a try. If only I knew what lay beyond death.

4

If only my mind hadn't been so confused and ravaged by conflicting thoughts which buffeted me helplessly this way and that like a discarded can of lager against the harbour wall in a storm. If only those bloody metal-framed windows hadn't been welded shut then maybe I could have propelled myself headlong from one of them onto the inviting hardness of the receptive concrete below.

I had paced up and down, down and up, up and down the soft-carpeted corridor on the ward a thousand times, if once, because my whole body was electrified with anxiety and couldn't rest. It had to move. It had to think.

Surely there must be a way to escape the watchful eyes of the staff? Surely I can find the courage and the opportunity to finish it all? Surely it would be right to do so – wouldn't it? Oh my God! If only my head were silent, just for a moment. If only I could find some answers to these remorseless questions.

But there were no answers, no opportunities, no courage – nothing! I couldn't even find the way out.

'You pathetic worm! How can you fight against God?' demanded the voice of my mind.

'How can you fight against the One who is all knowing and all powerful, against the One who has mapped out a pathway for you which leads to eternal damnation, against the One who entices you to take your own life but denies you even the tenuous comfort of having the conviction to know it to be the right thing to do – the conviction that would bring with it the requisite courage?'

Many was the time that I'd peered enquiringly, longingly, through the hospital windows onto the drop below. But there was to be no escape from the mental hell engulfing my frightened, desperate, psychotically deranged mind. My tormentor was mocking me, teasing me, laughing at me.

Don't jump! Think of your family!

How stupid. Didn't the man who'd spoke those words know that I had a wonderful family who, so I often believed, were sent to me from heaven itself? I loved them dearly, and they me. I had no wish to cause them pain of any kind, let alone abandon them. But the logic of my restless tormented brain, spinning helplessly out of control in a paranoid free-fall, told me that I could no longer return to being the husband and father they'd once known: I'd gone too far. I was now gripped by the punishing fury of an overpowering, vengeance-seeking God, for I had "crucified the Son of God on my own account".

'Vengeance is mine, I will repay,' saith the Lord. And I could almost see Him smirking with derision as He did so.

Biblical words of divine retribution spun round and round in my head with crushing, repetitive menace:

"For it is **impossible** for those who were once enlightened, and have tasted the Heavenly gift, and have become partakers of the Holy Spirit, and have tasted the good word of God and the powers of the age to come, if they fall away, to renew them again to repentance, since they crucify again for themselves the Son of God and put him to an open shame." [Hebrews, chapter 6, verse 6]

"It would have been better for them if they had **not** known the way of righteousness than, having known it, to have turned from the holy commandment delivered to them. But it has happened to them according to the true proverb: 'A dog returns to his own vomit, and a sow, having washed, to her wallowing in the mire'." [2 Peter, chapter 2, verse 22]

'Without doubt, without a shadow of doubt,' I thought, *'I am one of those people whom the apostle Peter was speaking about.'*

And the mire in which I was wallowing clung to me with painful adhesion. It was sucking me into its bog-like grasp and promising to finally overwhelm me. There, in Durham City's "County Hospital" – which treated short-term "acute" patients – I could find no respite from the torture of my own accusing thoughts. I found little solace in music and couldn't concentrate for long enough to read an article on the front page of a newspaper let alone attempt a jigsaw puzzle. I knew only the pain and deep deep depression of continuously rehearsing in my mind the reasons why I would never recover from this illness – an illness which God himself, so it seemed, had afflicted me with. The only respite I got from it all was when I fell into a short, drugged sleep at the end of every day.

If only I could bring it all to end, my family could then begin to rebuild their lives free from the curse which I carried with me.

Don't jump! Think of your family! By Christ, I wished that thinking of my family would have put it all into perspective and exorcized the madness.

I had a plan, though.

Having been taken off the "constant observation" suicide-prevention regime, I slipped out of the building after breakfast one Sunday morning and, in the small shop under the railway arches, bought a newspaper. If questioned on my return, I could produce it to use as an excuse for why I'd left the building without permission – permission which wouldn't have been given had I asked for it. Next, at the chemist, I bought a large bottle of Paracetamol which I then slipped into the inner pocket of my coat.

Back to the ward, and back to my room – unnoticed and unquestioned. Good! Write a short note to Jeanne. What shall I say? How will she understand? No need to say to too much; I've already said it all. She won't be surprised. Just tell her how much I love her and the children. Tell her how this is the best thing for all of us. Now, open the bottle. Start taking the pills.

One, two, three…

Without any shadow of a doubt whatsoever, all this madness was directly attributable to the way I'd been treated when I left the Jesus Fellowship Church back in 1982; attributable to the written judgement which Noel Stanton – the church leader – had pronounced over me for daring to question his authority and therefore rebel against God himself. In one paragraph of the letter I received from him, he'd written:

"We plead with you to return for a full reconciliation with Christ's body here and to take your covenanted place amongst us again. Should you refuse this (Oh, may it not be so) then the judgement the Lord states in Matt.18.17 must apply; in which case fellowship with you must cease. Even now you must understand that, until you respond positively and fully to our entreaties, we must consider you under discipline."

I hardly even needed to refer to my Bible to understand what was being said to me because the process of "church discipline" had been spelt out for us members many many times. We were all so familiar with its procedural stages and consequences that it had even entered into our jargon. It didn't used to be at all uncommon to hear people talk about "giving someone a Matthew-Eighteen".

"Moreover if your brother sins against you, go and tell him his fault between you and him alone. If he hears you, you have gained your brother. But if he will not hear you, take with you one or two more, that 'by the mouth of two or three witnesses every word may be established'. And if he refuses to hear them, tell it to the church. But if he refuses even to hear the church, let him be to you like a heathen and a tax collector." [Mathew, chapter 18, verses 15-17]

There were, so Noel had taught us, several stages to this disciplinary process, the first two being employed with the hope of "gaining back" the disobedient by urging them to renounce whatever sin it was they were being accused of. The third stage, that of being spoken to by the "the church", was someone's last chance to repent: failure to do so would result in their being given over to the judgement of God. This meant having nothing more to do with them, excluding them from all fellowship, denying them the right to share in the eucharistic signs of God's forgiveness (excommunication); treating them, in effect, as "heathens and tax collectors".

Noel had frequently warned us not to "harden ourselves" by refusing to listen to the corrective entreaties of our brothers and sisters. He had always insisted that "being of one heart with the brethren" was a necessary precondition to share in the eucharistic meal – Holy Communion – and be availed of its redemptive power. Those who "hardened themselves" towards their brethren were, he insisted, in grave danger of becoming like those whom the apostle Peter referred to as having "crucified the son of God on their own account".

These were the ones beyond God's grace, the ones who no longer had the opportunity to repent, the ones who had embarked on the irreversible journey to everlasting damnation.

It looked as if I was going to become the JFC's first unequivocally certified apostate! Noel's letter claimed to represent "the church", making it quite clear that if I failed to repent, if I failed to return, then:

"the judgement *[the ultimate judgement of excommunication]* must apply".

Just for good measure, the letter also accused me of "prides, self-justifications; resentments; accusings and patronisings [sic]". And then Noel went on to quote another New Testament passage:

"reject a divisive man after the first and second admonition, knowing that such a man is warped and sinning, being self-condemned". (Titus, chapter 3, verse 10)

I had managed to shrug off these threats of judgement for more than six years before they finally began to bite. During those years I had been instrumental in getting the JFC excluded from both the Baptist Union of Great Britain and the Evangelical Alliance; both exclusions having a marked impact on the Jesus Fellowship's reputation and credibility. I'd also been involved in several media investigations which resulted in indisputably bad press. What's more, I'd written a ninety-page report about the "the Church Community at Bugbrooke" which I'd had photocopied and circulated within Christian church circles. Not to put too fine a point on it, I'd done more or less everything which was possible to compound my previous sins and invite the furious reproach of an avenging God. That's why I was there in the County Hospital; that's why I was counting off the number of Paracetamol pills that I'd swallowed:

...four, five, six...

PART TWO

The early days at Bugbrooke

Important note relating to future name usage throughout the book:

"The Fellowship" (with capital F to distinguish from the word "fellowship" in general) – This is the name I will often use to describe the Jesus Fellowship Church (JFC) as a whole – which includes the New Creation Christian Community (NCCC).

"The Community" (with capital C to distinguish from the word "community" in general) – This is the name I will often use to describe the NCCC and thereby distinguish it from other JFC entities.

Whilst I will try to use "the Fellowship" and "the Community" where one or the other seems to be most relevant, it is often the case that, given a particular context, the two names are virtually interchangeable. This means that there may well be instances where I have chosen to use "the Community" when someone else may have felt "the Fellowship" would have been more relevant – and vice versa, of course.

"Fire in Our Hearts" by Simon Cooper and Mike Farrant – 1997.

I will frequently refer to, and quote from, the above historical narrative of the Jesus Fellowship Church, sometimes in a seemingly critical context. I should like to make it quite clear, however, that I mean no unkindness towards either Mike or Simon themselves, both of whom I counted as friends and whom I respected as men of considerable integrity. Simon was the principal author, and what he wrote was, of course, largely a product of his membership. I could easily have written much the same whilst a member, and very nearly did so for a university-based research thesis about the JFC – sponsored by the Fellowship itself. Any strong language I use in relation to "Fire in Our Hearts" should primarily be taken as being expressed towards to the content of what was written, not the author of it.

CHAPTER TWO: In the beginning was Noel Stanton

Within all religious movements that are – or are believed to be – cults, there is always one key person who holds, or held, supreme leadership during their tenure or their lifetime. This is as simple as it gets: it is an essential sociological feature of a cult; a requisite condition – but not necessarily a good enough reason in itself – of being identified as one. Noel Stanton was the key person responsible for the birth, growth, structure and expansion of the Jesus Fellowship, a period lasting from the early 1970s to around 2017. His death in 2009 marked the beginning of the era in which the Fellowship began its prolonged death throes; the period in which it imploded and collapsed under the weight of its own abuses.

Noel was born on December 25th. 1926, hence his name. Ironic, really, for a man who would go on to disparage the Christmas festival no less intensely than Oliver Cromwell did: both men were responsible for forbidding its celebration amongst their subjects. Leaving school at sixteen, Noel worked as a bank clerk for a couple of years before being conscripted for national service in the navy. When I held a structured interview with Noel in 1980 as part of a sociological project he'd asked me to undertake, he spoke to me about his time in the merchant navy rather than the Royal Navy. It's unclear, therefore, exactly which service he was referring to when he spoke *publicly* about his "time in the navy". We do know, however, that during his national service he held the rank of "Leading Seaman; clerical division". Back in civilian life he returned to his parental home and spent some time working with his father, who was a tenant farmer. Moving on to work for an accounting firm on a part-time basis, he was also able to study at the All-Nations Bible College for the London University Certificate in Religious Knowledge. His qualification enabled him to take up another part-time post as an assistant secretary with the West Amazonian Mission, a prelude to fulfilling his ambition of travelling to the South American interior as a missionary. Had he done so, he may not have then gone on – during his Bugbrooke years – to reproach all those who gave money to missionary work or charitable relief for *wasting their money on the unredeemed world and its people.* It was one of Noel's teachings that always jarred with me, and I was never able to reconcile myself to it despite his insistence that I should.

It would seem that Noel also harboured ambitions to become a successful businessman, and this would certainly go a long way to help explain all that was to happen in respect of the JFC businesses. Back in the late 1950s and 1960s he established a stationery business in Bedford: Stanad Ltd. He was the majority shareholder with a holding to the value of £3,000 at the business's inception. The Bedfordshire Archives show that Stanad Ltd., located at 115 & 117 Midland Road, fell within the category listing of "stationers, office equipment, toys and games".[2] In later years, Noel insisted that all those who joined the NCCC should sell everything they owned and hand over the proceeds to the Jesus Fellowship Community Trust (JFCT). For some, this involved huge sums: the proceeds, for example, of house and property sales. It will therefore come as something of a surprise for many, if not a shock, to learn that Noel still retained at least some of his shareholdings until as late as 1978. In fact, these holdings were only eventually sold during a period when Noel felt that the Fellowship was coming under intense media scrutiny and when he feared his continued possession of them might be unearthed by the press.

The nineteen-fifties were years when Noel was teasing out and testing the long-term direction of his Christian faith. He took on numerous evangelical preaching engagements and certainly "put himself about" in his seemingly earnest intent to spread the good news of the gospel. I have located several archive newspaper clippings which refer to him as a guest speaker, such as the one that appeared in the "Edinburgh Evening News" on April 7th. 1956:

CARRUBBER'S CLOSE MISSION
Great Saturday Rally
7 p.m. in
St. John's Tolbooth Church, Castlehill.
Rev. STANLEY COLLINS
In Upper Hall of Mission.
Sunday 3 and 7 p.m.
MR. NOEL STANTON
West Amazon Mission

And this from the "Bedfordshire Times and Independent" on February 19th. 1954:

WOOTTON
The Baptist Young Life Campaign Choir, under their leader, Mr "Tom" Dix, with Mrs. A. Redman as accompanist, gave a sacred concert at the Methodist Church last week. In addition to items by the whole choir, there were solos, duets, quartets, a recitation by Mrs. G. Woodland, and wood-saw playing by Mr. G. Woodland. Mr. **Noel Stanton** presided.

Also this from the same newspaper on December 24th. 1954 (one of my favourites):

GAMES AND SONGS
About 80 young people, leaders and others, were at St. John's Hall squash which was organised by **Mr. Noel Stanton**, General Secretary of the Crusades. Games were followed by a sing song and meeting.

Those of us who knew Noel from later years may well read these press clippings with a wry smile, unsure what to make of his involvement in activities – games and singsongs, for example – which he came to revile with such intensity. In our smiles, some of us may well be thinking back to a Noel whom we thought we knew; thinking back to the times when, deep in our hearts, we wished he could remember his younger self and rediscover whatever it was that had been consumed by the sense of prophetic destiny which finally overpowered him. *What exactly was it that had made him become so inflexible and domineering?* We sensed a deep insecurity in there somewhere, but we also knew him to be a man of deep passion who was capable of demonstrating sincere love and understanding – and even occasional humility.

Those who met him when he first came to visit the Baptist chapel at Bugbrooke village near Northampton in 1957 described him as a smartly dressed, passionate but polite young man. Apparently, he first arrived at Bugbrooke somewhat dramatically on his motorbike. The chapel congregation had been without an "official" pastor for several years and so Noel had been invited for what would effectively be a job interview. The key figures in the congregation, the deaconate, approved of the person they met and offered him the position of lay – part-time – pastor. At some point following his induction ceremony, Noel began to assume the title of reverend: the Rev. Noel Stanton. This is significant insofar as it provides us with a scent of the oblique and foxy nature that Noel would become increasingly willing to assume as the purpose suited him. The tile, of course, gave him the aura of credibility that he wanted. The blunt truth of the matter, however, is that, whilst he was acknowledged to be the bona-fide *pastor* of the congregation at Bugbrooke Baptist chapel, he lacked the credentials necessary for the Baptist Union to recognize him as a minister on whom they could confer the title of "Reverend" or simply "Rev".

In the book "Fire in Our Hearts" by Simon Cooper and Mike Farrant – a largely eulogistic and exonerative in-house history of the Jesus Fellowship – we're told that Noel was "called" to the chapel as a **full**-time pastor rather than a **part**-time one. Simon then explains that we should understand Noel's part-time status to be in consequence of a *voluntary* offer he made to help ease pressure on the chapel's finances. The offer, we're told, was for him to continue the pursuit of his remunerative business affairs *alongside* his pastoral duties – an act of generosity. Simon Cooper – the lead author and henceforth "SC", or, by virtue of his being a good friend of mine from days past, just Simon – goes on to talk about Noel's formal induction ceremony in such a way as to leave us with the impression that "that was that": the Rev. Noel Stanton now officially appointed captain at the helm of the good ship which was Bugbrooke chapel.

For much of the nineteen-sixties it would seem that Noel steered his ship through what many would regard as fairly conventional evangelical waters, with plenty of enthusiasm for outreach and growth. Those in the flock approving of a visionary style may well have welcomed the zealous way in which Noel led from the front; conversely, it might have all felt too much for those of a more traditionalist churchmanship. Even so, there were few signs of sufficiently rocky waters to excessively destabilize the vessel. There was, undoubtedly, a lot going on. Without yet having prefixed "Rev" to his name, Noel continued his public speaking engagements and organized a number of evangelistic rallies. The following clip comes from the "Northamptonshire Evening Telegraph" on January 20th. 1966

SATURDAY JANUARY 22nd,
At 7.30 p.m.
Moor Road Youth Centre,
RUSHDEN
Welcome return to our speaker:
NOEL STANTON
Group: The Followers
Make a date then —
This Saturday, Right!

The pivotal time of substantial change came in 1969. It followed on from Noel's personal experience of what has generally come to be known within the Christian vernacular as "baptism in the Spirit". From John Wesley's epiphanic moment when he found his heart "strangely warmed" to the dramatic, life-changing experiences of such as Nicky Cruz (a former New York gang fighter),[a] receiving the "baptism in the Spirit" has been a transformative event for both practicing Christians and the newly converted alike. In Noel's case, as in many others, it issued into praise for God through "talking in tongues" – a Pentecostal phenomenon visited upon the early Christians as described in the New Testament.[b] He has described his baptism in the Spirit as having been an occasion which lasted for hours and from which he took a long time to "come down".

---

[a] The story of Nicky Cruz and others from certain violent New York gangs, together with accounts of miraculous healings, is told by David Wilkinson in his book, "The Cross and the Switchblade"
[b] The book of "the Acts of the Apostles", chapter two – commonly known as "the second chapter of Acts" – describes the Christians as talking in different languages: ones which those listening were themselves able to understand.

CHAPTER THREE: And then there was fire

In "Fire in Our Hearts", SC tells us that Noel began actively encouraging others to discover the baptism in the Spirit for themselves. Initially, a group of teenagers proved to be most responsive. Simon describes what happened:

"The teenagers were very excited and encouraged one another along. Stories flew around of talking in tongues and seeing visions. The youngsters prayed together almost every night for revival to hit the chapel. Sometimes they ended up on the floor laughing in the Spirit. One of the lads felt something like a warm electric current come upon his head and travel down to his toes. The joy was immense and he shook for an hour."[3]

There are also accounts of the miraculous, such as:

"Saturday nights were times of discovery as the delighted pastor [Noel] stepped back and allowed the Spirit to move. They didn't know what would happen next. One lad jumped up, took his glasses off, and peered out of the window. 'Hey! I can see the "Baker's Arms" [pub] sign really clearly now!' he shouted."[4]

Simon writes about events such as this with an uncritical hand: *this is how it was; this is the verbatim account of what happened*. Regardless of one's take on events which sound more like drug-fuelled or hypnotic ecstasy, or one's attitude toward accounts of spontaneous healings which lack medical explanation or confirmation, the immediate years which followed Noel's baptism in the Spirit saw a change in the style of worship at Bugbrooke chapel that attracted many people – and by no means only the young – who wouldn't normally have had much truck with Christianity, as such – or at least not with what they considered to be stale, institutionalized, boring, church or chapel attendance. That there was something new in the air – the wind of change – is indisputable. And it wasn't just about the newly introduced handclapping, talking in tongues, waving of arms, tambourine playing and musical vibrancy. It was as much about a wonderful sense and discovery of *love* – both the love of God through Jesus Christ and love of one another. Many spoke about the very real love which Noel had shown towards them; and they had eagerly responded to his entreaties to love their Christian brothers and sisters as they loved themselves. For those looking for meaning and substance, this felt like what they'd been waiting for their whole lives. Nor was it restricted solely to the idealistic young. Miss Campion, an elderly lady whose Bugbrooke forebears had their name adopted by the local Campion Secondary School, was but one amongst those of the chapel faithful who supported and welcomed the changes taking place.

Although the new "Charismatic"[a] style of worship had initially been restricted to smaller, informal meetings held in the chapel's adjacent manse or elsewhere, Noel gradually introduced the loosely structed, so-called "free" worship into the Sunday services at the chapel itself. Inevitably, some left. Through my own research of yesteryear I came across the names of forty-three adults who terminated their association with the chapel between 1970 and 1974. In anticipation of the way he would respond to future opposition, Noel attributed the criticism of those who'd spoken with their deserting feet as being an inevitable consequence of "moving with God": it was, he explained, "the clearing away of dead wood". Despite the loss of some, the successful outreach amongst Northampton's bikers and hippies meant the chapel numbers began to swell. They were augmented by disaffected Christians from other local churches – and some from further afield – who became aware of what was happening at Bugbrooke and wanted to be part of it. Yvonne Roberts, writing in the "Northants Chronicle and Echo", provides us with an interesting snapshot of "the Bugbrooke scene" as it was in 1972:

"They meet in the Baptist chapel and for some it has meant the end to drugs and violence ... The people who meet each night from Sunday to Wednesday at Bugbrooke Baptist chapel range in age from early teens to late twenties, and in size from a group of 40 to as many as 130.

Their meeting is revivalist with speaking in tongues. Jesus is the focus and their message is uncomplicated by dogma. Religion is seen visually for them in the shaking of hands, the 'smile' stickers, and the 'Jesus Loves You' slogans; and it is community based. It means friendship and an end to loneliness for some who adopted derelict houses and the steps of All Saints' church, Northampton, as their base and others who turned off routine and turned on to speed, LSD, and in some cases 'Big H' – heroin.

Noel Stanton, Minister at Bugbrooke for 15 years, opened the church to the concept of 'The Jesus Movement' three years ago with the support of the established fellowship. Only a handful of young people came at first, but in the past few months the numbers have rapidly increased. This increase perhaps says as much for the vacuum in the believers' lives

---

[a] "Charismatic" worship – often featuring exuberant praise, talking in tongues, experiences of healing and declarations of spiritual knowledge – takes its meaning from the Greek "charismata", meaning "gifts of grace" or "spiritual gifts". In the modern era, those Christian assemblies adopting such worship have collectively been called "the Charismatic movement". Strictly speaking, the "c" in charismatic isn't capitalized. In order, however, to provide clarity between "charismatic" in a broader sense, and "Charismatic" in reference to the use of spiritual gifts, I shall refer to "Charismatic worship" and the "Charismatic movement".

before their 'baptism in the spirit' as it does for the power of the non-institutional religious message. An ex-president of a Hell's Angels' chapter, mid-20s with a suspended sentence for violence, originally came to a meeting to 'bust someone's head in':

"I came over here and created a disturbance during a meeting, but by the end of the meeting I really felt that I'd found some kind of truth. People were happy. I didn't know what was happening really, but the same evening I took off my colours and broke my stick in two. I'd used the stick to bash peoples' heads in."

Not all the Jesus People have such graphic backgrounds to their conversion. But those who do not have their personal miracles draw their strength from their peers. They quote the story of a heroin addict of 16 months standing who was baptised and successfully came off the drug (although he had failed previously even with medical help), but his arms and legs – ulcerated and swollen were still giving him problems. The fellowship prayed, they say, and overnight his arms were healed. Again, a Satanist attended a meeting to disrupt it with help from the occult. Instead he fell into a trance and has now joined the group. Proof perhaps! But is it all stickers and spontaneous spiritual combustion – or a more permanent commitment? The Fellowship think that it is the latter and their work seems to prove it.

Every Thursday they have a Bible class, Friday a God squad preaches to an often-oblivious Northampton, and there are now plans to set up a hostel for a dozen homeless boys. At present the manse, Noel Stanton's home, doubles as a temporary home for emergency cases. A meal and somewhere to sleep serve as a stop gap measure while parents, in some cases, are contacted or a more permanent arrangement made. But a hostel is necessary. Already, in one Sunday's collection alone, £600 was raised, but a lot more is required before a housing association can be formed and property bought. Mr. Stanton is unperturbed by the problem: *'Jesus will provide,'* he says, and it is very easy to believe him."[5]

What was happening amongst the Bugbrooke Jesus People, as reported by Yvonne Roberts, was in close alignment with what would become known as the "House Church movement", especially in relation to the informal style of Charismatic worship, reports of the miraculous, the sense of communality, and the sense of growth and revival. Already, however, Noel had begun to distance himself from too close an association with house churches. He certainly rejected any possibility of sheltering under the umbrella of their leadership or "covering": his own flock would go it alone under his sole authority. And he emphasized the need to avoid what he identified as the behavioural laxity which featured elsewhere: a lack of personal holiness and purity in obedience to Christ. Following baptism in the Spirit, he taught, Christian believers should leave their old life behind and begin to lead a new one characterized not just by joy and love but also by righteousness.

The sections of "Fire in Our Hearts" which cover this formative period make frequent reference to Rufus's story. Rufus may possibly be considered to have been an archetypal, long-haired, drug-fuelled spiritual seeker who is often imagined as stereotypical of the hippy generation. Although partly true, there was much more to him; not least the potential he'd once shown to become a film actor. He'd been cast, for instance, in the role of Petya alongside Anthony Hopkins, Morag Hood, Alan Dobie and others in the BBC's 1972 TV series, "War and Peace". Having moved away from his parental home in the early seventies, Rufus, together with his wife, Jessica, began to rent – and then buy – a terraced house in Argyle Street, Northampton. Over time, they were joined there by several others of similar lifestyle persuasion: Justin (Jessica's brother), Ralph, "French" Mary, Alan, and Chris. Jessica has told me about the amazing life they shared as a communal company of friends, well before Noel Stanton introduced them to his own style of community:

'We just used to put whatever cash each of us could afford into a teapot,' she recently explained to me.

'From it, we paid the essential weekly and monthly bills: mortgage payments, rates, utility bills, repairs and the like. No one ever checked who had put in how much; we just gave whatever we could afford.'

Jessica also told me about the fun they had together.

'We used to have fantastic meals,' she said, 'with all kinds of different food, and also' – at which point her eyes widened into a beautiful smile – 'lovely ice cream and chocolates.'

After the meals, she said, Alan and Chris – ex-buskers from London – would sometimes pick up their guitars and they'd all sit around together happily singing. In Jessica's recollection, at least, it was a time to look back on with nostalgic happiness. But then Rufus met Noel somewhere in Northampton and things began to change. Noel, it seems, took a particular interest in Rufus and often personally picked him up to take him back to meetings at Bugbrooke.

'We used to dread Rufus coming home after these meetings,' laments Jessica. 'He began to start insisting that we should change our lifestyle and he began to introduce house rules which he expected us to obey: no more ice cream or chocolate for example.'

Rufus had begun to uphold the righteous, self-sacrificial Christian behaviour which Noel felt was lacking in the house-church movement and which he was determined should feature as a product of his own ministry. As

1972 progressed into 1973 and beyond, the emphasis placed on leaving the old behind and embracing the new became increasingly strong: "new creation" became a leitmotif kind of buzz word. With it came a concomitant stress on the need for the flock to take up its cross in pursuit of a radical, revolutionary lifestyle. Noel began quoting from no-nonsense Christian leaders such as Watchman Nee (author of "The Ordinary Christian Life" and "Love Not The World") and A.W. Tozer (author of "The Root of the Righteous"). These men had spelt out the need for separation from the world to become a distinctive church; a city on a hill with a shining light. This meant a complete re-evaluation of everything which was "worldly" – TV, sport, entertainment, and much else.

A book that had a particular influence was "A New Way of Living" by Michael Harper. It described how, back in 1965, the Church of the Redeemer in Houston, Texas, had studied and taken inspiration from the account given in the second chapter of Acts about how Christians in Jerusalem had "shared all things in common" within a communal lifestyle. This had inspired the Houston Christians to create their own community. During a retreat to Malhamdale, attended by over one hundred of the growing Bugbrooke flock, a similar vision gripped hold of many: the foundations of the New Creation Christian Community were being dug.

For now, I only want to provide an outline sketch of the Fellowship's growth into what it had become when I first visited in June 1977. The essential elements of the how it all came together and worked, together with the spiritual concepts underpinning everything, will be explained and become quite clear as my story progresses. Those interested in a more chronological account of what-happened-when will find it in "Fire in Our Hearts", written engagingly – even if uncritically – by SC, someone who was actually there through it all.

Before proceeding with my sketch, however, I'd like to jump forward to 1975, the year when about two hundred people from Bugbrooke met for their summer retreat at Ashburnham Place in Sussex. This was the second year at Ashburnham, a large Christian Conference Centre set in acres of serene woodland and gardens that had been landscaped by Capability Brown himself. This was the year, SC tells us, when "restoring the fortunes of Zion" took centre stage. Most of us must surely know the infectious Boney M. song, "By The Rivers of Babylon"? Those who do will also – from its lyric – have heard about the lamentation of the Hebrew exiles who wept when they "remembered Zion". In Old Testament Israel, Zion was a hill within Jerusalem – also called "David's Hill" – which came to represent the meeting point between God and man; the symbolic place where God poured out blessings on his chosen people. When, following Babylonian conquest, the Hebrews were forced to relocate, they understood their exile to be God's punishment on their errant ways. They hoped and prayed for the restoration

19

of God's favour and a return to their homeland, Zion. Their longings were realized when the Persian conqueror of Babylon known as "Cyrus the Great" set them free. Those who have witnessed the capacity of Jewish people in Jerusalem to celebrate at Bar Mitzvahs will easily be able to imagine – and almost feel part of – the dancing, the marching, the tambourine playing, the joyful shouting, the drum beating, the sound of music everywhere, and the general euphoria that must have accompanied the returning exiles as they reclaimed Zion for their own.

Noel compared the Hebrew captivity in Babylon to the demise of Christianity throughout the Western world. By contrast, he explained at the Ashburnham gathering, the restoration to Zion would be seen in the outpouring of God's blessing as the nascent Bugbrooke community of believers came together to dedicate their lives to one another and rebuild God's kingdom. SC quotes Noel as having said:

"There's a movement abroad in which God is restoring glory to his church. The call is to be his Zion. We have heard that call and it has taken us into community."[6]

Also:

"Brothers and sisters, we give ourselves to the perfecting of this Zion. We have barely skimmed the surface. Zion is holy. Zion is distinctive. Zion is beautiful because it is magnificent with God's presence and power."[7]

To properly get to grips with what the JFC was all about, it's vital to understand what "belonging to Zion" meant for us. It was totally removed, of course, from modern day Zionism as a movement. Nor was it in any way xenophobic in a nationalistic sense. "Belonging", "devotion", "dedication", "beauty", "joy" and "love" are perhaps some of the best words to describe what came into our minds when we thought about Zion. One of the "Zion songs" we often sang together was penned by a brother with a unique ability to capture the right mood within the lyric and melody of his verse. Based on Psalm 126, we sang:

"When the Lord restored the fortunes of Zion
We were like those who dreamed.
Then our mouths were filled with laughter
And our tongues with shouts of joy
As they said among the nations
'The Lord had done great things for us'."

Reading these lines purely as poetry, it's impossible to convey the intensity of emotional energy experienced when five hundred or so people of all ages, backgrounds, class, education and colour sang this beautiful psalm together with open eyes of wonder and hands swaying in non-orchestrated union. *"This is it"*, we felt; we had arrived home. Most of us remained astonished – and yet elated – at the reality of such a diverse group of people coming together and being united in such intense commitment and love. As we looked around, our eyes fell on others to whom we believed ourselves attached in almost unbreakable bonds of friendship. We felt as though we would do anything or sacrifice anything for them: we loved them, even though "them" included many of those with whom we wouldn't previously have formed close friendships. As we sang, I used to find myself marvelling at the thought of all those who'd become as family to me and whom I now loved dearly; even Kelly Bartholomew – regarded back then as Noel's right-hand man – whose somewhat stern appearance had unnerved me when we first met – as it had many others. A hymn we sang by Charles Wesley, "happy the souls who first believed", captured the same sense of belonging:

> "Propriety was there unknown,
> None called what he possessed his own:
> Where all the common blessing share
> No selfish happiness was there. . .
> Oh what an age of golden days!
> Oh what a choice peculiar race."

So what went wrong? How did the dream of Zion fade? I hope that by the end of my story such questions will have been largely answered. For the present, however, I need to touch on one part of the explanation which will come to some as a shock – as it did to me – and which some will refuse to countenance. Testimony has emerged in recent years – from people whom I personally trust – revealing that, during the early seventies, Noel had apparently begun grooming certain young men within the flock to become recipients of his homosexual attention. This testimony came as a bombshell to those of us who, all along, had given Noel the benefit of the doubt when it came to rumours concerning his sexual proclivities. It was even more of a personal shock when I became privy to credible allegations which suggest that a vulnerable young brother was subjected by Noel to an incident of attempted rape. Unless, therefore, both my readers and I are willing to accept this aspect of Noel's character – a fundamental aspect of who he was and what motivated him all along – then the Bugbrooke story to follow will suffer from the dishonesty and dissimulation which has been a feature of so many others.

In 1974, using the proceeds from donations and income which had begun to be pooled in household "common purses", the Fellowship bought

Rufus and Jess's house in Argyle Street to be used as the first "Jesus Welcome Home": another one was later bought in Harlestone Road to become the second. But more important in terms of translating the vision of Zion into an earthly communal reality was the purchase of Bugbrooke Hall, a massive, imposing old building that had been used as a rectory and was set within several acres of grounds. Renamed as "New Creation Hall", it eventually became home to about thirty residents. A 64-acre farm was added to the property portfolio in 1975, providing a home for another thirty or so residents within the main farmhouse and converted outbuildings. The purchase also meant that commercial farming as a means of employment for some of the residents could now begin in earnest. House of Goodness Ltd. was founded as a registered company to incorporate both the farming activities and a new health-food shop, Goodness Foods, that had been bought in Northampton – alongside the clothing shop, "Jeans Plus". "Skaino Services Ltd." was born from the garage service used to maintain the Community's growing fleet of cars and minibuses, and it also branched out to begin providing building services to the general public. By the time of the 1976 summer excursion to Ashburnham, four large houses had been bought and established as community households with common purse arrangements i.e. the pooling of all income earned by each resident. Many more people had bought homes on Bugbrooke's modern housing estate, preparatory to a move into one of the larger homes as space became available. The estate homes were opened up as community households for other brothers and sisters who'd committed themselves to the Fellowship but, like their hosts, weren't yet able to take their place in one of the "main" houses.

Alongside the Community's growth, other characteristic aspects of the Fellowship's lifestyle became firmly established: a formal system of discipleship and shepherding; a clear-cut separation from worldly activities across a very wide spectrum; strict control of methods used to bring up children, including the encouragement of corporal punishment; segregation of the sexes; and an emphasis on the need for women to be meek, subservient, and wear only such clothes as could be considered both feminine and modest. SC's account of such developments consistently suggests they were "organic" ones, as when he writes:

"So much sprang from sincere love for Jesus and an innocent conscience."[8]

My own experiences of the Community suggest otherwise. *Significant* developments in the lifestyle or direction of the JFC *always* came from Noel himself. In fact, Noel trod *so* heavily on what he perceived to be organically generated initiatives – always fearing they threatened his authority – that it's impossible for me to believe that what *preceded* my membership was substantially different to what happened *during* it – nor what happened *after* it. I noted with a little wry smile Simon's description of the way in which Noel addressed the faithful at Ashburnham 1974:

> "'*Wake up, beloved! Wake up!*' he shouted. '*Let's not be duped any more!*'"[9]

My smile was on account of having heard Noel shouting at us all and rebuking us far more often than I – or any of us – should have tolerated. The truth was that he didn't so much shout as *bellow* – a screeching ululation announcing his refusal to court disagreement or challenge. From at least as early as 1974, if not before, Noel had begun to enforce his ascendent prophetic vision on the church and brokered no deviance. It's hardly likely, of course, that 1974 had been any watershed year in this respect.

Came June 1977 when I first visited Bugbrooke, the Fellowship's foundations had been well and truly established and the edifice of community already built on them was recognizable as the place which would forever be Zion, the centrepiece dwelling of God's restored people. The businesses were growing continuously and there were now five large houses and three Welcome Homes forming the nucleus of communal life: the housing estate was gradually being emptied of New Creation households as brothers and sisters moved "upward" into full community.

PART THREE

My preparation for membership of the Jesus Fellowship and life within the New Creation Christian Community

In the late summer of 1977 I became the new brother on the block at New Creation Farm. I was to learn that some of the brothers in other households would supposedly have given their back teeth to live at the farm; but for some reason I'd been invited to move straight in. I turned up one evening in August having driven from home, near Luton, in my recently bought Ford Cortina estate,[a] fulsomely equipped with a duvet and a holdall containing nearly all my worldly possessions: clothes, mainly. I wanted to hang on to my flared jeans as long as I possibly could; the thought of having to wear someone else's cast-off straight-legged jeans made me shudder.

How had all this come to happen?

---

[a] An elderly model with a bench seat at the front and a column-shift gearstick that had set me back a full one hundred and fifty pounds.

CHAPTER FOUR: The makings of Heavy Evy

After quite a few tumultuous years in my late teens I'd finally begun to grow up and settle down somewhat. I'd experienced a classic born-again moment at a Charismatic-movement church in Dunstable; I'd got through my first year at university with flying academic colours and had made wonderful friends in the Christian Union; I'd managed to get my finances into some kind of order such that David Copperfield's impoverished but ever-hopeful friend, Wilkins Micawber, would have glowingly approved of how my annual income now exceeded my annual expenditure; and I was, so I felt, beginning to grow up and appreciate the natural beauty and wonder of the world by which I was surrounded. If ever I could have been called "the original mixed-up kid", then it certainly wasn't true of me any longer. So what was it that made me not just willing but also unquestionably eager to cast in my lot with a bunch of zealots who appeared to be taking away much of the standing-up-on-my-own-two-feet independence that I'd painfully teased out from my earlier troubles? *We need to revisit a few events from my past to fully get the measure of what was going on inside me.*

In my early childhood I'd known a good measure of happiness and security, but also both emotional and physical cruelty. Memories of my birth father are sketchy as he'd left my mother when I was still a toddler and all contact with him stopped after mum was granted a divorce on the grounds of adultery when I was four: she married again fairly soon afterwards. My stepfather, David, someone who I would later find out had himself been mistreated, was often repressive as a parent. It's hard to forget the occasions when, in out-of-control fits of temper, he hit me repeatedly with his bare hands until he'd fully vented his fury. Once, after I'd stupidly managed to muster a derisive smirk when the beating had stopped, he launched into a retributory repeat of lashing out until he'd managed to subdue me sufficiently. I ought, perhaps, to add that these occasions weren't those which can correctly be called corporal punishment; they were assaults. Heaven only knows there were plenty of times when I deserved serious chastisement of some kind or another: I wasn't nearly so angelic as I looked in my choirboy photographs! But the occasions I've referred to weren't the consequence of any misbehaviour, they are best described as confrontations – times when David had lost patience with me purely because I'd annoyed him, like the time when he told me to play with my balsa-wood aeroplane somewhere else because he wanted me out of the way. I went away reluctantly, audibly complaining that I'd not been able to find anywhere else with a decent slope that would allow the plane to actually gather enough speed to take off from the ground for just a few feet. I still have no real understanding of exactly why this made him snap or why it provoked such a physical response.

Even though David was far stricter with me than I sensed most of my friend's dads were with *them*, I don't recall feeling that my home life was a troubled one. His lack of emotional warmth was more than compensated for by the very close and loving relationship I had with my mother – and, to a lesser extent, with my sister, Jane. And, within the constraints of his own constrained personality, David tried his best, so I believe, to demonstrate love through the way in which he ensured his family were properly provided for – even if Jane and I often went without by comparison with quite a few other village children. There were occasions when he showed surprising kindness, and he certainly tried hard to be as generous as possible. Our annual family holidays, mainly taken in Devon or Cornwall – so long as the old vintage cars that David insisted on buying cheaply managed the long journey – were essentially happy ones.

We lived in a small village between Luton and Hitchin called Breachwood Green. Even though it was only a mile from the end of Luton Airport's runway – as the crow flies – it was set firmly and squarely in the heart of rural Hertfordshire and was surrounded by rolling hills, open fields and numerous large woods where several herds of feral deer lived. The surroundings were idyllic for a youngster who day-dreamed about "outlaw" adventures such as those had by William Brown from the "Just William" stories. In many ways he and I were genuinely one and the same person: I was precocious but well-meaning; I ran my own boys' clubs; I romped freely around the village, through the woods and over the hills whenever the weather allowed; I climbed trees to a perilous height; I organized a village football team; and I wasn't always sure where the boundaries were drawn between being mischievous and being misbehaved. It was me who had the bright idea for us – myself and a few other village boys – to make an elaborate den out of farmer Tom's straw bales and smoke a cigarette inside it. It was most definitely not me, however, who experimentally put a lighted match to a blade of protruding straw. It was reckless Pug-Nose Paul – the village's very own Billy Bunter – who did so, presumably without realizing the inflammatory consequences. The ensuing conflagration was quite spectacular! As was normal, and in order to assuage my anxious feelings of guilt and discovery, I confessed the whole affair to my mother, who advised that the best bet was to "keep mum". Farmer Tom never did find out who the culprits were, even though he questioned me about it on several occasions when I was passing by his farm at the top of our road.

In addition to being a tearaway, however, I craved knowledge: knowledge about the world and about God. What I learnt from lessons at primary school was never enough, so I would read extensively at home and take the opportunities when they occurred – and as the mood grabbed me, I should add – to discover and learn more about, say, Romans in Britain or lunar missions or commercial aviation. Significantly, in terms of my later convictions, I was a compulsive and dedicated churchgoer. This wasn't simply because I loved singing in the local choir; it was also because church was where I felt closest to God – whoever he might be and wherever he actually was. Aware from a very young age that there was much about myself I didn't like and much I needed forgiveness for, Sunday evensong was an occasion above all others when I was able to find a reassuring sense of peace. The sung "Nunc Dimittis" was the high point for my sense of sanctity and safety:

"Lord, lettest now they servant depart in peace,
According to thy word.
For mine eyes have seen thy salvation,
Which thou hast prepared before the face of all people.
To be a light to lighten the Gentiles,
And to be the glory of thy people, Israel."

Puberty and adolescence hit me like a mysterious and unwelcome developmental tsunami: I was totally unprepared and didn't even understand some of the basics about sexual intercourse. It would never have been possible for David to talk with me about these matters; and for all the closeness I shared with my mum, she preferred, I think, to hope I would never have to suffer the encumbrance of finding myself sexually aroused – so she avoided all talk about "dirty" things. That might be just a bit unfair, but she certainly didn't approve of any open discussion about bedroom activity or anything which smacked of sensuality. And given that she thought all premarital relationships should be entirely chaste, she perhaps had felt I was far too young to be worrying about the changes which were happening to me. Unbeknown to me at the time, it was an attitude – a very strongly held attitude – which would affect me deeply; especially when her disapproval concerning my teenage sexual behaviour was expressed with such complete disappointment.

At much the same time as the prospect of undressing girls was starting to excite my aspirational imagination, I sat for a scholarship exam to try and grab one of the six places offered annually by Hertfordshire County Council to the public schools of Eton, Rugby and Winchester. Exactly how I managed to proceed to an interview must now forever remain a mystery – or possibly it had just been a mistake of some kind. The syllabus we'd followed for my first two years at Hitchin Boys Grammar School simply hadn't equipped me to provide suitable answers to many of the exam questions, so I waffled my way through most of them. Perhaps the mitigatory report which the juniors' headmaster wrote on my behalf was sufficiently explanatory. And perhaps an explanation for his extenuative generosity was actually his wish to see the back of me; a wish I'd given him ample opportunity to justify. The long and short of it all, however, was that I spent nearly four years of my teenage education as a "Flemming Scholar" at Eton College. I should love to write extensively about my time there, which was full of many highs and nearly as many lows. But, for now, I need only say that at the tender age of just-turned-seventeen, my school days were to end ignominiously. Following a hellish night spent in my housemaster's study whilst under the hallucinatory, hypnotic grip of an LSD trip gone wrong (a "bad trip"),

I escaped expulsion by a benevolent whisker: the headmaster, Michael McCrum, gave me one last chance to redeem myself.

Annual Eton Picnic with Family [a]

For eighteen months or so prior to finding my name entered into the headmaster's all-too-real "black book", my behaviour had been plummeting downwards in an out-of-control spiral whose intensity caught even myself off guard. By the time I'd finished my O-levels, aged only fifteen, I realized emphatically that Eton would only become an uphill struggle from thereon in. Whatever the rights and wrongs of it all may have been, I was finding it an ever-increasing struggle to fit in and accept the disciplinary restrictions of public-school life. Pursuit of my adolescent fantasies and libidinous aspirations had become far more compelling than studying for exams. Back in my home village, and especially in nearby Hitchin, I'd begun hanging out with friends who were a year or two older than me and whose seemingly harmless, gig-going,

---

[a] Annual celebrations at Eton on June 4th. originated in the 18th. century to mark the birthday of George III – a school patron. By tradition, the boys' families picnicked on "Agar's Plough" playing fields. Some of the picnics – a minority – were grand affairs with white-clothed tables from which food and champaign were served by liveried servants. Our picnic – with myself, sister Jane and mum in the frame – was a rather humbler affair, but still splendid.

party-going, drug-experimenting social life was far more alluring than being curfewed at Eton every evening and having to keep the company of peers whose social background and expectations were becoming increasingly difficult to stomach. But my pleas to be allowed to leave Eton and go to the local sixth-form college in Hitchin fell on unreceptive ears both at home and at school: I was persuaded that staying on would be the best thing for me. I gave it another wholehearted try for the next term and was rewarded with academic commendations that twice took me to the headmaster's study for all the *right* reasons. But it was an effort I couldn't sustain and gave up trying to. By the summer of 1973 my main interests in life were listening to music that I felt had some kind of "attack" or meaning to it;[a] going out with girlfriends; smoking dope when I could get my hands on some; practicing my drum-playing; and wearing clothes of the era that I felt good in: Loon Pants were a cheap favourite, even though they completely lost their shape after the first wash. Even my passion for playing football and my support of Luton Town FC had dropped way down the league table of my interests – but thankfully neither were relegated beyond recovery. The somewhat sarcastic new nickname, "Heavy Evy", that I'd teasingly been anointed with at school – replacing "Kenny" – was aptly earned and began to stick.

---

[a] Bowie, Led Zeppelin, the Doors, Genesis and Mott the Hoople were favourites at the time.

CHAPTER FIVE: Turning on and tuning out

In August 1973, whilst my parents were away for a couple of weeks and I was supposed to be staying with my much-loved-but-easily-biddable gran, I togged myself out in my best "freak" clothes – including a rather pretentious cowboy hat – and set off hitchhiking with my best friend, Mark, to the infamous free music-festival at Windsor. Hawkwind, so we understood, would be one of the bands performing there. I was all of sweet sixteen, comparatively innocent and thoroughly naïve. We arrived in the near-complete darkness that had fallen on Windsor Great Park. Away from city lights, and with none of the compulsory safety lighting required at today's council-vetted festivals, we had to creep around carefully within a small pitch-black wooded area to find a space where we could pitch our tent in amongst all the others. Once settled in, we both set off to try and score some dope, a mission which proved to be strangely unsuccessful: no one seemed to have any for sale – or at least that's what they told us.

Even when daylight came we still didn't have any luck in our quest for some cannabis or whatever else might have been available. In the end we simply gave up for the rest of the morning and afternoon. It had turned out to be a blisteringly hot bank-holiday weekend when the sun shone continuously, which proved to be just about the only enjoyable aspect of the occasion. The, ahem, "organization" was chaotic throughout. Anarchy prevailed at what would prove to be the last massive and genuinely free gathering of its kind – in England at any rate. There was only one loudspeaker, which was used for announcements, but no proper stage or associated PA system. Throughout the day we were repeatedly told that the stage was "on its way", and once or twice we heard a request for volunteers to "go to the top of the hill by the road" so they could help to unload it from the lorry. Mark and I excitedly went along up to offer our services, but... no lorry; no stage!

Evening finally came and some unknown band started to play on an improvised stage area using their own portable amplifiers, which were powered by a solitary generator. We made our way over to where the sound was coming from and lay back on the warm grass to soak in the atmosphere. Whilst they were playing, however, something truly miraculous happened: Hawkwind turned up with their own very distinctive "Orange" PA system which was hastily rigged up – we were going to have "proper" entertainment after all. Taking part in an event like this was something I'd dreamed of for several years, and now here I was laid back on the grass surrounded by hundreds of "my kind of people" (including some lovely-looking girls); no one to tell me what I could or couldn't do; and the prospect of an evening filled with "my kind of music". The only thing lacking was a joint to share around. It was Mark's turn to go in search of some gear and, at my bidding, he duly did so.

Mark returned dope-less. Instead, however, he'd got two pills of brown microdot LSD. I'd "tripped" on "acid" maybe three or four times before, but the most I'd ever taken was half of a tablet. Microdot was a fitting name for these pills, which were no bigger, and probably smaller, than a Piriton tablet. A sharp knife and flat surface were needed to cut one in half, and even then it was tricky; impossible, probably, in our present situation, especially without any tool for cutting. Inwardly, I took a deep sigh and told Mark I didn't want one. Previous experiments with acid – which is all they'd been – hadn't resulted in much: they'd made me feel a bit hyped-up and giggly, and also seemed to make everything around me look much sharper and more vivid – possibly as if a deeper layer of 3D had been added. Apart from this not being the kind of "high" I'd been wanting whilst lying there in the fading light, I knew that acid could sometimes have serious hallucinogenic effects which distorted reality and, in consequence, made people do bizarre and dangerous things. Sometimes, so I'd read, people even launched themselves from buildings, mistakenly believing they could fly. Crazy things like this were, presumably, associated with the experience of having a "bad trip", something else I'd read about which gave me the shivers and didn't want to experience firsthand. Staying in control whilst intoxicated by drugs or inebriated by drink remained a restraining influence on me. Yes, I'd been well and truly drunk on a few occasions, but I much preferred the far less sodden state of just being pleasantly heady.

Somehow or another – although I don't suppose it was too difficult for him – Mark managed to break down my resistance and persuade me to go ahead and join him on a trip: much better tripping together than alone. I remember very clearly just closing my eyes, breathing deeply, and then swallowing the pill. *There, I'd done it. No point in worrying about it now.* Just in case, though, I silently rehearsed the Lord's Prayer in my head as if were a mantra: a kind of enchanted verse which would ward off all evil. *Everything would now be fine.* With that, I lay back and tried to relax. Hawkwind had finished their set and another band had started playing – still using the Hawkwind PA equipment. After twenty minutes or so I wasn't aware of any change in mood. Some of the girls around us were sharing a flagon of cider, so I asked to have some in the hope it would help to get things going. Not long after I became aware that one of the guitarists in the band looked inexplicably weird. As I looked closer, I saw that his arms and legs had become vastly elongated and were somehow merging into one another. I was still with it enough, though, to appreciate that what I was seeing was somehow linked to the effects of the LSD. *Evidently, it had begun to work.* Then I looked up into the clear dark sky and saw a sustained shower of gold dust pouring down like transformed raindrops in a thunderstorm. It was breathtakingly beautiful and I lay there watching it, utterly transfixed. I tried to sit up but wasn't able to. This troubled me!

'What will happen at the end of the evening when everyone gets up to go back to their tents?' I asked myself.

I tried to force myself up and must have moved a little. In response, Mark lent over me playfully and started to flicker his fingers in front of my eyes,

33

unwittingly scaring me even further. Suddenly, I began to panic. My head felt as if would burst open from the deafening noise surrounding me, the cackling demonic roar of devils mocking me. And there they all were, thousands of gargoyle-like grotesque faces peering at me from within a huge oak tree that towered over us. I tried to sit up and take flight but my body froze as in the type of nightmare where it becomes impossible to flee the terror nor cry out for help.

The very next thing I knew I was on my feet and running through the crowd. All around me were bodies with faces that eerily transmogrified in front of me. Eyes sunk back into their sockets until only blackened holes which oozed blood remained. Everything and everybody I looked at took on the appearance of something which could only have sprung from the dystopian imagination of a psychotically crazed film director. I kept running, kept trying to escape the madness all around me: the sights, the smells, the noise, the physical sensation of oppression. It was all to no avail. I soon realized I was in a loop, running through exactly the same scenes repeatedly. As in a dream, I moved from one phase of events to another in the early stages of this trip with no memory of how they were connected; they just happened. At one point I found myself running across the road where a large phalanx of police officers was stationed. Bumping into one of them, I managed to speak at last. I pleaded for help, able only to explain that I was having a bad trip – that much I still knew even though the experiences of the trip had taken on a reality no less material – so it seemed – than the one we live in every day. In other words, I fully believed at the time that all of this was real: it was *really* happening. Instead of taking me away in the back of a van (I very much doubt I would be here writing this should he have done so), the saintly policeman took me to the "Release" area; the place where staff and volunteers from the drug-support agency, Release, had set up a base.

I have no way of knowing how long I spent with Release. There wasn't anything they were able to do with me; no magic antidote they could give me which would set things right. I just lay there on a blanket being bombarded by the menace in my head, the warped visions in my sight, and the accusing cacophony of voices I could hear compounding the message of doom. I believed myself to have entered hell itself. At some point I got up and wandered off. Some kind soul whom I bumped into offered to help and had me sit down with him and rest my head on his lap. I cried tears of sheer joy and thanksgiving as the trip changed direction and took me into a heavenly phase where I believed for a time that the very secrets of the universe were being unravelled right in front of me. Having seen what I'd seen, I knew I could never go back to "normal" life again; and yet I still hadn't quite entered into the rest of heaven. There was something keeping me back; something I hadn't yet been able to let go of. More phases of the trip followed, each with reduced intensity. Then, suddenly, I felt perishingly cold for the first time that night. Dawn was breaking and I'd been out all the time wearing only a T-shirt and jeans. The sensation of tiredness also began to grip me. At last, I guess, my body was beginning to respond to external stimuli in the way it should do. I went back into the wooded area hoping to find our tent and get some sleep. After much searching I eventually found it, trampled to the ground; and nor was there any sign of Mark. The sleeping bags were still there, so I lay down, drew myself tightly inside one of them and fell into a deep sleep for several hours. On waking, my five senses appeared to be functioning normally once again, even if my thoughts within were anxiously asking me how I could possibly ever make sense of what had happened. The fear of having sustained permanent psychological damage began to enclose me in its grip.

Back safely in Breachwood Green, with four or five days gone by since my bad trip, I felt the inability to make sense of what I'd experienced would drive me insane. I'd begun to enter a state of continuous anxiety and was unable to find comfort of any kind. Making it all worse, I think, was the thought of having to go back to school the following week: there was no way I could possibly have done so in such a state of mind. I shared all my anxieties with Tim, my sister's fiancé. He seemed to have some insight into what having a bad trip was all about.

'Look, John,' he told me bluntly, 'you've just got to tell yourself it was all nothing but a bad dream.'

Simple as that.

'What else was there for me to do?' I wondered. 'Would I be able to convince myself that this was all it amounted to? A kind of wakeful nightmare?'

To my amazement, and immense relief, his advice worked; and it worked quickly. Within just a few days I'd regained my senses and had slipped nearly effortlessly back into my previous persona. I felt genuinely able to look back on what had happened as being of no real consequence: an unfortunate result of having taken some "bum" acid. Hadn't I read about the "dodgy brown microdot" in one of the festival handouts? Yes I had! I'd known all along that I should never have taken it; certainly not a whole pill. So blasé did I become about the trip that I even came to take some kind of pride in having survived a rite of passage which now gave me the true credentials of being a thoroughbred teenage rebel.

The following winter term at Eton dragged on and on. I could no longer muster any enthusiasm for studying and the John whom my housemaster had once written about in a report as being "friends with one and all" now came to hold many of his peers in contempt: privileged bores who knew little or nothing about life "out there". More and more I yearned the company of my female friends back at home. One dark evening, a friend – a young Lord who was two years my junior – told me he had some acid for sale. Surely I could come to no harm, I told myself, if I were only to take a fraction of a pill. Longing for some kind of thrill, I suspended all rational thought and took what I believed to be about a third of a microdot pill. Half an hour later during collective evening prayers in the house dining room I'd become childishly giggly. Once we'd all dispersed I went to my room and sat listening to music through headphones. There were no visual hallucinations this time to suggest the LSD was leading me once again into an altered reality, but a moment came when I found myself literally plunging into a trip of equally disturbing intensity to my previous one. One second I was OK, the next I'd stepped through into a nightmarish world that presented itself as being both corporeal and incarcerating. I fled out of the boarding house and into the pouring rain wearing only the white collarless shirt and pin-striped trousers of our fabulous-but-famously-antiquated school uniform. One of the school chaplains found me next to the college chapel spinning myself around on the spot in response to some compulsive inner command I couldn't break free from. My recognition of him broke the spell and I sought the shelter of his umbrella. I was taken back to my housemaster's study, where I sat for the rest of the night completely mute whilst my trip passed through similar phases to those I'd experienced at Windsor.

I had to endure a prolonged interrogation from the headmaster, Michael McCrum, the following morning with the dark cloud of probable expulsion hanging over me. After the Headmaster graciously told me I *wasn't* going to be expelled, I immediately set about trying to pass it all off as a bad dream; just as I'd done only a few months previously. And I was equally successful. Having been given one last chance to prove myself, I set my mind to do so: there wasn't long left to go but I would work flat out to try and get decent A-level results. Walking down an enclosed shopping arcade in Hitchin just a few days before Christmas, however, the volume of surrounding noise began to intensify within my head uncontrollably. This was the only warning I got of the LSD flashback experience about to happen. For just a few seconds I was transported back into the unmistakeable horror of being on a trip: it was as real and intense as the trips themselves had been. But before I could begin to take any kind of stock I found myself walking out of the flashback and back along the arcade just as it had been a few seconds previously. To say that I was scared by the flashback would be a massive understatement. From then on, the awareness of being on the threshold between two distinct realities was one I couldn't shake off, no matter what I was doing; not even when I was back at Eton and playing football – a time, normally, when all my cares were suspended for the duration of the match. Repeated flashbacks no longer caught me off guard: I soon learnt how to anticipate them. To an extent, therefore, I was able to exercise some kind of mental control and prevent them overwhelming me in the way the first one had. Now, however, I was no longer able to dismiss the experiences as ultimately being of no consequence. They became of *huge* consequence, and I began to live in continuous fear they were the product of some far-more significant reality that was sucking me into its destructive control.

CHAPTER SIX: Ripened for harvest

I dreaded going back to school for the spring term: I knew I'd only get worse back in surroundings which would continuously remind me of that second awful trip. My housemaster was as kind and helpful to me as he'd always been, but I was sent home after just two weeks when my need of specialist medical help became apparent to all. My parents had been amazingly supportive when I'd told them about the trouble I'd got myself into at school; and they'd also proved themselves willing to help in whatever way they could after I'd started getting flashbacks. David had even bought a small portable TV to watch after all these years of us not being allowed to have a TV at all. At least the limited viewing allowance I was permitted gave some kind of distraction from the mental disturbance which had fallen on me. When I was sent home from school, however, David's tolerance began to crumble. Why, he asked, couldn't I just throw myself into studying and thereby forget all about these grand metaphysical issues of existence which seemed to be imposing themselves on me. It must have been very hard for him to understand just how scared and lost I was. As the weeks passed it became quite clear that he was increasingly coming to regard me as a hopeless case. Not knowing what else to do, he shut me out of his mind in much the same way as he wanted me to shut my own problems out.

Following a consultation which my mother had managed to wangle on the cheap with an eminent psychiatrist in Paddington, Dr. Elizabeth Tylden (Betty), I began to find some kind of hope that recovery was possible: an outcome I'd as good as given up on. She'd treated many others with drug problems, including those who, like me, had been floored by their misadventures with LSD. Her confident-but-caring approach gave me the assurance she was someone with real insight into my state of mind and would therefore be able to help. The Valium she prescribed for me *certainly* helped: it had an almost immediate calming effect which straight away lessened the cloud of oppression under which I'd become trapped. Put in plain language, I suppose I immediately began to feel much calmer. And the Valium also provided me with a defence against the threat posed by flashback experiences: when I felt myself "on the edge" I found I could chew a tablet – which wasn't unpleasant – and become quickly sedated enough to ensure control of what went on inside my head. After three visits to Betty my improvement was undeniable, even to myself. She was adamant that I needed to leave Eton and even rang the school authorities herself to give them her opinion. For David, I think this was last straw. All he could see was someone running away from his problems. And without that paternal attachment from knowing me to be the son of his own seed, he found it impossible to disguise the rejection he couldn't help but feel towards me.

Fully recovered, so I believed, later on in 1974 I enrolled at Stevenage College to make another stab at getting myself some decent A-level results. Garnished from her extensive drug-treatment experience, Betty had been able to provide me with compelling psycho-social explanations about the nature of LSD trips that went much of the way to satisfy my desperate need "to understand", and I'd finally managed once again to consign my troubled memories to that part of my brain's extensive storage system where they no longer overwhelmed my ability to get on with living. But I very nearly crashed out of college, once again, after one too many clashes with David. He'd refused to give me any kind of financial help beyond allowing me to continue living at home rent-free. And mum, having now started a late-in-life teacher-training course, had no spare money to provide me with regular support. Casual earnings from my weekend job on the deli counter at Safeway in Hitchin had to suffice, but it was all a bloody hard struggle; there's no better way of putting it, really. It became even harder when I switched jobs to a supermarket in Stevenage that paid slightly more and also enabled me to work longer shifts. On the downside, there was no bus service to Stevenage; so I had to get up early and walk the whole eight miles through country roads. Occasionally I managed to hitch a lift, but not often.

David made life at home far more difficult for me than it needed to have been. He still wanted me to obey certain restrictive rules with which it became impossible to always comply. There was still, for example, an evening curfew of ten-thirty. On one memorable evening I was coming back from Hitchin on my little old moped and knew that I'd be about ten minutes late. So maybe I was riding too fast – if that's possible on a moped. It was definitely too fast for the freezing conditions because when I hit a patch of black ice at the bottom of a hollow I lost control and skidded along the road underneath the moped for twenty yards or so. Although grazed, I was basically fine; but the bike had sustained sufficient damage to mean I couldn't continue riding it. I still had two miles to go along some seriously hilly roads – Breachwood Green itself is situated on a hilltop plateau – and had to push the bike all the way. As I entered the house, David appeared at the top of the stairs and began shouting at me. He'd had enough, so he thundered, of my refusal to obey his rules and there would be consequences – as yet unspecified. I explained what had happened but was told it was no excuse: ten-thirty was ten-thirty – regardless. He didn't even ask if I'd hurt myself.

My behaviour ended up coming under close scrutiny from *both* parents, not least on account of the music I listened to: "the Devil's music" so I was told. Bands such as Genesis may not have been to everyone's taste, but I have no recollection of finding any satanic influences in what I listened to. It became hard not to think I was failing on all fronts. Mum complained that I must be oversexed after I'd had a succession of fairly casual relationships. Even after I'd begun what would become a long-term relationship she accused me of promiscuity, something she abhorred with a vehemence equal to that of Mary Whitehouse's – if not stronger than it.

'Why oh why can't you be like one of the Mant boys? she often asked me despairingly.

Put simply, I had no wish whatsoever to be like James or Ian Mant, who apparently never ever stepped out of line, who dressed "sensibly", and whom I unkindly – and probably totally unfairly – thought of as being boring "straights". Besides, despite what mum may have thought I was still a virgin; there had only been two or three occasions when I'd come anywhere close to having been deflowered. There was never any doubt about the depth of my mother's love for me, nor mine for her; and I was always confident she would be willing to make any kind of sacrifice to ensure my welfare. But she was who she was and couldn't conceal her disapproval of my lifestyle, often appearing to be disapproving of me in person and little knowing how much it hurt. A few years previously, when I'd begged to be allowed to go and watch Luton Town play, she told me – in all seriousness – how ashamed she was to have a son who had all the makings of becoming a football hooligan.

'Why else,' she insisted, 'would you want to go to a football match?'

Why else indeed if you support the Hatters?

David's disapprobation wasn't softened by love in the same way that mum's was: he made it quite clear that he thought me to be beyond the pale. So a day came in early 1975 when we had one argument too many. I can't remember what provoked it but remember the outcome all too well. One insult led to another, as happens in rows, and he ended up detailing a whole litany of complaints that he'd obviously been nurturing.

'Both your mother and I,' he claimed, 'are thoroughly disappointed that you've become a drinker.'

Whaaat? Yes, I used to have two or three pints two or three times a week down at our local pub, the Red Lion. And there were occasions, I admit, when I'd go beyond two or three pints on a Saturday night out with friends in Hitchin at the notorious Red Hart pub. But these occasions of inebriation weren't nearly as often as I perhaps would have liked: I just didn't have the money, however much I begged, borrowed or even stole – the small trade in stolen tobacco which I ran with Christine, my partner in crime, was, praise be, never rumbled by the management of the supermarket where we both worked and where our contraband came from. When David had finished itemizing my behavioural shortcomings, I remained silent for a while. I wasn't at all happy with who I was and had no idea, really, who I wanted to be. I often felt adrift and vulnerable to the pull of different social attractions. Despite wishing otherwise, I had no clear sense of where I should be going and how I should get there – wherever it might be. But David had left me hurting and feeling totally misunderstood.

'Look!' I said 'I don't think you understand how hard I'm trying to change; how hard I'm trying to grow up and stand on my own two feet.'

He then gave me a disparaging taunt which entrapped me for far longer than I care to think about:

'That's all very well,' he began, 'but you're turning out to be just like your birth father. You won't ever change! A leopard can't change its spots.'

39

Hold on a moment! My birth father? The man who, so mum had told me, was a womanizing drunkard incapable of responsible behaviour. I was stunned. Floored. I was also intensely angry.

'*Christ!*' I thought, '*doesn't it mean anything to him that I've just narrowly escaped being crushed beneath the weight of a complete mental collapse?*'

Seemingly it didn't.

The next day I announced that I was off to live in my sister's house at St. Albans. And off I went. I then needed to work much longer hours in order to support myself – Jane wickedly made me pay rent. In nearby Radlett, stockbroker territory supreme, many of the magnificent houses had huge gardens to match; and these needed tending, of course. A door-knocking campaign to offer my gardening services was successful, but it came at the price of neglecting my college studies. My burgeoning little enterprise came to an end, however, when I sustained serious leg burns from a bonfire accident: the petrol I'd been throwing over the reluctant-to-burn garden pyre was to blame. Mum pleaded with me to come home so she could look after me whilst I was recovering, and I ended up staying on back at home indefinitely. One last gargantuan academic effort gave me three semi-decent A-level results a few months later; and these, together with the astonishing praise lavished on me in a reference from my former history teacher at Eton, resulted in an interview offer from Exeter University and an unconditional offer of acceptance from the University of Kent. Much to the chagrin of Michael Kidson, the legendary history teacher whom I'd kept in regular contact with, I took the later, not feeling confident enough to believe I would hold my own at Exeter.

Before taking my place at Kent, I spent a year working at a newly established Home and Garden Centre near Hitchin: "One Stop". My finances initially remained nothing less than chaotic; and I reached the nadir of my shame when a driving instructor from the BSM – British School of Motoring – called at our house to complain about what he called my "rubber cheque".

'*It's bounced as high as a house,*' he told mum, who'd answered the door.

I would never ever allow such a thing to happen again, I promised myself. And I didn't: neither in that year nor in any of the ones to follow. In fact I'd managed to save the goodly sum of one hundred pounds to augment my student grant by the time October 1976 came around. I'd also bought my first car: a mustard-coloured Hilman Imp that was forever breaking down and was more suited to the scrapyard than the public highway. Nonetheless, I grew very fond of it – as you do.

Perhaps the most significant aspect of these months was my wholehearted acceptance of Jesus Christ as lord and saviour: my born-again experience if you like. I'd never stopped fairly regular attendance at our local parish church, whatever else may have been happening with me. I even donned a cassock and surplice to sing in the choir from time to time, despite the unpredictably squeaky noises emanating from my teenage vocal chords no longer being either pleasing or in tune. Church was the place where I felt safest, where I felt everything was going to be OK, where I felt closest to God – even if he still seemed to be far far away. I wanted to find out about God almost as strongly as I wanted *anything* else in my life. All different kinds of spirituality intrigued and attracted me, and yet I always returned to Christianity as the faith which I hoped would ultimately lead me to the truth. And I finally found what I'd been looking for at St. Hugh's in Dunstable, a church which was very much part of the Charismatic movement.

Becoming born-again didn't happen in some kind of blinding flash; it was a process that took place as I spent an increasing amount of time with other young people from St. Hugh's. Even so, there was a very clear moment when I knew that something life-changing had happened; a moment when I felt – for the first time – that my many transgressions could be truly forgiven and when the love of Jesus Christ become far more than a worn-out cliche. By the time I went off to university at the end of the sizzling 1976 summer I was a noticeably changed person. I hadn't by any means renounced all aspects of what might be called my "worldly" lifestyle, and the company I kept was by no means exclusively Christian. But I had an enriched appreciation of the world, and mankind in general, which had made a profound influence for good on my attitudes and behaviour. I was even able to reassess my relationship with David. I shan't casually try to pretend this came without a struggle, but I knew I should at least attempt to show the same forgiveness God had shown to me – and so I gave it my best shot. With the unembarrassed forthrightness of a new convert I spoke with him about the new faith I'd found, and with my mother too. They both responded positively to "the new John" and began to explore ways in which they could deepen their own rather staid and conventional faith. I hadn't become anywhere near saintly, that's for sure, nor had I overcome all my personal problems; but I'd certainly begun to enjoy a lifestyle that was far more promising than the one I'd been buffeted about by as an adolescent.

CHAPTER SEVEN: Bugbrooke's kingdom

I woke up in the very early hours one morning sensing that something wasn't right. As I lay there in my student's study-bedroom I could feel the onset of another LSD flashback close at hand. I took some deep breaths, closed my eyes, and tried to fight off the sensations using mental determination. The flashback was averted but I found myself staring at the disturbing sight of where I would have ended up if I'd taken just one more step and fallen over the precipice into the hallucination-filled chasm below. There was no one to turn to for help; I was on my own. *Or was I?* I'd had one or two similar experiences in the previous year, but this was easily the most intense: I'd still not moved *completely* beyond the place where the influence of residual LSD damage could reach out to afflict me. Needless to say, perhaps, I felt decidedly freaked out. *Would my faith in Jesus Christ be able to sustain me? Or maybe heal me completely?* I'd received some pretty stunning "answers to prayer" since my born-again experience, some of which came very close to being beyond rational explanation – although I had, and still have, a deep reluctance to call them miraculous: they weren't. One of these involved certain problems within the family of a work friend, Sue, from the "One Stop" Home and Garden Centre where I'd been working. I promised to pray for her during my not-always-remembered bedtime prayers; and on this occasion I managed to keep my word. Events which subsequently took place stunned both Sue and me alike, and they were all verifiable. *But did they happen because of my prayer?* At the time I believed so. And yet, lying there awake in my university room, the helping hand of the Lord seemed nowhere to be found now that I perhaps needed it most. I didn't even have the help of any Valium. Without it, I feared another psychological collapse – another nervous breakdown if you like.

It was about four or five weeks into the term and I'd not had very much Christian company since arriving at university in Canterbury. I'd been along to a Christian Union (CU) meeting during freshers' week and had enjoyed the address given by a visiting preacher who went by the wonderfully zany name of "Winkey Pratney". But I hadn't been back again. The bottom line is that I'd been distracted, not least by my unsuccessful quest to meet someone attractive at one of the many discos being held around the campus and get hooked up with her. In addition to a blossoming social and sporting life, I'd also begun to tackle my course studies with something approaching gusto. My Christian faith had begun to take a back seat – evangelical Christians would probably have called it backsliding.

In spite of the fears provoked by the night-time LSD experience, I found out that I'd developed enough mental resilience to fight back against them. But I'd been given a sharp wake-up call and knew I needed to take action to get my Christian fellowship back on the right track. Thereafter, the CU itself – together with the friendships I made within it – quickly became central to my university life; of equal importance to my academic studies, if not of more. Listening to Christian music from people such as Graham Kendrick on my little old-fashioned record player was soothing therapy as I lay alone at night-time, and it helped me fend off being spooked by the occasional visitations I had from the stubbornly implacable LSD menace. Friendships matured, including the chaste one I had with Liz – a lanky, immensely attractive Welsh lass. By the summer term of 1977 I'd become so immersed in the CU that my name was being touted for the following year's presidency. I was ascribed considerable kudos on account of my home church being St. Hugh's at Dunstable, a fellowship which had become venerated within certain Christian circles after its vicar, Colin Urquart (a Charismatic-movement celebrity), had introduced the experience of being baptised in the Spirit and subsequently built up a congregation which filled the modern church-building to overflowing. I came across to others within the CU as being quite confident in my faith, and a number of friends looked to me for guidance on certain controversial issues. One of these issues was "Bugbrooke".

There were four or five CU members who'd caused considerable unrest as a direct consequence of the influence which the "Bugbrooke community" – as it was known – had had on them. A couple of them became committed members of the Community, and the others began an extremely close association. One of this little group, Debbie, had a room close to mine in the same college – Keynes – and we'd become close friends. She'd begun to have doubts about the authenticity of the Fellowship and had stopped travelling up with Clive Chitty – one of the committed members – on his regular weekend excursions to Northampton. Rumour had it that these Bugbrooke people were under the authority of "elders" who told them what they could or couldn't do. This, I felt, was "heavy shepherding" at its best; domination at worst. Also, apparently, those within the CU who'd taken the Bugbrooke command had created the impression of believing that everyone else should be doing likewise: *all other Christians are second best to the ones of us who live communally* appeared to be their message. What nonsense it was, I thought, if that's what they *really* believed. Neither did I think, as the Bugbrooke posse seemed to, that everyone should feel compelled to be baptised in the Spirit and engage in the more extreme forms of Charismatic worship, which included talking in tongues. I myself had always held this kind of worship at arm's length, despite my membership of St. Hugh's. I didn't really understand what talking in tongues was about and thought that the worshippers had been taken over in some way, that some external entity was doing the actual talking. This worried me, even if it was the Holy Spirit himself who'd been doing the taking-over. Because of my LSD experiences, I wanted to make sure I was always firmly in control of anything which happened to me.

Some of my CU friends were actually quite keen for me to visit Bugbrooke so that I could report back. Many of us wanted to find out exactly what lay behind the rumours we'd heard. After resisting the idea of visiting for quite some time, I eventually came round when I began to feel it was unfair of me to make judgements about Bugbrooke without having been there myself. When Clive found out that I was keen to visit, he came to see me in my room to offer a lift. Significantly, this was the first time he'd shown any interest in me or spoken with me face to face. I accepted his offer, however, and thankfully Liz did too. This gave me the reassurance I needed of not, for example, having to face the dreaded elders alone. So one fair summer's morning, a Saturday, the three of us set off north.

On arrival in the village of Bugbrooke, Liz and I were taken by Clive to New Creation Hall, a huge old former rectory set within several acres of grounds. I was almost immediately struck by unrushed, relaxed, friendly atmosphere. It would have been almost impossible not to be aware of it: the ambience could very nearly be described as having been corporeal in its intensity. Within the space of a few minutes we met at least a dozen or so people who were all as welcoming towards us as if they'd been looking forward to our visit for a very long time and had been preparing themselves for it. One bearded man called Victor, probably in his late thirties, grasped me by the hand and said:

'It's really good to have you with us, bro. I hope you enjoy being here. It's always good when people from Canterbury come up to visit!'

Until – dim witted as ever in some respects – I realized it was short for brother, I was puzzled by what would prove to be the much-repeated use of this word "bro". I'd never actually heard people address one another in this sort of language anywhere else; here, it was common parlance. At Bugbrooke, all men were called "bro" (brother) and all women "sis" (sister). *All* of the sisters were dressed in long flowing skirts or dresses and other loose-fitting apparel; *all* of them had long hair, and many had it contained within a headscarf covering. They weren't dowdy, however. In fact I remember having a strong impression of how colourful their clothes looked. As the day went by I noticed the sisters were all engaged in tasks of a domestic nature: cooking, ironing, looking after children, or cleaning. Not that they came across as being downcast; they just seemed to go about their duties with a cheery disposition, some of them singing quietly to themselves as they did so.

Out on the front lawn children were playing in the sunshine. Clive told me that there were several nuclear families living at New Creation Hall, each within their own allotted suite of rooms. This afforded them a measure of privacy, but they shared mealtimes with the unmarried brothers and sisters who made up the bulk of the thirty-five-strong household "family". I learned that the brothers shared dormitory-style bedrooms in one section of the hall, the sisters in another – the strict segregation of men and women being an important feature of their lifestyle.

We managed to have a brief look around the hall and its grounds before some other Community members arrived to take Liz off to the house where *she* would be staying for the weekend. No sooner had they all gone than a young man dressed in denim wandered casually over to join Clive and I on the lawn. He had chiselled, handsome features, and very long, straight, brown hair: he could easily have just come from a practice session with Status Quo for all I knew from his appearance.

'*Hi, bro!*' he said, putting his hand on my shoulder. '*My name's Jonathon. I'll be sort of looking after you for the rest of the day.*'

We went back inside the hall into a large lounge: previously, I presume, a grand withdrawing room; but, under its new management, all traces of grandness removed. It was furnished with well-worn armchairs and the atmosphere was pleasantly relaxed. From outside, through an open window, I could overhear the light-hearted banter between two brothers who were working in the garden.

'*What you up to, bro?*' one of them asked.

'*I'm purging this bed of elders,*' the second replied with a light-hearted laugh that was immediately reciprocated.

My ears pricked up.

'*Well,*' I thought, '*this little skit I've just overheard shows the elders aren't **so** fearsome that they can't be joked about.*'

Jonathon then drove me in one of the communally-shared cars to a village some three or four miles away – Nether Heyford – where "New Creation Farm" was located – and where Noel Stanton lived along with about thirty others. Whilst showing me around, Jonathon explained that many Community members had secular jobs *in the world* (as he described it), but there were also others who worked for one or another of the Community's businesses such as the health-food shop, the building and transport-services firm, the clothing shop in Northampton, or New Creation Farm itself. Jonathon also told me about the farm being a place where students or visitors came to work while they were staying in one of the Community-owned houses in the neighbourhood.

The farmyard itself was a scene of intense yet apparently happy activity. There were those who were getting on with their chores (mucking out the pigsties, feeding the hens, shifting straw, tending to the bees, repairing tractors and machinery, or packaging food in one of the converted sheds for distribution to the shops); children playing around in the garden or on the grass triangle at the front of the farmhouse; and those, like me, who were simply there to look around. Again, the atmosphere was one of friendship and welcome; smiles were everywhere. The warmth of the sunshine helped to reinforce the attraction of this other-worldly environment, which presented itself as a pocket of utopian escape from a chaotic, frenetic, unsympathetic world.

I was taken inside one of the timber-built pig-houses, where a long row of iron-barred cages enclosed the sows who'd recently given birth. The young piglets squealed and squirmed behind their mother under the warmth of the artificial lights. Had I then understood what was meant by "factory farming", I may well have recoiled at the incongruity of what I was observing with the world-renouncing lifestyle espoused by this Community. And the knowledge that the piglets were being injected with growth-enhancing hormones might also have given me early-warning signals which I would have done well to heed. Such environmental sophistication, however, lay some way ahead for a young man whose social and political worldview was still in its formative infancy. All I saw, therefore, were lots of delightful-looking, well-fed, pinkish piglets who, for all I knew, were as happy as a pig could be – even though they were soon to be prematurely weaned and clustered together for intensive fattening in "flatbed" containers at the other end of the pig hut. No different, it must be said, to hundreds of other pig farms around the country. But there again, this didn't purport to be a *typical* farm.

Jonathon proved to be an immensely patient guide, even though I subjected him to an almost uninterrupted barrage of questions about the issues which had been bothering me. His thoughtful replies helped me begin to understand how the whole setup worked; albeit that the impression I thereby developed was, in truth, no more than a skeleton outline which would require considerable fleshing out to give it authentic shape. *How was I to know that, once I'd attained sufficient maturity and experience to see clearly what I then only saw as through a glass darkly, my repellent assessment of everything would be far stronger than the attractive one I formed from first impressions?*
The guided tour had introduced me to many things which were strange and new, but I couldn't help myself from tingling with a restrained excitement. I sensed that this lifestyle *worked*. People were happy! They didn't look repressed or downcast but had gladly embraced a radical new way of living based on the principles of holiness, equality, and obedience to what they saw as being the way of the Bible.
'What could be wrong with that,' I asked myself, 'even if it flew in the face of what many might consider to be reasonable?'
Like a closed flower exposed to warmth and sunlight, I began to find – almost against my better judgement – I was opening up to what was going on at Bugbrooke, and I couldn't help considering the possibility that God had indeed led me there for a specific purpose.
With the time for us all to attend the Saturday-evening meeting in the chapel drawing close, I began to feel quite ashamed for ever having been so critical of these Charismatic Jesus-People, not least because in the past few hours alone I'd met a remarkable array of people from widely diverse backgrounds and age-groups. The way in which they all appeared

to be living together in an atmosphere of mutual acceptance and friendship, cultural and class barriers apparently overcome, was an achievement that I perceived to be unique. *Surely it was only the Spirit of God himself who could have established all this?* And if indeed it *was* the Almighty who'd engineered it all, then maybe I needed to revise my prejudiced attitudes on other issues which the Fellowship held to be important: issues which included baptism in the Spirit and talking in tongues. Again, I "opened up my heart" – Bugbrooke-speak – to Jonathon about it all. I tried to explain how scared I was about the effect which LSD had had on me and how uneasy I therefore was about losing control if I opened myself to experiences beyond my understanding. I felt sure that I could trust Jonathon; we seemed to have so much in common.

'The best thing you can do,' he said reassuringly, 'is "go up for ministry" after the meeting tonight. The elders will help sort you out.'

'What exactly do you mean by "going up for ministry"?' I asked, still getting used to the jargon which all institutions have a way of adopting.

'Well, bro,' he replied, 'after the meeting, Noel will ask anyone who wants to be baptised in the Spirit, or who needs help of any kind, to go to the upper room in the chapel extension where the elders will be there to talk with them and pray with them.'

I could hardly wait, although I was still by no means certain that the experience of meeting the elders was going to be a comfortable one.

To get to the chapel from the hall, where we'd gone back to at tea-time, we had to walk along a hedged pathway taking us through the older part of Bugbrooke village. Jonathon had an acoustic guitar slung over his shoulder and could easily have been mistaken for a festival-bound hippy. At one point we walked alongside the local parish church, so I thought to tease out from Jonathon his attitude towards it.

'What's this church like, Jonathon?' I asked.

A cheeky smile came to his face and he looked at me with a glint in his eye.

'Well, the bricks and mortar look alright to me. What do **you** reckon?'

I had no reply. I knew only too well that the most substantial asset of many such rural churches was the building itself – this could hardly be gainsaid. And yet Jonathon had managed to convey what he'd thought without being unnecessarily offensive or haughty. I returned his smile; we walked on together.

Bugbrooke Chapel in the 70s

I should have liked to have been better prepared for what was to happen that evening, although the effect on me would probably have been much the same. The chapel itself was a very simple, stone-built structure, set back some ten yards or so from the main village road; and it would have blended quite inconspicuously with the surrounding yellow-sandstone buildings had the words "Jesus Lives Today" not been emblazoned in bold red lettering across the front facade. The small car park in front of the adjacent manse was already packed full with a fleet of ageing minibuses by the time we ourselves got there. And more were still arriving, dropping off their passengers and then moving on to be parked elsewhere in the village. People were also arriving on foot from literally all directions; so many that it was hard to imagine how we could possibly all fit into this small building. I met up with Liz again on the front steps before we were taken inside to reserved "visitor" seats right at the front – where the altar rail would have been before the chapel was stripped of all furnishings deemed unnecessary under the new regime.

A more buoyant sight you could hardly have imagined. The building buzzed with literally hundreds of garrulous brothers and sisters pressing in to fill every available seating space, either in the original wooden pews that had been left in the main body of the chapel or on the plastic chairs which had been crammed into every nook and cranny elsewhere. It compared in my imagination with descriptions I'd read about the first-century crowds who packed into the buildings where the early apostles preached, especially because I remembered about one poor man, Eutychus, who could only find space on a window ledge and ended up falling through the opening to his death – only to be miraculously restored to life, so we're told, by the apostle Paul himself. It wasn't just the sheer numbers that amazed me, though, it was also the impression created by the casual appearance of the crowded company; vastly different to any other Christian assembly I'd been to. These folk weren't uniformly clothed in collar-and-tie or Sunday-best-hat but came dressed as they had been for the rest of the day. And although long skirts or frocks were evidently some kind of dress code for the sisters, there was no shortage of colour and different styles.

Not that *everyone* looked like a young hippy! There were those who weren't just *older* but distinctly *elderly*. There were children of every age, infants in their mothers' arms or in carry-cradles, and casually dressed adults just that bit too old to feel comfortable in faded jeans and T-shirts. All around, people were greeting one another as long-lost friends, hugging one another, waving to one another, laughing, or signalling to indicate an empty seat. No-one-but-no-one seemed to be anything other than excited that Saturday night had come round again.

There was no mistaking Noel Stanton, a bachelor of fifty, when he made his appearance. He came from a small room at the back of the chapel to take his appointed position on a small, unoccupied section of the elevated platform just three or four feet away from Liz and me. He was dressed in a smart suit (unlike anyone else), his unbuttoned jacket revealing a shirt stretched rather tightly around his somewhat corpulent midriff. He was tall and had quite long, rather straggly, thinning grey hair – swept back over the top of his head in the style favoured by those men who wish to disguise the lack of hair beneath. The murmur of chattering voices quickly subsided as he came to the front. He stood there for a while composing himself, then looked around, smiled, and addressed the assembled company:

'Greetings, beloved brethren!' he began. 'Good to see so many of you here tonight. I'm sure God's blessing awaits all of us. Put your hand in the air if you want to be blessed by God tonight. Come on. Right up... Yes! That's good!'

Just about everybody's hands were lifted high, although Liz had a struggle to get hers above shoulder height. I could sense how stiff she felt.

'Come on then, brethren,' he continued. 'Let's make the world tremble shall we? Let's show who is **truly** Lord. **We** are the people of Jesus Christ and are proud to announce it. Let the demons take note and flee. Let no one be left in any doubt that the kingdom of God is here with us **and that Je-e-sus Ch-rist is Lor-ord**,' each syllable thrust out with considerable force.

His voice rose in crescendo to a shout as he concluded his introduction with this triumphant declaration. Then he gave a brief nod to the rather dour-faced looking sister – so I thought at the time – sat at an electric organ to his right-hand side. She, in turn, gave a chord of introduction, and several hundred voices pitched into a full-throated statement of intent as they belted out the words of a Community-written chorus:

49

"Tremble oh Earth at the presence of the Lord,
At the presence of the God of Jacob;
Tremble Oh Earth at the presence of the Lord
for Israel is his dominion.
The sea looked and ran and the waters turned back,
The mountains skipped like rams;
The sea looked and ran and the waters turned back
before the chosen people of Israel."

It was so loud and so intimidating that I was quite shaken. Hands were raised in the air, almost in defiance. It could easily have been the marching song of an army set for battle, confident of victory.

'How can this be Christian?' I thought. *'It's too aggressive.'*

Almost in that very instant, however, I perceived a fresh element of Christian faith which had never really occurred to me before. Because I'd been accustomed to thinking of Christianity in terms of love, forgiveness, gentleness, kindness, patience and the like, I'd never thought too much about the loftier issues of spiritual warfare and victory.

'But why shouldn't we Christians announce in triumph that our God has been victorious?' I found myself thinking.

'Why shouldn't we serve notice to the world that the God of Jacob has chosen to demonstrate His glory through the people who are subject to him? Why should we always be so timid about declaring there is an omnipotent God who is in command of what goes on in the world?'

When the chorus was being sung for the third or fourth time, therefore, I found I could join in and enjoy it.

After an extended period of singing choruses, various people talking in tongues, and everyone collectively "singing in the Spirit"[a] such as I'd never heard before, Noel launched into a powerful address from where he stood at the front. This must have lasted for the best part of an hour and was delivered with great passion, straight from the hip. Although the content must have been carefully thought through and prepared at some time or another, its presentation came across as convincingly extemporaneous – albeit that a few years later I'd heard a standardised version of the same talk more times than I cared to remember. His main theme concerned "the kingdom of God"; how the church was meant to be a manifestation of it here on Earth, thereby reflecting God's power and glory. The hub of his argument was that God hadn't saved

---

[a] *Singing* rather than *talking* in tongues, each person using their own unique melody which, somehow or another, blended harmoniously with everyone else's singing – generally, that is, but not always.

us through the work of Jesus Christ in order for us to remain as individual Christians "doing our own thing"; rather, He intended us to join together as a church, as a kingdom, as a community with Christ at the centre: a community where the poor and needy could be looked after and where the greed of the world was done away with.

In one hand Noel carried a large, black, leather-bound Bible which he frequently waved in the air but seldom opened up to quote from: he seemed to know most of the New Testament off by heart and had no need to refer to the written text. He became extremely worked up at times and literally bellowed out his words in pursuit of his theme, the blood vessels protruding visibly from his forehead as he held his Bible aloft and rhythmically beat it with his free hand. It would hardly have been surprising had he collapsed with a heart attack, such was his animation. (And I cannot deny there were to be future times when, secretly, I came close to wishing he would.)

'Brethren!' (he shouted)

'I'm fed up!' (he stamped his foot hard down on the ground)

'Fed up of yellow-bellied,' (he thumped his Bible with one hand)

'weak-kneed,' (he thumped his Bible again)

'namby-pamby Christians' (he thumped his Bible once more)

'who say they've been saved but won't let God be the God of their pockets.' (he paused)

'You cannot,' (he slapped his Bible)

'I say **cannot**,' (he slapped his Bible and stamped his foot on the ground simultaneously)

'serve God **and** the world.' (he shouted at the top of his voice)

This certainly wasn't the standard fodder or normal mode of delivery that you could have expected from pulpits up and down the country in a typical church gathering. And Liz – good, "solid", evangelical Christian girl that she was – decided to check something he'd said in the pages of her *own* Bible: her surety that what he was saying was correct. As she turned the pages, so Noel turned to *her*.

'Sister!' he demanded. 'You don't open your Bible to check up on a prophet when he's delivering God's anointed word. I can assure you that everything I'm telling you about is there for all to read, even though you might wish it wasn't. Why don't you just go ahead and tear the page out of your Bible if you don't like it?'

He paused a moment and it seemed that he would carry on preaching. But then, sounding just a tad kinder, he turned to Liz again:

'You can talk to any of the leading brothers afterwards if you like. But pay attention while I'm ministering!'

Talk about "fire and brimstone"! I'd heard the doom-and-gloom merchants peddling their wares on the streets of our busy towns and cities, urging us to repent before it was too late; I'd been subjected to robust homilies from the pulpit of the local Baptist chapel in Breachwood Green; I'd sat through impassioned expositions of the gospel message from visiting speakers to the Christian Union, sometimes with a voice raised sufficiently to be classified as a shout; and I was well aware of the style used by some "professional" evangelists to impart their message. *This*, however, was going to take some beating. Whether you liked the style or not (which I didn't), there was no doubt the man knew what he was about: he left you with no scope for taking the middle ground. This wasn't a sermon you could have taken notes on and then gone away to chew over the cud of its content until you'd reached a dispassionate, informed opinion about it. This didn't leave the opportunity to sit on the fence undecided which way to jump. This required a reaction, a response.

It was possible, of course, that the man was deranged. But looking around me at all the wonderfully enthusiastic people – including a good number of successful lawyers, doctors and other professionals – who'd literally left everything behind to follow God in the Bugbrooke way, I doubted whether anyone at the helm of such a beautiful company could be away with the fairies. Alternatively, then, there was the apparently undeniable conclusion that the man was *indeed* someone with a message: a message that anyone wanting to be wholehearted in their Christian lifestyle would do well to heed. I didn't like the shouting; never had done. But I couldn't deny the growing conviction that, through this man, God was speaking to *me*. *And what had I achieved in my Christian life? How could little me be so proud as to suppose I knew better than this man who was building a Christian society at Bugbrooke which challenged the greed and corruption of British society – both world and church?*

Noel Stanton *wasn't* a man with immediate charm. He was quite unlike the slick, handsome, well-oiled charmers who with tear-in-eye and smoothness-in-voice can have the American public reaching for their chequebooks and falling over in the aisles in their rush to "come forward and be saved". Nor was he a man who could have been described as immediately attractive and likeable; not the sort of man whom you instinctively felt you could trust. He lacked true charisma – despite the forcefulness of his delivery. And although his use of words was intelligent and his biblical exposition well researched, he wasn't eloquent in the sense of being able to make a subject come alive for a spellbound audience: *he certainly lacked oratorial finesse.* There can be no doubt that unless you believed him to be who he said he was, an anointed messenger of the Lord, you may well have found him unattractive, abrasive and offensive. It was the *content* of his message, not the person delivering it, to which I responded. He used all his skill, his intelligence, his bulk and his volume to ensure that his message was being listened to and plainly understood. In doing so, he found, in me, a receptive vessel. Those who heard him and were inclined to feel – sensibly – that the man and the message had to be taken as a complete package may well have walked away from Bugbrooke Chapel with serious misgivings – unless, that is, they had actually enjoyed the experience of being shouted at.

After Noel had – finally – concluded his outpourings, he gave the invitation which I'd been waiting for:

'If you feel the Lord has been speaking to you tonight,' he announced, *'or if you need prayer for anything, or if you want to be baptised in the Spirit and released in tongues, then make you way to the ministry room upstairs to my left. The brethren will be waiting there to minister to you. Don't miss out on what the Lord wants for you!'*

Noel Stanton

As I negotiated my way up some narrow stairs to the ministry room, I passed a sister – Ruth – who'd visited Debbie at Canterbury and whom I therefore knew; so I greeted her with a warm hug – this seemed to be the way in which things were done here and I was genuinely glad to see her. Somehow, though, I felt she herself was awkwardly unresponsive towards me. In fact the poor girl must have been quite shocked by my forwardness. I felt rather red-faced when I later realized that I'd breached the protocol required by holiness: brothers hugged brothers, and sisters hugged sisters – but unisex hugging was *prohibited.*

The upper room was filling rapidly. I was shown to an easy-chair and almost immediately surrounded by four brothers. They knelt on the floor at my feet, and the one called Ralph spoke first.

'What can we do for you, bro?' he asked.

Ralph was a young man in his mid-twenties who had kind-looking, handsome features, with long ginger hair and a scraggy beard – many of the brothers, I noticed, had beards. He was very thin and wore the near-uniform blue jeans and T-shirt. He spoke gently, but also with clarity and apparent authority. When he drew breath between words, he let out a soft but audible whistle as the air passed between his teeth, rather like "whispering Bob Harris" from "Old Grey Whistle Test" fame. He was instantly likeable. But I'd *expected* to be talking with one of the elders and, as such, thought that I might be getting short-changed with Ralph. Or was *he* one of the elders? Surely not!

'Are you one of the elders?' I asked, quite brazenly.

'Yeah. Certainly am,' he said, kneeling to an erect position of playful authority. He drew breath in that characteristic way of his and, laughing quietly, carried on:

'Why? What did you expect? We're not really all that fierce you know. We ain't gonna eat you.'

He looked round at the others. Smiling kindly at me with understanding eyes, they all nodded in agreement. I felt surrounded in the security of warm friendship as they encouraged me to "pour out my heart". I explained how much I wanted to keep my feet firmly on the ground and how uneasy I therefore felt about the baptism in the Spirit. I also told them about the experiences I'd had with LSD and all the residual anxieties I'd been left with. Then I asked:

'Do you know much about LSD and what it does?'

Ralph again laughed quietly; and he did so without making me feel my own experience was inconsequential but rather that I was amongst people who knew what they were talking about.

'Yeah, quite a few of us have done bummers [bad trips] you know.' he answered.

This was all too much. St. Hugh's church had been good for me; very good. The Christian Union had in some ways been even better. But just about all the Christian friends I knew and loved had come through their teenage years almost unscathed by the temptations and traumas which I'd plummeted into, headfirst. As such, we didn't always speak the same language. There was still part of me which felt they were sometimes inclined to be a bit drippy, even though I would *never* have used this word to describe them: it's too frequently employed in derision of those people sensible enough to avoid the ridiculous extremities of the very people who would label them as drippy.

Ralph and his cohort were the first Christian people I'd met to have experienced anything like the adolescent turbulence which I'd been through, and yet they were the very "elders" of whom I'd heard such fearsome reports. *How could that be?* Regardless of what other people may have said about them, all I knew at the time was that they measured very tall against the intuitive yardstick I used to weigh people up and determine how highly I regarded them.

Moreover, I felt confident these Bugbrooke brothers would be able to help me exorcize the dreaded LSD spectre which had refused to lay down and die, which continued to inhabit the loneliness of my mind, and which, I felt, restricted me from ever completely becoming the person whom God wanted me to be – and whom, naturally enough, I myself wanted to be: someone who was fully "free" and comfortable with himself.

After we'd talked for some little while, the brothers said they would pray for me; each of them laying their hands on my head while doing so. They asked the Lord to take away my deep-rooted anxieties and give me increasing assurance of His love; then they spoke very quietly in tongues. I relaxed as I felt a warm glow of content take hold of me: nothing sensational or highly emotional, nothing which was an unmistakable visitation from the Almighty, just a feeling that I was with friends whom I could trust and that God was going to look after me. The brothers had made me feel very special, almost as if *they* were the ones who were privileged to have had my company, and not vice versa – which was how *I* felt.

That night I was to stay at a terraced house in Daventry – one of the households they called Welcome Homes. I squeezed into a packed minibus with others who were going there – or being dropped off along the way – and found myself sitting next to the same brother Rufus whom we've met in previous chapters. He wasn't a man, I discovered, ever short of a word or two; all part and parcel, I guess, of the thespian background he'd come from. During our conversation he kept referring to "the kingdom" as if he was talking about the Fellowship itself. I asked him to elaborate.

'Well, bro,' he said, 'of course God's kingdom is a lot bigger than just this Fellowship. I know that! And Noel has taught us that any true church is part of God's kingdom. But for us, you see, **this** is the kingdom where we live, and it's the kingdom we belong to. So in that sense it really is "the kingdom" – if you get what I mean.'

This worried me, as it reinforced what I'd been told – that people from Bugbrooke actually thought *they* belonged to the best of God's churches.

'What about these other "true churches"?' I objected. 'Do you **really** think they are as much part of God's kingdom as Bugbrooke is? What exactly do you mean when you talk about a **true** church?'

'Well, bro,' he said again, leaning forward as if he was about to take me into his confidence, 'different churches have had a different amount of light given to them, and everyone has to act according to the amount of light they've been given. A true church is one that is being obedient to the light it's been given. Here at Bugbrooke, because we have a prophet who has led us in the way of righteousness and holiness, we've been given a **lot** of light. We've been shown how important it is for a church which wants to move on in the Lord to have an organizational structure that's based on a community lifestyle.'

Then, as if he was aware of being mischievous, and with the kind of wry grin with which I was becoming familiar, he began to speak in much plainer English:

'Look, don't quote me as saying this, will you?' he began, whilst also putting his arm around me. *'And you'll have to forgive me if I sound a bit kind of proud – which I know I shouldn't be. But I've not heard of anything to beat what we've got here. I reckon we're out there in front somewhere, you know.'*

I was disarmed by his cheeky honesty and didn't feel the need to pursue the matter further. In any case, I was beginning to think there was probably a lot of substance to what he was saying.

At the house in Daventry, the dozen or so people who lived there had gathered in the living-room for a hot drink. I was offered one but didn't relish the idea of meeting yet *more* people: I'd taken just about all I could for one day.

'No thanks,' I replied. *'I think I'd like to get off to bed now. I just end up getting ratty if I get too tired.'*

This was quite true. But amongst these people I would soon have to learn that tiredness was no excuse for being ratty; nor an excuse for missing out on "fellowship with the brethren".

CHAPTER EIGHT: Robbing the world

Sunday in the Jesus Fellowship Church and New Creation Christian Community was no day for the fainthearted. The first morning chapel meeting I attended lasted nearly three hours and was again presided over by Noel Stanton. This time, he gave a lengthy biblical exposition which concentrated on a small passage of text from one of the New Testament books. Week by week, so I found out, he would progress through the same book, taking just a few verses at a time and analysing the meaning of each phrase in minute detail, often expounding on different inferences that could be drawn from a particular word when considered in the original Greek or Hebrew text. Not that he was a classical scholar in his own right, but he used the knowledge he'd acquired from a number of well-researched and respected Bible commentaries. These Sunday-morning "Bible Studies", so called, were no short affairs (they often went on for well over an hour), and it was surprising to find that the subject of "community" could be so clearly discovered in texts which, to the layman, were apparently quite unrelated. Sometimes there were people in the assembly whose body language or facial expressions must have clearly shown that they didn't find Noel's exegesis either comfortable or comprehensible. He wasn't a man given to the easy toleration of dissent and, if he noticed any such "cynic", was quite likely to interrupt his theme in order to address the now-more-pressing concern.

'So, we have a brother with us who's decided he doesn't agree with the Bible after all, have we? Go on then, my brother,' he would shout. *'Be real! Burn your Bible!* **If you don't like it, burn it.**'

The chapel would resound with his full-bloodied, thunderous reproach, no one daring to move or indicate further disagreement. After a short pause to let his words penetrate their target, he would then complete his reprobation in more subdued, if not somewhat sarcastic, language:

'It's funny how some people no longer like their Bibles when they understand the hard language in it. But please don't say you've got an argument with **me**! *It's the mighty apostle Paul who you want to argue with. He's the one who wrote these words, not me.'*

After the first of my many – too many – exposures to Sunday morning chapel (which certainly gave me plenty to think about), everyone went off to have a simple cooked meal at one or other of the large houses: for me it was back to New Creation Hall. No sooner had all the plates been cleared away and washed up than it was time to return to the chapel for an afternoon "praise meeting" led by Kelly, Noel's trusted lieutenant. The third and final meeting of the day – another marathon session led by the great man himself – followed on from late-afternoon tea and took us through to nine or ten o'clock. Altogether, some seven or eight hours of the day had been spent inside Bugbrooke chapel.

On the journey back to Canterbury after that first visit back in 1977, which took us deep into the night, I sat next to Clive and enthusiastically chatted with him about the weekend's experiences; Liz sat quietly in the back keeping her thoughts to herself.

'What about people wanting to leave the Community?' I asked him. *'Does it happen very often? Is it actually allowed?'*

*'Yes, people **do** leave,'* he replied. *'And it's common enough for us to have jargon for it. We call it "splitting".'*

He made it sound perfectly normal; nothing to get too worked up about. I felt thankfully reassured.

In the days that followed I could scarcely disguise my enthusiasm about the Fellowship while talking with other friends from the CU, although I did my very best not to do the same as some of the other Bugbrooke enthusiasts had: using the language of uncritical praise, they'd managed to convey the impression that they believed the Bugbrooke Fellowship to be the supreme example of what a Christian church should be like. Debbie, of course, was particularly keen to hear what I had to say, and I made no disguise to *her* of how deeply influenced I'd been. I also told her how keen I was to revisit the Fellowship as soon as possible. Having heard what I had to say, she more or less immediately decided that she'd been wrong to distance herself from a place which she still, deep within herself, regarded as her "spiritual home". We *both,* therefore, made arrangements to travel up with Clive on his next fortnightly pilgrimage to Bugbrooke. Liz wasn't keen to go back again, which didn't surprise me at all.

Word got back to me through Clive that one of the Fellowship brothers, Shaun, whom I'd met in the chapel and spoken with at some length, was keen for me to be his weekend guest at New Creation Farm. I was quite happy about this because I'd found him to be likeable, honest, and easy to talk with; whereas I'd already discovered that *some* of the brothers were far more inclined to use approved Community-speak in their conversation – by which I mean they spoke in a doctrinaire style and their answers to questions were, I sensed, more influenced by what they felt expected to say, or had heard others say, than by carefully-thought-out attitudes of their own; attitudes which would, inevitably, include subtle deviations to the party line. Shaun was one of the brothers who seemed willing to talk about the warts as well as the wonders of the Fellowship, and I was therefore more than happy to accept the invitation to be his guest.

Sometime on the Saturday of my next visit Shaun took me into Northampton to have a look at the shops which the Fellowship owned. But had it been intended that I should be impressed, the effect was quite the opposite. My head was particularly set-a-spinning by what I observed in "Jeans Plus", the high-street fashion boutique which sold the same kind of clothing you'd have found in similar shops under different ownership. In the first place, I was quite stunned to find that one of the sisters who helped in the shop – a very attractive girl with long, light-brown flowing hair and wraith-like figure – was herself wearing jeans, the normal dress code for sisters having been waived in favour of her commercial duty to promote the goods. Nor were the advertising posters necessarily any more discrete than elsewhere, there being nothing improper, it seemed, with displaying close-up views of tightly clinging denim around the shapely form of male and female buttocks. Anywhere else, I dare say, this would have hardly caused offence, and Lord Longford himself may have found the pictures innocuous. But to my naive, innocent and impressionable young mind, it was a clear display of double standards. In pursuit of the very highest standards of sexual purity, Fellowship members were forbidden from wearing provocative clothing. Yet here, in one of their shops, they were promoting the same kind of apparel all the local lads and lasses would be wearing on a Saturday night when they hit the clubs of Northampton intent on "pulling".

'And why did they sell incense and other eastern-style, pseudo-mystical regalia in the shop?' I asked myself. *'What was that all about? How did **that** fit in?'*

I was going to need some convincing answers to settle my nerves. But Shaun was unable to give them, unsure himself if he could see anything wrong with it all. My opportunity to seek reassurance at the highest level came when I was taken into Noel Stanton's private room at New Creation Farm to be introduced. Having been taking a rest in preparation for the evening's meeting, he was lying on his bed.

'Hiya, bro! How ya doin?' he said, in a deep, paternal, warm voice – quite unlike the one I'd heard as he stood bellowing at us from the front of the chapel.

'It's real good to have ya with us – I've heard all about ya from Shaun. He's taking good care of you I expect?'

His use of affected lazy slang, unnecessary and seemingly out of character, came across as quite strange. I could only conclude that he'd developed this style of speech in order to equip himself with an easy colloquialism for talking with the young brothers and sisters by whom he was surrounded, and also to distance himself from the stuffiness of middle-class culture: being middle class was apparently synonymous with being greedy, stuck-up, compromised, money-loving, selfish and insincere – it was a condition of near-unforgivable shame. *Whatever* the reasons may have been for the way he spoke, there was something strangely hypnotic about it which made me feel uneasy, which made me feel subject to him, and which made me feel very inadequate. Even so, I was determined to put my question.

'There's a few things I'm troubled about,' I said after the exchange of our introductory pleasantries. *'Is there any chance I can talk to you about them?'*

'Go ahead, bro. I'll see if I can be of help,' he replied quite straightforwardly, with the air of one who had nothing to hide – which was *before* he knew what I wanted to ask him.

'Well, what's troubling me most,' I began to explain, 'is why you sell what you do in the shops. It really upset me just now when I went to look at "Jeans Plus" with Shaun because I couldn't understand what was going on. I mean, I didn't think you approved of tight-fitting clothes and incense and stuff like that. Isn't it wrong for you to sell things which you disapprove of?'

Had I been more self-confident I would probably have realized the irritation I discerned when he began to respond was *his* problem, not *mine* for having spoken honestly. Somehow, though, he made me feel that this kind of questioning was the product of wanting to find fault where there was none.

'I do get a bit edgy about this kind of criticism, bro,' he said, not harshly, nor haughtily, but *now* with the air of one who is weary of inconsequential irrelevancies.

'Why,' I wondered, 'should he have so swiftly inferred criticism when I'd only been trying to get things straight in my own mind?'

He carried on with his reply:

'Most Christians have too much of an individualistic faith. They don't understand that God wants to build his church, his kingdom. God doesn't want to "save the world", you know; he wants to save a people from **out** of the world. What you've got to understand is that the world itself is fallen, that it's been given over to the prince of darkness; so there's no point in Christians wasting their time trying to make it "a better place". We mustn't be taken in by the kind of self-righteous and misguided nonsense which makes Christian people think that they should influence unsaved people to lead "better" lives through the example of their own ones. The aim of our commerce is always to make profit, and that's what we have to think about in deciding what to sell in the shops.'

And the conclusion he drew from all this went straight to the very core of what life in the Bugbrooke Community was all about:

'In our businesses, bro, we're robbing the kingdom of the world to build the kingdom of God!'

The colloquial friendliness had gone from his voice; he'd become a teacher. I realized I would get no further in pursuing the matter: continued questioning would only reflect my unwillingness to accept his authority. Nor was my experience of life or my intellectual prowess sufficiently mature to grasp the full import of what was being said. I just knew at a gut level that I didn't like it, understand it, or even feel my question had been properly answered.

I *now* understand far more clearly that his response was a classical statement of using the end to justify the means. It stopped some way short of suggesting that *any* means could be used in the Fellowship's commercial pursuits, but it nonetheless clearly implied that irrespective of whether they actually *approved* of what was being sold, and provided the funds being "robbed" were being employed in the service of constructing God's kingdom, there was nothing wrong in selling to the world those goods which worldly people wanted to buy – *"robbing the kingdom of the world to build the kingdom of God"*. I wonder where the shaded area of legitimate means would have crossed over from grey to black? *If it was okay to sell fashion clothing shunned by the Community members, then what was wrong, logically, with selling slinky, female lingerie?*

Nor did I fully realize in a way which I could have translated into words how much Noel had belittled God by reducing him to the level of reliance on human enterprise in order to demonstrate his majesty: not so much *using* human hands to build his kingdom as actually being *dependent* on the business acumen of his created beings to do so. I saw what he was getting at, though. The Fellowship wasn't trying to influence people from the world to lead "better" lifestyles, and it wasn't trying to raise public standards of decency or exercise any moralistic influence for good. How those people – the ones deaf to God's voice – behaved themselves in their careless passage through *this* life on the pathway to destruction was up to them – and best just to let them get on with it! At the same time it was apparently perfectly righteous to make use of shrewd trading with such lost souls to obtain funds which could then be used to build Community homes and finance Community evangelism; funds which could be used to facilitate both the practice and the preaching of the gospel message; funds which could be used to convert souls to Christ and then bring them *out* from the world and into God's kingdom, into a society of justice and equality where they could be nurtured and cared for – loved and accepted by their fellow brothers and sisters.

With the passage of time I began to understand how what I was hearing about "the kingdom versus the world" was the logical conclusion of the Calvinistic doctrine of *election*: the gathering together of the Elect – the Saved – and the inevitable damnation of the Lost. It should hardly have come as any surprise to me, therefore, when I began to hear the Fellowship brothers and sisters referring to people "out there" as *worldlings* – a derisory label which I hated and could never bring myself to use. Whilst compassion and warmth were shown towards *anybody* – even a worlding – who was seen to be a candidate for salvation (a candidate to join the Elect), the others – all those who were *completely* careless to the gospel of Christ – were regarded as having no place in the kingdom of God; they belonged to the kingdom of the world and were left to get on with their own affairs within it. The two kingdoms and their inhabitants were mutually exclusive, there being no point whatsoever in trying to make the kingdom of the world a better place for worldlings to live in. Poor Mother Theresa! No wonder Noel belittled her achievements when, during an address in the chapel, he bellowed out the rhetorical demand:

'And tell me, brethren, does anyone persecute Mother Theresa?'

The inference of his demand was that although she had laboured tirelessly amongst the poor and needy of Calcutta, punishing her own body to ridiculous limits in her desire to show the love of Christ to those impoverished orphans and social rejects whom she deeply loved, she hadn't perceived, alas, that good works of this kind were more or less a waste of her precious Christian energy – the Almighty having no concern to help improve people's lives within the kingdom of the world but only with helping them *out* of that kingdom and into another one. Because the saintly lady hadn't actually been helping to build the kingdom of God in such a way, she wasn't hated or persecuted by the world – she hadn't *offended* the world! She hadn't offered those poor worldlings the chance to come *out* of the world, find salvation through Jesus Christ, and build themselves into a saved community of God's people.

The theology of "the two kingdoms" was central to an understanding of the Jesus Fellowship as I came to know it, turning much of what I'd perceived Christianity to be about on its head. I was puzzled, for example, by how the parable of the Good Samaritan should be understood: it seemed to clearly suggest Christian neighbourliness was all about helping people in need, even though they might be strangers to us. This was a parable which through the ages had inspired many people to offer a helping hand of kindness to those who'd fallen into trouble along the wayside. Wasn't it teaching us that *all* people are our neighbours, that we should be concerned for the wellbeing of *all* alike – even worldlings?

I think Noel found the persistent questioning of mine throughout my Bugbrooke-years to be something of an irritant, and I exposed myself to the dreaded accusation of being too "mindey" – of thinking about things too much. But I could never completely forget these kinds of issues. They kept surfacing; they burned within me to be explored and explained. Needing to understand, I approached Noel after one of the Sunday meetings to ask why it was that the Good Samaritan parable seemed to contradict his teaching of what our attitude should be towards "unsaved" people out there in the world.

'*You misunderstand the intention of the parable, bro,*' he began to explain – wearily.

'*Too many people think that Jesus was trying to teach us not to be like the priest or the Levite – who passed by on the other side of the road to the wounded man – but to be like the Samaritan, who crossed over and came to the man's help. That's not the point of the parable, my bro! You have to bear in mind the initial question to which Jesus was responding: "who is my neighbour?"*'

The Pharisee who asked the question, Noel went on to explain, had wanted to justify his restricted pharisaic attitude of who his neighbour was – *God forbid that it should be a Samaritan!* But that's just who his neighbour proved to be. Jesus wasn't so much teaching that the man lying by the wayside was the Samaritan's neighbour, rather that it was the Samaritan himself who proved to be the neighbour of the injured man – the Jew. The meaning of the story, according to Noel, is that our neighbour is "the one who shows us kindness and mercy". The answer, then, to the Pharisee's question – as conveyed by the parable – is that the Samaritan proved himself to be a neighbour to the injured Jewish victim. Put more simply: the pharisee's question, *who is my neighbour?* is answered, within the scope of the parable, as *the Samaritan.*

'In the same way, therefore,' Noel concluded, *'we have to understand that it's the* **Christian** *brothers and sisters we live with who are our neighbours, regardless of whatever race or background they may have come from. They are the ones, after all, who have shown mercy to us.'*

It was with reluctance – and indeed sadness – that I accepted the explanation; with reluctance that I accepted the point of the parable to be different to the one which for years I'd believed it to be, the one which seemed so obvious; with reluctance that I accepted his insistence that the focus of our love should be predominantly towards our brothers and sisters within the kingdom of God – the neighbours who had shown mercy to us – and not towards people out there in the world.

Aside from the issue of attitudes towards outsiders, there were other aspects of the Fellowship's restrictive, dogmatic ways which made me feel peculiarly uncomfortable and uneasy. This, of course, begs the question of how I was nonetheless so very drawn to its lifestyle and came close to believing it uniquely favoured by God himself. Looking back, I can see quite clearly how, early on in my involvement, I must have allowed myself to go through a self-deceiving mental process which I hope never again to repeat. This process was one which involved subordinating my own views and opinions – which were more intuitive than clearly defined or clearly developed – to the black-and-white, forcefully expressed canons put forward by Noel as the authoritative expression of God's will for his people. Even though it was an almost head-in-the-sand thing to have done, it nevertheless helped me some considerable way towards resolving and reconciling all my uncertainties, insufficiently answered questions and anxieties.

On the one hand I'd seen evidence in the Fellowship of a society which I positively yearned to be part of on account of the equality, caring and love I'd witnessed within it; and also on account of the people who lived there, who I strongly felt were *my kind of people*. On the other hand, there were aspects of it all which I found disquieting. Because the first set of these considerations seemed to heavily outweigh the second, I decided that any reservations I had could be put "on hold". I was confident the Fellowship's leadership knew what they were talking about, and I therefore believed that I too would one day fully embrace even those aspects of the Bugbrooke lifestyle which I couldn't feel comfortable with there and then.

CHAPTER NINE: Ashburnham

It was almost inevitable after only my second visit that I would end up joining these Bugbrooke people. Not because I necessarily agreed with, or even understood, *everything* that they stood for and taught concerning the Christian faith and lifestyle – I had begun making the arrangement with myself to defer my reservations. It was almost inevitable because of what I'd found within its membership: a companionship which was extremely invigorating, and a depth and breadth of character that was unparalleled in any other church I'd been to. And whilst I knew well enough that it was Noel Stanton at the helm, I honestly believed it was God himself in the engine room.

But that wasn't all. The single-minded way in which the flock were determined to leave all self-interest behind, deny the world, and follow what they believed to be the way of Christ was irresistible to someone like me who'd always been attracted by the in-for-a-penny-in-for-a-pound approach to life and had now become convinced that the Christian lifestyle should be all-or-nothing. Nor can I deny having been emotionally bowled over by the love and attention I'd received: love and attention as a heavenly poultice on the wounds – especially the self-inflicted ones – from previous years, bringing with it further relief from pain, further healing, and further re-establishment of self-esteem. I was an idealist. I yearned to be part of a better society and believed that God had led me to Bugbrooke for a purpose. I just needed some kind of final reassurance that this purpose was indeed for me to join up.

I think more than anything else I'd been stunned into a deep affection for the Fellowship at Bugbrooke because of the undeniable love the members had for one another. They were unfailingly happy to be in one another's company, unfailingly willing to accept all types and all kinds of people; cliques appeared to be unknown. You felt, when you were there, that you'd found friends who would genuinely "lay down their life" for you. This is what the kingdom of God was all about. This is why many referred to the Fellowship as *the kingdom,* or sometimes *Mother Zion*, or *Jerusalem*, or even their **true** family. I think I honestly believed that such unselfish dedication to one another was everything it appeared to be. *It was to come as a painful blow to innocence to gradually discover that, in reality, this glorious utopian society was chimerical. It was flawed – as such societies always are – by human frailty in the form of pride, deceit, abuse, ambition, arrogance and stubbornness: no more so at Bugbrooke than anywhere else, probably, but far less immediately obvious.*

In the quietness of my own room back at university, and especially during an extended stay in the sick bay with some kind of fever, I began to read quite extensively on the subject of the baptism in the Spirit – how different people had experienced it. One particularly gripping book was called "Run Baby Run", the autobiography of a one-time New York thug, Nicky Cruz, who'd compulsively taken part in violent, gang-based knife fights. The story of how he'd found faith in Jesus Christ and been baptised in the Spirit was also told in another book, "The Cross and the Switchblade", authored by the near-legendary evangelist, David Wilkinson – the man who'd held his nerve whilst Cruz held a knife at his throat and boldly proclaimed,

'Jesus loves you, Nicky!'

Having read these books – and other less-dramatic ones – I came to understand about the baptism in the Spirit being a gripping internal awareness of God's presence that actually made *some* people feel physically warm and radiant. The most important aspect to it, however, seemed to be the deep implanted love for Jesus Christ which people found within themselves, leaving them unmistakably aware of having been "visited" by the Holy Spirit. Understood like this, I knew it was something I'd already experienced both at St. Hugh's and within the Christian Union, and I therefore didn't allow myself any further preoccupation with the whole issue. In a way, it all came down to the use of language; and I now felt quite certain my own experience had been as genuine as anybody else's.

With this newfound confidence about the authenticity and acceptability of my own spiritual history, I was also more relaxed about talking in tongues. I'd previously believed, I guess, that something pretty dramatic would need to happen if the phenomenon were to be genuinely "of God", like some kind of angelic force moving my jaws up and down. Instead of waiting for such an event, I lay on my bed, closed my eyes, and began to make sounds – any sounds – while trying to concentrate my thoughts on Jesus Christ at the same time. Within a short space of time these sounds were being made with as much fluency as I'd heard from anyone else. And although the "language" might just as well have been Cantonese for all the sense it made to me, it was still a pleasurable experience. In "Fire in Our Hearts", Simon refers to one occasion when a Malaysian student identified another person's "tongue" as being Mandarin Chinese.[10] I have never myself heard, nor even heard about, any other occasions when talking in tongues has been recognized as a genuine language, either extant or dead. If pressed to be brutally honest, I would have to say that anyone, so inclined, could speak in this way: it is, when analysed objectively, no more than the repetitive use of a limited number of sounds and syllables, with different levels of sophistication utilized by different people.

For the remainder of that summer term further visits to the Fellowship simply weren't possible because I needed to concentrate almost all of my time and energy on revising for first-year exams. Keen, therefore, that I shouldn't lose or forget about the enthusiasm I'd shown towards their lifestyle, Ralph and Shaun invited me to join them on the annual summer retreat to Ashburnham Place in Sussex. The environment there could hardly have been more conducive to a feeling of well-being with its wonderfully landscaped grounds, its leisurely woods, and its magnificent lake. The days were long and sunny, allowing us – brothers only – to swim in the clear waters. For the first time in my life I saw fireflies and glow-worms in the warmth of the night: magical creatures that captivated my imagination. I was growing up and blossoming out, allowing myself to relax, expanding my vision, beginning to appreciate and enjoy the beauty of nature, and finding pleasure in people and the world around me in ways I hadn't known since losing the irrecoverable innocence of childhood. *It was unfortunate, perhaps, that these aspects of maturing – a continuation of a process that had been happening for some time – should have coincided with my new allegiances since the two seemed so closely connected as to be cause and effect.*

For long hours of the day we sat packed into the main conference room while Noel outlined, in considerable length, his vision for the development of the Fellowship and Community. But we also had enough free time to go for unhurried lazy walks around the lake and in the woods. Through the conversations I had with others whilst out and about, and through the "ministry" given by Noel, I gradually developed a more comprehensive understanding of what it was I'd be joining – if and when I made such a complete commitment. Only later did I *fully* realize what an honour it was to have attended the retreat. This was essentially a week for the *initiated*, and it was only because some of the brothers believed me to have such a "good heart" – Community-speak – that the invitation to be there had been given. No doubt I was seen as an apple ready for the plucking. *I had no idea that friendship so freely given could also be so easily withdrawn!*

The subject of relationships with girls was one of those which the retreat gave me opportunity to explore. Although I had no objection, as such, to the emphasis given on the need to forge friendship bonds with one's own sex, I had no wish to spend the rest of my life confined to male company alone. I wasn't, so I hoped, about to become a eunuch; there was, I'd observed, no shortage of attractive young females amongst the sisterhood.

'*So don't you ever want female company?*' I asked one brother – John "Good" – as we sat on a grassed bank leading down to the side of the lake.

'*Yeah, course I do,*' he said, casually chewing a piece of the grass and looking wistfully at the sky.

'*D'you think we're all poofs or something?*' he added, almost challenging me to speak my mind.

The possibility had indeed occurred to me. And who wouldn't have at least *considered* the homosexual explanation if, as I had, they'd seen some of the brothers lying down close together on the same bed, sometimes with one of them resting his head on another one's chest? During my time in the Community this kind of brotherly intimacy became less common. When in vogue, it had been considered an acceptable display of friendship – compared by Noel with that displayed between David and Jonathon, the masculine biblical warriors who, according to the Bible, had *lain on one another's breast*. Noel himself, in his private room at New Creation Farm, sometimes had young teenage brothers come to lie beside him on his bed. To my way of thinking, even though – back then at least – I'd not seen or heard of any sexual contact, it all bordered too closely on misinterpretation and I believed it to be inappropriate, certainly on Noel's behalf. All of this raises important issues which I shall return to in detail later on. For myself, I would never have been able to express my friendship towards another brother with such close physical contact and I was glad to see the end of it all when the phase passed.

'*No, I don't think you're poofs,*' I replied to John, '*though I find all the hugging and lying down together all a bit much. Sometimes I can't help wonder...*'

I paused for a moment, unable to find the right words to say exactly what it was I *did* wonder. I'd never encountered such close brotherly friendship before and didn't quite know what to make of it. I felt genuinely loved by the brothers I'd met and thought they were terrific people; and yet it was all still somewhat enigmatic, somewhat perplexing, somewhat... *strange* – if I was perfectly truthful. John turned round and grinned at me; he understood the way I was feeling.

'*Yeah, yeah, dig wot ya mean!*' he said, sheepishly. Being labelled as middle class was, as already explained, a stain on your character of near-demonic severity, so the use of language like this – even though it was borrowed from an entirely different culture – had become widespread; a defence against being considered bourgeois.

'*Noel says there's real problems of unholiness between men and women, even in the church,*' John continued. '*So livin in community, like we do, we need to be really careful to make sure everything stays completely pure. That's why there's such a rigid segregation, bro – it's the way of holiness. When we've all got a bit maturer in the Lord, we can get together wiv a sister. But it's best for now, you see, if we try and "die to it". Best if we concentrate on our friendships wiv other bruvvers.*'

'*And d'you find "dying to it" easy?*' I asked.

'*No, course I don't. But my elder's told me it's wot God wants for me right now!*'

If I were to join the Community, I knew I would find this aspect of things really hard; *so* hard I could scarcely contemplate it.

Later that same week, Noel *himself* addressed the assembled company on this very subject of courtship within the Community. And in doing so he established the guidelines followed for years thereafter. He urged *everybody* to seriously consider embracing, in the first instance, what he called "the gift" of celibacy – the "higher calling" of Christian discipleship. To remain unmarried, he explained, gave you increased freedom to be devoted to the Lord; more time to be an evangelist; more time to be a teacher or carer within the Community; more time to utilize *whatever* gift it was you may have been given in order to serve Jesus. It was only when you were certain you *didn't* have the gift of celibacy, so Noel told us, that you should think about courtship leading to marriage; and this wouldn't normally be countenanced until the brother – always the one to *initiate* a relationship – was twenty-five years old, or thereabouts. This magical age attained, he might then be given permission from his house-elder to explore the possibility of "relating" to a particular sister. The elder, if satisfied the brother had "purity of intent" (whatever that may have meant), would next need to approach the house-elder of the sister in question to discuss whether she was actually "available": she may, for example, have herself made a decision to remain celibate, or she may not be willing to begin a relationship with this particular brother. Any brother lucky enough to get through all the pre-courtship investigations and checks – my words, not Noel's – would then have to wait for a while in case an elder from another household came forward with the name of someone else whom he knew to have an interest in the same sister – in which case the lucky sister would be allowed to choose between potential suitors. Once the final green light had been given, the brother would be allowed to meet with the sister so they could begin to forge a relationship; begin "relating to one another" as it became known. The "relating" would be closely monitored by the elders and needed to pass through predetermined stages of intimacy, there being no question that any of these stages would be even remotely sexual in nature until marriage itself had been solemnized.

That the sisters themselves would have no role in the whole affair except to say yes or no – or choose between two or three brothers – should not be a cause for concern, Noel insisted, for he was confident it would "all be sorted out in the Lord". He therefore wrapped up his lengthy discourse with the comforting reassurance that none of the sisters need fear being left on the shelf. *Fine words! But Noel himself didn't need to comfort the many Community sisters who, with aching hearts for male companionship, often wept themselves to sleep in the loneliness of their single bed.*

That anyone could have possibly joined the Fellowship knowing full well the rigours of this strange, draconian arrangement is, on first reckoning, totally incomprehensible. To make sense of it, one first needs to understand how deeply trusted the elders were to "get things right" and not abuse their authority. Not all of them proved to be as understanding, sympathetic and gentle as whispering-Bob-Harris Ralph. But even so, they had all proved themselves – apparently – to be men who could care for others with spiritual maturity and discretion. They were held in esteem as "bishops" of the flock, their charge being to guide us with a shepherd's staff into rich pastures – not coerce us with a rod to eat thistles. So it came down to trust. And I firmly believed I *could* trust these men, not only to lead me in "the paths of righteousness" but also to ensure no harm came to me through the rigours and self-denials of the exacting commitments which would be required – to ensure I wouldn't be disappointed in the faith I'd placed in them to treat me as God wanted me to be treated.[a] The courtship arrangements were alien, bizarre and hard to stomach. But the way I came to see things was that if God wanted me to be at Bugbrooke, *He* would have to give me the strength to accept them and live by them.

The critical question with which I struggled while at Ashburnham was whether God *did* want me to join the Fellowship. I needed to know *for sure* because I was well aware that the courtship restraints weren't the only ones I would find extremely challenging. As the week progressed, I became increasingly familiar with the uncompromising position taken by the Fellowship in its world-renouncing lifestyle. In general *all* those aspects of secular life regarded as being primarily for personal enjoyment and gratification were labelled as *worldly,* and they were therefore denied to Community members for their own entertainment, education or relaxation. Non-Christian books; magazines; televisions; radios and any music-playing equipment were amongst the most obvious of the normal household items *not* found in any of the Community homes. Even newspapers were initially taboo, but the broadsheets later came to be regarded as acceptable if read purely as a source of information.

Rejection of worldly pleasure resulted in a list of *don'ts* which was far longer than the list of *dos*. Clubs and pubs were strictly out-of-bounds – unless being visited for evangelistic purpose. No surprises there. Nor, perhaps, that the cinema and theatre were tarred as unclean with the same brush – irrespective of the film being shown or the play being performed. Harder for some to understand was the extension of prohibition to include just about everything which was non-Community based. Visiting museums, art-galleries or historic buildings; going out to a restaurant for a meal; going away on holiday; even just going out for the day: all these things were blacklisted by virtue of the opportunity they afforded for the indulgence of the selfish, fallen human nature.

---

[a] Only whilst rereading this paragraph have I properly appreciated the poignancy and relevance of the apology which the JFCT would issue in 2023 as part of their redress measures. I, like many others, had entrusted the whole of my life to the care of others in the belief I would be treated fairly and kept safe. Consider, then, one of the statements contained in the JFCT apology:

"On behalf of the Jesus Fellowship Community Trust, we are deeply sorry for the experiences you suffered during your time in community and for the distress and harm that these have had on your life; it is matter of profound regret that they were able to happen at all, and in the very place where you should have felt safe from harm."

One of the most controversial of all the prohibitions, especially insofar as it affected the children growing up within Community families, was the one relating to sport – competitive or non-competitive. Even though the Community organized its *own* schooling arrangements for those of a preschool age (and also for *all* ages during school vacations), the state school system was generally used in the normal way. Community children, however, inevitably found themselves differentiated from the worldly schoolchildren, not simply because they didn't mix with them socially *after* school but also through their exclusion from extracurricular activities – which included, amongst other things, organized sport. For me, sadly, Community membership meant no more football, either as a player or a spectator – though I cannot deny that I'd reached an age where sporting self-denial wasn't quite so difficult as some of the other privations required of us: the rejection of all worldly music being a case in point.

Without wishing to deny I had many faults, for the duration of my membership I somehow managed to become a loyal and obedient Community brother whose transgressions were not typically those of worldly indulgences. Even so, it should hardly occasion great surprise if I reveal that my one secret link with Babylon, unknown and unconfessed to anyone else (and regarded by myself as completely harmless), was that of following the progress of Luton Town in the sporting pages of the Sunday newspaper. Not that I avidly read the match reports; but I just couldn't help needing to know how they were doing in the league. I never forgot you, dear Hatters, even then! *This was evidence, no doubt, that my death to the self-life was tarnished and incomplete. An explanation, perhaps, for the seed of rebellion which was to take root, push up, grow strong and burst out.*

By the end of my week at Ashburnham the questioning from Community brothers had changed from *'do you think you will join the Community?'* to *'when will you join the Community?'* I wasn't one of those Christians too much given to looking for "signs" as an indication of God's will; and because I so much *wanted* – despite all the rigours and demands of their lifestyle – to be part of this radical, resolute, happy and exciting company, I took this strength of feeling to be evidence *in itself* of God's intent for me. It was therefore agreed by mutually enthusiastic consent that later in the vacation I would take my place as a Community member in the New Creation Farm household.

The remaining months of the long summer vacation were spent living at a Sue Ryder nursing home near Breachwood Green, where my parents had taken a job as joint wardens. A day job back at pre-university "One Stop" doing all kinds of menial work enabled me to save up enough to buy an old Ford Cortina which I planned to use for weekend journeys to Northampton after I'd gone back to university. This was a summer untarnished by the excesses which had handicapped me so seriously in the past; a summer

I enjoyed through and through. A new world had opened up in front of me. I found within me a broadened attitude and love towards one and all: a love which didn't so much want to take from people but, wherever possible, give something to them and appreciate them. I shall never forget – I hope – the rewarding pleasure that came from spending long hours chatting and laughing with the patients in the nursing home, most of whom suffered from the awful debilitation of Huntington's Chorea, Parkinson's Disease, Multiple Sclerosis or some other neurological wasting illness in an advanced state of progression.

Outside Sue Ryder Home – 1977

I didn't hold back from socializing with some of the younger staff members in the evenings (especially the nurses), and we often repaired to the local pub together – albeit that I now only drank in propitious moderation, if at all. I had no need! I was sufficiently intoxicated by the excitement I found in living itself. I loved the company of others and hadn't yet embraced the separation from the people of the world that would become necessary once I went to live at New Creation Farm. I was, however, far more circumspect in my relationship with the nurses than I would have been in the past.

I knew I had to behave with probity, but it didn't stop me going for long walks with Liz, a very beautiful-yet-fragile young woman who was working at the home as a volunteer and had recently been involved with a strange religious organization called "the Moonies" – a cult which I heard about for the first time through this friendship. Like many of the Bugbrooke sisters, Liz kept her hair in a headscarf: an expression of her religious convictions concerning femininity. She preferred her own company to that of the small gang of us who went out and about together. Shy, and reluctant to open herself up to others, she wasn't initially very communicative. As she became aware of my own faith, however, she began to confide in me and ask all sorts of questions about Jesus Christ: who he was, how he made himself known to people, how he wanted us to live. She never referred to her time with the Moonies and I never asked her about it, although the hurt and confusion within her were all too apparent. Wanting to help her break out of the mental prison in which she was confined, I thought of asking her to visit Bugbrooke with me. I didn't do so, though, because apart from doubting whether she would come (she was too timid in one way, and too self-possessed in another way), I had this strange, unaccountable instinct that, for her, it would have been like going from the frying pan into the fire; *and I had no wish to be instrumental in breaking a bruised reed.* I cannot properly explain how I can have felt this way whilst retaining such a strong conviction that the Bugbrooke Community was the right place for *me* to go and live.

I had agreed with *the brethren* – a term often used in reference to brothers holding authority of some kind – a date when I would move into the farm. The day drew close and I knew I had a particularly painful farewell to make. It was with Hazel from St. Hugh's at Luton, one of my most faithful pen-pals while I was away at Canterbury and someone with whom I'd grown increasingly close. Hazel simply wasn't the type of girl who would ever have foisted herself on anyone, yet it was quite clear how much she wanted our friendship to progress beyond the platonic. And had I not intended moving to Bugbrooke it may well have done so – not that I'd yet come to *fully* understand how the one completely precluded the other. I was perfectly well aware, of course, that I was about to become subject to the Community's courtship procedures. But because it was all so new to me, the stark truth that this would mean there could *never* be any possibility of a romantic attachment with a non-Community sister – not even with one so dedicated to the Christian faith as Hazel – hadn't penetrated beyond my naïve mental defences – defences which were ever prone to substitute an impression of the way I *thought* things should be for what they actually were. I think that I just didn't have the mental capacity to comprehend how *anyone,* even Noel himself, could have objected to the choice of Hazel as a partner; she was one of the most pure-hearted and innocent girls that I've ever met. Or maybe I thought that she might herself become a Community sister. I'd taken her with me on several visits to Bugbrooke over the summer months and she was by no means out of sympathy with the Fellowship. I can no longer say *exactly* what it was I must have thought, but I know I didn't completely rule out the possibility of there being a more serious liaison between the pair of us at some point in the future. It wasn't *all* down to my simplistic naivety, though. For the very reason that I knew I needed guidance about the long-term future of my relationship with Hazel, I discussed it all with a brother who knew about our mutual fondness.

'*I shouldn't worry too much about it all, bro,*' had been his reply, '*I'm sure that "in the Lord" things like this can be sorted out one way or another.*'

His misdirection had been in his failure to spell out exactly what was meant by "sorted out".

A few days before I was due to drive up to Bugbrooke in my mark-one Cortina estate (which belched thick black smoke from its exhaust with embarrassing profusion), the St. Hugh's young persons' group met in Hazel's house for a Bible Study. I began to make my farewells after it finished but was aware that Hazel had suddenly disappeared; so I went to look for her. She was stood in the kitchen looking extremely forlorn and had tears in her eyes. Never before had I seen her so disconsolate, though it didn't take a Claire Raynor to work out what was going on. I offered her some crumpled-up tissues which had been stuffed in my pockets.

'*Come on, use these you daft thing,*' I said, trying to be as kind and positive as possible.

'*We've just got to try and think about what the Lord wants for us – that's what we've got to try and do. I know what you'd been hoping for, and maybe it will happen one day. Maybe we **will** get together. But I've got to be obedient and do what I believe God is telling me. I'm sorry it hurts you so much – really, really sorry.*'

I reached down and took both her hands firmly in mine. I couldn't possibly have been more genuine in what I was saying and wanted her to feel my affection: I too was hurting. She dried her eyes and we were able to spend a few comforting moments talking honestly and openly together. Then she gave me a gentle kiss on the cheek and we said goodbye. If there *had* been any residual hope left within her of a future relationship between the pair of us, I knew when I'd been living in the Community only a short space of time and was told I should have nothing more to do with her – not even write to explain anything – that I'd been wrong to offer such a tenuous lifeline. The guilt and pain I felt about our enforced estrangement took a long time to settle.

One of the first things I wanted to do after moving into the farm was visit Jonathon and his wife, Sue, at New Creation Hall. The warmth of their welcome during my first visit had been extremely meaningful and I knew they'd be over the moon now that I'd joined with them in membership. I spoke to Rufus about it.

'*I don't think it would be a good idea for you, my bro,*' he said firmly. '*It's best you just stay at the farm and get to know the brothers here.*'

I was rather taken aback by his response and couldn't understand it. *Were my movements within the Community going to be restricted? Was I to be confined to a discipline of almost monastic obedience?* Not quite. But I *was* being shielded from exposure to things which Rufus thought would be harmful for me. I accepted the restriction which was placed on me without knowing that Jonathon and Sue had become disaffected with the Community and were on the point of "splitting". In a matter of days they were gone, as was the opportunity for them to poison my fledgling commitment with their misgivings and grievances.

In spite of all the assurances which I believed I'd been given, the Fellowship *wasn't* benignly tolerant and philosophically understanding about "the breaking of covenant", so called, occasioned by those who "split" – those who broke rank and left. This was to be no easy-come-easy-go affair. It was, so I came to understand, meant to be a lifelong commitment; and those who broke their promises of everlasting loyalty did so in disobedience to God himself. When such treachery – packing your bags and leaving – had been perpetrated, we were often expected to sing a dreadful dirge about a biblical "traitor" called Demas who parted company with the apostle Paul and thereby became apostate: a salutary reminder of what lay in store for any of *us* who might choose to travel a similar path. The message was forcibly communicated in another, easier-to-remember chorus which we also sang on these occasions:

> "Some turn back, believe it,
> Some turn back; we've seen it.
> Don't be taken unawares,
> Don't fall into Satan's snare,
> Or let a root of bitterness
> Spring up in you heart consciousness!
> Love Messiah's chosen race,
> Do not doubt your honoured place
> Do not thwart God's perfect grace for you."

Entry into full membership was through the act of adult baptism, or – for those who believed themselves to have already had a valid baptism by full-immersion elsewhere – through a ceremony known as *the giving of the right hand of fellowship*. In both instances the sacramental ritual was meant to signify that a "covenanted" commitment had been made, a commitment regarded as being lifelong and unbreakable: an expectation of enormous consequence given that many young people, like me, were baptised into membership after little more than a few weeks of living in the Community. It was, however, to be some considerable time after my arrival at New Creation Farm before I came to experience and fully recognize the intensity of the stigmatizing reprobation which was heaped on the heads of those who, having entered into membership, dared to split – dared to part company with the Community.

In those early days of moving to the farm, like any new recruit to a strict organization, or even like a monastic novice setting out on a life of poverty and obedience (a prospect which had always given me the jitters to even think about), I was ready to keep my head down, buckle under, and do what I was told. I could see no other way of accommodating myself to a lifestyle which I knew would challenge my independence to the limits but which I had determined within myself was God's will for me. I was a bit like Tom Browne during his first few weeks at Rugby: willing to do whatever was asked of him, and more, so he could fit into the public-school life he had so earnestly wanted to be part of.

As my experience of life in community progressed, I began to realize there were *many* aspects of our lifestyle which I'd previously only understood superficially but which were now becoming far more intelligible. Acknowledgement of "the lot" of the sisters was one such epiphany. I'd accepted the Fellowship's dogma about women needing to be submissive to male authority in general and, if they were married, to the authority of their husbands in particular.[a] And I'd also accepted their role within the Fellowship as being a "supportive" one; similar, perhaps, to the role of support staff within a large company or institution: sisters weren't expected to be visible or take credit, yet they toiled away in the background providing essential services.– domestic ones in particular but not exclusively.

As part and parcel of the same submissive package, sisters were required to be modest and discreet in everything, which included the way they dressed: headscarves were often worn as an emblem of submission, whilst long skirts or frocks were an expression of femininity. Initially, I'd thought the womenfolk and girls were quite happy in their divinely appointed roles as male helpmates, going about their day-to-day chores with a gay and contented countenance. But if I'd originally believed that "cheery" was a good descriptor for the sisters, then "cowed" would have been a better one after I'd realized how downtrodden they really were. Typical of their treatment was the era when it became the "done thing" to make sisters sit in the back of a car, even if there was space in the front passenger seat. Ian Callard, one of the Community's senior elders whom I lived with for a while at Stockton House in Warwickshire, deeply offended me on one occasion when he made a joke along the lines of "putting sisters in their proper place" by making them sit in the back of a car on a journey. I'm proud to say that, in this respect at least, I stood my ground and didn't yield to such nonsense: I *always* invited a sister to sit in the passenger seat if we were sharing a journey, despite most of them initially making a beeline for the car's back doors. Another humiliating example which stuck in my gullet was the occasion when, in my role as household deacon, I had to ask Debbie – my dear friend from Canterbury university – to show me her holed shoes before I could authorise her to request a new pair from the FDC – the so-called Food

---

[a] Looking back, my accord with such an attitude is one for which I feel deep regret, shame and sorrow. It was an attitude towards women which, so I believe, caused no end of harm.

Distribution Centre which had expanded to become a central supply centre for most of the households' everyday-shopping requirements.

Given the oppressive attitudes which the sisters had to tolerate, together with their total inability to initiate any kind of romantic relationship, it was hardly surprising that many of them were frequently in tears or "under the weather" – if not medically ill. Some of them – far more than one would normally imagine in the workplace, for example – seemed to be in possession of a cold with a regularity that bordered on constancy; some were fatigued beyond explanation, and some displayed symptoms that came close to being those of diagnosable depression or neurosis. That there were those who were genuinely happy in their servility isn't something I would wish to challenge, although I have no idea how many of such sisters there were. As a generalized observation, the underlying reality of unhappiness within the sisterhood became quite apparent to me: beneath their cheery exterior image lay insecurity, anxiety and frustration.

The colour and variety of the sisters' attire also began to fade. As "old faithful" items of clothing eventually wore out, they were replaced by standard issue from the FDC or handmade from the same rather-unexciting rolls of material also used by many others. In time – not too long after I'd left – Jesus-Army-themed clothing had a further significant impact on the increasing uniformity of the clothes which sisters were able to wear.

In spite of my growing recognition of the effects caused by the submissive regime within which the sisters had to live, for many years I agreed and went along with the Fellowship's teaching concerning the position of women. And, yes, there *were* plenty of smiles; plenty of lovely gentle sisters, both attractive and not-so-attractive, who shone brightly in spite of their situation – or maybe *because* of it as I thought at the time – and enriched everyone's lives with their apparent contentment and ministry. Some had beautiful singing voices and delighted us at meetings with what we called "psalming", an entirely extemporaneous song delivered with or without guitar accompaniment. Typically, such "psalms" would extol the joys of living within Zion and the deep sense of belonging it provided; also, the happiness engendered by being bonded in a covenant love with all the other sisters, the security felt under "the covering of the brethren".

But – and it's a very big but – I gradually came to understand that few aspects of the Fellowship's lifestyle were what I'd once supposed them to be, not least in respect of the sisters' wellbeing. Just beneath the surface lay discontent, even for some of those regarded as rock-solid leading sisters who were role models by virtue of their submissive-yet-fulfilled lifestyles. Even many of *these* sisters were theatrical conspirators in the wonderful-Zion masquerade so many of us felt obliged to act out. It would have been beyond me to recognise all this quite so clearly during my time of membership even though my eyes were gradually being opened to it all. I knew about the loneliness and struggles many sisters had to endure, but for a long while I too was in much the same boat: someone who was managing to sufficiently subdue my negativity and misgivings to the point where what others saw was my "kingdom heart" shining through like the sun itself. Likewise, I supposed these highly regarded sisters – these "daughters of Zion" – to be irrevocably knit-in with the Fellowship and incapable of being rocked by either Hell or high water. I was wrong! Some of the first sisters who left the NCCC after I did were those whom I would previously have bet large sums on being ones who were wed to Zion through and through.[a] These were sisters who not so very long ago had been singing beautiful psalms inside Bugbrooke chapel, songs which simply sat on top of their underbelly of discontent. But they weren't false in any way; they were sincere right to the bitter end. A time came, however, when they could no longer keep the lid on the swelling urge for liberty, an urge so very clearly apparent amongst large swathes of the sisterhood for those with the eyes to have seen it.

Given the expectation that we should all work in some way, I was initially asked to help out in the pig yard. It was a demand that made me have to endure an offensive swine stench that clung to every part of my exposed flesh and clothing. It became ingrained in your fingernails and couldn't be completely removed by even the most vigorous scrubbing when you took a shower at the end of the day. Mucking out pigsties for the rest of my life wouldn't have been a vocation willingly entered into, yet I tried to cope with the pain of blisters and weary muscles cheerfully; likewise, the tedium of repeated tasks. I have to confess, however, that I was very nearly overwhelmed when asked to clean out the deep pit under the farrowing cages where voluminous quantities of urine and excrement had collected. As I descended into it, the obnoxious and nauseating odour was all too much; I was very nearly physically sick. I had never been a person to shirk the demands of strenuous physical labour but found the avaricious arrogations of the pig yard – which I was unaccustomed to – exhausting. When confronted by the hellish pit beneath the farrowing cages, I came very close to raising the white flag of surrender.

---

[a] Assuming, that is, I'd been a betting man – one of the few vices I've managed to totally avoid.

CHAPTER TEN: Working obediently at New Creation Farm

I was too servile or too proud – I really can't say which – to make any articulated plea for clemency concerning my duties in the pig yard, although my weary deportment must have told its own story. Besides, I knew that aspects of the Community's lifestyle, such as our work responsibilities, were all part of finding a "new creation identity", as sung about in another Fellowship chorus:

"I've found my new identity, my new creation self."

To inherit this identity was by no means a simple case of removing one set of clothes and putting on another. To become the person whom the Lord wanted you to be wasn't a matter of simply "having faith" and relying on God to make you into a better person; it involved *dying to the flesh* – the process of renouncing your own self-life in order to avail yourself of the new, restored, re-created character God had in store for you. As such, we grew to learn there were, effectively, two forces at work within us: the work of the flesh and the work of the Spirit. The work of the flesh comprised everything dirty, selfish, rebellious, lazy and fallen – everything inherited from "the first Adam", the progenitor of fallen mankind; the work of the Spirit everything wholesome, unselfish, obedient, pure and strong, everything given us by "the second Adam", Jesus Christ himself, the saviour of redeemed mankind. At last I now understood the meaning of the words immortalized in the famous hymn, "Praise to the holiest in the height": a hymn which is sung every Sunday throughout the land but whose words are often lost within the swell of the mighty pipe organs and the clear, unfaltering mellifluence of the choirs:

"Praise to the holiest in the height,
When all was sin and shame,
A **second Adam** to the fight
And to the rescue came!"

Believe me! If ever a fight was waged between the flesh and the spirit, it was during those days in the pig yard. If ever anyone could have said "the spirit is willing but the flesh is weak", it was me. I just had to keep reminding myself that there was a good purpose to it all, that I should regard it as a "discipline" to help me acquire my new identity. In fact it was quite normal for people in the Community to *deliberately* give one another *disciplines* for that very purpose, and it would be hard to forget the occasion in chapel when Noel asked the assembly to volunteer examples of them.

'I've got a good one, bro,' Rufus shouted out. If anyone could be relied on to respond enthusiastically, Rufus was your man. Just by the way he spoke when he was in one his "bubbly" moods, you somehow sensed that one way or another you were in for a treat.

'*Tell us about it then, brother Rufus,*' Noel replied.

'*Well, bro, my wife, Jess, seems to be a bit squeamish about things to do with the countryside, if you know what I mean – smells and messes, things like that. So I gave her the discipline of treading in a country pancake. I told her to take her shoes and socks off and stand in it for a while to help her "get the victory" over her squeamishness.*'

A few gave quiet moans of sympathy at the very thought of what poor Jess had been expected to do. Most people, including Noel, were silent, thoughtful – even, possibly, a little embarrassed. Had Noel himself thought this was taking things just a bit too far, he would have done well to reflect on who he should blame. If a dog is trained to protect the home, then its owner shouldn't curse the animal if it goes further than intended one day by inflicting serious wounds on an intruder. The trainer, not the trained, is the one truly responsible.

Although the cowpat tale had made me shiver in disgust at the very thought of what was involved, a few years' further on in my Community membership I heard about another "discipline" which, this time, left me smouldering inside with an anger I had no obvious way of venting. It involved a young sister, Hilary, who became one of my partners in the street-evangelism which took place every Friday night in nearby towns and cities. These were the few occasions when brothers and sisters teamed up together. Because Hilary was anxious to keep her figure in trim, she'd made the confession to her household elders that she believed herself guilty of vanity. They rewarded her honesty with the discipline of making her take extra helpings at every meal until told she'd put on sufficient weight.

It wasn't long before the effects of Hilary's dietary discipline were clearly noticeable in her figure. For all I was worth, I wanted – in friendship – to shake her, shake her, shake her, to get through to her that she was daft to have made such a confession in the first place. Yes, we *were* meant to be perfectly open and honest with one another, we *were* meant to confess our sins and weaknesses to one another; and I believe I was as conscientious as most in purging my soul in this way. I had the good sense, however, to know what was sinful, what was vanity, and what was normal, reasonable, acceptable human behaviour. This wasn't a sister who vaingloriously preened and prided herself, nor did she display anything but considerate modesty and gentleness both in the way she dressed and in the way she treated everyone. Furthermore, although she was genuinely attractive she didn't have the figure of a fashion model: she was, shall we say, "nicely average". If, then, her desire to retain such discrete proportions was in any way the sort of concern with one's appearance which can be labelled as vanity, I suspect we shall all of us be found wanting when the secrets of our hearts are revealed on the day of judgement.

But if this lovely sister should have had more sense than to have confessed to vanity in the first place, then how much more culpable the man who deemed such a perverse discipline to be appropriate. I found myself questioning what earthly or heavenly good could be achieved by making someone eat more than is good for their bodies. Perhaps – who knows? – there *is* some merit in an act of penance; the execution of an arduous task to expurgate the soul from the effects and the guilt of sin. Certainly there are Christian churches that espouse such a doctrine – the Roman Catholic church, for example. But *our* church wasn't amongst them. *Disciplines* were not meant to be acts of penance, a way of making atonement for sin; rather, a pragmatic means of helping brothers and sisters to adorn themselves with holiness. If, therefore, I'd wanted to shake Hilary, then I wanted to shake the brother responsible for this ridiculous imposition much more vigorously, demanding him to tell me:

'How in God's name will this small-minded, high-handed discipline help this sister to become holy? How will it help her to overcome her wish to remain in reasonable shape? And what's wrong with such a wish anyway? Are we all meant to be overweight in order that we shouldn't be vain? And who is going to give Noel a discipline to help him overcome the self-conscious vanity which makes him brush his remaining hair over the top of his balding head?'

In addition to teaching me about holiness, my membership of the Community certainly taught me about anger and how to best manage it.

There is a Christian tradition, far wider and older than the Community at Bugbrooke, which teaches that obedience is good for the soul. So I guess it may have been argued that Hilary was benefiting from the act of obedience in its own right. The obedience lesson was well learnt one day at the farm when water supplies to the pig-farrowing shed were interrupted. Immediate action was needed, the well-being – not to mention commercial value – of the young piglets being in jeopardy. Noel organized all the available brothers into a long chain reaching from the farmhouse to the pig shed and had them pass buckets of water from one to another in order to replenish the drinking troughs. The sight caused some amusement to one brother as he came up the farm drive on his way home from work at a nearby electronics firm. Graeme Bird (aka Graeme Merciful) wasn't known for his diffidence!

'What's going on here?' he asked. Noel explained the problem to him.

'That's daft,' Graeme then objected. *'Why don't you just fill up the water tanker and get someone to pull it round to the pig shed with a tractor. The buckets can then be filled up from there.'*

Noel took the suggestion with bad grace and muttered something about "obedience". Later in the evening, as we all sat round the tables in the farm dining-room for our evening meal, he gave us a reproving little homily on just that subject. Referring to his short period of service in the navy by way of illustration, he emphasized the importance of obeying orders from the officers irrespective of the opinions of the ratings.

'The little exercise this afternoon,' he explained, *'showed me how much we need to understand the importance of "obedience training" within the Community.'*

And so, after all, the debacle had a value and purpose that none of us had realized at the time.

After I'd been a Community member for several years, this whole issue of "obedience" began to give me enormous problems. *Were we meant to be obedient to the eldership of the Community at all times and in all instances? Is that what Noel meant by "having a good kingdom heart"?* If so, I was worried; not least because I'd grown to trust some of the elders far more than others. I knew that the ones I *did* fully trust were unlikely to require of me anything which would deeply offend my conscience or sense of proportionality. The others I wasn't so sure about. I would most definitely have wanted rights of appeal to a higher authority had anybody told *me* to take second helpings at every meal. And at the top of the authority-pyramid was Noel himself. The use of the words *Noel says so* were often spoken as a verbal trump card which, when played, brought all disputes to a conclusion. That was it! If Noel *says so,* then it *must* be so – end of argument. This being the case, I found myself growing increasingly worried that, taken to its logical conclusion, my obedience to those in authority ultimately meant to Noel himself. And there lay my dilemma. What safeguards did we have to control any present or future demands he might make of us under this concept of "obedience"? Noel had referred to his time in the navy – and most understood him, rightly or wrongly, to mean the Royal Navy. But even within such a regimented institution there is accountability. The officer giving instructions is himself a man under authority who is restricted by defined parameters of jurisdiction. Even in combat he cannot assume to himself more command than that which his rank and rules-of-engagement allow. Nor so the man right at the top of the greasy pole, the Admiral of the Fleet himself. He too must give account to the Secretary of State for Defence, who must give account to Parliament, who must ultimately give account to the electorate. And within the Church, with its plethora of "orders" and "armies" and "missions", there is nearly always a framework of accountability which inevitably exercises a controlling influence. *What such safeguards did **we** have? What such safeguards in a Community where we had been told that "democracy is the enemy of a **true** church"? To whom was Noel accountable?* I knew that other church leaders were being told that he was no more than the senior pastor amongst a controlling group of elders. But if *they* were reassured by such statements, *I* definitely wasn't.

There were all manner of aspects to the way we lived which reinforced the Community's ownership of us. Many of us were even given a new name, a "virtue name", especially if we were a John or a Steve or a Dave and needed to be distinguished from all the other Johns, Steves and Daves. I became John Diligent, known to most simply as "Diligent", or, to my closest friends, just "Dil" – much better than the *Heavy Evy* moniker I'd been dubbed with at Eton. Moreover, even though we weren't forbidden from keeping contact with our natural families altogether, we were explicitly encouraged to treat our brothers and sisters in the Community as being our *true* family. So although many, like me, continued to enjoy reasonably regular communications with our parents, our loyalty to the Community was nevertheless *always* expected to take precedence over any residual loyalty to our kinsfolk. In fact it wouldn't be untrue to say that continuing to have links with our families was allowed more as a way to fend off criticism than anything else. Acknowledgement of birthdays, going home at Christmas, buying presents; all kinds of conventional indicators of attachment such as these were beyond the limit of what was considered acceptable. This being so, it was inevitable there would be some parents who felt snubbed and rejected by their children. They blamed the Community of course, and there was a lot of acrimony. The consequence of it all was that several of the brothers and sisters became more or less *totally* estranged from their flesh and blood.

To emphasize the finality of the move we'd made from one kingdom to another, we were sometimes encouraged to burn possessions which had been of value to us. Standing in front of a bonfire at New Creation Farm one day, I threw onto it my small but highly valued record collection. Amongst others, on went Mott the Hoople's "Wildlife" album, on went The Eagle's "Hotel California", and on went Pink Floyd's "Dark Side of the Moon". Some of the things I'd burned would be replaceable in later years; others were irreplaceable, such as my Eton College shirt collar with personalized messages and autographs from all five original Genesis members – collected after they'd played a gig in the school hall. When I tell friends the story of what I did with it, they shake their heads with melancholic expressions and say, *'oh dear.'* I can tell they are too polite to say what they're really thinking: *'what a plonker.'* I shudder to think how much that collar would fetch at a rock-memorabilia sale if I still had it. Anyway, there it was, gone for ever, the ashes blown to every corner of the apple orchard. I knew as I walked away from the flames that I'd taken an immensely important step in burning my bridges with the past, in turning from the old and facing the new. I felt within myself that I'd "let go". I'd been obedient in this and could now be obedient in almost anything.

It wasn't my struggle with the whole notion of "obedience", however, which led to the relief I felt when I was asked to work in the tractor repair shed instead of the pig yard. The problem I had working with the pigs wasn't anything to do with obedience, as such; it was all to do with how completely knackered I was at the end of every day. It was in the tractor repair shed, under the patient guidance of Steve (aka Steve Stalwart), that I stripped down and rebuilt my first diesel engine. What a proud moment it was for me when the old Fordson

Major purred back into life on the very first depression of the starter-button. She continued for many years thereafter to offer her uncomplaining help with the harvesting operations in the orchards – far out-powered by the larger tractors we would buy, but never overshadowed.

My relationship with the old David Brown wasn't to be nearly so convivial, a serious big-end problem that it developed giving me the opportunity for my second major engine-rebuild. This time, though, it needed to be without Steve's help because he was busy with other things. Armed with the workshop manual, I nervously set about the task; and once I'd successfully restored the engine to operational condition, the tractor was returned to its duties in the cattle yard shifting tons of dung and silage. Another job well done! It therefore came as something of a surprise to receive a report from the cattlemen just a few days later of what sounded like another serious engine failure. Steve and I drove off to the yard, half-a-mile or so away, and had the tractor's sump dropped in no time whatsoever. To our horror, it was immediately obvious that the crankshaft had sheered in half. Another rebuild would be needed. It was while so employed that I discovered a groove in the big-end-bearing thrust-washers which needed to be fitted facing *inwards* to facilitate the smooth passage of oil. Sufficient time has now elapsed for me to confess that I have no idea whatsoever which way round I fitted the thrust-washers on the previous occasion. Had they been fitted with the groove facing *outwards,* it would go a long way to explain the premature – and otherwise *inexplicable* – failure of the crankshaft: a critical component that wouldn't last long without proper lubrication.

The farm was run on a fairly tight budget. So, in the first instance, I decided to visit Curly Bell's scrap yard in the hope he might have a replacement crankshaft from an old tractor. Curly was a rough character if ever there was one. He always had a tatty old woolen hat pulled low down over his unshaven dirty face, and he didn't so much talk to you as snarl at you. It may say something about the man to know that outside his yard was the hand-painted-yet-clearly-visible notice which read:

"Trespassers will be sexually assaulted"

On my very first visit to his yard I'd made the terrifying mistake of questioning Curly about something he'd told me. His snarling response made me think he was just as capable of committing physical assault as he was of sexual assault. Visits to Curly Bell's scrap yard were never pleasurable, but sometimes necessary. Once bitten, twice shy! I did my very best never to provoke him again. Thankfully, he *did* have a crankshaft from a David Brown, and I successfully fitted it into our own tractor after it had been reground at a local engineering firm.

Perhaps it was just as well that the David Brown and I didn't see too much of one another because I could have sworn it was out to do me mischief, a suspicion strengthened by what happened when it was in the workshop to have a fault with the rear-hydraulics repaired: the lift-arms had stopped working. Due to my seriously limited experience, many problems of this kind were new ones to me; sometimes the successful repairs I'd made were the result of little more than inspired guesswork concerning diagnosis of the fault. Having a practical-minded brother called Ivor helping me on this occasion was therefore very reassuring. We cleaned out all the relevant hydraulic hoses and made extensive investigations, but we didn't appear to have found any cause of the fault. The only thing we could then think of doing was to refill the hydraulic-oil reservoir in the hope that we may, by chance, have managed to free up some blockage. Refilling it proved to be an extremely slow and tedious process, so we decided to start up the engine to try and get some fluid pumped around. While Ivor went to turn the ignition switch, I remained sat on the rear concrete-filled barrel – slung between the lift-arms as a counter-balance weight – pouring in fluid. I remember thinking to myself as soon as I heard the engine noise, *'My god, what will happen if the barrel starts to lift?'* But before I had time to reach out for the hydraulic lever, I was thrust forward by what felt like a pair of aggressively powerful robotic hands. I shouted out to Ivor in panic as the leading edge of the Power Take Off (PTO) guard began pressing into the front of my upper leg – which, without much doubt, would have been severed had the lift-arms continued to rise. Fortunately, he ignored my plea to come back and operate the control lever but hit the engine stop-button instead. The barrel then dropped an inch or two and I eased my leg away. In intense pain and unable to stand, I fell to the ground, where, screaming pitifully, I writhed about. A few brothers had soon gathered around me.

'Has anyone got a ministry of healing?' one of them shouted out. Had I not been in so much pain I may well have gone straight for his throat.

'Bugger a ministry of healing,' I thought, *'I want a doctor, and quickly.'*

I expose the secret thoughts of my mind not as a flag but a confession.

Word was sent back to the farm office, a doctor *was* called, and Noel himself came quickly to the scene. Together with another brother, he supported me back to the farmhouse and laid me on a bed. There were occasions when Noel could be immensely paternal, kind and reassuring, when you felt confident he had everything in control. This was certainly one of them, and at least *he* didn't start wittering on about praying for me to be healed. The doctor, Alasdair, himself a Community brother, soon arrived. My jeans were cut away to reveal a deep, reddened indentation running all the way across the top of my leg, so precisely formed that it almost appeared to be a natural feature of the limb. Alasdair, who was quite taken aback by what he saw, knew the pain must be excessive. He immediately gave me a shot of morphine into my arm, followed by another into my buttock. I gasped as the rush of drug flooded my body. The pain abated, but only slightly; so the kind doctor repeated the dose into my arm and backside. By the time the ambulance arrived to take me away, I had already "gone". I spent the next few hours in dazed oblivion, and I was almost totally unaware of the passage of time while being treated in the casualty department of the local hospital.

Surprisingly, the X-rays taken didn't reveal any broken bones, and later that same day I was taken back to the farmhouse by ambulance again. The paramedics who carried me up to my room in a stretcher-chair had to pass through the large entrance-hall of the farm, which, at the time, was packed full of about thirty or forty brothers and sisters who'd assembled for one of the weekly house-meetings – smaller versions of chapel meetings. What the stretcher bearers must have made of it all, I don't know. As for me, I was still too stoned to care. I just about managed to give the gathered company a pontifical wave from the glory of my elevated throne as I disappeared off up the stairs. The indentation in my leg remained with me for several years; the mental horror much longer. I've been awakened on many nights with a vivid recollection of the incident and haunted by "what ifs". I *still* shudder to think about it, whilst fully aware that the exercise of rehearsing what *might* have happened is futile. The concrete-filled bucket *wasn't* raised higher! The engine *was* switched off! Try and stop yourself fretting about *might-have-beens* when you can be thankful for *have-beens.*

I might just as easily be using this same philosophy in reference to another tractor accident involving Nigel, the ex-heroin-user farm manager who would become a close buddy. We could scarcely have been called the best of friends in those days, often at drawn swords with one another. This was very nearly inevitable given that we were perfectly ill-suited together. *He* often came across as brash, loud, and assertive, characteristics which I looked down upon; whereas *I* was softly spoken, diffident and sensitive, characteristics which Nigel thought were falsely virtuous and wishy-washy. I did my very best not to let him browbeat in the way he did with some of the other farm workers, but I wasn't always successful: he had the upper hand over me by virtue of his designation as farm manager and consequential close association with Noel.

In the seasonal calendar of work at the farm, the early-summer months were important as a time for harvesting the long meadow grass: the base-product for feeding to the cattle as silage over the winter. Generally, I enjoyed driving tractors; but not when I had to play second fiddle to Nigel – as I did during this particular exercise – because I was well aware of the speed with which he drove. Being, so he always used to remind me, the more competent and experienced driver, he invariably chose to drive the lead tractor – the one that pulled the grass-cutting forage-harvester behind it. I was always detailed to drive the second tractor, the one that pulled a deep-sided trailer to gather the grass cuttings as they were discharged through the forage-harvester's funnel. While needing to constantly stay within a few feet of the lead tractor's wheels, I also had to continuously fine tune my *exact* position in order to ensure an even distribution of the cut grass within the trailer. Keeping up with Nigel like this, while trying to avoid the ever-present danger of locking wheels with him, took every ounce of concentration I could manage (and considerable skill, I might add).

On the day in question we were cutting grass in a meadow which fell steeply away from the adjacent A5. Regardless of it being a small, uneven pasture with sharp corners, Nigel, completely careless of my own need to manoeuvre a trailer very nearly full with several tons of cut grass, hurtled around at a breakneck pace. As we sped along parallel with the road, and therefore leaning away from it, I saw his tractor bounce up and down after it had hit extremely uneven ground. Driving so close together, there was no opportunity to slow down or take evasive action. Instinctively, I knew these bumps and furrows were going to make it very hard for me to control my tractor. To my amazement, though, I passed over them relatively easily, my correct position maintained as the rear wheels bounced out of the hollows. I breathed a sigh of relief and quietly mouthed "praise the Lord" – the benediction used by most of the brothers and sisters dozens and dozens of times every week, if not every day. But my thanksgiving was premature. Scarcely had the words left my mouth than I found myself being propelled away from the open-topped tractor as it was flung violently upwards and over towards the ground. Because my left foot was trapped behind the clutch pedal, I flopped down headfirst beneath the side of the tractor – now suspended at a dangerous angle only a few feet from the ground. It would surely have rolled on top of me had it not been locked in this position by the draw-bar pin attaching it to the trailer. Nigel came running over and managed to disengage my foot so that I could crawl clear. I was then able to see exactly what *had* happened. Although the tractor itself had indeed ridden safely over the bumps, the trailer – with a far higher centre of gravity – had crashed to the ground with its tonnage of grass, taking the tractor with it like a die-cast model. I owed my life, possibly, to the particular way in which the draw-bar pin had buckled, thereby preventing the tractor from making final contact with the ground.

When Noel arrived at the scene, he was furious with Nigel.

'We'll need to get this trailer upright as soon as possible, bro,' he said. And shaking his head in vexed frustration as if all the forces of evil had colluded together against the Fellowship, he added:

'They'll all be laughing at us in the pubs tonight if anyone sees **this** from the road.'

It was one of a number of statements made by Noel which I could hardly believe I'd heard, which I stored without further ado in my mind until I should understand the man with greater illuminance. Steve Stalwart came down from the workshop armed with ropes and a more powerful tractor. He had the overturned trailer upright in no time; and within an hour I was back at the wheel. For the rest of *that* particular day, anyway, Nigel drove with far greater caution. Better still, on future occasions when I partnered him he was hardly able to complain if I signalled that I wanted to slow down – although the beggar did his best to make me feel a wimp for doing so.

CHAPTER ELEVEN: Excitement and happiness in Zion

Many of the anecdotes and illustrations concerning Community life so far related took place during the university vacations, when I lived and worked at New Creation Farm. Back at the university itself I was full of the evangelistic, proselytizing fervour so peculiar to those recently converted to a new lifestyle, be it that of non-smoking, socialism, environmentalism, or even vegetarianism. Notwithstanding either previous promises I'd made myself or how objectionable I'd found the same kind of behaviour in others, I wasted no opportunity to sing the praises of the Fellowship I'd joined, enthusiastically partnered in doing so by Debbie, who'd made a renewed, unassailable commitment to the brotherhood. Clive, having graduated, now lived at New Creation Hall.

We made the pilgrimage to Bugbrooke nearly every weekend and often invited people to travel up with us: journeys I can now look back on with some amusement but which weren't necessarily much fun at the time. Uppermost in my mind is the occasion when we'd been allocated a three-wheeled, fibre-glass-bodied Reliant Robin to travel in – Yes! The saloon version of the "Trotter's Trading Company" van – and there were *five* of us making the one-hundred-and-forty-mile journey. Somehow, somehow, we managed to squeeze everyone into the diminutive vehicle yet still hurtle down the M1 fast enough for the speedometer to register seventy miles an hour. It was really quite frightening. Every time an articulated lorry rattled past, the little Robin, caught in the slipstream, lurched dramatically to the left and I found myself driving on the hard shoulder. This was no vehicle to drive at speed on a motorway! In *those* days, however, I lacked sufficient clout in the Community to influence such absurd decisions concerning vehicle allocation and just had to make the best of it. Fortunately, it was soon realized by those with more seniority that our transport was unacceptable, and we were then given a comfortable Morris Marina to travel in; luxury indeed.

It wasn't too long before Debbie and I were joined in our commitment to the Community by four of those who'd been our weekend guests: Sue, Angie, Clive and Steve. This meant we needed a second vehicle. Initially we were given a beautiful, green Morris Minor, the car one senior brother described as the only one he'd ever driven that gave him no pride of life whatsoever when he was behind the wheel. The man must have had a shrivelled soul. I myself thought the little "Moggie" was quite wonderful: the gentle throb of the engine was distinctive, the staid stability of road handling reassuring, and the spoked steering-wheel a delight to handle. It was a sad day when we were given a characterless Ford Escort to replace it.

The six of us formed ourselves into a small pocket of Bugbrooke in the middle of Canterbury. We travelled together, eat together, lived together, and pooled our finances in a common-purse system akin to that operated in the other Community households. The other two brothers and I lived in an old, virtually derelict, badly heated farmworkers' cottage in Herseden; the three sisters in a modern bungalow at Sturry. Through our endeavours to promote the Bugbrooke brotherhood, we managed to make ourselves very nearly despised by erstwhile Christian friends; and the charge was frequently made against us that our only interest in associating with the Christian Union was to try and steal away others to join us in the Community. We denied such an accusation vehemently and complained that we were being persecuted because of the lifestyle we practised. If the truth be known, though, those who charged us with such indictments weren't too far from the mark. And they did well insofar as they managed to restrict the influence we otherwise may have had on several people who, at one time, we thought we'd won over to swell our numbers. Looking back, the way we behaved at Canterbury was undeniably condescending and very nearly unforgivable. Nor is there any doubt that it was, primarily, myself at fault: I was the one consumed with proselytizing zeal. So to those of you to whom I made myself odious, I would say I am very very sorry. But please remember that I myself had been influenced by others.

The Canterbury days shouldn't be passed over without mentioning the affection I began to develop for one of the sisters: Angie. Not that I ever had any way of finding out from Angie herself whether my feelings were reciprocated. Having become a faithful brother, obedient to the Community way of doing these things, I never spoke with her directly about affairs of the heart: I had to rely on intuition and disclosures made by her own elder, Kelly, to reassure myself of what I *thought* I saw whenever our eyes met. Whilst together at university, we enjoyed one another's company in a way denied to most of the other prospective couples in the Community – and despite the rigid segregation there were many. I was well aware how hard it was going to be for me come the time when I'd graduated from Canterbury and would only see Angie infrequently: at chapel maybe, or on the occasions when she came to work on the farm.

Our relationship – if it can be called that – had known conflict as well as tenderness. Without being a bona fide elder, I was nevertheless deemed to be the "shepherd" of the little Canterbury flock. As such, I saw myself to be responsible for ensuring the lifestyle we adopted was as close as possible to the one practised within the Community itself. Angie was quite headstrong and didn't always take willingly to this. Neither did she readily accept I had any authority over her. And nor did I, except that afforded me by her intent to become a Community member: an intent which, initially, was rather volatile and uncertain. I was often worried she would be enticed away from our little circle by the strong attachments she continued to maintain with other members of the Christian Union, or that she would capitulate in her struggle to relinquish the independence pulling her in other directions. Getting Angie to knuckle under, reigning in her strong, healthy, independent will, was something like – and no better than – the taming of the shrew. And the high-handed attempts

I sometimes made to bring her into line, believing them to be for her own good, gave her every reason not to like but to resent me.

It was in my final year at university that I decided the only obvious career I could follow with any conviction or enthusiasm was teaching. But these weren't the kind of decisions you made on your own; not if you were a member of the New Creation Christian Community. Major decisions like these needed to be discussed with and approved by the elder to whom you "submitted" – in my case Rufus, a man who, always with the best interests of the kingdom at heart, was quite capable of making decisions and speaking his mind without having first considered all the relevant whys and wherefores. Only a few weeks after I'd moved into the farm, as a case in point, he asked me to find out about transferring my degree course to a local polytechnic so that I wouldn't have any need to be away from the Community during the week. This had been a real problem for me. Considering all the struggles I'd been through to get there, I would have found leaving Canterbury a devastating wrench. And it wasn't even as if I would have been the *only* Community member away at college. Fortunately Noel himself, having got to hear about all this, had intervened, insisting it was important for my self-esteem – if nothing else – that I stay at Canterbury.

Another of the occasions I had reason to be thankful to Noel for taking a direct interest in my welfare was when I arrived at the farm one weekend and found out I'd been taken off Sunday-morning pigsty duties. I felt enormously grateful. Not because I minded the actual task of getting up early to go and muck out the pigsties (in fact I quite enjoyed it), but rather because of how exhausted I used to get on our late-Sunday-evening journeys back south. And I do mean exhausted! I used to be a danger to both myself and everyone else on the final stretches of the motorway through Kent. Sometimes, my eyes would deny all the rational, life-preserving attempts I made to fight off the slumber which begged them to close. It wasn't at all uncommon for me to give myself an almighty startled fright when I suddenly realized that I'd driven up dangerously close to a vehicle in front: the very same vehicle which I was sure had been some considerable way ahead in the dark distance of the night the last time I noticed it was there. But at the least the resulting surge of adrenaline helped me to regain control of my eyes for a further few miles. It was Noel himself who'd recognized the inflexible way in which the farm elders had refused to have one rule for some and another rule for others: *everyone else has to do work on the farm, so why shouldn't John Diligent?* Nor had I myself *wanted* to be treated any differently to the rest. The truth of the situation, however, was that no one else in my household had needed to make such a punishing journey late of a Sunday night; nor had they been virtually "on the go" since the Friday night – which was when we used to leave Canterbury. Observing all this, Noel made the necessary reproaches to bring change: change which meant I was able to enjoy the bliss of an extra few hours Sunday-morning sleep without having solicited such a privilege in any way whatsoever. Noel also took careful note what had become known as "the Canterbury scene", and he often used to congratulate me in my endeavours to "expand the kingdom". Although it was just the six of us who remained at the nucleus of this scene, there were others who became Community members as an indirect consequence of our proselytizing efforts.

In 1979, at a time when my star of spiritual status had risen to a position of some ascendancy, there was a general consensus within the brotherhood that it would be a good idea for me to stay on at Canterbury to shepherd Sue and Angie – who were slightly younger than the rest of us – through their final year at university. Against this background, I didn't have much doubt that Rufus would agree to me enrolling on a post-graduate course at a teacher-training college in Bexley Heath, an outer suburb of South East London which was just about within commuting distance of Canterbury. His blessing formally given, I applied to the college and was offered a place. The evil day of being taken away from Angie's company had been deferred for another year.

But my plans for teacher-training were changed when Noel asked me to look into the possibility of doing sociological research, with the Bugbrooke Fellowship as the subject. This was because the popular press had been giving the Fellowship a considerable amount of bad publicity with allegations which included brainwashing, family-splitting, and cruelty towards children. Noel was of the mind that a properly researched publication, academically authenticated and highlighting all the sociological benefits of the way we lived, would prove invaluable. Enquiries within the academic circles of the university led me to a professor who was both enthusiastic about the field of study I wished to pursue and willing to include me amongst his research students. The arrangement was ratified when it was confirmed that I'd managed to get an upper-second in my finals; so I cancelled the offer of a place at teacher-training college. This was done with no small measure of regret since I had little ambition to pursue purely-academic studies of which I'd become weary.

During the summer vacation following my graduation, Noel promulgated his vision for the Community of "enlarging the tent" by establishing "satellite" communities throughout the Midlands. For me, this meant all-change again. Deemed to be someone with a successful evangelistic ministry, Noel insisted I should move into the newly purchased "Harvest House", near Coventry. In consequence, I also had to make arrangements to transfer my research studies to Warwick University. I was well aware that Noel would be neither influenced nor pleased if I appealed to keep my place at Canterbury just because I wanted to remain near to Angie. Besides, I *did* have what everyone called "a kingdom heart" didn't I? I *did* want to do what was best for the whole of the brotherhood, not just for myself, didn't I? If, in fact, I *did* have a kingdom heart, I'm afraid it didn't help ease the pain of knowing that I would now only see Angie on the occasions when our paths fortuitously crossed while we were engaged in some common Community activity. I was only twenty-two years old. Twenty-five was the magical age when courtship could be countenanced: I'd therefore only served eighteen months or so of the prolonged romantic sabbatical enforced on me. These months had seemed long enough even though I'd seen and talked to Angie just about every day. *How would I get through the next three years?*

I'd also made the dreadful mistake one day, at the height of my zeal for Zion, of suggesting to Noel that I thought maybe, just maybe, the Lord wanted me to take the "higher calling" of remaining single. Believing it to be the proper calling for a brother regarded by many as having a key role in the vanguard of the expansion which God was apparently meant to have in store for the Fellowship, from that day onwards he marked me out as a celibate. Not that I was alone in this whole business of contemplating celibacy. There were many of us who, under intense social pressure, had at some point given serious consideration to it. Sometimes it seemed to be a more manageable commitment than the stark alternative of living with uncertainty. Better to be sure of where you stood, maybe, than to live with years of hope which may finally be dashed.

As the months rolled past, and as I began to have confidence that a future relationship might be possible despite all the talk of celibacy, I began to have longer conversations with Angie whenever the opportunity arose – and to hell with any purist who may have wished to criticize me for doing so. *Was I just imagining it, or was she in no great hurry to bring our chats to a close?*

Weeks turned into months turned into years. It would be a misrepresentation of the truth to deny that I enjoyed many happy days cradled in the bosom of a Community which I believed to be wonderful; to be Zion itself. I formed many valued, enriching friendships, the like of which I'd never known before. And life as a Community member wasn't *all* unmitigated intensity and self-denial. There were occasions of great laughter and merriment, times of great camaraderie, times of great poignancy, and times which I shall return to again and again with melancholic fondness as I daydream about the past.

But nor can it be denied that some of this pleasure was *in spite of* rather than *because of* the Community. Like the time when Shaun and I went to the Knebworth music festival with several other brothers on an evangelistic expedition. The pair of us, having spurned our inhibitions and fears of rejection and embarrassment, had spoken to countless numbers of festivalgoers, many of whom had snubbed us, but some of whom had come back with us to our camp site to talk further – and at depth. With the evening drawing out, we were tired – very tired; so we just flopped to the ground at the back of the main concert area. Led Zeppelin were coming to end of their set. For their reprise, they began to play "Stairway to Heaven". It was worldly music, of course, but still able to create a tingle in my spine. I closed my eyes, forgot about the Community, and allowed myself to be stirred by the familiar sound of the music.

As we left the festival site, we did so in the company of a hundred-thousand others, all crowded together as they funnelled through a narrow field: a slowly moving dark ocean of bodies who had become, somehow, magnificent in their sheer magnitude, illuminated only by moonlight.

Nor was life in the Community devoid of excitement. On Friday nights, for example, a whole gang of us went out and about to evangelize in different local towns. Intent on engaging people in conversations about our faith, we simply approached passers-by in the street or mixed with people inside the crowded pubs. The friendships and associations we made *sometimes* led to the recruitment of new members (although we would have objected to using the word "recruitment"), but they also led to diverse and fascinating experiences as we travelled here and there to nurture and strengthen the links which had been forged. One Friday evening, out on the streets of Leamington Spa, we couldn't help but be aware of not only a most unusual atmosphere in the town but also the surprising absence of passers-by. We'd arrived late on in the evening and were wondering quite what to do with ourselves as we stood forlornly on the edge of the park by the Spa Centre. The main parade behind us, lined on both sides with stately Georgian buildings, was deserted. Suddenly, a couple of skinheads came running towards us. I knew I had to seize the opportunity, so ran alongside them.

'Hold on. I'd like to talk with you for a moment, please,' I panted, glad that I'd been bold but feeling rather stupid as I tried to keep pace with them. The next thing I knew, I was looking down the sharp blade of a long knife held menacingly close to my face. I would have loved to do-a-David-Wilkinson and tell them *Jesus loves you*, but it would have been a borrowed phrase, hollow and meaningless. Leaving them to run on, I drew back.

Shortly after, another small gang of skinheads came past, one of them being helped along by the others. He was clutching the side of his head, which, even in the diffused amber glare of the street lighting, we could clearly see was covered in blood. He'd been attacked, no doubt, by the pair whom we'd just seen legging it: the pair who may, I suppose, have thought that I'd intended to try and confront them. No sooner had the small gang passed by than the whole street seemed to be crowded with skinheads who were waving their scarves above their heads and shouting,

'C o v e n t r e e e, C o v e n t r e e e, C o v e n t r y e e e.'

They were followed fairly soon after by a rival gang chanting:

'B i r m i n g h a – a m, B i r m i n g h a – a m, B i r m i n g h a – a m.

And then, on the edge of the park just across the road from us, there was open warfare: punching, shouting and kicking such as I'd only ever read about in the press or seen on the TV news. One of the youngsters, who surely-to-god couldn't have been older than twelve, fell to the ground. Four or five of the older youths were on to him immediately, each of them repeatedly using their sixteen-hole docs to deliver brutal kicks at every part of his body, including his head. The expression "putting the boot in" couldn't have been more apt. It was truly horrific.

Gentle by nature – an old softie – some may consider me, but there have been several times in my life when I've rushed to someone else's defence even though angels themselves may have feared to do so. Nor has age tempered my tendency to be sometimes far too impulsive for my own good. On this particular occasion, however, I remained firmly planted to the spot where I stood – and it had nothing to do with any unwillingness to help worldly people. There must have been fifty or more of these crazed boot-boys, and to have entered the fray would have been neither wise nor brave, just totally mad. A fiery young brother called Nick, however, allowed his gallantry to get the better of him and began to cross over the road. Knowing full well there was nothing he could do, I pulled him back: he would probably have ended up being pulverized himself without having been of any help whatsoever.

Thankfully, his help wasn't needed anyway. The whole crowd of them, both gangs together (including the youngster who'd been pummelled on the floor), suddenly began running off in the direction of the railway station: they'd seen the blue flashing lights of an approaching police car before we had. It was only later on in the evening that we discovered they'd all come from a punk-rock concert at the local civic hall – a concert which had finished just shortly after we'd arrived in the town. Who would have thought such a thing in regal, stately Leamington Spa? Obviously the local townsfolk had known only too well what was likely to happen and had stayed safely at home or in the pubs.

I could possibly fill a whole book with anecdotes about the exciting times of Community life and would love to do so – but mustn't. These adventures mitigated the sense of captivity which often contained us; and it's one of the reasons why leaving became so unthinkable. The adventure of a trip to Nelson Green's bulldozer graveyard in Lincolnshire is one that I simply can't miss out. We used a very old "Drott" bulldozer on the farm to load pig manure into a muck-trailer which then spread it onto our fields as a fertilizer. We simply called it "the Drott". On one memorable occasion, down at the Shalom-farm cattle yard, one of its rear idle wheels broke and became detached from the track. Steve Stalwart and I were called on to rescue the situation. One thing we knew for sure: Curly Bell would definitely not have a replacement in *his* scrapyard – this was a specialist item. Steve, however, managed to locate a second-hand bulldozer dealer in Lincolnshire, Nelson Green, who told him that he'd be able to help out. It was a sunny Saturday afternoon when we set off in a little Mini van to collect the replacement wheel.

On arrival we discovered that Nelson Green's business operated out of a disused WW2 airfield. From the main compound, filled with bright yellow, freshly painted, newly restored machinery awaiting export, we could see an untold number of old bulldozers lining the former runway for its entire length – well in excess of a mile. Nelson himself welcomed us with a broad smile:

'*Well,*' he said in a broad Lincolnshire accent, '*it's good to see two young lads working on a Saturday afternoon.*'

'*Little does he know,*' I found myself thinking, '*that sometimes, when necessary, we might well work from dawn to dusk **every** day.*' This was certainly true at harvest time when we needed to bale the freshly cut straw – bought from other local farmers – and take it back to the farm, where we built huge straw stacks with it: winter bedding for the cattle. Sunday was our only "day off"; chapel meetings were sacrosanct – except, that is, when Noel deemed it necessary for some of us to continue working.

We drove behind Nelson out to the runway, and then along it for several hundred yards. He abruptly pulled up alongside one particular vehicle and began to offload his oxyacetylene cutting gear. Pointing to the adjacent Drott, he told us that the rear idle wheels were identical to those on our own machine apart from a small lug on the inner-bearing cowl. The explanation given, he got to work with his cutting torch and had one of the wheels removed in next to no time. I was absolutely astonished by how he must have known every one of those bulldozers inside out. Not only had he taken us straight to the right one – there had been no hesitation whatsoever – but he also knew about this tiny little lug. In his own field, the man was a genius; and a highly likeable one to boot. He may have been a "worldling", but I never had any doubt that my life was all the better for having met Nelson Green.

Back at Shalom farm, we set to work on the broken-down Drott immediately; and we carried on, using artificial lighting, until late at night. It was one of the few occasions when I was excused from attending a Saturday-evening chapel meeting, the commercial imperative of getting the Drot back to work being apparently more important. Nelson Green had been entirely correct: we needed to grind off the small lug in order to fit the replacement wheel.

The brotherhood at Bugbrooke was ready to accept *all* types, shapes and ages of people from a vast array of different backgrounds. It came very close to being a truly classless society, and many people who were misfits in other environments found a welcoming acceptance in the Community. There were also many people who would have attracted *plenty* of friends and admirers in whatever company they found themselves; beautiful girls, for example, who'd sacrificed the lure of worldly admiration to adorn themselves with a beauty which they wanted to come from *within* themselves.

Small wonder we all felt we were part of something very special indeed. Small wonder many referred to it as "the kingdom". Small wonder we jealously guarded the Community from criticism and were prepared to put our loyalty towards it above anything else in our lives.

CHAPTER TWELVE: Power corrupts

Having set my hand to the plough, having pledged myself to membership of the Community, I was determined not to look back. So, despite the upset of being parted from Angie's company, I applied myself to making a success of life in the new Warwickshire household in the only way I knew: with diligence. I'd managed to find two academics in the sociology department of Warwick University who were keen to exercise joint supervision of my research, and it was agreed that the Fellowship would fund the study on a part-time basis. I was more than happy with this arrangement as it left me with two or three days a week when I could continue to work in the farm's repair shop with Steve: I often felt more comfortable up to my eyes in grease, oil, piston-rings and final-drives than I did with tedious and turgid sociological texts.

Regardless of the damning words which I could so easily use in any attempt to express most appropriately what it is I *now* feel about the Community, I cannot be anything but thankful for the rich memories I was to be plenteously provided with through my work on the farm. The expansion of agricultural experience and the increase of competence in things-mechanical which the non-academic half of my life gave me was something I always enjoyed and valued, strange though its juxtaposition with the other half may have been. And the skills acquired have always served me well.

During my final year of membership I moved to another newly bought Community home in Warwickshire: the rather grand "Stockton House". I was also invited to join the ranks of the eldership as a junior member. The respect afforded me from many others, especially as a leader in evangelism, had been acknowledged by Noel; hence the invitation. It was given, however, at a time when – had he but known it – my allegiance to the brotherhood was on the turn. Had the option been available to me, and had I been more self-assured about the strength and validity of all my misgivings and concerns, the most honest response would have been for me to decline the invitation. But I wasn't yet either strong enough or sufficiently disaffected to come clean about what was going on within me. In consequence, I found myself attending the regular elders' meetings held in the living-room of the farmhouse; and through so doing I became even further aware of how brazenly "bullish" Noel could be on the subject of business life within the Community. He had, I discovered, no qualms whatsoever about referring to others in the room by name when he wanted to make an example of them for being insufficiently business minded. Nor was he concerned about their feelings when he castigated them for being "wet". And to explain what the word meant, he recounted the telling anecdote of a local businessman. The man, apparently, had stood to become *extremely* wealthy following the buy-out of his small firm by a much larger company. On discovering, however, that several of the employees were to be made redundant, and even though it was at considerable financial disadvantage to himself, he had initiated moves to buy back the firm to protect their jobs. The year was 1981. Margaret Thatcher had begun to deploy the broom with which she'd promised to sweep away socialism and all its attendant wastefulness in commercial life: the result, she believed, of having put consideration for the welfare of workers on a higher pedestal than maximization of profit.

'Brethren!' Noel entreated us earnestly. *'Make no mistake. The man I've told you about was wet when it came to business life. And there are some of you here in this room who are also wet. But you mustn't be! We are in business to make as much profit as possible: profit which will be used to build the kingdom. I hope you all understand this. I will* **not** *allow us to be weak and inept in our business affairs, even though I can tell that some of you, because you still have wishy-washy attitudes, aren't finding what I'm saying very comfortable.'*

Did he know, I wonder, that I was one such brother? I bitterly regret neither having had the clarity of thought nor the courage to stand up and shout back:

'No, brother Noel, you're wrong! Maybe it's true that some of us aren't well suited to the cut-and-thrust of commercial life. Maybe there are some of us who, because we lack the single-minded determination to make profit, wouldn't make successful businessmen. But that doesn't make us "wet" any more than the man you've told us about was for having done what he believed he ought to.'

How I wish I could have then added:

'How dare you call him wet! He wasn't. He was strong. Strong in what **he** *believed to be right.'*

For all that I'd grown to deeply love the fraternal strength and companionship of this Community I belonged to, I was still haunted by the ferocity with which Noel prosecuted his understanding of "the two kingdoms" and the consequences his doing so had for the way the businesses were run – the sale of brightly-wrapped Christmas parcels in the "Goodness Foods" shops being a case in point. It was Noel himself who'd described the Christmas festival as being pagan and ungodly, Noel himself who was primarily responsible for us not taking part in any of the Christmas festivities. But no harm, so he must have reasoned, in joining in with the ways of the world and taking advantage of the Christmas season when it came to bringing in more profit through the shops. *No harm in robbing the kingdom of the world to build the kingdom of God.*

Stockton House in Warwickshire

My disaffection with the Fellowship had begun to take undeniable shape well before I became an elder; probably during 1979, the year when I moved to Warwickshire. In fact, my disquiet was compounded by the very study which Noel himself had asked me – if not very nearly *compelled* me – to take on. I'd read George Orwell's brilliant "Animal Farm" while studying at Kent, a novel which had alerted me to the way in which a utopian dream can be corrupted through the exercise of power. At Warwick, I furthered my understanding of such processes through detailed sociological research into sectarianism and the characteristics of cults, and I was remorselessly pressed at my weekly meetings with Ian and Ivan – my academic supervisors – to be objective in my reflection. On the other hand, Noel himself, although he was a man of considerable intelligence, seemed to have little understanding of the rigorous, "scientific", sociological method and was more interested, evidently, in the subjective and exonerative aspects of the project. As the weeks and months slipped past until I'd been at Warwick for well over a year, I found myself increasingly pincered between two demands on my loyalty. My *head* was telling me there was much about the Fellowship to classify it as a cult; my *heart* was struggling to keep pace with such a devastating conclusion. But it was there for all to see; we had most, if not all, of the characteristics commonly used to define a cult. We had a pyramid-shaped authority structure with *one* man at the top having supreme authority; we believed in, and practised, a lifestyle which inevitably separated us to a large extent from the world and our families; we acquired new identities as Community members; we regarded those who left the Community as rebellious or backslidden; we believed ourselves persecuted when criticized by people from the world; and we were taught to regard aspects of the Community's lifestyle and dogma as secret amongst ourselves.

These "kingdom secrets", as Noel called them, were only openly spoken about when we all assembled in Bugbrooke chapel on Wednesday evenings for yet another meeting. It was largely restricted to the Fellowship faithful; an esotericism which Noel justified by reference to the biblical injunction "not to cast pearl before swine". Without such restrictions, he argued, there could be those present who might not be able to appreciate the spiritual value of his teaching and who might, therefore, use their twisted understanding about these "secrets" to persecute us.

"Do not give what is holy to the dogs; nor cast your pearls before swine, lest they trample them underfoot and turn to tear you in pieces." (Matthew. Chapter 7, verse 6)

It was during these Wednesday evening sessions, in particular, that Noel outlined *specific* details concerning the development of our lifestyle: the use of birch rods to "discipline" – rod – children, restrictions on sex within marriage, courtship arrangements, attitudes we should hold towards backslidden "traitors" – and other matters of like kind.

It would have taken a huge amount of self-deceit to deny what I could plainly see: the key characteristics of a cult were in our DNA. I also knew that *power corrupts and absolute power corrupts absolutely,* and that Noel would have to wear the cap bearing this inscription if it fitted him: which it did. Be that as it may have been, I was also acutely aware that *any* church which took the dogmatic teaching of the New Testament at face value and allowed it to lead them courageously into a radical new lifestyle would appear to many as being a cult. *How then could the counterfeit be distinguished from the real?*

I had almost come to envy cults and sects like the Moonies, the Scientologists or the Jehovah's Witnesses, who surely, I thought, must be able to relate the foundational doctrine of their lifestyle directly to the unique influence of their own leader or founder. In contrast, our *own* beliefs and structures, so we believed, originated from the literary canon known by the church through two millennium as being the New Testament: a book which *all* Christians believed to be divinely appointed, and which therefore underpinned the authenticity of our lifestyle. *How could I work out if our own "cult-likeness" was the product of a genuine, radical Christian lifestyle or the product of having "gone off the rails"?*

Approaching the autumn of 1980 I was all too well aware of the inner turmoil which was beginning to rack my mind. The evidence of my experience, reinforced by the conclusions of my academic research, had led me to believe the Fellowship I belonged to had become – if it hadn't been all along – an institution which, sociologically, must undeniably be labelled as a cult. *But so what?* In my heart there was still so much about the place which I loved, which gave me great happiness, which I believed to be of God, and which I felt was very nearly worth dying for. *What was I to do? I couldn't possibly break my baptismal promises and leave, could I? Where would I go to? Who could I turn to for advice?* I was now so well indoctrinated with the Fellowship's dogma and ethics that the only people I really trusted to "give it to me straight" were those within it. And I knew what *they* would say if I aired the misgivings wheeling around in my head. It felt like a marriage going wrong; a marriage you no longer fully believed in because you felt cheated by your partner. But still a marriage holding you in obedience to nuptial vows, still a marriage where the desire to make it work lived on – primarily through the memory of how things *used* to be, but also through the effect of sometimes falling into one another's arms with sufficient passion to bitterly regret having even *thought* you'd been made a cuckold.

My vacillating deliberations acted like a wedge forced into a crack of mistrust. I began to find certain things which went on within the Community increasingly distasteful; and this acted like a hammer, driving the wedge ever deeper until the crack had become a wide-open cavity. All my suppressed reservations and suspicions then came flooding out of the yawning chasm, presenting themselves as matters of supreme importance which I'd been misguided – if not extremely foolish – to have put to one side. I also knew that sooner or later the wedge would be driven in so far I would have to act. I knew it in my *head;* but in my *heart* I still wanted to be faithful, to be obedient, to submit my independent spirit to the "communal wisdom of the brethren". I wanted to work things out. Despite all my inner turmoil, I was quite resolved that the effect of the penetrating wedge should have to be akin to that of dismemberment before I would be proved disloyal, for no other reason when push came to shove than my belief that *God* had led me to the Community – and surely, therefore, I would be betraying the Almighty himself if I were to leave.

Not that I very much liked any longer what God seemed to be doing with me. Not that I very much liked the person whom I'd become. Not that I could look back with pride on the way I'd once treated one of my roommates, Nick – the fiery brother with a distinctive mop of tightly curled hair whom I'd had to restrain on that evening with the skinheads at Leamington Spa. We were very close and often confided in one another about the agony of our respective fanciful love affairs, me with Angie and he with Janie – a sister who worked in the same shop as he did. In the openness we had with one another, sometimes pained, sometimes teasing, sometimes insouciant, we found a mutuality which helped us come to terms with both being considered too young for approved courtship.

Nick, more than anyone, was a forthright, honest brother, and his so-called "problem" with this sister was widely known. For reason's unknown to me, he'd been told by the eldership that he should forget about the possibility of a future relationship with Janie once and for all. Needless to say, he was very aggrieved. His perplexity had led him to become quite depressed and surly: he just couldn't block Janie out of his thoughts in the way expected of him.

Aware of all this, and knowing me to be Nick's close friend, Noel decided to ring me late one evening when most of the household had already gone to bed.

'Bro,' he said, 'we've got to get Nick sorted out with this Janie business. It's going to lead him to be unfaithful to the kingdom if it carries on, you know. You mustn't let him go off to bed until he's repented and got himself a good heart.'

Noel was quite comfortable about using various trusted lieutenants to do his bidding – to be his henchmen and do the dirty work.

Nick was *already* in bed. So, together with Ian, the house-elder, I woke him up and asked him to come downstairs to a small room which we called "the Gate", where some armchairs were arranged around the warmth of an open log-burning fire. We then set about the job of ensuring Nick was led to repentance. Sometime in the early hours of the morning Nick finally broke down in floods of tears, agreeing he'd been in the wrong, asking forgiveness for his disobedience, and lamenting the selfishness which could have proved to be a "seed of bitterness" taking root in his soul and eventually growing into rebellion against the kingdom. When the tears were dried and the exhortations finished, we all went off to our beds. We had "gained" our brother.

The Jesus Fellowship Church often vigorously denied that its members were brainwashed. There were, it's true, no systematic, organized sessions when members were exposed to repeated statements of Fellowship dogma under conditions overtly and obviously intended to overcome an individual's mental resistance. As such, it was all too easy for us to believe that we *hadn't* been brainwashed but had embraced the Fellowship's doctrine and lifestyle freely and willingly. After all, hadn't we joined-up of our own accord? *Where were the gates, fences and padlocks which made us stay against our will?* As I lay in my bed that night thinking about what I'd just taken part in with Nick, however, I understood far more clearly about the subtleties of brainwashing: how it needn't be premeditated, or even *intended*, and yet still be very effective. I realized that I'd become a moral robot, that I'd subjected another brother to a humiliating and intimidating experience which I would have hated to be inflicted on myself. Like a cowardly moron, even though I'd had no more wish for Nick's tender heart to be hurt than I did for mine to be, I'd gone through with the exercise. Blindly, I'd even believed our admonishment to have been what God himself had wanted.

'How could you possibly have thought such a thing?' I asked myself. *'Did you really believe that Nick's infatuating attraction to Janie was any worse than your own to Angie? And if not, then why in the name of God did you allow yourself to be party to the inquisition which he has just been subjected to?'* For it had been, in truth, no better than an inquisition, demanding confession and conformity as its objective. The only conclusion I could draw was that I'd taken part because *I myself* must have become brainwashed: I was allowing myself to do things and think things which with honest, objective reflection I wouldn't have wished to either do or think. So, I'd taken part in helping to brainwash Nick even though the *intention* to do so hadn't been there. *What was happening to me? What was I becoming? Where was the John who hated the idea of forcefully imposing himself on others? Where was the John who accepted one and all alike and who saw value in many different lifestyles and beliefs?* For all the chaos and trauma of my pre-Bugbrooke years, at least I hadn't then sat in judgement over others in the way I now found myself doing – and hating myself for. *Was I really any closer to becoming the person whom God wanted me to be than I was before I became a Community member?*

In went the wedge a little deeper!

It was during this difficult period of mental struggle that I heard my sister's husband had left her: it was something which I'd been expecting for some time. Even though I'd not kept up my relationship with Jane in the conventional way through regular phone calls, birthday gifts, and family get-togethers, I'd been careful not to cut myself off altogether and had continued to visit her occasionally – but not *too* frequently as this would have been discouraged. The fact was that I still cared about her; a lot! Regardless of what we may have been taught about belonging to a new creation family, she was still my sister, my *real* sister, the only one I'd got – and I still had enough savvy to know that I ought never to forget it. I felt the very least I could do now that she was living on her own would be to send her some money: I knew how little she had at the best of times. But charitable giving, as such, wasn't practised in the Fellowship. The words that *thousands and thousands of pounds of 'Christian money' have been wasted by giving it to help people who are under God's judgement* had always rung in my head like a huge, cracked, clashing, discordant bell. I'd *never* been able to come to terms with them. Nor the explanation that famines and disasters are an inevitable consequence of God's judgement on the world and that He doesn't expect *His* people to reach out with charitable missions of material and financial mercy to the ones affected. It tore at the very substance of who I felt I was when I heard about, read about, or saw pictures of desolate, starving children and was then forced to remain aloof and detached, unable to do *anything*, even just send a few pounds; and all because of that accursed doctrine of Noel's – that it was a waste of money to assist those who were suffering under the consequential effects of God's judgement.

But maybe I *would* be allowed help my sister, I reasoned with myself, given that we were trying as a Fellowship to prove to our critics that we *did* care for our natural families, and also given that we were prepared to pay out substantial amounts to those who'd suffered personal misfortune if we felt it was going to help lead them *into* the family of Christ. I approached Dave Hawker (aka Dave Resolute), the elder to whom I now submitted in my Warwickshire home, and put my request.

'Will it be of any benefit to the kingdom?' he asked me, quite sincerely – it was the way we approached things like this. It would have been easy to reply:

'Yes, I think it will be. I think the Lord is at work in her heart.'

The brutal logic behind such a reply – and I mean brutal – was the possibility that the gift of money might have acted as a kind of sweetener for her to accept an invitation from us to come and stay in the Community for a few days. And, if she had given her heart to the Lord while she was with us, she then might even have gone on to become a member herself. I can only possibly describe it like this from the safe distance of looking back. At the time, it would have been hard for any of us to believe this is what we meant by the expression *for the benefit of the kingdom.* But it was. That's why I couldn't bring myself to try and persuade Dave there could be any possibility of a spiritual payback: I didn't want to give my sister money for any other reason than to help out in her moment of need. *It was to be a gift given with no ulterior motives or it would have felt to me like dirty money.* I therefore replied:

'Well actually, Dave, I honestly don't know if will benefit the kingdom, as such. I just thought it would be the right thing to do. I just wanted to give her some money because – well, because she's my sister.'

'Sorry, my bro,' he said, not unsympathetically but more as a point of order, *'you know we can't give out money like that.'*

Inside I felt sick. I'd worked hard enough to earn my part-time wage from the farm business: a wage which went straight into the common-purse account along with everyone else's wage and was never seen or handled by myself personally. I had no great problem with such an arrangement in itself because – in *those* days anyway – I'd genuinely lost interest in money or material possessions (save for my precious denim shirt and flared jeans).

'But why,' I asked myself, *'shouldn't a small sum of "my" money have been made available for me to use at my discretion when I needed it for something like this?'*

The whole flipping caboodle suddenly screamed at me as being illogical, unfair and unnatural. *The Community could spend thousands and thousands of pounds on an evangelistic campaign yet deny one of its members the right to spend twenty or thirty pounds on a close relative in need.* Ouch! I felt a shiver of contempt run down my spine. There was, of course, nothing further I could do about the situation, an impotence that inevitably reinforced my awareness of the extent to which I'd relinquished control of my conscience, the extent to which I had to rely on others to make decisions of right and wrong for me – helpless to do otherwise. It was no good me *believing* a particular course of action to be right if I was powerless to act upon it.

The wedge went in deeper still.

CHAPTER THIRTEEN: Animal Farm revisited

In the early winter of 1980 a refreshing distraction took my tired mind away from its meandering perplexity: I was going to be flying off to the Middle Eastern sun for a week. My parents had gone out to Jerusalem the previous winter to begin working as managers of Christ Church Hospice, an Anglican complex which catered for pilgrimage-style visits and holidays. After they'd been there for the best part of a year I was fairly confident I'd be given permission to visit them. This was because we were going through a phase as a Fellowship where we were anxious to prevent further media criticism concerning insufficient contact with our natural families, and I knew that one brother had actually been *encouraged* to make a visit to *his* parental home in South Africa. Why! Jerusalem was just around the corner by comparison. I was regarded – unwisely – as being rock solid in my allegiance, and I had no intention of confessing to any compromising vacillations which may have jeopardized the approval which, as I expected, was willingly given to my request. I knew that not only *ought* I visit my parents, as a dutiful son, but that I also really *wanted* to see them as well. Nor can I deny looking forward to the consequential perk of a holiday thrown in, and I was in no mood to squander this opportunity by yielding to the interfering demands of any scruples which may have tried to make me consider the welfare of my soul.

Having been met by parents at Ben Gurion airport, I set off with them on the rugged ascent inland just after dusk had begun to spread out her mantle of soft darkness. The wide carriageway, hewn through the rock of the surrounding hillside, was flanked with rusting military vehicles left as a perpetual memorial to the bitter struggle for independence. Nearing Jerusalem, the air through which we drove became strongly charged with evening scent from surrounding pine forests, a seductive fragrance which forced its way into the vehicle and intoxicated my senses. Then, as we came around the edge of an imposing rock face to one side of the meandering carriageway, I caught my first sight of the city rising up above and in front of us; a city built from stone that blended into the hillside, a city illuminated with the golden glow of sodium incandescence. Another passenger in the car, a Jewess, let out an almost worshipful exclamation.

'*Look!*' she said, '*the Holy City!*'

For four years I'd been denied that pleasure which is derived from the excitement of travel, so it was probably only to have been expected that I found myself almost punch-drunk by this new experience. The flight itself had been pleasurable enough, the five hours airborne passing all too quickly. I soaked it all in and, carefully studying the land I could see below from my window seat, tried to work out exactly where we were with the help of the passenger flight-map. Onboard, surrounded by a fascinating array of cultures, I was particularly intrigued by the many orthodox Jewish men with their large black hats or kippahs, scruffy beards, sidelocks, open-collared white shirts, dark suits, unpolished shoes, and tasselled waist bands – prayer belts. I knew very little, if anything, about Jewish culture and was even unsure how to reply when the airhostess asked if I wanted kosher food. This was the first time I'd been on a long-enough flight to be served a meal, and I had no complaints about the content of the heated food packs whatsoever – it all did me very well, thank you. But there again; ever since crossing the threshold of palatal immaturity and discovering that Brussels sprouts didn't contain poisonous toxins *after all*, I've been very easy to please in affairs of a culinary nature.

It had been a bitterly cold November morning when I got on the plane at Gatwick, with sleet showers driven by a fierce easterly wind bearing down on the tarmac. As we taxied along the arrival apron at Ben Gurion airport I noticed palm trees silhouetted in the setting sun. The airport ground staff, directing the airliners to their allotted termini with their reflective paddles, were wearing only white, epauletted, short-sleeved shirts. In fact I was almost overwhelmed by the intensity of the heat gusting over my face in the strong breeze when I stepped out of the plane into the Israeli air for the first time. It felt good; very good. And dark dank England with its enigmatic, wearisome, bewildering Community was very easy to forget about: for the time being anyway.

I rose early the following morning and quietly slipped out of Christ Church Hospice's silent, stone courtyard, which was beautified with exotic, ostentatious bougainvillaea plants and vine-covered verandas. The amplified ululations of the muezzin from an adjacent mosque had begun calling the Islamic faithful to prayer. Already, the narrow streets were humming with the activity of traders organizing the delivery of goods to the nearby souk, which weaved its way up-and-down, above, below, and in-and-out of the congested network of buildings within the walls of the Old City like the proverbial rabbit warren. Donkeys, carrying packs far larger than I could have possibly imagined to be humane, were being urged on by their Arabic-speaking masters, neck-bells ringing away to warn people out of their path. Others were transporting their fare on bicycles laden front and back with huge panniers. Bedouin women mingled in with the busy noisy throng, seemingly able to balance huge baskets of goods on their heads as if they'd been born to the task, so natural it appeared to them. And as I passed by the head of the souk, the heated, entangled smell from the multiplicity of wares – including heaps of tropical fruit and fresh vegetables, Turkish delight, baclava sweetmeats, hoummos, incense, earthenware, olive wood, camel leather and dust – created a glorious perfume of Eastern promise which I would always thereafter fondly associate with the teeming, haggling markets of Old Jerusalem.

Passing by the market and leaving the Old City through the Jaffa Gate, heading in the direction of the newer, far larger part of the city which is Jerusalem, I walked a few hundred yards or so north alongside the ancient city wall. The sun had already gripped the day with its heat even though it was early in the morning and late in the year. I sat on a small stone wall by the edge of the road to enjoy the sunshine on my face as I looked back towards where I'd just come from.

The parapets of David's Citadel rose prominently above the Jaffa Gate, outlined against the clear deep-blue sky. Palm trees waved their branches gracefully in the air on either side of the pathway. I soaked myself in the contentment of the moment: it had been some considerable while since I'd felt so relaxed and gratified.

My parents took me just about the length and breadth of the small country during the all-too-short week; from the so-called "Sea of Galilee" in the North to the other diminutive body of water, "the Dead Sea", in the South; from Haifa in the West to Jericho in the East. We sat amongst pine trees on Mount Carmel to have a picnic on one of our outings, which was when I was introduced to the enticing taste of pitta bread and hoummos for the first time. To say I fell in love with the country of Israel may sound rather fatuous, but it would nonetheless be the most apt way to describe what happened to me during that week. Not that I became a Zionist or came to favour the Israeli territorial dominance: it was to be some years before I would understand the history and politics of the Israeli–Arab conflict sufficiently well to form clearly defined views on the subject. I just fell in love with the land: the vast expanse of parched but scenic wilderness and the cultivated splendour of the Samarian fields; the intense, stark, unforgiving, shimmering heat of the Jordanian rift valley and the hot, salty buoyancy of its sunken sea; the contrasting cultures, buildings, noises and smells of Jerusalem and the Mediterranean attractions of the Tel Aviv metropolis.

By the Dead Sea in 1980

On the last day of my visit we walked through the dusty, dinghy back-streets of Joppa and along to the westernized sea front of Tel Aviv itself. A fresh westerly wind was bringing Atlantic-style breakers crashing onto the sandy beaches, and the invitation to frolic in the frothy waters was compelling. We all swam together, although I myself lingered on in the water long after my parents had dried themselves off in the intense sunlight. I didn't have a surfboard – unsurprisingly – but I found that with my body outstretched I could mimic the action of surfing, catching the breaking waves at just the right moment and then being propelled breathlessly towards the shore, carried forward and immersed by the garrulous excited water. Time and time again I waded back for more until I had been sated with pleasure. Back on the beach, I buried mum in the sand – bringing back pleasurable childhood memories. Insofar as it was important, the past had been forgiven and forgotten; we could all have begun to enjoy one another's company as a family in a far more natural way if I weren't still encumbered by the restraints involved in my Community membership.

The battle of loyalties in my mind, however, was far from over. Even though I'd enjoyed the innocent pleasures of my week away, I knew I had to see it as no more than an unexpected interlude from the main programme, which was my life in the Community – and to which I must return, ready and willing to join with the brotherhood in the spiritual fight to advance the frontiers of God's kingdom.

I had left England in the sleet, and I returned to her on bitterly cold, icy, early-winter's evening. I didn't go straight back to Bugbrooke because I'd already made arrangements to include a visit to my sister and stay at her flat in St. Albans for the night. After Jane had left for work the next morning, I gathered up my travel bags and began to walk forlornly through the streets of the city to the station. The ice had gone, but it was a dreary, grey, overcast day. The small, single-platform station was completely deserted, meaning I had to rely on the unreliable information of a timetable to convince myself a train would eventually appear. Everything about me felt heavy: my legs, my arms, my suitcase, and especially—oh yes, especially my heart. Feeling close to genuine depression, I gave up pretending to myself I was the loyal, committed Community member that for so long I had been. In doing so, I allowed myself to seriously consider the possibility of not going back at all. My head spun with turmoil! *If only, if only I could be sure that God himself wouldn't be angry with me for splitting, then I could let the train go by and walk back up the hill past the abbey to my sister's house.* It would have meant leaving Angie behind as well, of course. But how could there possibly be any future together for us in the Community, I wondered, when I seemed to be growing so far away from what everyone else stood for and believed in. Above all, I wanted to be my own man again. I wanted to make my own decisions about my life – *and* my own mistakes. I wanted to treat people as *people*; not as objects for God's blessing or curse.

If only the train would arrive late so that I could resolve this one way or another in my mind.

But the train wasn't late. Nothing had been resolved as it drew alongside the platform. The moment of truth had come. I found myself slowly walking towards the carriage, mechanically, unwillingly, and with sad resignation. I opened the door, climbed in, and sat down. Nothing at all within me – save the prospect of a future relationship with Angie – wanted to go back; but I just felt, just knew, I *had* to. I took a long deep breath and then carefully expelled the air in a cathartic sigh of acceptance. I would return to carry on with the next chapter of my life at Bugbrooke.

Without overelaborating on all the finer points of what I'd been going through, I made a clean breast of things to Dave, my elder, when I got back to Warwickshire. He didn't, to his credit, make a big meal of it all, and I guess he must have just put my turmoil down to something which St. Francis of Assisi had once observed: *foreign travel is not good for the soul of a brother.* It was in spite of all this that a month or two later I found myself being invited up higher to join the ranks of the eldership. I was unable to say no, was unable and unready to defend myself at the court of enquiry which would have been convened had I been bold and honest enough to say how inappropriate the invitation was. Instead, I took my appointment to be the long-awaited "nod" I'd been looking for from the Lord to indicate whether or not he wanted me to stay at Bugbrooke – evidently, he *did* want me to. With some considerable reassurance, therefore, of God's blessing on what lay ahead, I once again resolved to try and lay aside all my misgivings and get on with the job in hand. I had no deliberate intention of betraying the trust bestowed upon me. Besides, I'd just negotiated my twenty-fourth birthday and was aware that my close friend, Graeme Merciful, had recently been allowed to begin a courtship with *his* long-standing love, Carole, even though he was some way off being twenty-five. I saw no reason, therefore, for inflexibility over mere months when it came to me pursuing *my* claim, and I became increasingly hopeful that it was now only a matter of time.

It was at an elders' meeting early in the new year following my trip to Jerusalem that Noel made an unusual departure from his habitual plea for celibacy amongst the brethren.

'It's time,' he announced, 'the elders began to set an example of "holy marriage". We need more of the elders to be getting married and showing how "marriages in the Lord" can be worked out with great success to the glory of God.'

This was a tacit acknowledgement that there were marriage problems within the Fellowship. Many of the difficulties that afflicted marriages out there in the world, from the mundane to the sexual, were also present in the kingdom. A senior elder once confided in me that he intended trying to make improvements in his relationship by spending at least ten minutes – *ten minutes!* – a day with his wife. And there were those, apparently, who, after some considerable time in wedlock, had been unable to consummate their union. Noel had often told us that "marriages in the Lord" ought to transcend such troubles, be they petty or of more consequence; hence his appeal for some of us elders to tie the knot and show the institution of marriage off in the best possible light. Surely this was the green light I'd been waiting for.

Both my own covering elder, Dave, and Angie's elder, Kelly, agreed with me at long last that the time was right; and neither of them made any perverse spiritual interrogation on *this* occasion about whether or not I had "died to my love". Had they done so, I wouldn't have been able to answer affirmatively: I hadn't – what a load of old tosh it all was! At the next elders' meeting, therefore, Kelly made the announcement which I'd waited several years to hear:

'I'd just like to let you all know that John Diligent wants to begin a relationship with sister Angie from "Living Stones"' – the name of another medium-sized Community home.

That was it, short and sweet, the intention being to give opportunity for the other elders to find out whether there were any eligible brothers within their own households who were also interested in having a relationship with sister Angie. Provided there were none, Angie and I would soon be able to start meeting together – assuming, of course, that she herself was happy about it all. But perhaps there *was* one further obstacle – Noel himself. He knew about my interest in Angie well enough – I should think just about *everyone* knew; even most of the sisters, probably. But he'd never relaxed his expectation that I would take the higher calling of celibacy. *How would he now respond? Would he be shocked? Disappointed? Disapproving?* His face hadn't noticeably shown any objection during Kelly's announcement, which I took to be a good sign. Later in the week, however, Graeme told me about a discussion that had taken place at the farm in which Noel, evidently, had been expressing his concern.

'You've got to tell me exactly what he said,' I begged of Graeme, who seemed unusually reluctant to be frank. *'I don't want you to spare my feelings. I just need to know!'*

'Well, bro.' Graeme replied, *'you won't like it, but he said: "If John gets married, it will mean either a disastrous ministry or a disastrous marriage."'*

Graeme paused, put his arm round me and carried on:

'I was really shocked! But I promise I stood up for you.'

If Graeme was shocked, then I wasn't; it was just the kind of reaction which I'd anticipated. Nor did I need further explanation about what was meant, it was all too obvious: if I were to marry, either my evangelistic ministry within the Community or my relationship with Angie would flounder – depending on which of the two I gave most attention to.

*'How **dare** he say such things behind my back,'* I thought. But I did my best not to get too chewed up by what had been said, which I tried to convince myself had only been an off-hand remark. I kept on clinging to the hope that it wouldn't be Noel who made any final decision. Surely it

would be up to Kelly and Dave, who had immediate charge over Angie and I – wouldn't it? *Hadn't Noel always claimed to outside critics that he was merely a humble member of the body of eldership, as much subject to them as they to him?*

I stoically carried on refusing to believe the worst, even when Noel reprimanded some of those present for not paying close-enough attention during the next Wednesday-night assembly in the chapel.

'Come on, stay awake,' he bellowed, puffing out his flabby jowls like a bloated bullfrog.

'I've got some important ministry to give as the evening goes on, and some of you aren't going to like it. But you need to hear it, so you must stay awake.'

'Deacons!' he shouted. *'Let's have some more air in the building through the windows. Come on, deacons, let's have **all** the windows open!'*

This wasn't an unusual instruction to the deacons – chapel stewards – even in mid-winter.

I knew—I just knew he was going to say something which would directly address my courtship ambitions, but I kept hoping against hope I was wrong. It was only right towards the end of his habitually lengthy discourse that he came to what he had referred to as *the most important part.*

'Brethren!' he announced, *'you are all well aware of the spiritual battle in which we're engaged. The forces of darkness are lined up against us. There's a battle going on; a battle which Jesus Christ has already won on the Cross, of course, but one with which we need to actively engage to avail ourselves of the victory. We are an army at war, and there are some of you who are in the front line! **Those** brothers shouldn't be thinking about getting married at a time like this. The whole of their energy, their thoughts and their determination need to be taken up with the battle. They shouldn't allow themselves to be distracted.'*

This was even worse than I'd feared; but still he carried on:

'Only when the battle's been won, only when the battle troops are visibly victorious and return home should marriage be thought about. But that victory is some way off. The Spirit of God doesn't want you to be thinking of marriage – he wants you to be all out for the fight!'

I looked across to where Angie was sitting and hoped she had *some* idea about what I was thinking: I would have liked to shout out:

'I cannot, I just cannot believe what I'm hearing!'

How quickly the Spirit of God had changed his mind. Why! Only a few weeks earlier Noel had told us that the Holy Spirit was wanting examples of holy marriage from within the eldership. Now, apparently, the Holy Spirit was wanting these same "officers", the ones in the front line of the battle, to put marriage out of their minds. So that was that! And Noel hadn't even had the decency to come and talk with me personally but had thwarted my hopes in a display of untouchable supremacy from the platform. When I went to see Kelly after the meeting there was little he could say save to confirm that he could no longer approach Angie on my behalf. He, too, had been taken by complete surprise despite his elevated position right at the top of the seniority pole. It didn't take long for me to discover that nobody was prepared to fight my corner. Nobody was prepared to stand up to Noel and say:

'Hold on a minute, Noel, you can't do this. Between us, we prayerfully believed that it would be right for John to begin a relationship with Angie. You can't just play about with people's lives in this kind of way.'

The next day was one of those when I worked on the farm; one of those when, inevitably, I met Noel during the course of my work. *'How ya doin, bro?'* he asked in a disingenuously avuncular voice, fully aware of how I must "be doin". I simply shrugged my shoulders and did my best to ignore the question, wishing I could have ignored the man altogether. Later that day, though, I just *had* to go and talk with him in his room to find out exactly what was going on. I soon wished I hadn't bothered. He made it quite clear that he wouldn't countenance my beginning a relationship in the foreseeable future. Apart from anything else, so he explained, some of the younger brothers who looked up to me with respect might see such a relationship as a green light for them to follow suit, and then there would apparently be all kinds of problems within the Community as a result. Exactly what sort of problems he envisaged, he didn't say; but I guess it was all related to this wretched business of celibacy and the example he felt I should be setting. Our interview was concluded with what I suppose he thought was some kind of reassurance:

'Who knows what may lie ahead for you after you reach the age of, say, thirty, bro. Who knows what the Spirit has in store for you. For now, however, you mustn't take your eyes away from the battle.'

For a long while afterwards I was silent and withdrawn. I knew I had to surrender all hope of ever having a romantic relationship with Angie: the ability to carry on hoping for one against all the odds was beyond what I could cope with. Not only that, but my trust in the Fellowship's high command had taken irreparable damage. My commitment to the Fellowship at Bugbrooke had been based upon the belief that the voice of God spoke through that of the corporate eldership: a notion which now appeared laughable, for how could the voice of God say one thing one day and another thing the next? And what was more, this whole bitter affair had given me the damn good shake up which I needed to make me pull my head out of the sand and start calling certain aspects of the way we were led, and had been led, what they were: blatant contradictions. If I was honest with myself, there were many things about the Fellowship that just didn't hang together, that needed some magisterial spiritual explanation if they were to be justified. Why did Noel himself, for example, not submit to many of the demands made on everyone else? Why was he the only person exempted from the manual labour of picking gooseberries in the annual harvest? Even old Charles – who was eighty – had had to spend long evening hours around the gooseberry bushes with the rest of us. Why was Noel the only brother who had his own room to sleep in? Some of the elderly sisters had a room to themselves, but Noel wasn't even elderly. Besides, he'd had his own room right from the start of community living. And why did he never submit to correction or criticism of any kind, however mild or well intentioned? And whose feet had *he* ever washed – literally – as the rest of us had in an act betokening the wish for a servant heart? The list of my concerns about leadership and lifestyle contradictions, along with those about convenient directional changes, began to look quite a long one. Wasn't such capricious inconsistency at the top at least *similar* to the goings-on in "Animal Farm"? Wasn't Orwell describing how the subjects of despotic leadership, thoroughly convinced they are working to build a wonderful new society, can be persuaded to accept dreadful contradictions in the behaviour and edicts of those in authority?

Disillusioned, it became easy enough for me to empathize with the bewilderment of the poor farm animals in Orwell's brilliant novel as they struggled to come to terms with the insidious rule-changes which were introduced by their masters, the pigs; easy enough for me to empathize with their bewilderment as the pigs tried to persuade them to believe that Animal Farm was *still* being run as it should be and that their worries were completely unnecessary. The common worker animals – mainly sheep – must have felt very ashamed for ever having got themselves so disturbed about the pigs sleeping in humans' beds when, as the pigs themselves pointed out, there never *had* been any such prohibition. They must have felt very stupid when they realized the pigs were right! They must have felt very put down when they looked at the seven commandments on the barn wall and saw that one of them was quite precise in its instruction: "*No animal shall sleep in a bed **with sheets**".* What a difference those last two words, *with sheets*, made to the sentence; two words which the pigs themselves had secretly added. Obviously, of course, there were no sheets on the beds which the pigs had begun to use.

There were other changes going on that they were also concerned about; changes which seemed to be going against what their erstwhile leader, Old Major, had instructed. It was Squealer, one of the leading pigs, who resolved the apparent contradiction between the new way of doing things and Old Major's instructions:

'*Are you certain that this is not something you have dreamed comrades?*' he asked them. '*Are these instructions written down anywhere?*' And since it was true that nothing of the kind existed in writing, the animals were satisfied that they had been mistaken.

I felt similarly confused. Maybe, for example, I'd misunderstood what Noel had meant when he'd urged some of the elders to consider marriage.

Maybe the contradictions which I thought I saw were just fanciful. It would have been all too easy for me to carry on just as Orwell's farm animals had done; all too easy for me to admit that *I* was the one in the wrong and that the contradictions were illusionary. In fact in some ways it would have been far more comfortable for me to take the party-whip than force myself to face up to the truth. But my wake-up call had been too shrill to allow any such mental capitulation.

For all my disenchantment, however, I still couldn't summon the necessary conviction I knew I needed to get up and leave. I couldn't help thinking of those dreadful reproaches made against people who split, the dirges we sang admonishing us not to become backsliders, and the teaching Noel had given about "making the demons laugh with glee" should we be disloyal to the brotherhood. I got in a car one afternoon and drove around the Warwickshire lanes desperate to find the mental certitude of "doing the right thing" that would equip me with the courage I needed to join the M1 and head south, and away. But it wasn't there. I just couldn't stop thinking about all my wonderful friends, the colour and beauty I saw all around me, the laughter, the shared tears, the joy, or the glowing faces on young men and women from disturbed backgrounds as they came out of the baptismal pool to begin a "new life in Christ". In particular, I couldn't stop thinking about some of the very special elderly folk whom we regarded as our spiritual mothers and fathers. They, more than any of us, had sacrificed so much to come and take their place in the New Creation Christian Community, not least the property and possessions which they had acquired over years and years of hard work. *How could I let any of these precious people down by taking wings of flight?* And yet how could I stay when I believed there were vital aspects to our communal life which were so horribly wrong?

For several months I carried on with this ridiculous charade, going through the motions and trying for all I was worth to do so with sincerity and conviction. Somehow, I kept telling myself, there had to be a way to rekindle the enthusiasm and belief which would drive away the demons of doubt and leave my mind in that state of willing compliance I'd once enjoyed. It wasn't to be. *The writing was on the wall, and it was to be Noel himself who delivered the final blow which enabled me to break free.*

It was Noel's insistence we should *take the central ground* which finally did the trick, an effect which was the complete opposite to that which had been intended. He told us he'd seen a vision of a dark circle representing the central ground of the Christian lifestyle. For too long, so he explained, this central ground had been usurped by demons; hence the darkness. Now was the time for the Church-Community at Bugbrooke to evict these intruders by strengthening the bonds of our brotherhood – making our commitment to one another even stronger and ridding ourselves of any lingering reservations we may have had about our communal lifestyle.

One of consequences of the drive for increased, uncritical dedication which resulted from Noel's vision was that we were told *not* to join in when we broke bread and drank wine at our communal meals – a non-liturgical form of Holy Communion – unless we were free in our hearts and minds of all criticisms and reservations. Failure to join in, however, apparently meant that we were in rebellion by refusing to avail ourselves of the cleansing power of the bread and wine – in direct defiance to the Lord himself. Talk about being caught between a rock and hard place! The solution, of course, was to rid ourselves of all reservations and criticisms and join in the ceremony with a pure heart. It cannot be said of me that I didn't *try*. But no amount of earnest soul-searching and repenting could rid me of my critical, rebellious thoughts, which now seemed to strengthen daily.

In the collective meetings at chapel we were told to raise our hands in the air as an indication that we had no reservations whatsoever about our commitment to the Fellowship. I waved my hands like a zombie along with all the others, too servile to be the only one with them down by his side yet thoroughly disconsolate with my own compliance. I felt as ridiculous and spineless as the gullible sheep in Animal Farm, the ones who'd insisted on continuously bleating: *'four legs good, two legs bad,'* but then, when Squealer the pig himself began to walk on hind legs, changed their bleat to: *'four legs good, two legs better.'*

Nothing less than the complete rooting out of any rogue attitude in our hearts towards the brotherhood was going to be good enough for Noel, and he wasted no opportunity to have us reaffirm our uncritical loyalty. All impure thoughts were to be repented of and renounced. We were instructed to humble ourselves before God, submit every aspect of our lives to the better judgement of the brotherhood, and vow to one another that we had *no reservations*. At one particularly memorable elders' meeting, Noel asked us to share any examples of how we'd managed to strengthen the bonds of brotherhood within our own households. It was in response to this that one elder made a statement which finally awakened me from my mesmerized blindness.

'I asked the household brethren to tell me what they thought commitment to the Community meant for ***them***,*'* the elder began, *'and one of the brothers came up with something which was so good that we decided to use it as a benchmark to measure our own loyalty.'*

'Come on then, bro,' Noel encouraged him, *'tell us what he said.'*

'Well, bro, what he said was this: "If everybody else splits and there are only two people left in the Community, those two people will be Noel and myself."'

A murmur of approval rippled around the room, which was packed with the thirty or forty so-called elders. *Was I really the only one who thought this dreadful? No thank you, mam! This wasn't for me!* This spoke to me, clearly and unequivocally, of allegiance to a man, Noel Stanton; nothing more and nothing less. If everyone else had left the Community, as in the illustration, there must be something dreadfully wrong with it.

'How,' I wondered, *'can it be thought to display anything other than mindless stupidity to suggest that commitment involves remaining loyal to Noel to the bitter end? No man deserves such unthinking allegiance; surely **all** men are fallible?'*

If uncritical fidelity like this was going to be taken as the benchmark of a true kingdom heart, then, whether I liked it or not, there was no way I was going to affirm my commitment any longer. I began to seriously consider my next move.

Early one morning at the farm, not more than a couple of days after I'd come to my senses but while I was still trying to decide exactly what I should do, Nigel came storming out to the repair shed in a state of considerable agitation with Noel. I'd always taken him to be unquestionably loyal and hadn't seen him in this light before.

'Flaming brotherhood,' he muttered, making no attempt to conceal his ire. *'I don't call it brotherhood, I call it wicked!'*

'What's the matter?' I cautiously enquired, trying for the life of me not to appear as too much of a kindred spirit: I was worried that he might clam up if he "sussed me out" to be a secret malcontent.

'It's that flaming man Noel,' he replied. *'He had us all up really really late last night ranting on-and-on-and-on-and-on about brotherhood till we were sick of it. Some of the young kids were so tired they were crying; they needed to go to bed. And still he carried on. The man's a nutter, I tell you, a flaming nutter!'*

I hadn't really needed any further *intellectual* confirmation that there was something terribly wrong with all this overkill on commitment. What Nigel's uncharacteristic bellyaching provided me with, however, was the *emotional* enragement I needed to say to myself, *'Right! That's it! Enough is enough!'* Both my head and my heart began to work together at last; and my anger equipped me with the mental tools I needed to force my way through the hidden-but-very-real locked door into the world beyond Bugbrooke.

Nigel, aware that he'd left me in stunned silence, immediately began to try and play down his derision for fear of any adverse effect on my soul. But the damage had been done: not by Nigel *himself* (despite the unkind accusations made against him when I eventually managed to get away), only by what he'd *told* me. Through his unyielding insistence on complete, uncritical commitment, it was Noel Stanton who had excluded me from any possibility of being able to conform. I wanted out – quietly and without recrimination. This was going to take a certain amount of guile because I knew I mustn't let anyone get wind of my intention to leave. If they *did,* there was little doubt I would be subjected to interminable entreaties and brotherly head-to-heads imploring me to reconsider. Not to mention, of course, the reminders I would be given, and the songs we would sing, about the judgement awaiting those who betrayed Zion. More than anything else, perhaps, I knew that those such as Margie, an elderly sister in our household who'd fondly mothered me and knew all my secrets, would be disconsolate. I didn't think I'd be able to withstand such diverse pressure. I wouldn't be able to stand my ground. I'd be persuaded I was in the wrong and, in repentance, would yield myself back into the bosom of the fold. But nothing would have been solved if *that* happened. It would only be a matter of time before the old grievances resurfaced and I would have to go through it all again.

Fuelled as I was with what I believed to be righteous indignation, I could, I suppose, have given angry expression to my frustration and stormed out there and then, shielded from reproach in doing so by the excitement of my animation. But although this was a distinctly possible way of going, it was neither my preferred option nor my style. Besides, I had no wish whatsoever at this stage to complain or pass judgement; all I wanted to do was be certain of making good my flight with as little fuss as possible. I certainly didn't think there was anything like the fifty ways of leaving that Paul Simon had sung about in his song "50 ways to leave your lover", but the advice he'd given Guss and Lee seemed sound enough:

"Hop on the bus, Gus
You don't need to discuss much
Just drop off the key, Lee
And get yourself free"

I knew that I'd need both emotional support and somewhere to stay. I also knew that unless I went about it all in the right way I could easily find myself floundering around in a sea of self-recrimination and regret. Everything would be much easier for me, therefore, if I were to wait until my parents came back from Jerusalem in just a few weeks' time for a short vacation. I could easily enough get approval to drive down and meet them at Heathrow; and then I needn't come back save to return the vehicle; to *drop off the key, Lee.*

Came the Sunday evening before I intended to split and nothing had deterred me from my chosen course of action. Nor had anyone suspected that I was anything other than a bit out of fettle – still licking my wounds over the whole Angie business probably. I had one almighty hurdle still to negotiate, though, as one of the brothers whom I'd helped lead into the Community – someone I'd met at Warwick University – was being baptised that same evening. Everyone would be expecting me to show my enthusiasm for the occasion with vocal encouragement of some kind – what we used to call "ministering" – whilst the brother was stood in the baptistry waiting to be fully immersed.. *How could I possibly remain silent without it almost being a public confession that I was well and truly out-of-sorts? And how would I cope with then being questioned by those who were concerned for my spiritual welfare?* I could just imagine the sort of question they would ask:

'It wasn't like you to be so quiet and look so downcast, bro. What's wrong? I just know there must be something. Tell me about it.'

I doubted whether I would either have the nerve or be sufficiently insincere to respond to such questioning with wilful deceit. But nor could I possibly be so blatantly hypocritical as to fake a genuine interest in the baptism when my full intention was to be away from the place the next day. It was amongst one of the longest meetings I'd ever had to get through. As I looked around at the jubilant faces of those I held to be such special friends, I was sorely tempted to crack and put away my wicked intents. *Where again would I find such a marvellous company of vibrant, dedicated, selfless, loving people? What was I giving away?* It wasn't hard to see myself as a traitorous Judas Iscariot. I just had to keep saying to myself:

'Stay angry, John, stay angry.'

And when I reminded myself how these lovely people had become little better than pawns in someone else's game, I knew I'd be able to see my plan through – for I was no longer doing it just for myself: it was for everyone.

We arrived back at the Warwickshire house late after the Sunday baptismal meeting. Amazingly, no one had questioned me about my silence during the baptism. Instead of hanging about for a bedtime drink and a chat with the others, as was normal, I just slipped up to my room, stuffed a few clothes into a bag which I hid under the bed (including, of course, my beloved denim-shirt), climbed *into* the bed, drew the covers up over my head, and feigned sleep until I *did* finally succumb to her much-needed embrace.

Up before anyone else in the morning, I carefully placed my pyjamas into the top of my bag and took it down to the car, feeling like some kind of escaping traitor as I did so: it was an act of betrayal which would have triggered every spiritual alarm in the building had it been observed. I'd been asked to drop a couple of sisters off in Rugby en route to the motorway; so, while waiting until we were all ready to leave, I carried on with the normal morning rituals and tried hard to appear cheery and casual. And then we were away. Having dropped the sisters at the bus station in Rugby, I turned back to rejoin the A5. It was all going just as I'd planned and, as a gesture to myself of my freedom, I pulled in at a roadside café to order breakfast with some of the pocket money

I'd been given for the journey to Heathrow. Normally, of course, I wouldn't have dreamed of indulging myself with such an expensive treat, but it proved to be one of the most wonderful breakfasts I'd ever eaten. Somewhat to my surprise I found that I had neither menacing thoughts of being under the judgement of God's anger nor bitter regrets concerning friends left behind – just sadness. In fact I had no equivocation whatsoever; just the most wonderful feeling of being free.

CHAPTER FOURTEEN: Leaving on a jet plane

'You're having me on aren't you, John?' Graeme anxiously asked on the other end of the phone when I called him from a public kiosk at Breachwood Green in the evening.

'No, Graeme, I'm not! Honestly! I'm deadly serious,' I replied. *'I **have** split. And I want you to tell Noel for me, please. Tell him I'll come back on Wednesday morning to return the car and collect my stuff. But I've gone! I'm not coming back and I don't want anyone to try and contact me.'*

I was uncharacteristically abrupt because I wanted to avoid any prolonged discussion with such a close friend: it might have tugged too hard on my fragile conscience and caused me to reconsider. I put the receiver down and wandered off along a quiet and shaded country lane, alone in the evening stillness of the rolling Hertfordshire countryside.

I felt like someone who'd been awakened from a charm, someone who now looked back on the mindless obedience caused by the spell with a cold shudder of disbelief. I felt myself to be right there alongside the little boy who was made so famous in the fable, "The Emperor's New Clothes". All around me, I could hear the crowds cheering, clapping and waving their hands in the air as they applauded the magnificent cut and cloth of the new outfit worn by the vain emperor to advertise his splendour. The young lad, sat on his father's shoulders, was looking at the crowd in mystified astonishment. Unable to understand what was going on, he turned his head back around to take a more careful look at the procession in front of him. Then, with a cheeky grin on his face, refusing to deny the evidence of his own eyes, he shouted out at the top of his voice:

'The emperor has no clothes on.'

I broke into a nervous run, reproaching myself for my stupidity.

'You imbecile. You great, impressionable fool!' I said to myself. *'How could you have been blind for so long? Why didn't you allow yourself to see what was going on and get out way before now?'*

I wanted to kick myself, unsure whether to laugh or cry with the liberating relief of facing up to the truth: the truth that if you want to believe something strongly enough and are with others urging you on, wanting to believe it themselves (and no one strong enough to let evidence take precedence over the hopes of their heart); if you fear isolation and rejection; if you trust others and mistrust yourself; if you have visions and dreams of greatness and believe they can be achieved; then, immersed in and pulled along by a surging flag-waving crowd, you could probably be persuaded to believe just about anything – that the Earth itself is the centre of the universe, that a naked fool is a wonderfully clothed monarch, that genocide will liberate a nation from its enemies, *or that a glorious new society can be created through the coercion of a bad-tempered bully-boy.*

Having slept at my sister's flat for a couple of nights I set off back to Northamptonshire on the Wednesday morning. David, having offered to be my chauffeur back to St. Albans later on in the day, followed behind in his own car. I'd decided that before I went to see Noel I would call in to try and find Angie at the local psychiatric hospital – where she was working as a librarian – in the hope I could have a talk with her. I'd no set plan for what I wanted to achieve from doing so, but I think – if I'm totally honest with myself – that I at least wanted to give her the opportunity of leaving with me, even though I had little hope she could possibly do so after being so suddenly put on the spot. Of more importance was the need I felt to explain all that had happened in my own words, and before anyone else could do so using Fellowship spin. Luck, or providence, was on my side, and she was able to leave her work for a while to come and sit outside with me on the front lawn. The sun, too, was kind to us with its warmth. I gave Angie a poem I'd written for her, which she read with evident pain: it seemed that she hadn't known the full strength of my feelings, even though she'd suspected I was more than just fond of her. After I'd given a truncated version of how my hopes of a relationship with her had been thwarted, it became quite clear that what I'd said was a massive shock: a bewildering shock. It was also obvious that I'd made her immensely upset, so much so that I began to think I'd probably done the wrong thing by coming to see her. We did, however, get the chance to talk openly with one another for a while, so I was able to explain all about my reasons for wanting to split. Angie, too, would come to similar conclusions as my own a few years later and would also leave. When I sensed we'd each said all we were able to at the time, I told her that I'd best be going. As I got up to do so, I found the courage to ask her if she wanted to leave with me; but I think I already knew her answer:

'I couldn't bring myself to leave all the sisters at the "House of Living Stones" and let them down just like that, it would all be too painful,' she said quietly. With that, we said goodbye for what I thought would be the last time.

I'd prepared myself mentally for the encounter with Noel at New Creation Farm by rehearsing over and over in my mind all the responses I would make when subjected to his entreaties. The most important thing, I felt, would be to keep things brief. I wasn't intending to walk out on the Fellowship all guns blazing, firing off from a magazine filled with accusative bullets concerning spiritual cruelty and the like. I just wanted to amicably agree, where possible, to differ – and then leave quietly. The bottom line, I promised myself, was that I wouldn't allow anyone to persuade me to change my mind. I asked David, who had said he would wait in his own car, not to let me go back on this pledge, not to drive away from the farm without taking me with him. He readily agreed, wishing me well as I headed off to sort things out in the farmhouse. Word was sent to Noel that I'd arrived, and he hurried from his office to greet me.

'Hello, bro,' he boomed in his most affable way. 'You've come back then. Come and let me give you a hug.'

I froze with frigid, unfriendly stiffness as he approached to put his arms around my shoulder.

'As I said on the phone to Graeme,' I replied, 'I've only come to drop off the car, say goodbye properly, and collect my clothes and other stuff; so I'd rather not give you a hug, thanks.'

'Tut, tut, bro,' he said, putting his arm around my shoulders anyway, 'don't be like that. After all, we **are** your family. Come on, let's go into the lounge and talk.'

'Oh, alright then,' I agreed. 'But only for a few minutes. And only so long as it's clearly understood that I'm **determined** to leave. My father's waiting outside for me in his car, and I've told him to make sure I leave here with him.'

He was clearly uncomfortable to hear this: the chagrin showed in the tightening of his facial expression. Apparently, so I got to hear some time later, he labelled me as a coward for having brought my father with me. While we sat and spoke together face-to-face, however, he showed only benign concern to "sort things out". If he'd only taken the aggressive attitude towards me which I'd heard him take towards other brothers who'd split (admittedly behind their backs), I would have been able to get things over and done with far more easily: I'd come prepared for *that!* What I *hadn't* anticipated was this softly softly approach in which he appeared to be willing to discuss where things had gone wrong. The last thing I wanted to do was appear to be unreasonable, so I patiently tried to explain everything. A few minutes soon turned into the best part of an hour.

When I couldn't bear the thought of David having to wait outside for me any longer, I again told Noel that I was going. But still he wanted me to stay and talk, to go over *everything;* and I'd barely begun to scratch the surface of all that *needed* to be said.

'Come on, bro,' he said. 'We can't just sort all this out in a few hours. I can see it might even take several days. You've got to be fair to us and give us time.'

Persuaded there could be no harm in "just talking", I was bold enough to state my terms: firstly, that I wouldn't under any circumstances stay in the Community overnight; and, secondly, that I needed the use of a car to travel back to St. Albans. These agreed, I went out to David, who'd already been sat there patiently far too long. *How would I now manage to persuade him to go back on the promise I'd made him give me?* It wasn't too hard, actually, after I explained about the deal I'd cut. I think he could tell that I wasn't going to be bullied into staying against my will, and so off he drove after I'd thanked him profusely.

Over the next few days I commuted between St. Albans and Northampton and spent long hours talking with Noel about all the misgivings

I had concerning life within the New Creation Christian Community and what it had become under his autocratic leadership. At *his* request, I made a clean breast of all the criticisms, reservations, resentment and bitterness which I felt towards the Community; not with the intention to seek redress (all I wanted to do was get away from the place), but simply because *he'd* asked that I should do so: *'to give me,'* he said, *'the opportunity to understand what this is all about.'*

The final agreement we struck after these protracted discussions was one which Noel himself offered me as a "first" for the Fellowship. We agreed that I would return to Stockton House for a period of four weeks as a demonstration of *brotherly unity and reconciliation.* Then, *with the blessing of the brotherhood,* I would be released from my membership vows so that I could fly out to join my parents in Jerusalem: they had already spoken to me about the possibility of living and working at Christ Church Hospice over the forthcoming winter months. In many ways I couldn't have wanted for anything better. I'd never wanted to be at odds with the Fellowship, to become an enemy or anything like that. It was just that so strongly did I disagree with what was now happening, I no longer wanted to be a part of it *myself.* Never before, though, had Noel suggested it might be possible for a committed brother like me to be amicably released from membership. The concession being offered me was, he said, something new for the Fellowship, and the opportunity to part company in friendship seemed to me to be an ideal solution all round. I believe, however, that the offer made was because I'd managed to make him understand that I was determined to leave come what may and was going to do so *with or without* anyone else's blessing.

During those four "reconciliatory" weeks I found I needed every ounce of the self-assurance I could dredge up from my reserves of confidence in order to ensure that the agreement we'd established was brought to its agreed conclusion. Nothing had been written down; and I soon found, now I was back within the enclosure of the fold, that misinterpretation – however motivated – was all too easy. Even though Noel himself knew perfectly well the terms under which I'd agreed to temporarily return and the freedom from pressure which I'd been promised, I still found all manner of accusations were made against me. And even though funds to pay for my flight were forthcoming, I seemed to be very nearly alone in my understanding that this would be a parting of the ways *without prejudice,* without there having to be a guilty party. There were many times when I heard people accuse me of having a critical heart. This was hardly reconciliation. This wasn't what I'd agreed to; there wouldn't have been any logical reason to do so. Given that nothing was going to deter me from leaving, what would have been the point in my agreeing to stay on for these four weeks if I was still to be regarded as self-willed and defiant? I need only to have stood my ground and said:

'Sorry, but I'm not coming back; not even for a few weeks. I'm going now and that's final.'

As I listened to some of the harsher things that were said about me, and as I contrasted them with what I'd felt to be, at the very least, the *spirit* of the agreement we'd struck, it would have been easy for me to feel my mind had begun to play tricks, that I was deceived and confused. I could almost hear the phantom of old Squealer whispering in my ear, *'are you sure this is not something you have just dreamed, comrade?'* Unlike the tractable animals of Animal Farm, however, I was damn sure I wasn't going to roll over and just accept that *I* was the one being awkward, that *I* was the one who'd misunderstood the intentions of my superiors.

The elders were told at their fortnightly meeting that my disaffection with the Fellowship sprang largely from what had happened concerning Angie. As such, then, the criticisms I'd been nurturing were only to have been expected: the explanation that I was leaving because I hadn't been allowed to have a relationship with a sister made me out to be someone whose main reason for becoming discontent was, primarily, purely personal; someone whose other complaints about the Fellowship could therefore be regarded as *peripheral* – the carping of someone who hadn't got his own way. But I was quite prepared to be cast in the role of a love-torn malcontent if it meant, at least, I could take my leave without being considered something far worse, a traitor, by the many whom I'd grown to love.

Far harder to live with were some of things said to the *rest* of the Fellowship at our chapel meetings.

'Don't be troubled, my beloved brethren, when you hear of a brother criticizing us,' warned Noel. *'Don't be troubled when you hear of him questioning the way the businesses are run. Don't be troubled when you hear of anything said against the "holy" pledges of loyalty and commitment made within the brotherhood. Don't be troubled when you hear him criticizing our emphasis on celibacy or our dedication to the bonds of brotherhood.'*

Time and again I found that the very same confidential issues which I'd talked about with Noel – at *his* request – were now being openly referred to in his chapel preaching. When I challenged him about this after one of the meetings, complaining that he was being unfair, I was met with denials.

'I can assure you, bro,' he said, *'it wasn't **you** I had in mind in what I said tonight. I don't know how you can have even **thought** it was.'*

It was hard for me to believe him given how the subject matter of his warnings corresponded so closely with what I'd spent the thick end of a week discussing with him. The bitter truth is that he wanted to make absolutely certain I didn't poison anyone else with my criticisms; something he considered to be an imperative which was, to his shame, far more important than keeping to his word.

And what can I say about the outcome of our agreement that I should be amicably released from my membership vows? After a week or so of my return I began to hear from others that they'd been told I was going off to Jerusalem for a "cooling-off" period of maybe eight months or so. This was, apparently, so I could have time to "reflect on things" and get over my disappointment about Angie; also, so I could humble myself before God and find a release from my residual worldliness and independence. *What? How could going off to Jerusalem achieve **any** of those things? If they couldn't be achieved **within** the Community, how were they going to be achieved **outside** of it?* No! This was another of Noel's perfidious untruths which he'd fabricated; possibly because he'd come to realize that many more brothers and sisters would seek to be released from commitment to lifelong membership if he allowed it for *me*. It stank! This had nothing to do with any desire to serve God; everything to do with empire preservation. I didn't, however, have the mental energy to try and correct the misinformation of which I'd become the subject, especially when it didn't really matter: I would soon be away from the place – my flight had been booked and I was counting down the days until airborne.

On every side of me, brothers and sisters alike tried to persuade me not to go. Some were genuinely tearful in their approaches; others more heavy-handed. I sat out in the garden at Stockton House one evening with an elder who inferred I was stubborn and proud.

'How can you believe,' he asked, *'that five hundred people can be wrong and you're the only one who's right?'*

This was a very hard accusation to cope with, and in many ways it went right to the heart of the matter. This is what made leaving a community like this one so very hard. If you needed to justify *to yourself* that you were "doing the right thing" (as I did), then you had to find an enormous amount of self-assurance and courage to stand firm *regardless* of what five hundred people were telling you. It would have been all too easy to concur with the accusations made, not only from others but also from within your own head, that you were being arrogant. It was important for me, therefore, to keep reminding myself that throughout history *whole* masses of people, nations even, have sometimes acted with one voice for wrong: might isn't always right and the judgement of the mob has long been regarded as unreliable. In any case, I also had another answer which satisfied my purposes.

'You can't make it so black and white,' I said. *'The fact that I feel very differently to the rest of you doesn't make me **against** you all. It certainly doesn't mean that I think I'm right and you're wrong. It just means, looked at from a very logical and practical point of view, that I can't actually be a member here any longer. How can I be when members aren't meant to have doubts or criticisms? How can I be truly committed when I know that I **have** got reservations, lots of them – and we've been told we're not meant to have **any**?'*

'That's just a cop out, bro,' replied the elder. 'We all have thoughts and attitudes which come from the flesh. What we've got to do is submit them to the Lord so we can get rid of them.'

'But I can't. I've tried! So what am I meant to do? Stay and be dishonest? Or be honest and leave?'

'What you've got to do is look at the fruit of what has been achieved here. You don't get good fruit from a bad tree. So you have to accept that it's genuinely God himself who is blessing the Fellowship – and that means there must be something within **you** that needs to change.'

'But that's just my problem. I've told you that I can't. It's not that I'm trying to say the Fellowship isn't being blessed by God, or anything. That's not really the issue,' I said, trying not to be forced into a circular argument about who's right and who's wrong.

'Look!' I carried on, 'the fact is that what Noel is asking for are members who are both outwardly **and inwardly** one hundred percent behind everything the Fellowship represents and stands for. So what happens to those of us who find that our thoughts – the secret thoughts of our hearts – refuse to behave in the way we're being told they should? What is it we're meant to do? Pretend to be something which we're not?'

'What you've got to do,' persisted the elder, refusing to give any credence to my dilemma, 'is "get the victory" over any rebellious thoughts and criticisms. And the only way you're going to do that is by repenting of them.'

'So that's it, is it?' I asked, exasperated with the apparent simplicity of it all. 'And the fact that I've **still** got doubts and reservations after all these years means, I guess, that I mustn't have repented properly. Okay, look at it like that if you want. But I'm fed up with all the robotic intensity of trying to conform and denying what's **really** going on within me. I'm fed up of trying to make myself think that Noel's teaching is inspired of God when I think some of it is a load of old codswallop and some of it is positively dangerous. And if that makes me profane, then that's the way it will have to be. Can't you see that it's best for **everyone** if I go?'

He was silent, and I could tell that what I'd said had struck a chord. Thank God I didn't yield to his persuasive reasoning because within a few years he too had come to the same conclusions about the Fellowship. He proved himself to be stronger and braver than I'd been because, before he left, he tried to bring change from within by making his feelings openly known. The product of his honesty, alas, was that in the end he was actually told to leave and take his dangerous criticisms with him.

Whenever I needed to reassure myself that I was doing the right thing, I reminded myself how angry I was with a society, any society, that made people into deviants purely on account of their questioning and criticising – thereby denying them their individuality and independence.

A few nights before my flight to Israel, Nigel asked me to join him on the night-time delivery of fruit products from the farm to the wholesale markets around the Midlands. As we drove off into the night and started chatting, I began to discover a Nigel I'd not known before: a Nigel who actually seemed to value my company when all along I'd thought he saw me as something of a nerd. After all the fruit had finally been dropped off at the various markets we also had to deliver some flour to our own bakery in Braunestone – a small village near Rugby. We pulled up outside it at around five in the morning. Because the baker – Big Trev – hadn't yet arrived, we slumped back in our seats – exhausted. The next thing we knew was when, having dropped off to sleep for maybe half-an-hour or so, we both, simultaneously, jerked ourselves back awake. There was something about the way we both woke up with such a start at exactly the same time, and both thinking more or less the same thing – *Crikey! how long have I been asleep for?* – which drew us together instantly. I cannot explain how such a strange and inconsequential incident should have signified the start of such an enduring and valued friendship, but in that moment a bond was formed which was undeniable. It was to be a year or more, though, before Nigel would join me out in the "big bad world" to pursue the friendship further.

Finally, finally, the day of my departure came. Graeme and Nick travelled down with me in the car to Gatwick, and we were all in good spirits despite the imminence of the farewells that needed to be made. Graeme, who'd brought his guitar with him, took up the refrain of *I'm Leaving on a Jet Plane* as he strummed away in the back of the car. He'd always been a joker! It was Graeme who'd walked into the farmhouse one day and found Noel sitting at a table with cheque books and financial documents spread out in front of him.

'Aha,' he said cheekily. *'The king was in his counting house, counting out his money.'*

Noel looked up without smiling: he didn't appreciate that kind of humour. But Graeme never had been one who was noted for deferential diffidence. He too has long since parted company with the Fellowship

Flying away from the United Kingdom, I knew that I'd been through one mother an emotional ordeal. It was hard to fend off absurd worries and insecurities as I wrestled with the possibility that I had, indeed, displeased God by betraying his people – and maybe, I thought, He would reveal his judgement on me with some awful air crash. As we flew through turbulence – which I hadn't experienced before – and were required to take our seats and fasten our safety belts, I had to steady my nerve by talking to myself in the language of reassurance. I longed for the Israeli sun and a long period of sustained emotional and spiritual convalescence, promising myself that if and when we landed at Ben Gurion I would banish all further doubts about God's love for me into the deep depths of the ocean. How I longed to hear the comforting squeal of wheels spinning along the runway and the reverse-thrust of the jet engines as the plane landed safely. Which, of course, under the capable control of the British Airways' flight crew, it did. I closed my eyes and silently gave thanks for what I genuinely believed to have been a deliverance. And as we walked out onto the tarmac I would have prostrated my body to kiss the ground had I not been so thoroughly British.

PART FOUR
The JFC exposed and unplugged

Much of what I've written so far has been anecdotal. I have been describing events, together with commentary, as they happened. The story in this form will resume in chapter twenty-one. For the next few chapters, though, I would like to take a more penetrative, in-depth look at various significant events which took place within the Fellowship and also analyse some key aspects of its lifestyle and doctrine. I covered some of this in the typewritten report I prepared in 1983 called "The Church Community at Bugbrooke" and I shall make quite a number of references to it. Writing in 2024, however, I'm now in a position to expand on what was written in the report through the insight I've since gained and the additional information I've been able to collect. I have yet, of course, to write about the extraordinary circumstances surrounding the recent – 2017 – demise of the Community and the closure of the Jesus Fellowship Church. That will come. In the meantime, without any longer having a need to continuously look over my shoulder and moderate the content of my writing, I shall be able to include certain material that I've previously withheld for fear of a litigious response – even though I've known it to be entirely accurate and true. Until now I've concentrated on getting as much information about the Jesus Fellowship as possible into the public domain and have endeavoured to ensure the content is such that the possibility of legal proceedings which might dimmish its impact is minimized: hence my caution. There are, however, no new bombshells to drop that will cause any deep intake of breath; the essential facts about the Fellowship's beliefs and practices have already been handled by myself and others in a wide range of formats. But I *will* be able to write with much more freedom in how I present the material, and especially in the choice of language I use to express the strength of my feelings.

CHAPTER FIFTEEN: Distressing deaths

I shall begin my in-depth look at various JFC-related events and issues by returning to February 1978, the month when Steve Orchard (aka Steve Faithful) met his death on a section of the mainline railway track close to New Creation Farm.

Following a coroner's inquest in June of the same year, the Northampton Evening Telegraph printed the following report:

"A question mark today hangs over the death of a young religious sect member following an open verdict after a three-hour inquest.

Stephen Orchard (19) was decapitated by a train near the headquarters of the Jesus Fellowship Church at Bugbrooke, near Northampton. A pathologist said his injuries were consistent with him having been lying on the track.

He was the second member of the sect, which discourages people from leaving, to die in 18 months. In February 1977, another youth died in a field from exposure." (June 28th. 1978)

The first death which the report refers to was that of Gavin Hooper. For some reason which I haven't quite figured out, SC refers to him as "David" in his book. This is how he describes what happened:

"David was a gentle young man who had recently transferred his job as articled clerk and moved up to Victor and Sheila's house on the estate. One Saturday in December he took his Bible and went for one of his 'prayer walks'. It was sunny but very cold and frosty and Dave had no coat on. When he didn't appear after lunch, Victor sent someone looking for him but without success. As the day drew in, he grew uneasy and organised a proper search. By seven in the evening we left off to attend chapel but continued afterwards. Perhaps he'd gone off somewhere on impulse, as he'd told us he was prone to do.

A time of great anxiety followed, especially for David's parents and for Victor's household. The next week, a villager walking his dog found his body in a strip of scrubland. Next to him was his Bible and, strangely, his neatly folded shirt, socks and vest. Accidental death from hypothermia was the verdict of the coroner. One symptom is the feeling of being hot and confused and this probably explains why David removed some of his clothing."[11]

Whilst doing further research for my 1983 report, "The Community-Church at Bugbrooke", I had the memorable pleasure of talking to Gavin's parents. They gave me their own story about what had happened, which, as much as anything else, was movingly sad. I pieced together everything I'd been able to find out about Gavin's death and wrote as follows:

"In February 1977 an incident occurred which, once again, made the Community the subject of local attention. A young man, Gavin Hooper, who had been living with one the Community's senior elders, was found dead in a local field. His body was half naked, albeit that the neighbourhood had been experiencing sub-zero temperatures.

The coroner's inquest into his death failed to establish a conclusive explanation concerning the circumstances of the tragedy. Even though a verdict of 'accidental death' was recorded, the coroner, Mr. Michael Colcutt, made the following remarks:

'It is an extraordinary thing that a young man should go out at 8 a.m. on a bitterly cold morning with only a shirt and no coat. And it is even more extraordinary in view of the time of year and the temperature that he was found in the circumstances which gave the impression of a man who had been sunbathing. The reason he was lying in this position will always remain a mystery.'

The inquest, needless to say, received a good deal of press attention, and there were various people who began to raise some serious concerns about the Community. Perhaps the most significant of these was the one raised by the Rev. Harry Whittaker, director of the Northampton association of youth clubs. He was reported in the Northants Post as being 'very concerned' about the 'absolute loyalties' demanded by the church. The newspaper reported him as being, in particular, unhappy 'about the way the church claims the absolute allegiance of its members against all other loyalties.'

Such a concern was also uppermost in the minds of Mr. and Mrs. Hooper, Gavin's bereaved parents. Their grief was by no means minimised by the response they received from the Community's leadership. They first heard of Gavin's disappearance – more than 24 hours after he'd last been seen – on Sunday 5th. December, not from the Community but from the local police. The first written communication which Mr. and Mrs. Hooper received from the Community was on December 17th. when they received a letter from Mr. Stanton, written the day previously.

Mr. Stanton's letter was written thirteen days after Gavin's disappearance and six days after his dead body had been found. To Gavin's parents such a seemingly casual regard for their grief from the Community's leadership highlighted the gulf which had grown between their son's loyalties to them, his parents, and towards his 'spiritual family' within the Community.

Mr. and Mrs. Hooper are convinced that, at the time of their son's death, he was experiencing an extreme conflict of loyalties. They are able to identify three areas in which their son was having difficulty. Firstly, he was concerned about the considerable financial resources which were becoming available to the Community. Secondly, he was finding it difficult to accept Noel Stanton's teaching on the Satanic nature of Christmas and the need for the Community members to have nothing to do with it. And, thirdly, he was unable to sort out how he should respond to the emphasis given which required the members to regard the Church-Community as being their true family home and hence deserving of their greatest loyalty. The Hoopers are convinced that Gavin died in a disturbed state of mind while endeavouring to resolve his inner conflicts."

Noel Stanton's response to the criticisms of Gavin's parents was one which he would deploy time and again: he dismissed it as the type of persecution which was only to be expected towards those who were true followers of Christ. He was unwilling to give any countenance to the concerns which the Hoopers expressed, especially those concerning torn loyalties. They served to highlight, however, an unsparing aspect of Noel's teaching about allegiance to natural families which was central to our lifestyle. He gave particular emphasis to the words of Jesus recorded in Matthew 10, verses 34–37:

"Do not think that I have come to bring peace on earth. I did not come to bring peace but a sword. For I have come to set a man against his father, a daughter against her mother, and a daughter-in-law against her mother-in-law. And a man's foes will be those of his own household. He who loves his father and mother more than me is not worthy of me."

Radical words indeed. And I can still hear Noel stood on the platform in Bugbrooke chapel, stamping his feet, beating his bible rhythmically and shouting:
'So! You don't like the Bible any longer do you? You'd rather these words of Jesus weren't there, would you? Well, be real then! Tear them out! Tear out those pages in the Bible which you don't like and then you won't have to take any notice of them.'
Few, if any, of us had an adequate mental defence against his logic, so we accepted it as being what he claimed it was – prophetic wisdom revealing the way of truth. Closely allied to his teaching about family loyalties was that of "discipleship", which meant a complete renunciation of one's "old life" in the world with all its habits, hobbies, attitudes, possessions, sports and ambitions in favour of a "new life" and "new identity" which Christ was offering within the Community. Noel taught that unless an individual renounced family associations sufficiently to enable him or her to become completely committed to the Community then they hadn't taken up the Cross to follow Jesus as a disciple. For many, Noel's call to community living represented an uncompromised,

honest and forthright adherence to Christ's words above concerning families; and it offered us the opportunity to join a church which was being honoured by God on account of its obedience to the discipleship demands made by Jesus himself. Noel frequently referred to his prophetic status, and we looked up to him as one with a special anointing to fulfil such a role. As such, his authority over the Community's members became one which was unquestionable and without challenge. This was why no one questioned *his* version of events after Steve Faithful's tragic death on the railway lines.

Noel wanted us all to accept that Steve's death was *another* tragic accident. He told us that all of Steve's body parts had been found *within* the two rail tracks, making it seem that he'd been hit – by a freight train – whilst crossing the line in darkness. His exact time of death was unknown as the impact hadn't been noticed by any of the train drivers that night, but there was a possibility the fatality had happened when a passenger train and the freight train had crossed paths. The theory presented was that Steve had crossed the line after the brightly lit passenger train had passed by and inadvertently walked into the path of the oncoming, largely *unlit,* freight train. Had this been the case, however, then Steve must have somehow missed the beam from the headlight of the approaching train's locomotive engine, something which would have been possible, of course, but unlikely. In answer to the question of *why* Steve had been down by the track late at night, the answer we were given was that *this was just the kind of thing Steve did*; it was the kind of person who Steve was, someone who loved the outdoor life. But the idea of a brother being out at night all alone, off on some kind of rural adventure, was completely unconscionable. It just didn't happen! Unless, that is, the brother was acting disobediently as a result of being out of sorts or something similar. The possibility that *Steve* could have been behaving in such a way was dismissed by Noel as entirely fanciful. He would tell the coroner's inquest that Steve had no doubts about life within the Community, that he had "found himself" and that he was perfectly happy.

I first heard of Steve's death from my friend, Shaun. It was during a telephone conversation we had while I was away in Canterbury, where I'd also been at the time of the tragedy itself. I'd not been a Community member for more than a few months and therefore still lacked a full understanding about the nature of the unquestioning loyalty expected of us. I hadn't anticipated Shaun's reaction when I asked if Steve had committed suicide. It seems that I'd come close to blasphemy and was told in no uncertain terms that it was only the Enemy who could put such thoughts into anyone's mind. *Of course he hadn't committed suicide! This was Steve Faithful, the brother whose faithfulness had been an inspiration to everyone within the Fellowship.*

I travelled back to Bugbrooke on the next Friday evening, as was usual, and found the whole brotherhood in very sombre mood. Steve's parents, Lionel and Marian, were also Fellowship members, as was his older natural brother, Maurice. None of his family were able to countenance anything other than Steve having been perfectly happy with his life in the Community; and most of the brotherhood, it seemed, were smitten by the thought of the grief Lionel, Marian and Maurice must be feeling. The evening chapel service on Saturday evening became, predominantly, a tribute to Steve's life and also a prolonged lamentation from a Fellowship-wide extended family made up of broken hearts. We all sang a beautiful hymn which had been penned for the occasion. It began like this:

"In the day of his life,
more were slain than in the day of his death:
Steve Faithful, how faithful, my Lord."

Early on in the evening, Noel had announced his expectation that all of us should weep in sorrowful memory of Steve before the end of the meeting. As we sang the above song, there literally wasn't a dry eye in the building. Tears were flowing from everyone's eyes and some were sobbing loudly, some uncontrollably. I cried too, even though I carried inside me a haunting secret which made it very hard to accept the unanimous verdict on Steve's awful death; a secret which I wouldn't reveal for many years. And yet, as my own tears started to issue spontaneously, I felt cut to the very quick with remorse and sorrow as I remembered the brother whom I'd shared a room with at the farm. I had indeed grown to love him as a true brother.

I can no longer be precise about when it was I recognized what happened that evening as having been attributable to the process of group dynamics; some kind of group psychopathy akin to running with the herd, and orchestrated by Noel himself. But it certainly wasn't *too* long afterwards before I could see it all quite clearly, maybe even within days. Without doubt, the surge of grief had spread through the assembly like a contagious Mexican wave of desolation. I've noticed similar kinds of mass despondency since then; most notably, probably, following the death of Princess Diana – albeit somewhat less acute than what happened at Bugbrooke. Many people in that chapel hadn't even spoken to Steve; some may have even disliked him given he was occasionally quite surly and dismissive; nasty even. And yet here was everyone behaving as if in some kind of hagiographic awe. It wasn't natural, nor did it pay Steve the respect he deserved: honesty and truth.

Life moved on and a plaque with the words of Steve Faithful's song was put up in the entrance hall at New Creation Farm. Above it was an enlarged photo of his unmistakable mischievous face and crazy mop of red hair; there he was, watching over us all.

The appointed coroner for the inquest was once again Mr. Michael Colcutt. Considering it was the second death within the Community he'd been called on to examine, and because he'd received a number of letters from concerned parents, he went to considerable lengths to establish whether Steve's death might be associated with anything untoward that might be of wider concern. The following report appeared in the Northampton Evening Telegraph on June 29th:

"A question mark today hangs over the death of a young religious sect member following an open verdict after a three-hour inquest. Stephen Orchard (19) was decapitated by a train near the headquarters of the Jesus Fellowship Church at Bugbrooke, near Northampton. A pathologist said his injuries were consistent with him having been lying on the track.

He was the second member of the sect, which discourages people from leaving, to die in 18 months. In February 1977, another youth died in a field from exposure.

The coroner, Mr Michael Collcut, said: *'The circumstances of this young man's death are far from straightforward. Just how much the young man, if he had wanted to leave, would risk showing other people in the community he was dissatisfied, I don't know.'*

'Whether or not he was depressed or wanted to leave we cannot be entirely certain. But, on the other hand, what is the explanation?'

Stephen's body was found on a railway line near the sect's New Creation Farm, Nether Heyford, on February 28.

Stephen's father, Mr Leslie Orchard, said Stephen had mentioned leaving the community, but it was nothing serious. *'As far as I know he was perfectly happy. Had he not been, I am sure he would have told me because we were quite close.'*

Mr Collcut said he felt bound to make a full inquiry because of letters he had received from parents anxious about the safety of their children. It was not for the coroner's court to question religious beliefs, he said, or the manner of the organisation, unless it had a bearing on the death.

'We have heard that a number of parents have expressed considerable concern about the activities of the fellowship and the community. I am not surprised this should happen where the parents do not hold the same beliefs.'

Mr Collcutt added it was clear the young man was lying on the rail when he was hit by the train. But because it was possible it had occurred accidentally, he was obliged to record an open verdict."

In the report the newspaper published the day previously, before the end of the inquest, the court reporter had written:

"Pathologist Dr Robert Sladdon told the court the head had been severed from the body, and death was consistent with multiple injuries received by being struck by a train while lying on the track. A railway inspector said blood and flesh on the train indicated Mr Orchard had been lying on the track."

Noel returned from the inquest shaken and angry. At the next chapel meeting he made damning references to the coroner's prejudice and accused him of being an instrument of Satan. Returning to a theme which had already become rather hackneyed, he dismissed the court's open verdict as another example of the Fellowship being persecuted and "hated by all men" on account of our radical Christian lifestyle. He stuck to his story that all of Steve's body parts had been recovered within the tracks, and many of us were unaware that the court had been told otherwise – that his head had been severed as a result of his lying across them.

Someone must have been lying – let's call it what it was. Either it was the pathologist or it was Noel Stanton. What motive could the pathologist have had for lying? It's hard to think he could possibly have had one, unless he was genuinely a mouthpiece for Satan. What motive could Noel have had for lying? It wouldn't be hard to identify plenty of reasons he may have had, and that's without even taking into account the secret I've already spoken about: that I knew for sure about Steve's troubled state of mind.

I first realized Steve was unhappy when he began reading late into the night. Although reading "Christian" books wasn't explicitly forbidden, at the farm you carried the risk of being reproached if you read them frequently for amusement rather than edification – just like Steve did. Simply from the way he spoke it was apparent that things weren't right with him, and it seemed he couldn't wait until the time of day when he could switch off from his cares and escape into the allegorical world conjured up by authors such as C. S. Lewis and George MacDonald. His problem, however, was getting his hands on the kind of books he liked, so he would sometimes ask me if I could possibly get some from the university library at Canterbury. Sadly, I wasn't ever able to locate any of the ones he asked me about. Even Steve's father is reported as having admitted to the inquest that his son had spoken about leaving the Community:

'Mr. Orchard said Stephen had mentioned leaving the community.'[12]

Much more significant than all this was the row I overheard him having with Noel. It was in the week before his death when I heard the angry shouts of a heated exchange coming from Noel's private bedroom – my own room was directly opposite. As I opened my door to find out what was happening, they both came out into the corridor and Steve marched off towards the staircase.

'*Come back, Steve Faithful!*' Noel demanded.

Without so much as looking up, Steve stomped off down the stairs whilst raising his arm aloft in a gesture which is normally taken to mean something like "get lost" – to be as polite as possible about the gesture. I don't know whether or not Noel was aware of my being there.

At the evening chapel meeting on the Sunday before his death, Steve had been sitting on the raised dais just to one side of where Noel stood to preach. This was nothing unusual. He looked quite forlorn throughout the meeting, but nor was *this* too unusual. What *was* unexpected, however, was the way in which Noel turned to him straight after the meeting had finished to ask him if he was OK. Even more surprising was the way Steve refused to look up at him but just remained silently sat there with his face looking downward.

How it was that Noel could have stood in a coroner's court and blithely dismissed any suggestion that Steve had been unhappy is only explicable when it's understood he was willing to be blatantly deceitful when necessary. Why? Was it simply that he wanted to defend the Fellowship against further criticism? Or was it anything more personal? It wasn't until as late as 2018 that I read about a brother who claimed he'd had to hastily escape from Noel's bedroom when he feared that Noel, who only had a bath robe around him, was on the point of making inappropriate sexual advances. Other credible reports recently made available to me confirm that this would have been entirely in accord with Noel's sexual proclivities. Had Steve himself been approached by Noel in such a way? Is that what the raised voices I heard had been all about? There is no way of knowing, of course, and I continue to think it highly unlikely. But to dismiss the possibility as unthinkable is simply to bury one's head in the sand. One thing is beyond dispute: Noel had shown himself to be a liar. I was never fully able to admit this to myself – let alone anyone else – whilst in thrall to his position as a revered prophet, and I certainly wasn't able to face up to the consequences of what it meant. Had I been able to do so, then I should rightly have left the Community there and then.

In various media reports which have featured the Fellowship since the time of my own membership, there has regularly been reference to *three* deaths that have been cause for concern. The third of these happened in 1986 when a young brother was drowned in a freshwater well at New Creation Farm. The only knowledge I have about the circumstances surrounding the tragedy are those I've gleaned from newspaper reports. It's best, therefore, if I restrict myself to the inclusion of the article which appeared in the Northampton Chronicle and Echo on June 14th.

"A 25-year-old Jesus Fellowship member has been found dead in an underground tank in Nether Heyford. The victim, was named today by the Jesus Fellowship as Mohammed Majid. A spokesman said he was on New Creation Farm, Nether Heyford when he complained to colleagues that he felt too hot. Mr. Majid said he wanted to go for a swim in the underground tank on the farm. His clothes were found nearby.

A spokesman for Northamptonshire Police confirmed that the body of a young man had been recovered from a fresh water well. They are not treating the incident as suspicious and said formal identification should be made later today.

The Fellowship statement said: *'Twenty-five year-old Mohammad Majid, who had been staying temporarily in a Jesus People house in Pattishall, was found drowned in an underground tank at the farm in Nether Heyford on Friday afternoon.'*

'He had been working voluntarily on the farm and had spoken of feeling hot and wanting to go for a swim in the underground tank'

'He was told this was dangerous and strictly forbidden. However, he disappeared during the afternoon and some of his clothes were found by the entrance to the tank. His body was recovered by firemen.'

A spokesman for the Fire Brigade said a tender and a pump from Northampton had been sent to the village well at about 5 pm yesterday. He said two firemen recovered the body."

In the absence of any further information, it certainly seems that this was genuinely nothing more than an extremely sad and tragic accident. I would, however, like to reference and discuss two more disturbing deaths – often unmentioned and overlooked – that needed investigating by a coroner's court.

Pete Fincher was killed when his motorbike skidded on icy roads near Towcester. I had worked with Pete quite often at the farm and therefore knew his reputation for being difficult to get on with was well justified. I would suggest, however, that his argumentative character was closely related to his need for the pursuit of truth in his Christian lifestyle. In fact, he was an honest, loyal, and direct brother who was devoted to his wife, Anne, a grand-mal epilepsy sufferer whose disposition was always radiant: she faced her disability with much courage and fortitude. I was also aware of Pete's timidity around machinery, a "weakness" which various brothers, including Noel, were constantly entreating him to "overcome".

Pete was using the motorbike to attend a TOPS vocational training course in Milton Keynes. His parents, Bob and Adelaide, questioned why he'd been riding one on a 56-mile-round journey when he'd previously shown such an aversion to them. And even more pertinently, why was he doing so in such icy conditions when he was only a very inexperienced learner driver? These were amongst the issues raised at the inquest, which ultimately concluded Pete's death had been entirely accidental. The coroner's court wasn't the appropriate one to answer the whys and wherefores of the "discipleship" processes to which the Community's members were subject; the only tribunal which could have done so was one which would have been able to dig deeply enough to attribute and apportion blame for requiring people to do dangerous things for which they weren't trained or suited. Although I cannot be absolutely certain about it, I strongly suspect that Pete was on a motorbike because he'd been asked to ride one as part of his discipleship training: I have absolutely no idea by who – but *someone* does. I only knew of one other person who rode a motorbike in the Community, a young brother called Ivor who lived at the farm but worked "in the world" as an electrician. He was an experienced rider who was perfectly at home on two wheels. No doubt there were many brothers who would have loved the opportunity to ride a decent-sized motorbike, but Pete wasn't one of them.

I shared correspondence with Bob and Adelaide Fincher after I'd left the Fellowship and found them to be humble people who'd born their grief with great dignity considering the circumstances. They'd become estranged from Pete since he joined the Fellowship despite having a strong evangelical faith themselves. In letters which Bob and Adelaide kindly shared with me, Pete had accused them of being "agents of the Devil" – and all because they'd opposed his membership. They also told me of the distress they'd experienced as Pete changed into someone openly hostile towards them; and nor could they understand why they'd been denied the opportunity to help care for Anne in the way they'd previously done – through the support they'd provided in helping her to manage her epileptic seizures, she'd become like a daughter to them. To crown it all, they'd had no personal communication from Noel Stanton concerning Pete's death or his funeral arrangements. In a subsequent letter, Noel explained that it wasn't unreasonable for him to leave such pastoral responsibilities in the hands of others.

I still have difficulty writing about Noel's attitude without finding myself welling up with incredulity and anger. So much for his boasts about experience of the Naval service, within which a commanding officer wouldn't dream of delegating responsibility to a subordinate for writing letters of condolence, even when there were many to be written during an armed conflict. *Who exactly did the man think he was? Had a death within the brotherhood become such a commonplace event that he was incapable of taking responsibility for expressing the Fellowship's sorrow towards loved ones who'd become the bereaved?*

Another brother was involved in a fatal road accident just a few months after Pete's. Paul Andrews, who was 27, died as a result of injuries he sustained when the car he was driving had a head-on collision with a lorry. Paul had failed to pull back to the left-hand side of the road after he'd overtaken the car in front. Evidently, there had been plenty of space and time for him to have done so. Although he'd been connected to the Fellowship for several years and was staying in a Community house at the time of the accident, he'd only recently committed himself to membership. The inquest, presided over for a third time by Mr. Michael Colcutt, heard that Paul was receiving psychiatric treatment and had been in disturbed state of mind when the collision took place.

A verdict of accidental death was recorded. Presumably this meant that, in the eyes of the Fellowship, Mr. Colcutt had redeemed himself for the "open verdict" he'd returned after Steve Faithful's death. It seems he must have quit the dark side and returned to the good one. The Northampton Chronicle and Echo, however, followed its coverage of the inquest with an editorial in which it called for an extensive inquiry into the Fellowship by the wider church authorities. It made the following comments:

"Evidence of a disturbed state of mind in other young people connected with the Jesus Fellowship was uncovered in our special investigation into the group earlier this year...

An independent inquiry should be carried out into the Fellowship in order to assess its influence and effect upon young men and women. The people with the moral authority to carry out that inquiry are other concerned Christians of all denominations."[13]

The plaintive request for help from concerned Christians was never responded to by those in a position to have done so; just as they didn't respond to the appeal I would make many years later for them to be courageous and recognize the Fellowship for what it was – a cult.

There would be further incidents of deaths in unsettling circumstances within the Fellowship, and I will refer to these in due course.

CHAPTER SIXTEEN: "FAIRgate" and others

With each passing year toward the end of the seventies, the theme of persecution became a subject which Noel increasingly addressed in his preaching. It felt as if he was becoming ever more sensitive towards criticism, especially so if it appeared in the local or national press. He invariably dismissed press criticism as persecution, and he frequently reminded us that it demonstrated we were on the right track. This, of course, is a classic misconstruction of two related conditions. You could say, for example, that all Premiership football teams can expect to be taunted by a section of the crowd at some point during the season. It's fairly obvious, however, that being taunted by the crowd doesn't mean that you're a Premiership team – nor does being persecuted mean that you're on the right track as a Christian church. Reversing these two conditions is disingenuous to say the least.

There were dozens of articles which appeared in print during the period from 1977 to 1982, some of them no more than a few column inches, some of them far more thoroughly thought through and well researched. We were also filmed for an episode of Sue Jay's "Jaywalking" series: "A City on the Hill". Before being allowed to film, Sue and her team had to give cast-iron assurances about the content of the final version, which included an agreement not to focus on issues which might adversely affect the Fellowship. Behind closed doors, Noel briefed us all on how we should conduct ourselves during filming; and he stage-managed the chapel meetings to such an extent that there was little about them which would have been of concern to most, even if their format was somewhat different to commonly held perceptions about "normal" Baptist chapel services. I watched a recorded version of the Jaywalking broadcast in the audio-visual studio at Warwick University: the first video cassette film I'd ever seen! I replayed the tape repeatedly until I'd made sufficient notes to give Noel a detailed report of its content. Given the constraints which had been imposed on the filming, it was hardly surprising that the documentary lacked depth or any kind of bite: it was undoubtedly interesting and informative – but rather bland. Noel's general verdict was a satisfactory one, which should be enough to tell its own story about the extent to which the broadcast had – or hadn't – plumbed the depths of life with the Jesus Fellowship Church and the New Creation Christian Community.

Listing and commenting on *all* that was written and spoken about us during the years in question would be unduly extensive and repetitive. What I'd therefore like to do is focus on three incidents of threat to the Fellowship which were blown up into quite a storm and which SC has also covered in his book. Each of these incidents was quite distinct in character; and yet the Fellowship's response was, with hindsight, predictably consistent. Cashing in on the post-Watergate craze for gate-naming sleazy, disreputable or controversial incidents, I shall take a look at what I've cheekily named "FAIRgate" (which spawned "Spudgate"), "Devilgate" and "Tapegate".

FAIRgate took place in 1978. FAIR – Family Action Information and Rescue – was an organization with a mission to support families of those people who found themselves entrapped within a cult. In response to letters they'd received from anxious parents about the JFC, FAIR produced a report which Noel responded to furiously. Legal action was threatened unless an apology was forthcoming. With plenty of wealth to back it up, the Fellowship increasingly used the threat of litigation as a response to unwelcome press. I never explicitly discussed this issue with any of my brothers, but I'm sure I wasn't alone in wondering why we, as a fellowship, couldn't put our trust in God himself to be our defender, or why we couldn't just proudly acknowledge the validity of some of the charges made against us. It was an incongruity which nagged at me persistently. I shall allow SC to explain more about FAIRgate through what he has written concerning some of the report's claims:

"Another document had been circulating for a couple of years from an anti-cult body called FAIR – Family, Action, Information, Rescue. This 'unfair' document passed between angry parents and critics, and became standard press material. It was inspiring, even entertaining – and libellous!

'Their fellowship is real and warm. Their adherence to traditional Christian values of selflessness and self-discipline is essentially beyond criticism.'

That was inspiring. Their portrait of charismatic worship, though, we found hilarious.

'Members go into a trance-like state, sobbing, muttering, and swaying with arms outstretched. Stanton preaches for two or three hours. The rest of the time is given to violent rhythmic singing, prayer, and individual rambling outpourings. This creates a state of emotional climax and abandon. Combined with late hours, poor food, and lack of normal emotional outlets, the members are continually swung between deprivation and ecstasy.'

It was a strange caricature! Noel (unbeknown to himself!) had been to the States, the hotbed of cults. The plebs suffered from a lack of veg and a surfeit of spuds. Members were pasty-faced and overweight. Children were subdued (ho! ho!) and undersized. We shared all our clothes and had little idea where our money went."[14]

My own recollection of events – as I wrote them down in "The Church-Community at Bugbrooke", and based on the journal I'd been keeping for my PhD research – is somewhat different. One of the "libelous" claims in the report concerned us being denied access to fresh fruit. In fact it was *semi*-true. I'm not completely sure that every household was identical in this matter, but at the farm household – *prior* to the FAIR report – we'd been rationed to two pieces of fresh fruit per week. The requirement wasn't monitored and it would have been easy enough to exceed this amount had your conscience allowed it. In a mischievous mood, we may even have seen such a felony as no worse than scrumping or the like. Yet I have no memory of breaking the rule myself, nor of anyone else doing so. And so far as the allegation made about "the surfeit of spuds" – what I've renamed as "Spudgate" – it wouldn't have been at all hard to locate the fire that had produced the smoke. The FAIR article was, in fact, just one amongst a number of reports containing references to controlled diets of some sort; reports which Noel tried to dismiss as fabricated nonsense. I often used to wish that "our" response to these claims had been more nuanced, not least because I thought the efficacy of such a response would have been far greater – especially when it came to Spudgate. I should have liked to hear Noel beginning his defence of the issue with something of a chuckle and a big grin on his face. He could easily have said something like:

'OK! I've got to come clean about the quantity of spuds we sometimes eat... it's a fair cop – guilty as charged. On the other hand, the reason why we eat so many of them is far more prosaic than certain people have suggested.'

Oh! Those accursed potatoes! There were times when we eat so many of the wretched things that we may well have ended up looking pasty-faced – or even spud-faced. We had several fields at New Creation Farm in which we grew potatoes. These were destined for sale in the chain of "Goodness Foods" shops which had multiplied during my membership. It seemed, however, that demand and supply hadn't been assessed very well, meaning there was often a Maris Piper, King Edward or Desiree glut. In order to tackle the resulting potato mountain, each household was given a weekly supply far in excess of what they normally would have needed or wanted. All manner of creative recipes were devised to ensure the spuds were consumed in a way which reduced the stodgy monotony of eating them boiled, roasted or fried; and most of us were amazed at how enjoyable the various offerings of potato cake, served up for dessert, could be. But there were limits to how far even the best of household cooks could disguise the humble apple-of-the-soil. It was a blessed day, indeed, when the surfeit had finally been eaten away – at least, that is, until the next harvest. So, yes, we *did* sometimes eat a lot of spuds; but the reasons for doing so were attributable to pragmatism rather than anything more sinister. At its worse, it was an imposition which many in the free world would have found intolerable; at best, it was a test of dietary endurance. In general, we had a diet which kept us well fed and healthy.

Sadly, nuanced diplomacy of the kind I've suggested wasn't Noel's style. In response to outraged protests and the threat of legal action, FAIR's chairman, Barry Morrison, agreed to visit the Fellowship to find out for himself what the truth of the matter was. The observations I made on the day of his visit are seared into my memory, the most vivid being the well-stocked bowl of fruit which had been ostentatiously positioned within the entrance hallway of the farmhouse. Likewise, the newly hung posters with straight-as-a-die evangelical themes and wording. The evening meeting at the chapel was to be one of those when several new members would be baptised by full immersion in the chapel's baptismal pool. It was normal on these occasions, as the ecstatic neophyte emerged from the water praising God "in tongues", for all the chapel brethren to erupt into praise themselves – hands raised in the air and cheering so loudly that it could easily have been described as "shouting in tongues". The overall effect was a cacophonic one: deeply inspirational to those who understood it to be jubilant worship; deafening, and probably frightening, to those who remained observant outsiders. Those in the latter group may well have described their experience in words similar to those used in the FAIR report: *emotional climax and abandon*. Well aware of this, Noel orchestrated the baptisms during Barry Morrison's visit in such a way that the eruption of praise was forestalled. Compared to normal it was all a very subdued affair. He also took care to ensure that most of the hymns we sang came from the conventional hymnal rather than from our own huge collection of self-penned verse. This gave an orthodox feel to the meeting, by which Noel had hoped our visitor would be influenced and impressed.

Later that evening, back at New Creation Farm, Noel was told that Barry Morrison hadn't been at the chapel for much of the meeting – evidently, he'd been detained at New Creation Hall by a couple of elders. I don't know whether this had been intentional; possibly a ploy to ensure he wasn't exposed to the glorious exuberance of the "normal" chapel meeting which these elders had anticipated. Or maybe it was just that they'd been engaged in a discussion which had seemed to them an important one. I wouldn't have enjoyed being in their shoes, however, when they discovered the extent to which, as a consequence of taking matters into their own hands, they'd apparently been used by the Enemy. Noel was visibly furious on hearing about it; and he launched into an explosive tirade in which he vilified the two elders for their stupidity and accused them of betrayal. It was one of the many times I witnessed him losing his temper, and each time for similar reasons.

Perhaps the fact that things hadn't quite gone to plan explains why the apology Noel had been pressing for wasn't given in the way it had been hoped. It was only after several months of negotiation that FAIR, as an organization, agreed – albeit under considerable duress and with the threat of litigation still being a concern – to circulate a letter which contained some of the corrections Noel had demanded. FAIRgate didn't play out in quite the way SC's account – the authorized JFC account – suggests.

After FAIRgate came "Devilgate": *"How Hardline Noel beats out the Devil"*, screamed the News of the World (NOTW) headline in April 1981.[15] The article was as scurrilous as one would expect from an unashamedly sensationalist gutter-press tabloid. Amongst its many allegations were those

145

of excessive child-beating, a Gestapo-style eldership, people leaving the Community penniless, and forced marriages. Few people would have expected the NOTW to be anything other than OTT (over the top), and it was unlikely that many would have given much credence to the feature's content: despite its title, the NOTW wasn't read for genuine information about world news so much as for cheap thrills from exaggerated and histrionic reports of the world's most shocking, disgusting and condemnable affairs. *Thank God I'm not like **them*** was the self-righteous, judgmental, feel-good response which the paper aimed to solicit from its readers. Not many would have therefore expected or predicted Noel's reciprocal OTT response to the article. Had he been able to just roll with the punches and taken it on the chin, then I'm sure he would have demonstrated his trust in God more convincingly and therefore commanded far greater respect.

Aware of when the article would be printed, he firstly sought to minimize the number of local people who would be exposed to its content. He did this by sending some farm brothers to the local newsagents in order to buy up all available copies before anyone else had a chance to set eyes on one. He then did something which was similar to what he'd done in relation to FAIR's accusation of restricted access to fresh fruit: he made internal changes to draw the sting. FAIRgate resulted in fresh fruit becoming available in all of the households at all times; Devilgate resulted in the return of capital funds to many who'd previously left but hadn't yet received a refund for their contributions. The formal wording of the JFCT document relating to such refunds was that they could be made "at the discretion of the trustees". Discretionary "relief of need" payments could also be made in certain circumstances. In practice, such payments required an application from the person in need, a hurdle which few felt able to face in the emotional aftermath of having split and been condemned for doing so. Following the NOTW article, Noel asked for a list to be drawn up of all those who'd left but hadn't had their capital contributions refunded. This list was then presented to us at an elders' meeting and we were asked to advise Noel of anyone on it to whom we felt a repayment would be expedient. Put bluntly, we were being asked to identify those whom we knew had either expressed disquiet at what they had, or hadn't, received back, or whom we thought might be "bought off" from making trouble at some future point if an unsolicited refund were made to them immediately. It was rank, self-serving hypocrisy. I believe I recognized this at the time, and yet I lacked the certitude or moral courage to object. It was slowly beginning to dawn on me, however, just how Noel treated people as little better than pawns in his grand masterplan: he tried to move them around the board as best suited his purpose. If it suited his purpose to withhold funds from those who'd left, then he did so; if it suited his purpose to repay them in order to secure their support, then he did so. Seen in this light, the people themselves were of little consequence to him;

all he was able to see is the way in which they could be best used in the bigger scheme of things.

The NOTW article had clearly riled Noel more than any previous press feature. Legal action was threatened, as was quite normal by now. And in preparation for such litigation he began drafting – as the basis for an affidavit – a thorough point-by-point response to what had been written about us. Once finalized, the document was made available for all the elders to read. At the elders' meeting following its circulation amongst us, one brave brother raised a concern about the technical accuracy of one or two clauses. Predictably, Noel openly rebuked him for being "petty". At best, Noel's reaction was unkind; at worst, dictatorial: the brother had clearly just wished to ensure his conscience would allow him to sign the affidavit as being entirely true. But we weren't permitted the indulgence of having an individual conscience; we had to submit ourselves to the "collective wisdom of the brotherhood" – which was little better than another way saying, "the wisdom of Noel Stanton". Noel arranged for a solicitor to be present at the next elders' meeting a week or two later. Each of us present had to swear on oath that the affidavit was entirely true and then add our signature to it. Any other elder who felt, as I did, that what we were doing was wrong would have suffered the same sense of shame as mine. To have sworn, for example, that "Noel was as much subject to the other elders as they were to him" was plainly and simply perjury – it may have been *constitutionally* true, but it certainly wasn't so far as the day-to-day workings of the Fellowship were concerned. Signing the document was an inexcusable act of cowardice. The only mitigation I can offer for my own culpability is that I did at least acknowledge to *myself* what I'd done. SC mentions none of this in the brief paragraph he has written about Devilgate – my own nickname for it all, of course. He does, however, attribute blame for Devilgate to the web of opposition which had been spun by "disgruntled ex-members and irate parents". Anyone who voiced opposition was labelled as "disgruntled", "irate" or some such term; blame was never apportioned to anything that Noel may have said or done.

The third instance of so-called persecution in this period which I want to write about is one I've named as "Tapegate". Portrayed by Dave Resolute – now acting as the Fellowship's press secretary – as simply a dispute between two churches, Tapegate reached the pages of the Northants Post in February 1982 beneath a headline which read: *"ANGER OVER 'BRAINWASH' TAPES – Pastor told to stop sales":*

"A cassette tape which claims members of a religious commune are brainwashed was at the centre of a row between two churches this week.

The Bugbrooke based Jesus Fellowship Baptist Church claim the tapes are libellous and want them withdrawn. They have sent a solicitor's letter to a Northampton pastor who has been distributing the tapes which contain a series of statements supposedly from ex-members of the Fellowship. The Pastor – who has asked us not to name him – has been operating a counselling service to help former members re-adjust after leaving the community.

On the tapes, which warn people off joining, the ex-members give alarming accounts of experiences they say happened when they belonged to the community. They talk of brainwashing techniques being used. And one ex-elder says the only way to get people out of Bugbrooke is to hire a helicopter and kidnap them.

The tapes were being sold for £3 each to people thinking of joining the group – which is affiliated to the Baptist Church. The Pastor told us:

'I've received many heart-breaking letters from all over the country from parents who claim they have lost their children'.

'Other people have contacted me asking about what is happening at Bugbrooke and I have sent them the tape'.

'It is simply the accounts of personal experiences'.

'The Fellowship contacted the local ministers of Northampton when the tape was first produced about a year ago, asking me to withdraw it. I am in no doubt they will take me to court unless I do as they wish'.

For the time being the Pastor has stopped selling the tapes. Instead he says he may put people directly in touch with the ex-members who talk on it."[16]

Sometime during the first half of 1981, the minister of an Elim Pentecostal church in Northampton, Pastor Cuthbert, had arranged a get-together for a group of the Community's ex-members during which he had asked them to share their experiences. These were recorded and then distributed on cassette-tapes by the pastor. The content included allegations of brainwashing, with one contributor humorously claiming that the only way to get people out of the Community was in a helicopter. Having found out about the tape, Noel responded with aggression. He had a solicitor's letter sent to the pastor demanding that the tape should be withdrawn or legal action would follow. I was present at the Fellowship's annual summer convention – now being held in Northampton's Nene College – when Noel denounced the devilish and demonic nature of both the tape and the man who had produced it. I was sitting next to Dave Resolute when we drove past pastor Cuthbert's Pentecostal church on our way home from one of the convention sessions. Dave pointed to the building and referred to it as "Satan's tabernacle".

SC refers to the tape's content as "very silly and unhelpful", a rather low-key summary considering the virulent denunciations pastor Cuthbert was subjected to and the high-handed response of legal threats. And yet somehow or another Noel saw no inconsistency between the approach he took and biblical appeals to "love your enemy". SC quotes a hymn verse, penned by Noel, which sums it all up nicely:

"Though false religion speaks against
And carnal Christians run to oppose,
These brethren stand, in Jesu's name
In faith and love, and bless their foes."[17]

Understood within its context, this was a warning to us, the brethren, not to be taken in by the claims of "carnal Christians" representing "false religion". Carnal and false, this is how we were urged to regard pastor Cuthbert and his ilk – those who worshipped in "Satan's tabernacle". Our response to falsehood, so Noel claimed, would be to stand firm whilst blessing our "foes" at the same time. If I could write about any of the ways in which we actually made good on the claimed intent to bless our foes then I would gladly do so. But the closest we came to blessing them was *singing* about doing so. Noel certainly knew how to play his audience, and I sometimes despaired at how easily certain reputable Christian leaders from within the wider church were taken in. That part of me which still sought after integrity longed for us to be open and honest about everything even if it meant we were to be damned for our beliefs and lifestyle. *What shame was there in that? It was certainly a far better kind of shame than that of being deceptive.*

Noel's deception skills had been perfectly illustrated previously, in 1980, following a report that was published in the Baptist Times – the mouthpiece of the Baptist Union. Taking up a story that had originally been featured in the Oxford Times, it ran the headline:
MP URGED TO PROBE RELIGIOUS SECT
Prior to publication of the Oxford Times article, Noel demonstrated his wiliness by inviting the journalists involved to attend a Saturday-evening Fellowship meeting at Nene College – due to space and parking constraints at Bugbrooke chapel, the college's assembly hall was now being used quite frequently. I made a specific entry in my sociological-research diary concerning this meeting as it was the one and only time Noel had used a small section of the Apostles' Creed – read from the Anglican prayer book – as the theme for his preaching, which was also unusually low-key. There was no shouting or Bible-thumping, and many aspects of the meeting were radically different to the norm. This, so Noel would have argued, was using the "wisdom of the serpent" as a righteous means of defence for God's kingdom. The journalists, however, didn't show up; but they went ahead with their prepared text regardless. The article spoke about the concerns of an Oxford couple who believed the Community was responsible for splitting up their family by taking away their son. It addressed other issues too, including the subservient role of sisters. These issues were then revisited a few weeks later on the front-page story ran by the Baptist Times.

Issuing legal threats to the editorial team of the Baptist Union's own newspaper was, unsurprisingly, not a response used on this occasion – the Fellowship's remaining supporters within the Union may well have been lost had it been. Instead, Noel appealed for help from an old friend, Lewis Misselbrook, now a Baptist Union official: he was asked to visit the Community and make his own assessment. Following his visit, Misselbrook wrote an extremely complimentary article for the Baptist Times, one which sought to correct what he believed to have been the mistakes of the original report:

"When I arrived, Noel was out in the fields working. He came in, mud all over his gumboots, and gave me the shy, welcoming smile I remembered so well. . . He is still the same quiet, deep man, but one held by a vision that by the Spirit the church is to be a visible and powerful expression of the kingdom of God. . .

Most of the criticism of the community has been unfair and uninformed, and some has been malicious. Bugbrooke is not perfect. Noel Stanton is not always right. But it is a bold venture of faith. . .

First, it is a genuine effort to express the Gospel in practice. . .

Second, it is a lay movement. . . every member plays his part. . .

Third, it reveals the kingdom of God as a true alternative and revolutionary society. . .

Fourth, for the Jesus Fellowship, mission and community are inseparable. . .

Fifth, it is a dynamic and ongoing movement. . .

At last week's Baptist Union assembly it was said that God is doing a new thing. . . If we are not too afraid of change to lift up our eyes to see, we may well be considerably enriched, whether we follow the Bugbrooke pattern or not." [18]

I cannot find any credible explanation for why Mr. Misselbrook wrote such an article. If I were being ungracious, I might advance the idea that he was seeking to enhance his own reputation as a sort of Christian statesman by demonstrating even-handed tolerance of radicalism whilst shying away from such extremism himself. Whatever his motivations may have been, Noel had played him like a fiddle and he became an almost perfect mouthpiece for the Fellowship's propaganda. The best that can be said is he showed dangerous naivety, not least in his description of Noel as some kind of humble farm worker mucking in with everyone else. That was entirely wrong! Noel's only work at the farm was managerial. In fact, I never once knew him to have actually joined in with any of the manual tasks required around the farm: he'd never experienced the fatigue of long hours shifting hay bales and had never dirtied himself by helping muck out the pigsties. Even when word went out for all able-bodied brothers and sisters to spend an evening at the farm helping out with fruit harvesting, Noel was the only person who didn't physically participate. He spent most of each day either in his private bedroom or cocooned in the farm office with Lizzie, his secretary. Once he'd finished leisurely reading a daily broadsheet in the office, he then dictated the text of letters and other documents that needed to be typewritten.

Attention to the Fellowship's administration and finances also took a lot of Noel's time, delegated authority in these matters being kept within strictly controlled limits. As for the idea of his being *quiet and shy...* my, oh my! Misselbrook clearly hadn't been exposed to Noel's prolonged rants, both at meetings and around the farm. SC was clearly aware that this was an issue needing to be handled cautiously. He therefore wrote about Noel "roaring on the platform and purring at home", or sometimes "roaring at home and purring on the platform". Bellowing or screaming would have been far better words to use than roaring. His raised voice was far more comparable with the aggressive screech of a jackal than the majestic roar of a feline apex predator such as a lion; his casual, "endearing" tone of voice far more comparable to the hypnotic, alluring lisping whisper of Kaa – the python from "Jungle Book" – than the soothing purr of a domestic cat. It seems, however, that Noel must have presented himself in such a way that Misselbrook, his erstwhile friend, was eating out of his guileful hand. *He couldn't possibly have been aware, could he, of the rancorous vitriol used by Noel to dismiss the "yellow-bellied" cowardice of all those compromised Christian preachers who hadn't led their flock out of the world and into the kingdom of God – into a community lifestyle where all things were shared in common? He couldn't possibly have been aware, could he, of how Noel thundered out reproach towards the vast majority of Christian ministers whom he dismissed as being "false shepherds"?*

Misselbrook also made some extremely sweeping, ill-conceived and thoughtless statements, such as when, for example, he asserted that most criticism had been "unfair or uninformed". *Most criticism? How could he have made such a claim?* He hadn't actually spoken to any of the critics, so he can only have been making a judgement on the basis of what he'd heard from Noel. The sad thing is that we ourselves – or, at least, *many* of us – knew a significant amount of the criticism Misselbrook had referred to was, truth be told, both fair and informed. We just couldn't admit to it, not even to ourselves. Deep within, however, we yearned for Christian leaders such as Lewis Misselbrook to speak out with a clarity which would help reinforce our shadowy doubts and give them sufficient weight and gravitas to enable us to hold them tight rather than try to rid ourselves of them – as Noel would have had us do. As such, Misselbrook was just another one of those who betrayed us.

CHAPTER SEVENTEEN: The constitution and institutionalism

Graeme Merciful, a brother whom I looked up to and who was undeniably more gifted than myself in just about every respect, once told me that the happiest days of his time in the Community were during the period when I was the new kid on the farm block – *his* words – and when the concept of brotherhood was one which still seemed fresh and exciting. It was Graeme's recollection – and mine too – that this was a time when many of us were genuinely eager to surrender our own ambitions and independence so we could more easily comply with the biblical injunction to "love our neighbour as we love ourselves", or, as Noel was constantly telling us, to "love our brother or sister in Christ as we love ourselves". In practice, this meant loving our Fellowship brethren; and in terms of our day-to-day experience of doing so it meant loving those within our own household – for Graeme and me this was the farm household. In consequence, many of us had formed entirely chaste same-sex friendships that enriched our lives in a way we hadn't previously experienced. We used to love being together, teasing one another, sharing our deepest secrets with one another, working with one another, worshipping the Lord together, and often laughing with one another. It was these friendships which made living in community such a wonderful experience: these were friends whom we held so dear that we believed we would die for them. Trying to put this experience into words for a project I was engaged with some time ago, this is what I wrote:

"Working on jobs around the farm with brothers who'd become such wonderful friends was often joyful: the anecdotes about happy times would be legion. And I did sometimes wonder if perhaps it wasn't heaven itself when I'd roped up my last trailer load of straw bales for the day, the brothers who'd been helping me had clambered onto the top of the loaded stack, and I got behind the wheel of the tractor to set off, contented, back through the beautiful Northamptonshire lanes towards the glowing colours of the setting sun: back to New Creation Farm to discharge our cargo, to maybe sit around and sing songs of Zion together, to laugh, joke and go off to bed tired but happy. And then, after the refreshment of sleep, we were ready to spend another day out in the harvest fields and the sunshine. No wonder one of the Community brothers wrote down his feelings in a song which began:

'Happy the days in Zion's fields
Enclosed away from Babel's strife;
Beneath the Father's open sky
We feel the Spirit's fertile life.'"

The brother who wrote this beautiful verse was, I believe, our very own SC – Simon Cooper or "Overcomer". Noel had often preached the theology of Zion to us. It's a theology which leads to the concept of being *God's chosen people – the Elect – living together in a city set apart:* a city whose purpose is to radiate the glory of God to the surrounding world. The concept, however, is an extremely problematic one which more often than not leads to a culture of insularity and superiority. There are similarities, too, with secular movements which seek the creation, or restoration, of some glorious confederation: the promise of a great – but illusionary – homeland has infamously been trumpeted by many deluded visionaries who have ultimately been exposed as power-hungry tyrants. There was a time, however, when many of us felt overwhelmingly thankful to be part of a homeland, a Zion, in which we felt the presence of God, of Christ himself, was unmistakeable. And the happiness we shared together was undeniable; the special friendships we formed felt intensely meaningful. These were the "best of times" which Graeme Merciful had identified as those he'd enjoyed the most. Had anyone tried to tell us that our experience of life in Zion was not the authentic one we believed it to be, or that future disaffection for many was inevitable, we would have easily dismissed such suggestions with the smug laughter of those who know best: even if we'd been willing to acknowledge certain shortcomings in the Community, we nonetheless knew that our home within it had been divinely ordained and we often felt breathless with the exciting momentum of our radical lifestyle.

It was with some concern, then, that I recognized the process of institutionalization affecting the Fellowship. At university, one of the first sociology textbooks I'd read – by two eminent sociologists, Berger and Luckman – was called "The Social Construction of Reality". One of the phrases I encountered on the very first page alarmed me so much that it has remained engraved in my memory:

"Institutionalization is the reciprocal typification of habitualized actions."

Taken on its own was bad enough, but it was part of a large paragraph written in the same wordy, esoteric vocabulary which, as a fresher, left me baffled. It made me seriously doubt whether or not I'd be able to survive the course. Thankfully, not all the texts were so inaccessible, and I slowly began to get my head around the sociological lingo used by academics who lacked the ability or intelligence to use understandable words and sufficiently-well-constructed sentences so that their arguments and explanations would make sense for most. I gradually came to understand how institutionalization – where reliance on commonly understood and codified ways of doing things replaces those from earlier and fresher, more-exciting and pioneering periods – was a widespread feature of many, if not most, institutions that had introduced ground-breaking procedures and had once known rapid growth. This was especially true of breakaway sectarian movements from the "established church" within any given era. The desire, and indeed the need, to preserve and safeguard what has already been built can all too easily sap the energy and radicalism underpinning an organization's growth and therefore take it off the boil. Left unchecked, institutionalization can spell the death-knell of radical movements, and this has often been the fate of many pioneering Christian movements. Even whilst the Fellowship continued to expand during the period of my membership (an "enlargement of the tent" that had issued from Noel's prophetic ministry), it also became far more structured and rigid. Although it would be failures of a far more heinous nature which finally "did for" the Jesus Fellowship Church, even SC acknowledged that, by 1982, the household at New Creation Hall – by way of example – had become *a little reserved and institutional.* In his own words, he conceded that *form without power was useless* and that a *spiritual dullness had settled over many parts of the church.* He then expanded on these comments:

"'Do we really want the presence of God?' I wrote in my journal. 'Would it be too troublesome? We've got it nicely wrapped up. We are a well-ordered community. Rushing wind and tongues of fire? The awesomeness of God? Oh no! We're content to know him in a relaxed way; you know — the "still, small voice". And so the Bugbrooke revival becomes the Bugbrooke "denomination" and dies in the midst of prosperity.' We were making outward changes — but where was the power of God? The joy and spontaneity? The miracles? The surprises of the Holy Spirit? 'Things have become routine,' wrote Mike "Rockfast" in his diary. 'We have almost succeeded in eliminating the unpredictable and taming the Holy Spirit.' We put on a brave face. People learned the ropes and were loyal. But there was unreality ..."[19]

These were honest, reflective words, written with an ache for reality and the demonstration of God's power and glory. They stand as another reminder – especially to me – of how, at the root of it all, the primary aim of those within the Fellowship was obedience to Jesus Christ; obedience to the call of the Cross; obedience to the call of the Holy Spirit. Recognition of institutionalization as a creeping danger – "well-ordered routine" to use SC's words – was nothing less than what one would have expected from those like Simon and Mike who, above all else, hungered for a lifestyle of radical righteousness.

One huge leap in the institutional direction was the creation of a constitution aligned with a formal statement of faith. The prima facie need for a written constitution was attributable to the complexity of organizational structure which had developed alongside the growth of numerous different entities within the collective whole. Put more simply (and using plainer language which

I hope is easier to understand), a comprehensive written statement which set out the function and purpose of the various charities, businesses and church procedures had become necessary. It was all the more important on account of the considerable collective wealth now being held, including, of course, all of the capital holdings: the Jesus Fellowship Church and its affiliates had already become a multi-million-pound operation.

The New Creation Community's property portfolio in 1979 included nine large houses with more than ten people in residence[a] – some of which were home to around thirty or forty – and about a dozen houses accommodating around ten or less.[b] The "House of Goodness" company included four "Goodness Foods" health-food shops, the "Jeans Plus" clothing shop in Northampton, a central distribution warehouse, and two co-joined farms – Shalom farm and New Creation farm. Fellowship-owned Skaino Services Ltd. had no central premises but was comprised of a growing building company and a haulage firm with its own garage. And Towcester Building Supplies (TBS) had begun trading from the first of its depots – others would follow. During this year – 1979 – these three companies legally consolidated, with House of Goodness (HOG) Ltd. becoming the holding company. The first annual accounting period for which I began obtaining records from Companies House covered the 1981 calendar year. These showed HOG Ltd. as having an annual turnover amounting to just over one-and-a-half million pounds and net assets of nearly nine hundred thousand pounds. In addition to the businesses already mentioned, the Fellowship also owned an architectural firm called "Heritage Design", and it had a holding interest in the large outdoor clothing and equipment shop in Northampton, "White and Bishop Ltd" – this was on account of a director, Sue White, being heavily involved with the Fellowship as a non-Community member. I will be looking in more detail at how these businesses operated in a later chapter.

During this era, the Jesus Fellowship Church comprised two categories of membership: those who lived in a Community household and those who didn't – Sue White, for example, whose husband wasn't involved with the Fellowship, was one of the latter. The constitution conferred an "official" status on these members as, respectively, "baptism and community" or "baptism only". The categories would be expanded over the years, but this is how they were initially identified. The funds received from capital donations, common-purse income, and any other financial contributions from JFC members were held, together with all the JFC fixed assets, in a central trust: the Jesus Fellowship Community Trust (JFCT). And to complete the portfolio of organizational entities there was the Jesus Fellowship Housing

---

[a] New Creation Farm, New Creation Hall, Cornhill Manor, Sheepfold Grange, House of Living Stones, Shalom Farmhouse, Festal Grange, Harvest House and Vineyard.
[b] Including the welcome homes at Harlestone Road and Argylle Street in Northampton, and Bady Road in Daventry.

Association (not normally referred to in abbreviation). All those who were deemed to be residential in a Community household, whether members or not, paid a weekly rental to the association.

Finally, the constitution needed to incorporate the Fellowship's charitable status into its content. The JFC itself wasn't registered as a charity – the separate charitable entities of the Jesus Fellowship Life Trust and the Jesus Army Charitable Trust would come later. But there were defined aspects of the JFC's activities which were recognized as being "charitable" insofar as they met the requisite objective: "the promotion of the Christian faith". The constitution would give formal clarity, acceptable to the charity commissioners, concerning the strategy for meeting this objective.

The chief architect of the constitution was Noel, of course. But he also drew on the administrative and legal help that a few Oxford graduates were able to provide. These were, Dave Resolute (Hawker), now a teacher; Ian Willing (Mason), now a solicitor; and Mike Rockfast (Farrant), now an accountant. Beyond the need for codification and clarification of how its different parts functioned and fitted together, the JFC's constitution – as in the case of the famous American one – was intended to enshrine and consolidate its foundational principles and operational structure. As such, it had been created to protect against future deviations from the way of truth already established – and hence the need for its close link with a statement of faith, a document which I'll also be looking at and explaining. The traction of institutionalization within *any* organization is immediately made stronger, of course, once such a document has been created and accepted. It cries out *this is how we do things*; and soon after comes the cry, *this is how we have always done things*. Unless a constitution is fluid enough to allow for almost continuous change, then it inevitable creates a fixed point which people refer back to. Looking forward becomes ever more shackled and difficult; behaviour becomes far more routine and repetitive.

In addition to the purpose of "pulling everything together", there were other issues which had influenced the need for constitutional legality. One of the most pressing had been to establish membership status and conditions which the secular authorities could recognize and accept. There had been situations, for example, when the Fellowship had found itself on the wrong side of judgements made by the Department for Social Security. This had been financially painful because there were a significant number of unemployed people living in the Community, especially within the cohort of those in the early stages of membership – those, for example, who had been "rescued" through the Fellowship's evangelism. Redundancy and reaching the end of fixed-term contracts also affected established members in the same way it affected their secular peers. No one, however, was allowed to stay in a Community house and be given a free meal ticket or free accommodation. *Everyone* was expected to make some kind of financial contribution to the household common purse, either from the full amount of their employment net salary or "in kind" through their labour – usually at the farm – if they were unemployed. And *everyone* was also expected to pay a given rate of board-and-lodging rental – from their housing-benefit allowance if they were in receipt of social-security assistance. In the same way that those who were employed handed over their pay cheque in its entirety to the household common purse, those receiving social-security assistance were also expected to sign over any giro payments they received. Eventually, however, the social-security officials stopped playing ball and began to cut up rough: they started asking awkward questions about housing-benefit eligibility for residential members of a religious community, and they also started questioning whether those who were expected to work at the farm in lieu of making a financial contribution could be categorized as "unemployed". *Were such people genuinely available for work, and looking for it?* Following the judgements made in various test cases, there was a significant reduction to the amount of state benefit received by JFC claimants – and hence by the JFC Trust itself.

Noel had been infuriated by such judgements. It's very tempting to say that he'd wanted "to screw every possible penny from the state coffers". In my most heightened moments of anger I've felt that such a comment would be no more than plain speaking. And yet I wasn't party to the negotiations which took place and have no authority or ability to determine the essential "fairness" of what happened. As a loyal Community brother, I'm sure I would have felt that Noel had only been acting shrewdly as a responsible custodian of the Fellowship's finances. I'm not able, nor is it necessary, to explain the detailed intricacies of how the constitution was designed so that issues such as those with the Department for Social Security could be resolved. One of the solutions it provided for, however, was that of making us – as Community residents – licensees of the Jesus Fellowship Housing Association. And daily work on the farm by the unemployed was certified as being *largely* voluntary, with sufficient time allocated for job seeking. Even back then, I thought there were aspects to all this that seemed to be financially dishonest and manipulative, that were rather like wanting our cake and eating it. I think, however, that I knew it was way beyond my remit to have any influence in these matters, and I had little choice – as we shall soon see – other than to accept things as they were.

There was yet another aspect to the constitution of vital importance; an extremely well-concealed one that I have often attempted – not very successfully – to expose. The constitution was a firewall! It was a barrier to any outside challenge against the Fellowship's behavioural correctness and orthodoxy. Many has been the occasion since 1979 when I've heard of either Noel or another Fellowship leader attempting to offer reassurance about members' welfare by referring to one or more of the constitution's clauses. The classic example I've often highlighted is that of the one-year probationary period for membership. The constitution stipulated that no capital donations would be accepted from anyone until they'd been living in a Community household for one year. At the same time, however, we were explicitly told that we would become lifelong covenanted members of the Fellowship either when we were baptised or when we received – for those who believed they'd already had a genuine baptism by full immersion elsewhere – "the right hand of fellowship". My own baptism took place just a few months after I'd begun living at New Creation Farm. The brother who was baptised in 1981 on the evening before I left had also only been with us for a few months – and there had been no discussion whatsoever with him about any probationary period. That was it! Should anyone have considered leaving *after* they'd been baptised or received into the church family, then they did so in breach of their covenant vows. As my own story illustrates, leaving the Community was a profound and potentially devastating experience. Anyone who had been accepted into membership would invariably go on to stay for well in excess of a year, which would then include, of course, the donation of their capital. The one-year probationary period affecting capital donations was little more than a smokescreen: in reality, it offered no protection against making a hasty membership decision.

It was much the same concerning the return of capital to those who left. I became frustrated and weary of hearing people being told that the Fellowship trustees had the constitutional authority – discretional – to return capital donations, possibly with interest. This claim made it sound as if the Fellowship leaders would be quite co-operative in helping people to leave, thus ensuring they need have little anxiety about how they would be treated were they to do so. I would suggest that for those who managed to disengage themselves from the Community (something which was even rarer for families than for individual brothers and sisters), the question of whether or not their capital would be returned was of secondary importance alongside all the other deliberations and choices they would have been struggling with whilst deciding whether or not to quit. There were far more complex and retentive issues we all had to weigh up and resolve other than those of our future financial welfare, even though all those who received capital reimbursement or other pecuniary support were, I'm sure, extremely thankful for it.

The existence of the refund provision didn't indicate a willingness of the Fellowship to engage with leavers in the conciliatory manner which was claimed. Nor were the "relief of need" payments provided for by the constitution handed out in the supportive way many were led to believe they would be. In my own case, for example, the only payment I received was for my flight to Jerusalem – and the implied "generosity" of it was something that Noel and others made much of afterwards. In fact, the flight cost less than the sum of money I donated following the sale of my precious HiFi unit. I had used pretty much the total sum of my wages from casual work – undertaken during vacation from university – to buy the equipment back in Easter 1977. Selling it so soon afterwards was as painful as making the bonfire to burn my small record collection. I had assumed the relatively small capital donation I made from the HiFi sale would be returned to me. It wasn't. And nor did anyone tell me I would need to *apply* for its return, something I would have been loath to do at the time. More significantly still; I had worked as a salaried employee of HOG Ltd. for two full years, and before that I'd worked on the farm as a general labourer and mechanic for *every* day of my university vacations. Despite the significant contribution I'd made to the Fellowship coffers over these four years (in kind and in pounds Stirling), when I left I was offered no financial help whatsoever – even though I went away with nothing but some books and clothes, and even though I had no career to fall back upon. So I repeat my claim that aspects of the constitution served as a protective firewall: they played a defensive role against external criticism but didn't, in practice, provide the safeguards which were claimed.

Closely allied to the constitution, as already mentioned, was the statement of faith and practice. This ran to forty articles and clarified our beliefs about theological issues such as "the trinity", "Christ the Messiah", "angels", "water baptism", "community", "the Bible", "exorcism", "celibacy", "male leadership", and "the last judgement". The all-embracing claim of the statement was that of being totally biblical, the Bible being the final arbiter of Christian faith. It included a complete recitation of "the Apostles Creed", "the Nicene Creed" and "the Athanasian Creed"; and it had been sent to Oxford-based theologians who were asked to check it for consistency and orthodoxy. Noel had always been determined that the Fellowship should be seen as a bona fide representation of radical but *orthodox* Christianity, and he'd been at pains to convey this by the inclusion of a much-shorter statement of faith printed on the notice sheet which was distributed at weekend meetings:

"This church upholds orthodox Christian truth, being reformed, evangelical and charismatic; practising believer's baptism and the New Testament reality of Christ's Church. We believe in God, Father, Son and Spirit; in the full divinity, atoning death, and bodily resurrection of the Lord Jesus Christ; and in the Bible as God's word, fully inspired by the Holy Spirit."

SC has written about his reaction to when the completed, full-length statement of faith was read aloud in chapel for the first time:

"The public reading in chapel was moving and some aspects were a little controversial."[20]

These are some of the statements – in a subsequently revised version – which may have raised eyebrows:

- "God's eternal purpose is to gain a people for His own possession and glory ... God made covenant with Abraham as the father of the chosen race of Israel. This promise is fulfilled through the New Covenant through Jesus Christ, which unites both Jews and Gentiles in the true Israel, the church of the living God.
- God's covenant people are not to love the world, nor the things in the world. As His temple they are to be a holy society that displays the fruits of righteousness and shows light to the world.
- God calls us to be holy, as He is holy. Where there is a consistent willful rejection of this call to holiness then apostasy must result.
- The regenerate should gather together in local Church-Communities in a voluntary covenant bond, with love and service, with various gifts and graces flowing through each member.
- Male and female are equal in new creation status, both being sons of God in Jesus Christ. In this present age, however, they are to be different in role, appearance and dress.
- There is no scriptural justification for keeping special days and seasons.
- Believers are to bear their own cross, suffer reproach and persecution for Christ's sake."[21]

The statement was, I believe, a genuine account of what we believed and how we lived – or at least a genuine account of the *theoretical* basis for our beliefs and lifestyle. It once again needs to be understood that the statement, together with the constitution, was part of the defensive firewall: what was written down and what actually happened didn't always sit together very snugly. Noel himself had much to answer for with regards to this discrepancy because of the unwavering way he controlled every aspect of our faith, lifestyle, and behaviour: he was a complete law unto himself and could deviate from his own proclaimed orthodoxy with impunity. I made specific reference to this issue in an entry I made in my sociological journal for Sunday December 7th. 1980. Something had happened which I thought was totally inconsistent with what we were *supposed* to believe about the "means of salvation".

One of our written articles of faith emphasized the need for God's mercy on our sins and the impossibility of finding salvation through our works but only through our trust in the person of Jesus Christ – good, sound, evangelical doctrine! But, on the Sunday in question, we had a young lad amongst us who'd only been "coming around" – as we called it – for a few weeks. We'd already given him a virtue name, however, so he'd become known as Mick "Accepted". Noel's preaching on that morning was – once again – on the theme of belonging to God within his kingdom. At one point he decided to address himself directly to Mick – someone who habitually wore a leather jacket. Noel told him quite specifically that he couldn't become a member of God's kingdom if he continued to insist on wearing his jacket. Apart from humiliating the young man, Noel had pinned his *true* theological colours to the mast: *salvation through a very blinkered interpretation of what it meant to lead a holy lifestyle.* Following Noel's further elucidation of what holiness meant with respect to how we dressed and looked, it was hardly surprising that conformity became increasingly prevalent. Very few of the brothers, for example, continued allowing their hair to grow beautifully long and curly, opting instead for the less flattering and less vain scissor-cut offered by those who had a "ministry" – a non-professional one – for haircutting. The results were unexcitingly uniform. Nor did they wear ragged jeans any longer, nor anything with individualistic flare. By and large, we became increasingly dependent on the rather dreary, cheap and sensible clothing which needed to be ordered internally from the central FDC. The move towards a very similar dress style was also true amongst the sisters. Quite a few of us sensed – and dreaded – that it wouldn't be long before we were expected to wear some kind of uniform.

Take another incident, too, that illustrates how careful we should be in accepting that the constitution and statement of faith were reliable as a means of illuminating what the Jesus Fellowship Church *really* believed and how it *really* worked. Several of the articles referred to matters of leadership and discipline within the church. From them, we understood that leaders were themselves – theoretically – ultimately accountable to the church members; and Noel frequently spoke of being subject to the body of elders as much as they were to him. The constitution reflected this in its requirement that every member of the JFCT should receive an annual "examination" to reaffirm their loyalty to, and agreement with, the faith and practice of the church. Elders were required to be examined annually by other elders.

Not many weeks after the constitution had been formally accepted by the church membership (more about this presently), I happened to be sitting alone in one of farm's rooms getting on with my studies when I heard a brother called Ed Hunt beginning a conversation with Noel in the farm's entrance hall. Ed was sometimes jokingly referred to as the Fellowship's archdeacon – the leading deacon. Appreciated by many as a long-standing senior elder, he also had an important administrative role – the senior event organizer if you like. I peered through the gap in the open door and saw that Noel was ensconced in his usual armchair close to the front door and Ed was actually crouched on his haunches in front of him.

'*I've been talking with a couple of other elders,*' Ed began courageously, '*and I've been delegated to come and talk with you, bro, about a rather delicate matter.*'

'*Oh dear, bro, I don't very much like the sound of this,*' said Noel – or words very much to that effect.

*'It's just that we were talking about how to organize the annual examinations for the elders when we realized, of course, that the constitution requires **everyone** to be examined – which includes yourself, bro.'* He paused for a moment before saying what he must have much rather not had to.

*'So we were wondering who will examine **you**?'*

It would have been oh-so-simple for Noel to nominate his right-hand man, Kelly: most of us would have felt he was the natural choice. Instead, however, Noel launched into an angry, petulant tirade about the pettiness of Ed's suggestion. With his voice still raised, as if he were preaching in chapel, he said the issue was just the kind of thing he'd feared with respect to the constitution, that there were those who would use certain of its articles for their own "selfish" and "manipulative" purposes.

'Of course I don't need to be examined myself!' he thundered.

Ed was then dismissed, very much with a flea in his ear. Was this, I wonder, what SC had meant when he wrote that Noel sometimes "roared at home"? The incident was actually of huge significance, giving the lie as it did to the Fellowship's claim of mutual accountability amongst the leadership – a principle that had supposedly been enshrined in the constitution. Noel held himself and his prophetic position with severe protective jealously, never fully able to subjugate his authority – or even his whims – to any challenge from other leaders. Simon has given us a somewhat different picture; but, then again, he never actually lived with Noel at the farm and probably didn't know him as some of us did. In his description of the "early days" at New Creation Farm, he tells us about Noel's willingness to let other leaders lead:

"Shortly after, somewhat apprehensively, Noel moved in and filled his little room with books. Surprisingly, he didn't take over! Noel had a great respect for Rufus' inspirations. Dave 'Elder' Lantsbery began pastoring the sisters and John [Gentle] led the brothers … During the evening grace times Noel would sit back and enjoy the ministry of his brothers and sisters. It felt good to be part of such a family and he sought to hear the wisdom of God through them. Community life required mutual submission. The lie was that independence brought fulfilment. It didn't."[22]

If only! If only this had been true, then everything may have turned out very differently. There was the incident concerning the talcum powder and deodorant, for example – trivial in one way; enormously significant in another. Perhaps I should call it "TalcumGate", or some such name. It was at some point during 1978 that Rufus and John Gentle decided we should stop using talcum powder and deodorant as aides to personal hygiene. Using these items, they explained to us, was just the thin end of the wedge which led to the use of cosmetics and scents: carnal indulgences which weren't necessary if we used soap when washing, bathing or showering. Exercising their authority as house elders, Rufus and John instructed the household deacons not to order any more of these luxuries. Word spread quickly to other households, who also implemented the prohibition: where the farm household led, others invariably followed.

Within a week or two, existing supplies of our pretty much bog-standard talcum and deodorant had been finished. Most of us just took it all on the chin, even though it seemed a bit severe and hard to get used to. To our surprise, though, at the next Wednesday-evening chapel meeting we were treated to a delightful little homily from Noel about the ancient Britons and how one could have smelt their encampments from miles away. Given our communal lifestyle, so he told us, we could end up in the same stinky state if we didn't use certain supplements to help us smell "nice". Needless to say, Noel himself was wedded to the antiperspirant toiletries we'd been using and, as was his wont, he asserted his authority from the chapel platform when a quiet word with Rufus and John would have been just as effective; there was no need to have humiliated them and forced them to make the policy U-turn which immediately followed – their leadership had been made to look limp in front of *everybody*.

As for Simon's description of Noel meekly sitting back during evening "grace times" – a euphemism – and enjoying the ministry of others... if Noel had something on his mind to say either before or after our evening meals, then he said it; as he did on that awful occasion I've already described when he kept everyone up until very late droning on and on about "taking the central ground". If Noel was happy to sit back and let the other elders "minister", then he did so; if he wanted the stage to himself, then he took it.

That any one person should ever have been allowed to exercise the absolute authority which Noel did is sometimes hard for observers to understand. It would seem to suggest that we were all little better than compliant vassals who'd surrendered every aspect of our independence to our overbearing leader. Even in the most tyrannical of secular regimes there are always those who will band together in the quest for liberation, and some of these will be prepared to endure torture, imprisonment and even death in pursuit of freedom for their fellow countrymen. *Where were these brave souls within the Jesus Fellowship?* Once in a very blue moon someone would summon enough composure and courage to indicate their disagreement with and disapproval of the Fellowship, as I guess I eventually did myself; but the invariable outcome of doing so was cessation of membership. Many, I'm sure, craved personal freedom from Noel's oppressive yoke and would have loved to challenge him on occasions; yet no one seemed able to fulfil such a longing whilst remaining part of either the Community or the broader Fellowship. Ultimately, those of us who were in some form of leadership need to accept that we ourselves, to a greater or lesser extent, were responsible – and therefore accountable – for the damage that resulted from allowing Noel to get away with his unchallenged dominion over the church for so long. We can offer naivety, immaturity, ignorance, coercion, brainwashing, confusion, poorly developed perception, and many other reasons for our behaviour, but we should never deceive ourselves into thinking we can absolve ourselves from responsibility for all that happened with the excuse that we were only doing what was expected of us.

Noel had managed to pummel us into believing he was one of God's prophets and that, in this capacity, what he was preaching to us was the anointed word of God. Should we have questioned his teaching, we would have been questioning the Almighty. This is beautifully illustrated by something I read in one of the letters which Pete Fincher – the young man who was killed in a motorbike accident – had written to his parents. Bob and Adelaide Fincher were kind enough to let me read and use the letters, which they'd kept. On one occasion Pete wrote:

"My best friend and I have been discussing whether Noel Stanton's teaching could possibly be wrong. But we are both agreed that since he preaches under the Spirit there is no possibility he could be."

These honest-but-revelatory words must surely be such as can only have come *straight from the mouths of babes and sucklings,* to coin an apt biblical quotation.

In the light of our surrender to dictatorial leadership, it's easy enough to understand why there were external critics who claimed we were brainwashed. But we were perfectly capable of shrugging this one off with a laugh:.

'Do we act like we've been brainwashed?' we would ask one another in a mock-zombie kind of voice.

Quite clearly we didn't – at least so far as our understanding about brainwashed behaviour went. In general we were healthy, well-nourished, often quite happy, and mentally alert – albeit that quite a few of us were frequently over fatigued and in need of a good long sleep. Besides, we hadn't ever been subjected to the kind of brainwashing techniques used by totalitarian regimes, nor the kind of one-on-one re-education sessions such as those used in room 101, the sinister brainwashing lair made famous in Orwell's novel, "1984". Those who made claims such as needing a helicopter to rescue us from the Community were actually scoring an own goal.

'Where,' we asked with bemusement, *'are the walls, the locked doors, or the guards who are forcing us to stay against our own will?'*

For me, part of the process of finally finding the wherewithal I needed to leave was admitting to myself that, despite our vociferous denials, I had indeed been brainwashed. I came to recognize that if I'd been able to somehow step outside of myself and look at everything perfectly objectively then I wouldn't be behaving, or thinking, in the way which I often did. The brainwashing had insidiously and unwittingly taken place in a number of ways: from the fear of disobeying God which Noel had instilled in us; from the exposure to frequently repeated themes concerning our membership of God's kingdom; from the near-constant requirement to confess any misgivings we might have had; from frequently being asked to raise our voices and hands in unison as an agreement that we were all of "one heart and mind"; from repeatedly singing about what happened to those who turned back and therefore betrayed God; and from the disciplinary processes imposed on us "for our spiritual good" or because there was some concern amongst the elders about our behaviour. Like admitting to being an addict, admitting to yourself that you *had* been brainwashed was a vital step in the process of enlightenment and then recovery.

Lest there should remain any doubt concerning Noel Stanton's iron grip over the entire faith and practice of the Jesus Fellowship Church, or over the introduction of the formal constitution as a means of not only consolidation but also as a screen to hide behind when required, then perhaps these might finally be laid to rest with a very brief explanation of how the constitution came to be ratified. It needed to be approved by a majority of Fellowship members[a] in order to achieve the legal status it required... I don't have a record of whether this was a simple majority or a higher percentage. Once the document had reached its final draft, its content was explained in some detail to all of the elders. Within each household a copy was made available for any brother or sister to consult, and everyone was quite at liberty to ask their own elder for any further explanation they may have required. It is extremely important to stress, however, that no formal opportunity was given for anyone to submit suggested *changes*, however small. Even so, the contention made by Noel and his lieutenants thereafter was that anyone *could* have offered suggested changes had they so wished... but evidently no one had wanted to. The truth is that we all knew better than to be accused of being critical, and therefore censured, by indicating anything which could have been construed as disagreement.

At the members-only Wednesday-evening meeting when the constitution was to be ratified and its sister document, the statement of faith and practice, was to be read out in full, those present – about four hundred people, I believe – were asked to vote for approval with a show of hands. One hundred percent of us indicated our consent, there being no abstentions nor anyone voting against. In future years, similar "extraordinary" meetings of the membership were required when additions or amendments to the constitution were proposed. No questions were ever raised on substantive issues or even points of order,

---

[a] Those who were contributing financially to the JFCT (Jesus Fellowship Community Trust) – virtually all of those living within the NCCC, and also recognized non-Community members of the JFC (Jesus Fellowship Church).

and the voting pattern was always the same: unanimous approval of every motion. Noel himself boasted that this was an indication of everyone being "of one heart and soul", but the truth is more correctly understood in the context of his coercive authority. Alarm bells should ring whenever there is such complete and consistent unanimity amongst so many people. I've recently renewed a friendship with Shaun, my erstwhile roommate from New Creation Farm who has spent most of his teenage and adult life in membership and is now incredibly glad to have been finally set free. One thing he has asked me is why there wasn't the sound of anyone banging a drum to warn about what was happening:

'Surely' he said, *'there must have been Christian leaders who understood the issues, weren't there?'*

The answer is that, yes, there *were* some. But the Fellowship did all it could to silence them or neutralize their criticism. Others, however, were duped and taken in; either that or they pursued the religious and spiritual equivalent of appeasement politics. Some would go so far as to become virtual collaborators, as we shall see.

As Noel pressed ahead with the institutionalization of the Fellowship's lifestyle and procedures, and as he also intensified and secured his own position of prophetic – or despotic – leadership, many felt and grieved the loss of something wonderful which we'd previously known. We grew weary, too, of the seemingly never-ending Quixotic fight against both real and illusionary enemies – against both corporeal ones in the here and now and against demonic ones in the spiritual theatre of warfare. We still had plenty to stir our hearts and plenty to occasion thanksgiving and rejoicing; but much of the sparkle had gone. Something about both the intensity of everything and the increasing formalization was having a definite dampening effect on the pioneering excitement which we'd once experienced together within our brotherhood.

A chapter endnote: Hypnotic influence and sleep paralysis.

There were times when I used to wonder if Noel had managed to exert some kind of hypnotic influence over us. But I usually ended up telling myself not to be so stupid. After I'd left the Fellowship, however, it certainly felt as if I'd woken up from some kind of trance, that I'd regained the ability to think clearly and see things as they really were once again. I have no wish whatsoever to press this line of thinking too far, which is why I'm including it purely as an endnote. All I want to offer amounts to little more than musings: the enquiry about things I experienced which I cannot properly account for but which I'm not quite able to forget about. I sensed having been exposed to experiences which were too powerful for me to do anything about other than wonder how it had all happened and what it had meant.

I knew from my sociological research that a technique used by cults as part of their indoctrination programme is to ensure members are kept in a state of continuous activity and therefore continuous fatigue. Professional interrogators are perfectly well aware, of course, that causing fatigue can be instrumental in breaking down a subject's resistance. I have never been able to accept that such a technique was used *deliberately* within the Fellowship as a means of control. And yet it's perfectly true that I for one felt perilously tired much of the time, and it's also true that this was a direct result of the lifestyle we led. There always seemed to be *something* going on, which included an untold number of hours spent in group meetings both large and small; and these were often at the end of long hard days, especially for those of us who worked on the farm. Further still, any theoretical "spare time" we had was largely taken up for many of us with evangelistic pursuits of one kind or another. Straight after work on a Friday, for example, evangelistic teams headed off to nearby towns and spent three or four hours trying to spread the faith, either to passers-by in the street or to those who frequented the clubs and pubs. It was tough going, often with little obvious reward. And we always ended up back at one or other of the Community houses, where we took some of those we'd met for late-night refreshments and further conversation. Busy, busy, busy, and yet even more busy; that's how life sometimes felt. We didn't have "days off" as such, nor any holidays as people generally know them. I remember joking – well, semi-joking – in the farm workshop with my friend, Steve Stalwart, about how the first thing we'd do when we got to heaven was find a really comfy armchair and have bloody good rest – although we didn't swear of course.

We grabbed the opportunity to sleep, to "crash out", whenever we could. Often, we found an opportunity to do so for about an hour before we went off to the evening meeting on a Sunday afternoon. We went to various different houses for a meal after the morning meeting, and later on – after we'd fulfilled whatever other responsibilities we may have had – quite a few brothers would converge on the household bedrooms to "bag" whatever spare bed was available and get a fragment of the sleep we desperately needed.

As a young adult in the Community I experienced what is known as "sleep paralysis" on three or four occasions. This is when – typically whilst falling asleep or waking up – you find yourself completely unable to move or speak. All you can do is wait until the paralysis lifts, usually within a few minutes. The first episode I ever had was especially frightening, all the more so on account of the accompanying hallucinatory sensations of elevation and piercing noise. It's only with the advent of the internet that I've discovered how common these experiences are, particularly amongst certain groups – including students and those with mental illness. Extreme fatigue can be a contributory factor to the event.

The hallucinatory aspect of the experience is less common than the paralysis itself, although it can present itself in several different ways. One of these is the sensation of severe chest compression, or even suffocation. Those who've experienced this have sometimes also reported seeing and feeling some oppressive being – known as an "incubus" – forcing itself on them. There is a famous painting called "The Nightmare" which depicts such a scene. It was painted by the Swiss artist, Henri Fuseli, in 1781.

I had the misfortune to experience such an episode of sleep paralysis and incubus visitation when I was waking from a Sunday afternoon "crash out" at the farm. The incubus pressing down and smothering me as I lay there took the form of Noel Stanton himself. Strangely, it didn't frighten or disturb me nearly as much as may have been expected. It was one of those times when I knew only too well that I simply couldn't risk dwelling on what had happened or trying to understand it. I just had to accept the experience and get on with life, not even knowing to what extent there had been any reality to it – maybe it had all been a kind of particularly weird dream? This way of dealing with it was all the more necessary given how it would be many years before I'd find out about sleep paralysis as a recognized neuro-scientific phenomenon. Until then, I just lived with the knowledge of what I'd experienced and tucked it away in my mind as deeply as I possible could; so deeply in fact that I virtually forgot about it for a long, long time.

Could there be any explanation of what happened beyond that of a medical condition which is known to affect certain people, particularly students and those suffering from mental illness and extreme fatigue? Is there any other way of understanding it? Likewise those thoughts I had of having been hypnotically influenced: impossible, surely? Since leaving the Community, I have never had another episode of sleep paralysis.

CHAPTER EIGHTEEN: Kingdom businesses

Without having yet explained about the Community – or "kingdom" – businesses in much detail, I feel sure that by now it will have become clear there were many who worked for one or other of these companies: HOG, Skaino Services, and Towcester Building Supplies (TBS) being the principal employers. When trying to explain to others the purpose of our businesses and how they worked, we often used Skaino Services as an example – especially because of its name, which had been chosen to reflect the apostle Paul's remunerative occupation. Skaino is an ancient Greek word meaning "tent making", a trade which Paul pursued in order to finance his apostolic ministry. Noel had often stressed how, in like manner, those who worked for a kingdom business would have greater flexibility to pursue Fellowship-related ministries – especially evangelism – than those in secular employment. Another purpose was to help provide the income which the Fellowship needed in order to both function and grow. And this profit motive, I believe, was a feature of the businesses which was of far greater importance in actual practice than providing, as was often claimed, the opportunity for flexible working. On a day-to-day basis, employees of HOG, Skaino Services and TBS worked in much the same way, and for much the same daily and annual hours – if not more – as those in similar agricultural, building or retail occupations: involvement in Fellowship ministries largely took place in the evenings and weekends, or during annual leave.

Work at New Creation Farm enabled the employment of about ten people as the main operational team. Activities included the rearing and raising of cattle, sheep and pigs; beekeeping and honey production; poultry farming; and extensive cultivation of potato crops. There were also about 20 acres or more of gooseberry bushes, apple and plum orchards, and strawberry fields. New Creation Farm itself covered about 64 acres, and the immediately adjacent Shalom farm added about 40 more to the total. In 1978, 40 more acres on the other side of the A5 towards Stowe were bought at what was locally considered to be the breathtaking price of £98,000 – £2,450 per acre. During the grass-cutting and crop-harvesting seasons, our total acreage was extended through financial agreements struck with other farmers to bale the hay and straw lying in their fields and transport it all back to our own farmland to be used for feeding and bedding the cattle and pigs over the winter months. Once, I had to drive a tractor and hay-laden trailer back from a field which was five miles away from the farm. The country roads were typically narrow and twisty, so it was a task I had absolutely no wish to repeat.

Within the core team of farm employees, Roger and Ian – who both had muscles like those of a body builder – were the pig-and-poultry men, Steve and myself were tractor drivers and mechanics, Dave was our bee-keeper and fruit expert (as well as being a walking encyclopaedia concerning everything rural), Nigel was another tractor driver, Irene worked in the packing shed and produced the bottled honey, and finally there were two more Steves (Zealous and Genuine) and John who were our tough-as-nails cattlemen. Nigel and Dave shared farm-management duties between themselves, which included responsibility for organizing all the many voluntary workers who came to the farm more or less every day either as visitors or as those on the threshold of becoming members. They were also overseers for those occasions, notable during the fruit harvests, when the plethora of Fellowship members whose help had been called on needed adequate organization and supervision. On a more wide-ranging basis, Noel himself kept a close eye on everything; and he often referred to himself as being the overall farm manager – something which caused noticeable friction with Dave and Nigel on occasions.

Another of HOG's arms was the "Goodness Foods" operation, essentially several health-food shops which would expand to become a regional chain over the following decades. There were eight who worked in the four shops we had in 1981, which included my roommate at Stockton House, Nick, who had the enviable physique of an athlete, tightly curled gingery hair, and was – as you may by now suppose – immensely handsome. In a previous life he'd been a beach-buggy-driving cool dude, now he was manager of the Weedon shop, where he worked alongside Janey – the dark-haired, attractively lithesome Scottish sister who'd melted his soft heart. Another four worked in the fledgling distribution warehouse that had opened in Daventry, and two more in the artisan bakery shop at Braunstone – including Big Trev, the baker himself. Alan, a laid-back, good-natured, cheerful, dependable brother, drove the HOG delivery lorry with its highly visible, bright-yellow curtain sides; and we mustn't forget the couple who worked at the Jeans Plus fashion shop: Kerry, the confident, straight-talking, huskily spoken manager; and Penny, the beautiful sister who – alone amongst the sisterhood – was able to wear jeans and show off just how good they looked on her model-like figure. That makes a total of seventeen.

Skaino Services employed the range of tradesmen typical of a small to medium-sized building firm. Dave, Rufus and Shaun were chippies; Alan and Ken were brickies; John and Ralph were plumbers and heating engineers; another Dave and Ken were plasterers and painter-decorators; Jim and Jo were general labourers; and Kelly was boss of the whole show – as well as helping out with most of the trades wherever and whenever needed. In addition to these, Skaino also employed three other brothers who, quite literally, kept the whole of the Jesus Fellowship Church on the road. As well as being hugely popular, patient and unfailingly cheerful, Jim and Derek were mechanics who kept the whole fleet of minibuses and household cars in good repair. Chris, an ex-hippy busker from London who was one of the Fellowship's "originals", also worked in the garage doing bodywork repairs and paint spraying. Lastly, but very definitely not least, was Russel the lorry driver. I make that to have been sixteen.

When we add on Lizzy (Noel's amazing personal secretary who somehow managed to remain helpful and happy even after being held in the farm office as his hostage every day), Cyril and Victor (architects from Heritage Design), Martin and his team from newly opened TBS, and a few others not accounted for within the formal fold of the recognized businesses, then we can reckon on about fifty people as those who "worked for the kingdom" during the time period I was familiar with. In keeping with the vision of creating as many Paulean-style, tent-making jobs as possible – to facilitate increased kingdom-building flexibility and, of course, increased profit – the number of employees in Fellowship businesses continued to increase year on year.

I have already indicated on several occasions how much I disagreed with – and disapproved of – the business model that Noel had fashioned: it was a key feature of the lengthy discussions I had with him when I was leaving. Anticipating events which will be properly covered in later chapters, I need to explain at this juncture that during the early years of the new millennium I created a website aimed at informing people about the dangerous practices – as I perceived them – of the Jesus Fellowship, now more commonly known as the Jesus Army. The Fellowship's business model was one of the key subjects which I attempted to spotlight, especially because I'd been astonished and angered by the brazen hypocrisy contained within a report about Goodness Foods called "Principles Before Profit" which I'd read on the BBC news website. If ever there was a red rag to a bull in the context of my dealings with the Jesus Fellowship, then this was one of the reddest:

"From the outside, Goodness Foods based in Daventry, Northamptonshire, could be any other company. It employs around 70 people and has a turnover of around £10 million a year. But go inside and you'll see they do things a little bit differently.

Ethical

Take the lunch break for instance. There's no canteen but a prayer meeting and hymn-singing, which the vast majority of staff, as Christians, attend every day. The company manufactures and distributes health foods, but is special in that it claims to run itself to the strictest ethical standards. All members of staff are part-owners of the business through share ownership.

Sharing

They all receive the same salary, from the warehouse workers and fork-lift drivers, through to the directors, and everyone is consulted before business decisions are made. Any money the company makes is either re-invested in the business, or donated to local charitable causes. In short, Goodness Foods, as its name suggests, tries to adhere to the ethos of principles before profits. But in the cut-throat world of business just how realistic is such a worthy aim?

'I'd love to see other companies do what we do,' says Lesley Cutts, marketing director at Goodness Foods.

'We are all about using profits for charitable causes and making life better for other people, rather than just putting money in directors' pockets.'

'We're here to prove it can be done, and that it works financially.'

Responsible

As well as adopting a more ethical approach, the company tries to be environmentally responsible. Members of staff are encouraged to share transport for example. On the recruitment level the company offers jobs to people who would otherwise sometimes struggle to find employment.

'Here we employ people who have been homeless, those who've had drink and drug problems, ex-cons, and asylum seekers, and they get restored here,' says Lesley.

'We train them to use a fork-lift truck, and they can take these skills elsewhere. It's a mobile environment where people choose to work.'

Chris Meadows has worked at Goodness Foods for several years. He used to be an alcoholic and drug addict, but he's adamant that this special working environment has enabled him to rebuild his life.

'Goodness Foods has done a lot for me really,' he says.

'I never worked before, just thieved. I'm a recovering alcoholic, and I enjoy it here.'

'It's given me a use after what I've gone through, and something to live for.'

Profitable

As a business, Goodness Foods' principle aim must be of course to make money, and in this respect it continues to go from strength to strength. The firm is rapidly developing its online operation, Goodness Direct, and the company is now one of the country's biggest distributors of health-foods. It all goes to show perhaps that businesses don't always have to be cut-throat and ruthless to be profitable."[23]

I know that Lesley, whom I knew personally, was only acting as a mouthpiece for others, and ultimately for Noel himself; but I'm sure she must feel deeply ashamed when she reflects on the deceits and outright lies that have been attributed to her. It could be argued that much, perhaps most, of the article's content is *technically* correct – or very nearly. This makes it all the more reprehensible that the Fellowship leaders were willing to deliberately utilize deception and twist the truth in order to portray the business operations as being something other than what they truly were, to effectively promote black as being white. Without unpicking all the distortions contained in the article, I shall focus on a couple of the main ones.

The very notion of *principles before profits* is a blatant reversal of how the businesses actually operated. You will remember, perhaps, the anecdote I told of how Noel reprimanded certain elders for being "wet" on account of their failure to accept the need for what many would call cut-throat trading practices. He used the example of a man who had bought back his company in order to prevent the redundancies being proposed by those who had recently bought it from him. "*The man was wet*," he had yelled at us, evoking the Thatcherite principles of putting profit first. And nor did Noel lose any sleep concerning the consequences of the abnormally low wage-costs which the JFC companies enjoyed; i.e. the consequential threats this posed to other local businesses who were unable to compete on a level playing field. That all employees were paid the same is quite true. But it wasn't on account of any inherent policy to promote socialist egalitarianism. In fact, Noel had once referred to socialist policies as being *the acme of self-interest*. Given that no one received any individual benefit from their wage (which simply went into the common-purse account), it made absolutely no personal difference to anyone how much salary they received. Everyone was equally paid a minimal wage in order to keep costs as low as possible and thereby maximize profit. This is what I meant in my claim that the BBC article contained statements which may have been technically correct but were totally untrue with respect to the underlying principle, or principles, claimed for them. Everyone did indeed receive the same wage, but not on account of ethical policy – principles before profit – but on account of business expediency – profit before principles.

Even more egregious is the reported claim that *any money the company makes is either re-invested in the business or donated to local charitable causes.* Lesley herself is quoted as having said, "we are all about using money for charitable causes". Where did you leave the voice of your conscience when you spoke those words, Lesley? Were you satisfied with being able to claim that what you'd said had been *technically* true? True, that is, to those in the know; but totally untrue in the impression given to both the BBC reporter and all those reading the article. I shall explain about the charitable donations more comprehensively in just a while. For now, however, it's sufficient to say that the charitable donations made from the Fellowship businesses were exclusively to their *own* ones: the Jesus Army Charitable Trust and the Jesus Fellowship Life Trust. Anyone reading the BBC article would most probably have imagined that the Fellowship, through its businesses, had given financial support to independent local charities which, for example, may have helped homeless people or promoted environmental welfare. They would have been totally wrong. As already explained, Noel vehemently refuted the conventional understanding of Christian charity. He claimed, for example, that many of the destitute were in such a position because of God's judgement on them. He insisted that seeking to alleviate destitution with either financial or material help was, of itself, a mistake. It beggars belief, therefore, that the Fellowship – through its mouthpieces – could have stooped so low as to have given an impression of charitable support that was entirely non-existent.

Before returning to the 1980s in the next chapter I'd now like to jump ahead to 2009, the year when I prepared various in-depth articles to read on the website I'd created: **jeanni.org** – **JE**sus **A**rmy **N**ews **N**etworking and **I**nformation. By reproducing one of these articles – revised and shortened – I hope to consolidate an understanding of the Jesus Fellowship's business structure, something I believe was of fundamental importance in its overall development and inextricably linked to the doctrine of "the two kingdoms". Although the businesses had grown significantly by 2009, and the charitable structures had matured considerably, what I shall describe will be immediately recognizable to those who were my contemporary members – the fundamental ethics of how everything worked also remained much the same. Rather than laboriously reinvent the wheel by completely rewriting my original article, therefore, I've integrated it into this chapter in the belief that it will be the best way to provide the comprehensive understanding I'm aiming for. *Please keep in mind, then, that what follows was essentially written in 2009 for the JEANNI website* (with most grammar, punctuation and spelling mistakes retained).

1. JFC businesses and "the two kingdoms"

A central feature of the JFC's belief system is the concept of there being two kingdoms: the kingdom of God and the kingdom of the world. All of us are deemed to belong to one or other of these kingdoms. Naturally, members of the JFC believe themselves to be part of the kingdom of God; and whilst they acknowledge that this kingdom has other inhabitants who aren't JFC members, they believe themselves to be the unique expression of it in modern day Britain by virtue of their community-based structure – a continuation of the model established by the very first Christian church in Jerusalem where the members had "everything in common" and shared all of their possessions (New Testament: second chapter of Acts).

The kingdom of God, then, isn't some linguistic concept to categorize a group of people: so far as the JFC is concerned, it's just as real as the kingdom of Great Britain. It is to be found wherever Christian brothers and sisters unite together in "covenanted" relationships with one another. You need to look behind the exuberant attention-grabbing covers of the JA street papers and publicity material to discover what the JFC is *really* about. What you'll find out is the ambition to build "Zion", a "city on a hill", the "new Jerusalem". The concept of belonging to the kingdom of God, or Zion, is made perfectly clear in one of the Jesus Army's "Flame" leaflets, also called "Zion: City of God".[24]

'Only as we gather, like the first Christians, in a community of "one heart and soul",[Acts 4:32] does God's Zion really shine out as light to the world... for us, that has meant setting aside every other interest so that a "Zion church" can arise in beauty in our midst. It has involved a lot of repentance, sacrifice, forsaking of the world, and coming together in continuous covenant love. But it's the warm brotherhood of Jesus that's good news to the poor. It's God's kingdom.' [25]

What you won't read about in the promotional literature, either, is the harsh spiritual attitude which lay behind the creation of the JFC businesses. I discovered it for myself as a naive twenty-year-old and have never been able to forget it; nor have I ever been given cause to suppose it has been renounced. Shocked at why one of the shops was selling tight-fitting jeans, Christmas boxes, and pseudo-eastern paraphernalia (products denounced as "worldly" within the terms of the JFC's radical Christianity), I asked Noel Stanton, the senior pastor, for an explanation. *'What you've got to understand, bro',* he told me, *'is that in our businesses we are robbing the kingdom of the world in order to build the kingdom of God.'*

In other words, the end justifies the means. Provided nothing intrinsically wrong is happening, the *methods* – the *means* – of "liberating" money from the kingdom of world don't have to be ones which square with one's own spiritual values and beliefs; all that really matters is to ensure the *end* use of the money should be consistent with building the kingdom of God. The chill I felt when I realized the implications of this was a very cold one; and I would soon discover that the end-justifies-means approach toward business life had many practical implications I considered to be unacceptable. In this respect, nothing has changed.

Once you've understood the core idea about resources being transferred between kingdoms, you will recognize it repeatedly as you read through the JFC "Flame" leaflet on the subject of "Wealth Creation". Consider the following statement:

'As Christians it is our privilege to transfer wealth from Satan's rule to God's, to be used for the growth of His kingdom.' [26]

That the so-called "kingdom businesses"[a] of the JFC are essentially all about "robbing the kingdom of the world – Satan's kingdom – in order to build the kingdom of God", there surely can't be any doubt; and nor can there be any concerning the adaptation of the end-justifies-the-means approach. Put another way; within the JFC businesses, lifestyle values are subordinate to commercial decisions. This is made explicit by reference to the choice of goods and services for sale:

'It does not matter what the goods or services are, so long as they are basically honourable. What matters is that they are something others desire and are prepared to pay for.'[27]

No matter, then, that the businesses thrive on the sale of products denied to their own members. The ethical black hole is apparently plugged by the ultimate use to which the funds are put – building the kingdom of God; and in particular its local expression as represented by the JFC. To my own way of thinking, however, the JFC business foundation and rationale is extremely hypocritical; especially when so much emphasis is given to the "goodness" theme without there being any genuine interest in the doomed kingdom of the world, except to rob it of its wealth and transfer as many of its people as possible into the kingdom of God.

2. JFC businesses and charitable giving

Noel Stanton, chairman of the Jesus Fellowship Community Trust (the non-charitable trust that holds all the wealth of the JFC and the House of Goodness group of businesses), has often berated other Christians for giving to Third World charities. Distressingly, he has claimed it is tantamount to wasting thousands of pounds of God's money by supporting people under the judgment of God. Given my own convictions about how we should respond to world poverty, famine and disaster, I've always been implacably opposed to the conclusions which derive from Stanton's two-kingdom preaching – and especially the inevitable effect it has on business operations. Using money in charitable support of welfare programs which seek to alleviate hardship and poverty, and especially using it to try and address the root causes of poverty, is not considered to be "God's work". God's work, according to the JFC, is inextricably tied up with "building His kingdom".

---

[a] How the businesses are referred to in the "take money from the world" section of Wealth Creation leaflet

You might think the situation was otherwise when you read certain articles about the businesses on the Jesus Army website. You might think that the businesses are there almost as a protest against the profit-motivated businesses of the world and that charitable giving is something to be applauded, not questioned. But questions *have* to be asked – and answered. Why? Because, to use a fashionable term, the JFC "spin" makes it very difficult to fully understand exactly what's going on.

The latest accounts which, at the time of writing, are publicly available for the House of Goodness (HOG) group of companies cover the twelve-month period up to 31st. December 2008. These show an income – turnover – of nearly £22,000,000 (twenty-two million pounds)[28] with a declared gross profit of just over £5,500,000 (five-and-a-half million pounds).[29] From this, £350,000 was given to the Jesus Army Charitable Trust under gift aid. In previous years, such as the year ending 31st. December 2005, a charitable donation was also given to the Jesus Fellowship Life Trust (the sum was £50,000 in 2005). **No donations to any other charities are recorded in the HOG company accounts.**

So, to follow the trail of money that constitutes the charitable giving of the businesses, we need to look at how it is used by these JFC-linked trusts.

The Jesus Army Charitable Trust (JACT).

When the Fellowship talks about giving hundreds of thousands pounds a year to "local charity", the main beneficiary is the JACT – whose declared charitable objectives are as follows:

'To assist people in need or suffering hardship because of their social and economic circumstances, to advance the Christian religion through the provision of places of worship and to provide facilities for recreation in the interests of social welfare.'[30]

These objectives are similar, no doubt, to those of many other Christian charities. But we need to be clear that the kind of charity being promoted, together with the money to finance it, remains entirely bound up with institutions and activities that are all part and parcel of the JFC "family" and its way of life. This is declared explicitly in the statement from the JACT trustees concerning how they are going to meet their charitable objectives:

'The current strategy for meeting these objectives is the operating of Jesus Centres providing care, worship and social facilities in major towns and cities around the United Kingdom.'[31]

This strategy can be spelt out in pounds and pence as follows:

The total gifted income of the JA Charitable Trust for the twelve-month period up to 31st. December 2008 was just over £1,000,000.[32] As already noted, £350,000 came directly from the HOG group of businesses and the bulk of the rest from either the non-charitable Jesus Fellowship Community Trust (JFCT – not to be confused with the charitable JACT) or members of the JFC through the household common purse surpluses. With the addition of funds from sales and interest, the total income was £1,337,326. From this total, £783,043 was spent in pursuit of the charitable objectives; all of it essentially related, either directly or indirectly, with operating the various JFC Jesus Centres around the country. The remainder, £554,283, was put into a holding fund which had accumulated over the years to nearly £5,000,000 (five million pounds).[33]

Collectively, these figures conclusively demonstrate that charitable donations from the JFC businesses simply end up – put crudely – sloshing around within the Jesus Fellowship itself. *This is entirely consistent with what I explained earlier concerning the JFC vision of building the localised expression of the "kingdom of God".* **The important thing to take note of is the END use of the declared charitable giving from the businesses.**

Jesus Fellowship Life Trust.

This charity received £25,000 from the HOG businesses in 2004 and £50,000 in 2005. Its declared charitable objective is as follows:

'The promotion of the Christian Faith.'[34]

The strategy for initially meeting this objective is:

'By supporting the charitable activities of the Jesus Fellowship Church. This is achieved through provision and promotion of public meetings and evangelistic activities, provision of literature and publicity, the production and sale of Christian resources and financial assistance to relieve material need.'[35]

Total gifted income during the twelve-month period up to 31st Dec 2005 (which includes the £50,000 gift from HOG and £350,000 from the JFCT) was just over £500,000.[36] Expenditure went principally on the organization of JFC-related meetings and evangelistic events, including associated literature and advertising. Only £8,982 went to "relief of need", although there is no further specific information about how it was apportioned. Relief-of-need payments are, of course, sometimes made to support members who have left and subsequently find themselves pretty much destitute. These aside, relief-of-need payments are made within the context of the charity's objective, *promoting the Christian faith,* or – to use more informal language – *spreading the gospel.* To refer once again to the "Wealth Creation" Flame leaflet:

*'The more money we take for God, the more we can make property and facilities, vehicles and equipment, literature and resources, bursary funding and **charitable relief available to spread the gospel.'*** (my emphasis)

Consider also what the JFC has to say, specifically, on the theme of *spreading the gospel* and the bigger picture then begins to come into focus and take shape:

'Without a "Zion church", our evangelism would be a flop. That's because it's only when God blesses our oneness that we can lead people to Christ. Equally, it's only when some people feel the genuineness of brotherly love that they have any desire to find Christ for themselves. But that's what the Lord predicted.[John 13:35]
Almost daily now, through the warmth and energy of the gathered church, we see Jesus healing wounds, bringing dead souls to life and baptising them in the Holy Spirit. Amongst us, new brothers and sisters are nurtured in a "family" atmosphere of togetherness, acceptance and patient love. "Zion" is a fruitful mother.[Is. 49:18-20][Is. 60:4][Is. 66:8] Without her many would go backwards.'[37]

So, spreading the gospel and "building Zion" are, effectively, one and the same thing. Likewise, charitable relief has to be understood within the same overall context. All roads lead back to the building the kingdom of God and the JFC's belief that this needs to be achieved through local church growth.

In summary, I've shown how the charitable giving of the HOG companies remains within the family of trusts that are an integral part of the JFC. Resources that have been taken from the kingdom of the world are ultimately used "for God" in ways which contribute to the establishment of Zion – or building the kingdom of God. Ultimately, these are terms which refer to the local gathering of God's people – the church – and therefore relate back to the JFC itself.

Personal Comment:

If there were one reason beyond all others for my disagreeing with the JFC, then it would be the alienation from other people that results from their rigorously "Calvinistic" approach to the fate of all those "lost" people out there in the kingdom of the world; the people who can only be helped by exposing them to the good news of salvation in Christ; the people for whom we have no other responsibility than to reach out and pluck them from the jaws of hell.

This means that the next time you see a terrified, starving, mutilated African child on the television, a child whose parents had fled their village in order to escape the rampages of a militia bent on ethnic cleansing, or a child whose parents had just been blown to pieces by a land mine, then you need to give yourself a bloody good talking to if you feel like ringing up a charitable help-line number to pledge a financial donation. DON'T WASTE YOUR MONEY! Especially don't waste it if you are a Christian! The money you have is money that has been plundered from Satan's kingdom and you shouldn't carelessly allow it to slip from your grasp by supporting those who are facing God's judgement.

Forgive me, please, for resorting to such dramatic, strident and emotional sarcasm, but the previous paragraph *precisely* illustrates the logic of what Noel Stanton taught us about the plight of orphaned children in the Third World and how we should respond. And the foundational principles of how money should and shouldn't be used are built into the warp and woof of the JFC businesses themselves. It's easy enough for Noel to make some relatively bland justification of his position such as *"we don't believe God is calling on the JFC to support Third World charities"* (which is what, in effect, he's done in his published interview with Roger Forster),[38] but it looks far more unpleasant and unpalatable when the full implications of his teaching about *"not wasting money on those who are under God's judgement"* are spelt out in the way I've just done – something I felt necessary to drive home just how hard it was for some of us to stomach.

Even so, there are those who accuse us JFC "critics" of being, at best, unfair and unreasonable, and, at worst, of being agents of the Enemy – and all kinds of things in-between; bitter and twisted, for example. Will someone please answer me how it is that ANYONE can harden their hearts to the very real plight of the young African orphans I've described? And if there are those of us who have felt strongly enough about how wrong – and even wicked – the consequence of Noel Stanton's teaching is, strongly enough to make a stand and speak out, then those of you who have dismissed us as being misguided – or worse – should be ashamed of yourselves.

Furthermore, if there are any Christian leaders who want to cosy up alongside the Jesus Army and disdainfully dismiss opposition to them as "amusing" (see the introduction to "Fire in Our Hearts"), then you too should take a long hard look at what is going on in inside. I would suggest you are either gullible or extremely blinkered.

I personally have a deep-rooted conviction that colour, sex, sexuality, gender identity, age, race and creed are of no importance whatsoever in terms of the responsibilities I believe I have as one human being to another. If, somehow or another, my charity is influenced or limited by any evangelistic desire to "spread God's word", then I consider it to be no charity at all. In fact I would consider it to be tainted and corrupt. When I give charitably, I hope it is either because it feels "right" to do so or because my heart has been touched. Anyone who denies me the freedom to act according to my conscience like this denies me my humanity... and I think I may as well not be alive if forced to accept such constraints.

I hope this goes some way to explaining why I'm so vehement in my opposition to the whole concept of "robbing the kingdom of the world in order to build the kingdom of God".

3. JFC businesses and "worldy" businesses

Two kingdoms: God's and the world's. It follows that if there are "kingdom businesses" then there are also "worldly businesses". In referring to them like this, it's inevitable they should be contrasted with one another and seen to have totally different agendas, one for God and one for Satan. To think of "non-kingdom" businesses as belonging to Satan may seem a bit extreme, but it's implicit – if not *explicit* – in the two-kingdoms' concept. Here's another quote from the Wealth Creation leaflet:

'All we own needs to be given to God. If we think of money, possessions or property as 'ours', then selfishness still grips our hearts and our wealth still belongs to Satan!'

So worldly businesses that don't have the explicit objective of giving their money to God but consider the profit they make to be their own are serving Satan – whether they realize it or not. Once again, this way of thinking has profound consequences for the attitudes and actions it leads to. Perhaps the most heinous consequence, from my own experience, was the way some members became dismissive and completely careless about the fate of *any* businesses apart from our own JFC ones and those which they – the JFC ones – needed to interact with, for supplies or sales by way of example. To these members, what happened to worldly businesses outside the orbit within which the HOG companies operated was of no consequence: they could be treated as entirely dispensable and driven to the wall for all that anyone cared. It was an attitude, of course, which was replicated in the attitudes held towards worldly people in general.

We also need to understand how the wage structure of the JFC businesses facilitated a considerable commercial advantage over their worldly competitors – and it continues to do so. When I worked at the farm, full-time employees of HOG were only actually paid for a limited number of hours each week and the remaining hours were deemed to be voluntary. Obviously this had benefits, not only in smaller wage bills but also in reduced social security and tax bills. Consider the following example.

During the year ended 31st. December 2004, the HOG group of companies employed one hundred and ninety-three staff. The total wage bill – excluding employers' social security payments – was £1,825,446. This works out to an average wage of £9,458, which is considerably lower than the national average of £21,840 in the same period.[39]

But there were, of course, industry variations which affected salaries; and I don't have specific information about the national part-time to full-time ratios which would be needed for an accurate evaluation and comparison. So, to make a more convincingly equitable illustration, I've compared the wage bill between the JFC-owned Towcester Building Supplies – TBS – and another building supplier close to where I live, Birtley Building Products – BBP. The average wage bill for TBS in 2004 was £9,945 and for BBP it was £19,968. I also found it interesting to note that the employers' social security payments were £578 per employee for TBS and £2,085 for BBP. *The total average annual staff cost for TBS, then, was £10,523; and for BBP it was £22,053.*

This wage structure was perfectly legal and continues to be so. But to my own way of thinking it's morally wrong for at least two reasons. Firstly, it gives the JFC businesses an unfair trading advantage over local competitors not linked in any way to product quality or productivity. And, secondly, it involves an avoidance of contributions to public funds normally incurred by corresponding businesses: funds we all rely on, for example, to fund the welfare system of which we can still be rightfully proud.

The JFC will defend itself in terms of the result – building Zion, where, amongst other things, vulnerable and wounded people can find shelter and employment. As I see matters, however, the outcome of *anything* must be corrupted if the means to achieve it are ethically wrong; so the much-vaunted "good works" which the JFC frequently refer to both on their website and in their literature ought not be taken at face value. Claims that needy people such as the homeless and addicts are being offered new opportunities is often used to slam the door shut on further criticism about the JFC's wealth-creation methods. Such claims, however, aren't sustainable when set alongside the motivations and operational methods of the kingdom businesses and charities.

None of this is armchair pontification: local businesses really *have* felt the pinch! On August 7th. 1981 the Northants Chronicle and Echo ran an article under the heading: *"Jesus Group 'Threat to Business' Claim"*. It began by explaining how a Daventry-based builders' merchant, SRBE Daventry Ltd., was losing customers to TBS because of being seriously undercut on the price of many products. Mr. Goad, from SRBE, is quoted as saying:

'TBS is now undercutting so drastically that they do not appear to be running on a commercial basis. Things like cement and sand are considerably cheaper there and we are losing custom.'

The Chronicle and Echo reported that it had also received complaints concerning Skaino Services Ltd. Mr. Ron Olivera, of Drayton Heating and Plumbing, had told the Echo he was unable to compete with Skaino. He said:

'I submitted a £50,000 tender for work on the Wheatsheaf Hotel which is being renovated in Daventry. I kept my estimates very tight but I understand Skaino won the contract and I understand on a figure considerably lower than mine.

I believe that Skaino operates on much lower labour overheads. I don't mind fair competition but I cannot match them.'

The article's closing comment was that a Jesus Fellowship spokesman had offered a "no comment" reply when asked about the criticism. Within the Northants farming community, too, there has been both surprise and consternation at the amount the JFC businesses have been able to spend on land and property purchases. Of course, none of this matters if you subscribe to the ideology of the two kingdoms and are therefore unconcerned about what happens to worldly businesses and their staff. However, in just the same way that I oppose the rampant march of economic muscle in the capitalistic business world – a march that has little regard for those unfortunate enough to find themselves in its path – I also oppose the economic muscle which the JFC businesses are able to flex by virtue of their uncompetitive operational structure.

CHAPTER NINETEEN: Hoodwinking and kingdom secrets

The Wednesday-evening meetings at Bugbrooke chapel had been phased out by 1981, much to the relief of neighbouring residents, I'm sure: the noise of several hundred people arriving and departing, together with all the associated minibus activity, must have been a continual irritant even though we behaved as respectfully as possible. Nor do I suppose I was the only one who offered prayerful thanks for what I perceived to be deliverance from having to attend them. I remember many late evenings when it felt virtually impossible to keep my weary little peepers open and Noel's voice had become nothing more than a relentless, unwelcome drone. I used to sometimes fantasize about bringing a white flag to chapel with me so that I could wave it about and shout, '*I surrender! Please, please let me go home and get some sleep.*'

As mentioned earlier on, these were the occasions when Noel shared what he referred to as "kingdom secrets" – aspects of our lifestyle which were deemed too hot to be handled by those who didn't have a "kingdom heart". The danger, Noel explained, was that these pearls of precious wisdom might not be understood or appreciated by some, and such people could well use the subject matter they'd become privy to as a tool to use against us, to smite us with. This didn't mean the meetings were entirely restricted to existing members, but we were each charged with ensuring – so far as we could – that any guests whom we brought along were suitably sympathetic to our lifestyle. My plan for the next two chapters is to look at a few of these secrets with some care and try, therefore, to get to the heart of what we genuinely believed them to mean and how we put them into practice: "synagogue evangelism" is the first one I shall examine.

The accusation made against us of "sheep stealing" was a fairly persistent one. In other words, we were charged with expanding our numbers by stealing away from their own churches those who were already born-again Christians. It was a charge which, if proven, would have only served to intensify the friction that existed between us and Christian fellowships elsewhere. Our reputation would have been particularly blackened if it came to light that we'd stolen sheep from fellowships regarded to be Spirit-filled, flourishing ones. This being so, we vigorously denied such charges whenever they were made. If there were those, we explained, who felt they were being led by the Lord to join us, then, after prayerful consideration, we wouldn't try to stop them doing so. But, no, it wasn't our policy to proselytize, to snatch other Christians away from their rightful spiritual homes and fellowships. Concerning our outreach – evangelism – in the Warwickshire area, here's what SC has to say on the matter:

"Many who came were interested Christians. Along with the new churches, we were accused of 'sheep stealing'. It would be wrong to say we didn't want Christians to join us. Rarely, though, did we go out to find them.

They came by word of mouth. Occasionally we visited Christian festivals to share with the unconverted, the searching or the backslidden. It was often a case of finding lost sheep."[40]

I often wonder how Simon must feel when he rereads what he wrote all those years ago. How does he now feel about his complicity in promulgating defences of the Fellowship which were at best misleading and at worst blatantly untrue and deceptive? His mention of the Christian festivals is pertinent, and one of those was the increasingly popular Greenbelt Festival which we first visited in 1979: it was as a prelude to doing so that Noel had introduced us to the concept of "synagogue evangelism". There would be occasions, so he told us, when it would be necessary to visit other Christian assemblies and gatherings with the specific intent of stealing away those who were in receipt of poor "shepherding" and giving them a new spiritual home amongst ourselves; somewhere they could receive *proper* shepherding. Noel justified such activity with reference to times when the early apostles visited the synagogues of their Jewish brethren specifically to preach the gospel of Christ: *synagogue evangelism.*

When I write about these kinds of issues and reflect on the indignant, straight-faced, and adamant denials we made in response to the accusations made against us, I find myself floating in and out of some kind of unreal dimension where truth itself is unknown. Did I just imagine, for example, how we stealthily engaged in synagogue evangelism? Had it all been some kind of lingering dream, maybe? *How is it that something which was denied so emphatically by intelligent and otherwise-trustworthy people could possibly have happened?* But I wrote it all down in my sociological journal, thank goodness, so I'm able to reassure myself about not being away with the fairies. And my own personal experiences, of course, were remarkably apposite to, and corroborative of, the sheep-stealing charge. After all, I myself had been stolen away from what was then considered to be one of the leading Charismatic fellowships within the Anglican church. St. Hugh's in Luton – featured in a 1975 TV documentary – had been spiritually regenerated under the empowering ministry of the Rev. Colin Urquart, a young, long-haired firebrand who was one of the leading lights within the Charismatic movement. It was there, within the pastoral fold of the youth group, that I'd experienced new birth in Christ. And although the shepherding structure practiced at St. Hugh's wasn't anywhere near as tight as that at Bugbrooke, its influence was key to my becoming increasingly serious and mature as a Christian disciple. If St. Hugh's wasn't considered by those within the JFC to have been a suitable spiritual home for young Christians like myself, then more or less every other church and fellowship must have also been deemed equally unsuitable. The elders of the Fellowship were perfectly aware of my situation; yet *they* were the ones who explicitly and earnestly encouraged my move into the Community. They *could* have suggested I stay at St. Hugh's and make the short drive up to Northampton every now and then for spiritual encouragement and nurture *if* they'd genuinely believed that sheep stealing was wrong and had behaved in the responsible way to which they laid claim.

I too engaged in sheep stealing whilst in the Community. I was responsible for stealing at least four others – and maybe *indirectly* six – from the Christian Union at Canterbury, all of whom were established evangelical Christians with a supportive church background. When Noel realized that the Christian Union (CU) at Canterbury was proving to be a fertile synagogue within which to evangelize, he had then suggested a team of brothers and sisters – led by Kelly – should visit the university specifically for that purpose. The planned visit was met by the CU members with understandable resentment, and they therefore greeted the Bugbrooke brethren from behind defensive spiritual barricades which the most outspokenly opposed of them had successfully managed to erect for the protection of all. In consequence, this particular episode of synagogue evangelism was singularly unsuccessful.

It was much the same story when I began my postgrad studies at Warwick University. A few others and I began to attend the CU meetings regularly, fully intent on "plucking off" those vulnerable students who hadn't integrated within it very well. Shame on us! To compound our duplicity, we also applied to become a recognized student-union society in our own right – just as we'd successfully done at Canterbury. Me, Graham (one of the few Asian Community-members), and Caroline responded to a summons we received requiring us to defend our application at one of the weekly student-union committee meetings. Having been briefed by members of the CU who were aware of what we were up to, the committee members gave us a thorough grilling which largely concentrated on the role of women within the Fellowship. Aware that this line of questioning was likely, we'd asked Caroline – herself a student at Warwick – to be one of our representatives. Between us, we did our best to convince our interrogators that sisters had far more liberty and responsibility than was generally supposed. As a case in point, we told them about Sue White, the owner-director of White and Bishop outdoor clothing in Northampton, who was named as a trustee of the JFCT – no matter that this was little more than an expediency required by the incorporation of her company into the House of Goodness group. Our defence cut little ice with the committee, which nearly unanimously – one "for"; eleven "against" – voted to refuse our application. It then moved straight on to the next agenda item and left me, Graham and Caroline sat there feeling unfairly treated, misunderstood, and somewhat dejected.

The "harvest" at Warwick University was by no means so rich as it had been at Canterbury, but we still managed to steal a few souls away, one of them being the brother whose baptism took place on the night before I split and drove down to Heathrow. I had begun reproaching myself for the synagogue evangelism I was involved with, and yet I still – mindlessly so it seems – went through the motions. It was whilst doing so that, by some kind of perverse circumstance, I managed to fish Steve out of the CU pond and transfer him into the Bugbrooke lake. This was very similar to how, even though he'd begun planning to split, Jonathon had had such an influence on me when I first visited New Creation Hall. I can maybe offer certain extenuating defences for my behaviour toward Steve, and yet I felt nothing less than a pitiful cad. In spite of the genuine spiritual turmoil I was struggling to resolve, and even though I simply didn't have the courage to have behaved differently (or any clear understanding of how to have done so), I need to accept a significant portion of responsibility for Steve's mistreatment: it was damaging, deceitful and quite simply wrong. I still carry the memory of what happened with considerable shame.

Our synagogue evangelism at the Greenbelt festival was equally duplicitous, and it was exposed in a most unlikely way. A group of brothers had apparently gone to one of the evangelistic tent sessions and offered their services as counsellors. When questioned about their motives for being at the festival, my close friend, Shaun, had – as was his wont – answered quite truthfully: *synagogue evangelism*. Yes! He used those very words. Shaun was refreshingly innocent and uncomplicated. Although gifted, intelligent, and in many ways very perceptive concerning character, he wasn't what you would have called a deep spiritual thinker, as such: he still tenaciously clung to a very simple and straightforward understanding of right and wrong and hadn't yet internalized Noel's injunction that we should be "innocent as doves, yet wise as serpents". Being wise as serpents sadly meant there were times when it was necessary for us to be a bit slippery, a bit canny if you like, with the truth. For Shaun, the difference between being canny and being deceitful wasn't an obvious one: lies were still lies in his book, so he just said things as they were. The offer made by the brothers to be counsellors was declined and "the Bugbrooke people" quickly became persona non grata. It had been all been a very strange experience.

For some long-forgotten reason, I had only joined the Greenpeace team as a last-minute replacement; a substitute, and a not-very-experienced one to boot. We each slept in smallish tents – as I seem to recall – and used a large frame-tent as a kind of base and kitchen. For our synagogue evangelism amongst the crowds, I was partnered with a highly respected and influential elder, Mark Turner (aka Mark Strong). Mark was the adopted brother of Steve Turner, the Christian poet who himself had a slot on the main stage. It was the first time I'd been involved in anything remotely similar, so I meekly accepted Mark's guidance when he said that, initially, we should just walk around the perimeter of the main-stage audience to "vibe them out" – his exact words – and make them aware of our presence. If that, indeed, was to be the outcome of our first sortie, then, even though I didn't really understand what would be achieved, I was nonetheless willing to take part in our show of deluded spiritual power and was therefore an accomplice to the underlying arrogance we displayed. I doubt we actually *did* achieve very much, apart from looking right plonkers to those who noticed us. Still, I enjoyed listening to Steve Turner's recital of poetry whilst we doing our "vibing out", and I also enjoyed meeting up again with some friends I'd made during a CU evangelistic mission that had taken place during my first year at Canterbury. Never easily deterred, we carried on with our synagogue evangelism at Greenbelt – and elsewhere – for many years afterwards.

Accusations about the Community's children being treated cruelly were made on a fairly regular basis. As with many of the other charges, it was a case of there not having been smoke without fire. In other words, there was nearly always some underlying truth about our beliefs or lifestyle which gave rise to the criticisms, even if the expressed allegations themselves had been exaggerated or off the mark. In the case of the child-cruelty charges, the principal underlying truth giving rise to them was that they were caned – or "rodded" as it was more commonly called. The full detail of how our children should be subjected to corporal punishment was definitely regarded as a kingdom secret. Had we come completely clean about it all, maybe the smoke which came from the fire wouldn't have been so blackened and acrid. So what *was* the truth about the discipline of children? What exactly *was* this particular kingdom secret Noel had elucidated when there were no swine around to trample the pearls of wisdom he'd cast underfoot?

Secretive issues such as these were generally recirculated verbally within the Fellowship, so there was rarely a trail of evidence that could be conclusively used to confirm the nitty gritty of Noel's teaching. I was amazed, therefore, when a year or so after I'd left I was given a twelve-page booklet, "Education and the Community", which had been written by one of the senior elders – Pete Mattacola (aka Pete Just) and contained a lot of sensitive material concerning the treatment of children. Pete and I, for the record, were well acquainted by virtue of having lived under the same roof at Harvest House for over a year. He was an extremely confident schoolteacher who was also regarded to be the headmaster of the Fellowship's holiday school. The booklet had been distributed, so I understood, to the majority of Community families and was clearly labelled: "For private circulation only". I'm not entirely sure Pete had received Noel's blessing for production of the booklet. Maybe, as head-teacher of the holiday school, he'd assumed it was something which was within his brief and didn't need further approval. What I *do* know is that distribution of the booklet was fairly swiftly curtailed and serious efforts were made to ensure that no copies found their way into the outside world – and therefore into the hands of those who were considered to be enemies of the kingdom, such as myself

The way children were treated can best be understood if we take a closer look, just briefly, into what we were taught about their inherent nature. At the root of everything was the belief that *all* newborns are congenitally "Adamic". This means they are all cursed to inherit the fallen, rebellious disposition of their ultimate ancestral predecessor, the first Adam. Eve, of course, needs mention as provider of the wicked assist, but it was Adam who was credited with having done the destructive deed that did for us all. We were taught that, left unchecked, the inherited Adamic nature would insidiously strengthen its grip on the lives of the youngsters until, ultimately, they would reject Christ and – even worse, presumably – leave the Community. If, however, through parental and Fellowship discipline the Adamic nature was held in check, then the reverse was true: at an age of responsibility the children would accept Christ and demonstrate having done so by the exercise of their own free will to become covenanted members of the Community. Retention of the second generation was taken to be guaranteed if the children were brought up correctly; it was a promise that God had given his people as recorded in the biblical scriptures:

"Bring up a child in the way he should go and he will not depart from it." (Proverbs 22. verse 6)

"For the promise is to you **and to your children** and to all who are afar off."(Acts 2. verse 39)

All this was neatly summarized by Pete on page 9 of his booklet:

"The child's soul can be seen in a state of balance, poised between the influence of Satan's world through its Adam inheritance and the influence of the Community in Christ and its Christian parents. The side exerting the greatest influence will gain the child. We have the promise of the covenant but must be earnest in God to tip the balance to Christ – and his people."

There were three essential components to minimizing the hold of the Adamic nature:
(1) the correction of bad behaviour
(2) the encouragement of good behaviour, and
(3) the avoidance of worldly influence

It was the correction of bad behaviour through corporal punishment that largely, but by no means exclusively, gave rise to the allegations of cruelty. It's been with considerable pain, and something of a fight to hold back tears and fend off melancholy, that I've revisited this subject and reread what Pete has written about it. Particularly difficult to accept as being either humane or Christian is his suggestion that corporal punishment should begin even before a child has reached his or her first birthday. In his pamphlet, he suggested that a smack on the hand should be sufficient up until then, but for those aged one and over he sanctioned the use of a rod:

"Foolishness is bound up in the heart of a child, but the rod of correction will drive it far from him." (Proverbs 13, verse 15)

I ought to stress that such punishment was only meant to be used for correction and not as an outlet for parental frustration or anger. Parents were encouraged to ensure that the child had a clear understanding of what it was they'd done wrong, and, so far as was possible, endeavour to help the child believe it was an act of corrective love which would also pain themselves as disciplinary agents. Quite how these aspects of the punishment could possibly have been conveyed to babies and toddlers remains a mystery to me, and I'm forever thankful I was never called on to strike a child with a rod – or anything else for that matter. I would also venture to say there were many parents who only used the rod against their better judgement and now regret having done so. Like most things which go against the grain, however, rodding a child became easier with each successive punishment, and even more or less routine in the long run. I've recently spoken to a sister, Vikki, who had a large brood of lively children to care for – I've yet to tackle the issue of contraception! A couple of her boys were especially mischievous and unruly as seen from the Community's behavioural line of sight. Vikki now winces at the memory of how, in consequence, she gave them more than their fair share of the rod. At the time, of course, she'd bought into the notion that she was treating them as a loving mother ought to, and this went a long way to numbing the emotional pain she otherwise would have experienced. It was even harder for Vikki herself, however, than for most. One of her particularly self-willed boys, Greg, often found himself being told off by a few of the other household sisters who, all too often, were unctuously zealous in their disapproval of his behaviour. Having received frequent complaints about Greg from these sisters, Vikki felt herself compelled to administer corporal correction far more often than she otherwise would have done left to her own parental judgement. Worse still was the fact that Greg often rubbed Noel himself up the wrong way, and *his* demands for corrective discipline were particularly hard to ignore. Poor Greg! In spite of all the rodding and correction, however, neither his Adamic nature nor his spirit was tamed; he left the Community as soon as he came of an age to do so.

Using the rod was primarily the responsibility of parents, but there were occasions when others also flexed their disciplinary muscles. Those others included teachers in the Fellowship's holiday school and those who had temporary care of a child, or children, in their parents' absence – maybe through illness, visits to the dentist or doctor, involvement with Fellowship ministries, or any other occasion when help to look after children was needed. In order to ensure a suitable instrument was available to administer punishment, a stripped birch twig – about a foot long – was positioned in various places around each house, usually above a door frame where it could only be found by those who knew of its location: we certainly didn't want visitors accidentally coming across one of them.

Our society has, by and large, already moved so far away from considering corporal punishment on children to be acceptable – not even the occasional smack – that we should safeguard against judging what happened within the Community through the ethical standards of 2024. Back then in the seventies – and even the eighties – corporal punishment of children was still legal and would remain so for some time to come. It was still considered an acceptable punishment in many schools, especially public schools, and was advocated by many well-respected evangelical Christian teachers as a suitable chastisement if applied with due proportionality. In spite of these considerations, however, when I wrote my 1983 report, "The Church Community at Bugbrooke", I had good reason to include the comment that *there is a difference between an act of correction and a thrashing*. Moreover, the instruction given to parents that they should apply the rod to a child's fleshy buttocks to reduce the possibility of visible wealds speaks volumes about the level of force that may have been used – at least by some. I remain firmly confident that Noel himself wouldn't have condoned thrashings and would have urged restraint. I also strongly suspect that he didn't anticipate the way in which some children would suffer at the hands of excessively zealous parents and others who had charge over them. This doesn't absolve him. It wasn't hard to predict how his disciplinary teaching would be employed by those, for example, who hadn't yet mastered their own emotions – especially those of anger and pride.

I have one specific, haunting memory of being witness to a rodding given by a senior elder in one of the houses well known to me, someone who went on to become a high-ranking leader after Noel's death. I have redacted his actual name from the final draft of this book from concern about libel, even though what I'm about to describe is entirely true. The elder's eight-year-old son had misbehaved at the communal dinner table and was taken away from it to be disciplined. I don't know what he'd done, but the look on his face was one of unmistakable fear. I have always believed that what followed was the consequence of the elder in question wishing to show off his disciplinarian prowess. Even if I'm wrong (which I may well be), I remain no less censorious of his behaviour. Rather than taking his son well away, to the family's private rooms for example, he chose to punish him within an adjacent room to the one where we were all having our meal. The sound of birch against flesh, together with that of the child's screams, was clearly audible to all of us. At least six strokes of the rod were given. It was deeply humiliating for the boy and it turned my stomach. If a senior elder could have treated his son like this, then what was the fate of those children whose parents were themselves demonstrably immature and lacking in self-control? There were some parents, for instance, possibly new members within the Community, who'd only recently begun their recovery from emotionally damaging experiences. Making rods available to those parents, and encouraging their use, was tantamount to serious neglect – an invitation to cruelty.

This incident had driven another nail into the coffin of my eroded commitment to the Fellowship, and it wasn't to be many more months before I threw in the towel altogether.

Corporal punishment wasn't the only means of restraining children's Adamic nature. As is normal within families, other means of correction and punishment were used; none of them – to the best of my knowledge – so susceptible to the overt cruelty which was possible from a rodding. A telling-off; isolation from other children for a while (a "grounding"); a withdrawal of something enjoyable; or an imposition of some unwanted task; these are all non-corporeal sticks which were used by Community parents in much the same way that they're used by parents the world over. Together with discussion of the punishments given to children, I feel it's also important to emphasize the strength of love they received. Almost all the parents I knew displayed a deep and genuine affection for their children; many of them were *slow to chide and swift to praise*. Although, as may be expected, there were differing levels of disciplinary severity within families, I don't believe that most of the children had any reason to doubt the sincerity of their parents' best intentions, nor the strength of their parental pride, and nor the veracity of their wish for them be as happy as possible – a wish born out of love.

In focussing on what is now being called the "systemic problems and failures" within the Fellowship, I – for one – can sometimes forget about the happiness experienced by young and old alike. Watching the young children gadding about and playing with one another, sometimes boisterously, it would have been hard to predict the troubles which were being stored up for later life. Some have even described many aspects of their upbringing as idyllic. An article published on September 18th. 2017 in the Northants Chronicle and Echo – confusingly under the headline: *Alleged victim of historic abuse reveals traumatic childhood growing up in the Jesus Army* – quotes Philippa as saying that her childhood was:

"idyllic in a lot of ways at the time, filled with long walks and picnics, a sense of belonging. It was free in many senses. I remember being allowed to help in the lambing season, we had a big garden that we enjoyed. My parents were really good at maintaining a sense of normality as well."

The article goes on to describe the repression and abuse Philippa experienced as she grew older. But her comments remain as testimony to the warmth and love which many experienced within family life – as they did within the Fellowship itself. And this leads neatly on to the second aspect of reigning in the Adamic nature: the encouragement of good behaviour.

The "stick and carrot approach" to bringing up children is a good way of describing the one utilized by Community parents, with the dangled carrot representing an enticement to trot along in step with the Fellowship's expectations. Praise is a powerful instrument that most mums and dads select – even if, for some, only occasionally – from their parenting toolbox, and the Community parents were likewise happy to utilize this tool whenever possible. Attention, affection, and approval were other tools they had to hand. Primarily, it was the mums who had sufficient time to shower their children with love and encourage them along the approved behavioural pathways. There were no "working mums", as commonly understood. Mothers were expected to give up their existing job – if they had one – to concentrate on childcare and domestic duties. Although this was, I suspect, inwardly resented by many, they would have nonetheless been expected to show a willing compliance – even if only as a facade. Which isn't to deny there were also those, of course, who may have enthusiastically embraced the opportunity to relinquish paid employment in favour of a more traditional maternal role. Whether the stay-at-home mums accepted their role under duress or eagerly, by and large they displayed cheerfulness and contentment with their lot just as all the other "domestic sisters" did – these were unmarried women whose role was comparable to that of a household servant.

Mothers, then, shouldered much of the responsibility for the loving, time-consuming nurture of children which would loosen the Adamic hold. They were also charged with ensuring that family-time-together wasn't simply playful but also focussed on leading the youngsters to become accepting and active members of God's kingdom – "discipleship" is the word Pete uses in his pamphlet for this aspect of a child's training:

"Family discipleship is the most crucial [aspect of time spent together]. It represents mainly a time with Mother when the Children come home from school. It is a time of quieting, relaxing, talking, heart-sharing, reading of stories, worship and prayer, spiritual teaching, practical tasks, relating with their natural brothers & sisters etc. It serves to counteract the harmful effects of the day's school viz. worldly vibes, speediness, humanistic teaching, and it re-establishes the harmony of the Kingdom life to their soul. It is a crucial time for Kingdom teaching which reinforces the life of Christ in the heart and negates the evil influences of the day. It is a time when hearts are directed and drawn into the Kingdom and gained by their mother. It is a time of discipline when Kingdom standards are insisted upon where there may have been laxity in school discipline."

Although this may have been Pete's *vision* for after-school family time, it amounted to quite a tall order even for the most exemplary Community mothers with the most compliant children: in practice, it remained an aspiration rather than an accurate description of what time-with-mother was actually like.

Within wider society, a common tool for rewarding children is the offer of a material gift. Without the tenpenny-mix-up of sweets which our youngest, Ben, looked forward to after primary school every Friday, I'm not sure that Jeanne and I could have managed even the small amount of control we had over his behaviour. Bribes, if this is what they are, come in many shapes and sizes: the tickets to see "Oasis" offered to our teenage children, as an example, were invaluable in encouraging them to study sufficiently for their exams. The list of rewards and bribes given by most parents is normally quite long. Some from this list may have proved successful, but many of them, I'll wager, will have been unsuccessful even though they were quite expensive and indulgent. There were far fewer rewards and bribes, however, available for use by the Community parents. Everything classified as "worldly" or as "worldly entertainment" was strictly *verboten*: dummies; dolls and teddies; most toys; sweets; radios, cassette players and stereo equipment; TV; concerts; films; theatrical plays; ball sports; swimming; clubs; boy-scouts and girl-guides; dances; discos; secular literature; parties and pubs were just *some* of the objects, activities and places forbidden to Community members, young and old. Nor was playing with or socialising with non-Community – worldly – children permitted. So the choice of rewards was mainly restricted to those which didn't require expenditure or engagement with anything worldly: being allowed to feed the farm cattle, having a sleep-over with a friend at a different Community house, or sitting next to a favourite brother or sister on a minibus journey to chapel were amongst those simple pleasures that Community children came to value and look forward to. I had a young friend, Dave, who very nearly begged parental permission to sit beside me on some of the bus or coach journeys to meeting venues; and I was by no means alone as a brother whose company was, with innocent affection and esteem, in demand by certain youngsters. Dave and I *both* valued the relationship, and we certainly laughed a lot together. These "treats" could be permitted by parents as a kind of reward; but they could be refused, too, as a far milder punishment than reaching for the rod.

Provision of toys for the children was restricted to those approved ones which were believed to offer some kind of educational benefit. When, at one of the "open days" which were held periodically from about 1980, Pete was questioned about the provision of toys, he is quoted in SC's book as having replied:

"Ugh! Consumerism gone mad. We like simple creative things like Lego and Meccano . . . and word games."[41]

Apparently, his wife – Carol – added pots-and-pans to the list. And what parent can't testify to the hours of amusement a child can derive from such "toys"? Ben made his first drum kits from them. Sometimes, he banged away at them for literally hours – we were lucky enough to have had a spare downstairs' room where he was able to do so with minimal disturbance. Cardboard boxes, too, were often appreciated far more than some of the shop-bought toys we gave our children. The Lego Pete referred to must have been of a quite basic nature, nothing like the complex, movie-themed sets which are available nowadays. To the best of my knowledge, however, *new* sets of *any* type of Lego or Meccano were never bought for the children to play with: they would have had to make do with any hand-me-down or second-hand bits and bobs that some of the luckier ones might have managed to get their hands on. Most of them had to be content with the pots-and-pans variety of toys that Carol referred to. In his education booklet, Pete had this to say about toys in general:

"Educational toys have only a limited value if one sees mothering and human interaction as being the most educative of experiences. Never-the-less they do often encourage motor skills and a certain amount of ability to think logically or three-dimensionally. They also serve to fill in time when, for various reasons, a child could get bored. But it would seem good that the child feels they are only available with parent's permission and not as the child's right."

Much bad blood was spilled over parental refusal to let outside relatives give gifts or treats. When children's grandparents, for example, wanted to treat them to a cinema outing or give them a present (especially on birthdays or at Christmas time), their offer would invariably be rejected. Not only was the celebration of Christmas forbidden, but birthdays too. Presents weren't exchanged on these occasions, which were treated as any other day of the week.

The third restraint against Adam's grip on our children was to minimize worldly influence. The most problematic aspects of doing so resulted from their attendance at state schools – primary and secondary – where they were subject to influence from worldly children, worldly teachers, exposure to humanistic curriculum content, and the attraction of extracurricular activities. Influence from other children – worldly ones – was, perhaps, the easiest to tackle: so far as possible, the Community youngsters were prevented from close association with them. Here's the advice that Pete gave:

"Always give children lunch at home if at all possible. Some of our children have found themselves in difficult straits due to forming unhelpful relationships with other children. Every parent real}y ought to be aware of which children their own child is befriending. Family discipleship is the ideal time for encouraging a child away from its problematic relationships. Each child should be encouraged to find its best friend within the Community."

There isn't really much more that needs to be said. The long and short of it is that children attended state schools primarily to comply with legal requirements and little more: educational achievement wasn't highly valued in its own right and social interaction with worldly children was positively discouraged – it was impressed upon our young ones that non-Community children should be avoided. At the Campion secondary school in Bugbrooke village, therefore, cliques of Community children gathered together at break times thereby inviting further criticism of the Fellowship itself. It wasn't until the mid-to-late teenage years that some of the adolescents felt confident and emboldened enough to begin challenging parental restrictions, although many still found it expedient to keep their heads under the radar by continuing to behave with apparent compliance. Up until their later years at secondary school, most of the children seemed to have accepted their parents instruction to avoid worldly children. I was told of one young girl, Gloria, who'd woken in a state of fright from an infantile nightmare. *Had she seen demons at the bottom of her bed? No! She'd seen a **worldly** child sitting there.* I think this neatly sums up just how developmentally and socially damaging the Fellowship's segregation policy could be.

The children didn't just need protecting from their worldly peers but also from the influence of their worldly teachers. Pete didn't have a very high opinion of teaching standards in general, and, in consequence of the pride he believed his teaching colleagues derived from inculcating humanistic attitudes amongst their pupils, he accused them of being self-righteous. No doubt his attitude would be applauded by those who currently believe there is some kind of liberal agenda to indoctrinate schoolchildren with lefty, secular beliefs. Pete made his views quite explicit when he wrote:

"Teachers, in general, don't like to admit that they are failing with children or that they are not able to exercise good class discipline or that there is anything wrong with their method of teaching; i.e. teachers easily have the heart of the pharisee ...

Teaching is fast becoming a relatively non-remunerative occupation when compared with other jobs undertaken with similar qualifications. Consequently people who go in for teaching do so for a multitude of reasons. Some of these we ought to consider, namely reasons of propagation of humanism and fulfilment of self-righteousness."

Parents were encouraged to make sure that in their family-discipleship times they unearthed any teaching given to their children which needed correction, especially if it smacked of humanism or what was considered to be spiritual self-righteousness. Put bluntly, however, the charge of "self-righteous humanism" was levelled against more or less any kind of morality which the Fellowship – meaning, ultimately, Noel Stanton – disagreed with or disapproved of. "Keep Sunday Special", for example, was a contemporaneous Christian initiative supported by those opposed to a relaxation of the existing Sunday-trading legislation. But it was lumped together with the rest of all that was labelled "humanism" because Noel Stanton didn't believe there was any "kingdom" or "Zion" basis to it. Our own main meetings were held on Sundays primarily from expediency, not because the day had some kind of familial Sabbath quality to it. Noel went so far as to proclaim that support for Keep Sunday Special was *sickeningly self-righteous.* In similar vein, the disapproving and dismissive stance taken by the Fellowship towards so-called humanistic schoolteaching meant there was much which needed to be unearthed and rejected. And because it was felt that the task of re-educating the children was too much for parents to tackle alone, at some point early on in my membership "Community holiday school" was introduced. It continued to be held for a number of years after I'd left but proved unsustainable in the long run. So having explained the main reason for its introduction, all I feel it necessary to do is reproduce a section from my "Church-Community at Bugbrooke" report:

"'Holiday school' takes place – as you would imagine – during the school holidays and is compulsory for the children of committed Community members. Children are required to attend for three and sometimes four days a week. The headmaster of this school is Pete Mattacola and his staff is comprised of other brothers and sisters whose 'worldly' occupation is that of a schoolteacher. Children are allocated to classes according to age and the classrooms are various of the large rooms within the Community houses.

Holiday school has several basic functions. Firstly, children receive additional tuition in the subjects which they are already being taught at 'worldly' schools. Secondly, they are given instruction in the values, attitudes, and doctrines of the Community. Thirdly, they are taught to have a 'correct' attitude (i.e.'Fellowship' attitude) to the world and to their life at normal school – as seen through the eyes of the Community.

As part of the holiday school's programme children will spend several days throughout the holiday on New Creation Farm and girls will be expected to spend at least one day a week helping their mothers with domestic responsibilities around the community house."

The final feature of Adamic repression, restricting the children's involvement in extracurricular activities, was probably the most contentious aspect of the measures taken to combat worldly influence. However accepting a child may have been of the Community's beliefs and lifestyle, many of them would undoubtedly have welcomed the opportunity to play in one of the sports teams, take part in a dramatic production, or to go on a school trip – possibly abroad. These were the things which, for most of us, gave some sparkle to our school days and helped make them bearable.

Although children were permitted to join in with organized sport during school hours, they weren't allowed to take part in any out-of-school-hours sporting activity however skilled they may have been. When questioned about such exclusion by the press or school authorities, Noel, Pete and other Fellowship leaders often tried to wriggle out of truthful disclosure by claiming that such decisions, ultimately, lay with the parents. True, it was the parents who actually *communicated* their refusal for a child to become a member of, for example, a hockey or netball team, but the actual decision didn't belong to the parents themselves. I was present when Noel and others were discussing how to deal with a teacher's request for one of our young lads to represent his school in the main football team. Apparently, the boy had shown considerable flare during sports lessons and would himself have liked to be in the team. Although the answer to the request was a foregone conclusion, the whole matter seemed to have escalated into one where some kind of spotlight was going to be shone on the Community. It therefore, apparently, needed to be handled with extra care – hence Noel's involvement. There can be no doubt where the Community stood on such matters, especially after reading another section of Pete's didactic prose:

"The educational reason for Sport in schools is fulfilling the concept of 'educating the whole child' i.e. developing the muscles and co-ordinating abilities of the child. We would not argue with the principles involved here. However, like most things in Adam, proficiency – or even semi-proficiency – in sport also develops egotism, showing off, big-headedness, enjoyment of praise, and the competitive spirit. For example, football develops the Adam ego much more than the physical body ...

Schools like children to do well at sport because it fosters school pride and reputation. Teachers like children to do well at sport because they gain 'Ego renumeration'. These two reasons often comprise the driving force behind school complaints to parents about our children not taking part in competitive or representative sport."

It seems that Noel had a particular dislike of football. At our annual summer gathering in 1981, Noel told us all that *there is something distinctly sinister about kicking around an inflated bag of leather.* Like a good many others, including those in secular society, he clearly hadn't acquired any real idea of what the Beautiful Game is all about. We should, perhaps, treat those who have such a blind spot with pity rather than disapproval: they, after all, are the ones who are losing out.

We should also consider what Pete wrote about drama in schools:

a) Don't be deceived into thinking that drama is valuable and important.
b) Don't let children take part in productions as it encourages Adam problems and trains a child to hide their heart.
c) In Family Discipleship, influence the children against pressure they may feel along the lines of missing out on the "togetherness" which there is in school productions and any desire they may have in their own heart for adulation.

So much, then, for the disingenuous claim that parents had the freedom to make their own minds up about these matters! That they were under instruction about what they should and shouldn't allow their children to do is quite plain. So too is the explicit injunction they were given to indoctrinate children with Fellowship values – see (c) above. Thankfully, though, there wasn't a *total* ban on all school trips. Permission to go on one depended on the household elder's agreement with the parents that there would be some "educational value" from the child's doing so. The problems with such trips, Pete pointed out, were that, a) they cost money, b) they ventured into worldly scenarios, and c) children got *very much taken up with the spirit of the occasion.*

It's surely little wonder that so many of the children – now adults with their own families – have recently been claiming financial redress for the emotional abuse they received. *The kids certainly weren't alright!*

CHAPTER TWENTY: More Hoodwinking – Sex and celibacy

Fornication for procreation only was at the core of the JA sexual ethic, but it was closely guarded as a secret that few on the outside would understand. It was hard, therefore, for those who questioned us to get an entirely straight answer on the subject and we were very noncommittal in what we said. This was another example of our being unnecessarily defensive. It wasn't even as if the Fellowship stood alone in its sexual teaching: it was an anti-sensual, anti-contraceptive, anti-abortion ethic that has long been associated with certain sections of orthodox Christianity, and still is – the Roman Catholic church being, perhaps, the most powerful advocate.

Married couples within the Community were told that pregnancy should be the specific aim of their coming together; or – by way of a reluctant, expedient concession to those who lacked self-control – pregnancy should at least be a welcome outcome of coitus. The use of contraception, therefore, was regarded as being contrary to the will of God. To ensure couples avoided unnecessary temptation they were told to sleep in single beds. This issue, however, was frequently fudged when it came to any form of public discussion. Further on in the book I shall have the pleasure of writing at some length about my experiences when asked – in 1993 – to take part in an episode of a rather whacky late-evening ITV programme called "Dial Midnight" – an episode which featured the Jesus Army. For now, I only intend referring to what happened fairly briefly in order to address the issue of Community sleeping arrangements for married couples. John Campbell (aka John Perceptive), who had replaced Dave Resolute as the Fellowship's spokesman, was sat on a gaudy red settee – more about that anon – alongside the programme's presenters. Asked specifically by one of them, Anastasia, whether it was true that couples had to sleep in single beds, he replied by suggesting it was something which couples decided for themselves. It was an almost perfect example of the deceit used (for that is what it was), when required, to try and present black and white issues in various shades of grey. In fact, when I recently replayed the Dial Midnight video for the first time in over twenty years, I was astonished – once again – by John's straight-faced duplicity and willingness to tell what he plainly knew to be lies. Consider this word-for-word transcript of his interview:

Anastasia: *There have been accusations from ex-members that children are beaten with rods; sex is for procreation only – and not for emotional pleasure; celibacy is enforced, even for married couples; members are not allowed to socialize outside the Community or enter romantic relationships without the permission of the leadership... is this all true?*

Whilst Anastasia was speaking, the camera gave shots of John with his lips slightly curled up into a bemused smirk of a smile; one which would have had us anticipate his thoughts as being: *'Yes, yes! Heard it all before!*

This is the kind of stuff which people often say about us – and it's all nonsense.'
His actual reply, therefore, was predictable:

John Campbell-Perceptive (henceforth JP): *No! That's pretty wild and largely over the top.*

Anastasia could hardly contain her disbelief at his reply, so her next question was somewhat spluttered out in astonishment:

Anastasia: *What? Is there **any** truth in this? About the socializing ... are members in the Community not allowed to socialize with people outside of it?*

JP: *No! That's not true. Obviously, our emphasis on Christian community is about being together… attempting to serve Jesus… to serve God. But of course lots of people have friends outside; people have jobs outside.*

Anastasia: *And what about married couples and the sex side of it? Do they all sleep in single beds as we've been told?*

JP: *How people sleep is up to them!* (Oh, John! Shame on you!) *We certainly have lots of married couples… lots of children.*

Every so often I find myself experiencing a deep sense of unreality when trying to unravel some of the breathtaking deceits to which various Fellowship leaders have been party – and in such a straight-faced way. They've managed to express what is so transparently untrue in such a casual, calm and convincing tone of voice that one ends up feeling they must have genuinely *believed* what they were saying; and on occasion it feels as if truth is something which you no longer properly understand. On the same Dial Midnight programme a clip was shown of an interview with Noel in which he was asked about people being pressurized. With some kind of convincingly reflective sincerity, and in a reassuring, softly-spoken tone of voice (his feline "purring mode"), he spoke to the camera of having no wish that anyone should feel under pressure but that they should find their own freedom and self-purpose within the fold of the Community. Contrast that with what happened to a newly married, much-respected elder – let's just call him, say, Dave – who quite simply refused to accept sleeping apart from his wife: he pushed their two single beds together. In justification of his action, Dave explained that he and his wife wanted to sleep alongside one another purely for the purpose of companionship and nothing more. Noel, however, was having none of it. Referring to Dave's action – in the hearing of myself and several others – as being *disgraceful and disreputable;* he said that Dave wasn't fit to be an elder if he didn't agree to comply with the single-bed injunction. A couple of other elders were charged with bringing Dave to heal. When, after several attempts, they managed to do so, Noel offered them his congratulations.

Consider also the way in which Noel sometimes used others as his personal attack dog, and then try to square such methods with his denial of using pressure. One of my deepest regrets is having allowed myself to be used in such a role more than once. My deepest moral descent came on the occasion when I was charged by Noel, late one evening, to correct my brother Nick for his wanton refusal to repent of his attachment to the sister whom he'd set his heart on. I have already described the incident back in chapter twelve. I cannot, simply cannot, understand how Noel – how anybody – could have possibly denied the use of pressure in the light of everything I've explained; and it's this seemingly irresolvable fissure in my understanding which brings with it the sense of unreality.

Leaving aside the practical implications which the Fellowship's sexual ethic had for married couples, we also need to understand the effect it had on attitudes towards sexuality in general. Given we were told intercourse was only acceptable to God when performed to produce offspring, it followed that all non-procreative sexual thoughts and impulses were to be considered impure and unclean. Put bluntly, they were supposedly nothing more than pure lust... the potential for repressed sexuality need hardly be spelt out. Philippa, the ex-member who told the Northants Chronicle and Echo about the idyllic aspects of her upbringing,[a] also tells us about the time when, as a child, she drew some sexualized stick-figure sketches of a naked body. When the sketches were found, she was hauled off – as she describes it – to a room with a fireplace; a suitable location, apparently, for an elder to perform an exorcism over her – presumably the demon possessing her was to be driven off into the fire. I have received quite a number of similar accounts from others who contacted me through my JEANNI website. Philippa subsequently faced damaging psychological struggles in consequence of growing up with the belief that there was something wrong with her sexuality. Her story is an almost perfect example of the damage I believe can result from teaching people that sexual awareness and thoughts disassociated from procreative activity are unclean and lustful. What utter nonsense! Small wonder that Noel has been ridiculed by the press for preaching to young men and women about their need to let God be in control of their genitals.

Throughout most of the developed world there are indeed special circumstances in which some couples specifically plan their lovemaking around the desire for children, especially when – possibly due to problems achieving pregnancy – key fertility times of the female cycle need to be

---

[a] See page 192

identified and utilized. This aside, marital sex is pretty much like most other sex: an indulgence of erotic urges. In saying this, I am merely trying to be honest about what is going on: trying to cut through the hypocrisy that would attribute "higher" motives to what, essentially, is a natural base instinct common to most animals... so let's not dress it up in sanctimonious spiritual language. True, it can also – though not necessarily – be an expression of deep love, but that doesn't change the essential truth that the urge to join bodies comes from sexual excitement. If the fornication-for-procreation ethic is to be taken seriously, however, then couples who come together purely for sexual satisfaction are deemed to be yielding to the temptations of the flesh and, as such, being sinful in sight of God.

It's my contention that this is an unnatural and unhealthy attitude towards sex. Any provision for its being mutually enjoyable is missing from the ethic, and the attainment of sexual pleasure is entirely secondary to the procreative imperative. Unfortunately, it's the female who is therefore most likely to suffer sexual frustration in consequence of failing to achieve orgasm. There is no place for experimentation with techniques that allow **both** *partners to achieve orgasm because that ISN'T what sex is meant to be about according to the teaching of those such as Noel Stanton. To deny women the experience of sexual satisfaction, as the JFC's sexual ethic must have done for many, is – in my opinion, anyway – extremely callous and selfish. Conversely, proper consideration for one another's physical satisfaction within the sexual act can be a genuine expression of unselfish awareness and care.*

On a somewhat lighter note, writing about such chauvinistic attitudes towards sex has made me remember and chuckle about Robin Williams's wonderful portrayal of Mrs. Doubtfire (Annie) in the eponymous film. Disguised as Annie – a widowed nanny – in order to infiltrate his ex-wife's new home and be near to his children, Williams's character finds himself (herself?) in a heart-to-heart conversation with his unsuspecting "ex" concerning marital issues.

'How it was for you and Mr. Doubtfire?' his ex asks "her".

'Oh well, you know', "she" begins wistfully in her plaintive "Scottish" lilt, *'he just used to say: "Brace yourself, Annie".'*

How we miss you, Robin Williams!

Given the importance placed on the virtue of sexual abstinence, it isn't too surprising that marriage was regarded as being second best to celibacy. The following passage was often quoted:

"It is good for a man not to have sexual relations with a woman. But because of the temptation to sexual immorality, each man should have his own wife and each woman her own husband." (Corinthians, book one, chapter 7, verse 2)

Put simply – and ironically in the light of the foregoing discussion – this passage was used to support Noel's view that the institution of marriage exists as a concession to those who've been unable to master – "get the victory over" – their sexual impulses. It once again draws attention to the way in which the Fellowship lumped together sexual impulse with "uncleanliness"; and it's also a denial of there being perfectly natural and approvable reasons for non-procreative matrimonial sex beyond the fulfilment of selfish lust. "Conveniently", the very next sentence to the one I've just quoted from the first book of Corinthians was seldom mentioned – if at all. It reads:

"The husband should give to his wife her conjugal rights, and likewise the wife to her husband."

In my early days at New Creation Farm, I asked my elder, Rufus, if he thought marital sex was OK when it was a genuine expression of love. Shooting straight from the hip, he replied:

'Yes, I guess so. So long, that is, as you don't just want to get under her knickers.'

Rufus had an amazing way of making his point – and making me laugh, too.

The idea that sexual impulses and thoughts are unclean also became a visible feature of the way we lived. No one who spent any time with members of the Fellowship could have failed to notice the very strict segregation maintained between the sexes. SC has explained it thus:

"We had kept a degree of segregation since first establishing mixed community at the Farm. Men shared their feelings mostly with men, and women with women. That encouraged depth and avoided the subtle dangers of flirtation. We mixed together in company but avoided being left alone together."[42]

Reading this makes it sound as if segregation was introduced as a precautionary expedient within a communal lifestyle. Although probably true to a certain extent, a more honest explanation of the segregation is the way in which physical proximity was believed to invite sinful thinking. Thoughts about the sexual attractiveness of the opposite sex were deemed to be just as bad as sexual encounters themselves. Out-of-sight-out-of-mind was considered to be an effective way of suppressing both intimate thoughts and intimacy itself. The segregation also existed so that romantic attachments couldn't flourish secretively and without the prior consent required. But even before such consent might be given, brothers and sisters alike had to demonstrate their capacity to form deep and healthy same-sex relationships, whilst also needing to prove – to themselves and to their elders – that the higher calling of celibacy wasn't the one that God had chosen for them.

As with the business of sleeping in single beds, the Fellowship leaders did their best to suggest that remaining celibate was simply a matter of choice, that it was a "calling" which some of the brothers and sisters had joyfully embraced in their deep desire to serve the Lord. SC has written quite extensively about celibacy in his book, especially the sense of freedom and purpose which was found when the free-will choice to remain single was decisively taken. Here are some examples:

"Janie from the Farm was now a leader amongst the sisters. She'd considered celibacy before but it was unheard of in the circles she'd moved in. After joining us, she soon found a deep fulfilment in community, took hold of the celibate gift, and sought to live 'in undivided devotion to the Lord' (1 Cor 7:35).

Piers was another enthusiastic advocate of this path: *To me celibacy was the highest way according to Scripture, and I didn't want second best! I reckoned I could handle it temperamentally, so I laid it before God. Shortly after that I was struck by an article in New Wine magazine about being single for the Lord and I knew God was telling me to 'Go for it!' ... I didn't want to get bogged down in the cares of life. I never regretted it or hankered after marriage. I just wanted to follow Jesus and travel as light as possible! Time is short and there is so much to do. Celibacy is priceless! It's pure! I love the freedom it brings."*[43]

"'Celibacy!' Lesley said, 'I love it! Jesus said, "Seek first the kingdom". I made a pact with God and expected him to meet my needs. Celibacy is like getting into a new car. The sun is shining, God is with you, and you can explore.'"[44]

By 1982 the Fellowship had begun holding specific celibate-only meetings. The status of this "higher calling" was endorsed and accentuated by targets set for an increase in the number of those who'd taken a vow of celibacy. By 1992, SC tells us, this number had reached two hundred:

"The 200-strong meeting of vowed and probationary celibates excelled in worship as one sister recorded: *It was incredible! When we started to worship I sensed fire racing through our hearts. I was weeping to God to so cleanse me that the fire would stay and never go away. I heard instrumental music and angels with really high voices. An amazing spiritual song swept around the hall in ever increasing waves. After that we all broke out in thunderous Jesus claps and cheers.*

A celibate power-switch was thrown and the whole spirit of celibacy became futuristic."[45]

To read all this, you might think – as it was hoped you would – there was a veritable host of young men and women whose hormonal urges and romantic desires had been almost celestially displaced by the glorious attraction of remaining single within the kingdom of God. There are those the world over, of course, who genuinely feel they've been called to remain single – and not only in pursuit of *religious* goals. But for the vast majority it goes completely against the grain and involves the renunciation of a deeply embedded instinct, the one that craves the affection and companionship of someone from the opposite sex – or same sex – with whom a physical attraction is shared. This was as much true for the Fellowship brothers and sisters as it remains true for many today. In reality, therefore, the vow of celibacy taken by many in the Fellowship didn't prove to be a key which unlocked the gateway to a life of freedom and joy in the service of Christ. Vows of celibacy, so I would claim, were taken primarily because of the immensely strong internal social dynamic of the Fellowship – and it was a social pressure I believe to have been harmful and the resulting vows largely unsustainable: many confessed celibates have left the fold of the Community over the years and renounced their vows by themselves entering into wedlock.

So paramount was the emphasis on celibacy that, in 1995, the Fellowship began producing an annual/biannual periodical called "Undivided" which was dedicated to celibacy issues; it's subtitle was "Celibacy Inspirational Newsletter". In the October 2000 edition, the brother who would succeed Noel Stanton as leader of the Jesus Fellowship, Mick Haines, wrote about his own calling to celibacy:

"I received the gift of celibacy over twenty years ago, when I was thirty. Looking back over the years, I am so thankful to God for His grace and for so many opportunities to serve Him and build His church. The gift of celibacy is built into my foundation as a man and fires up my other gifts. I find a continual passion for Jesus and His church. It is great to be set apart for service with few distractions. I would always recommend that every single person considers the gift of celibacy and if they are able, to receive the gift."[46]

But even Mick Haines – acknowledged for many years as the Fellowship's "leading celibate" – has shown that the much-vaunted call and delight of celibacy was largely chimerical – a self-perpetuating fantasy created by the enormous emphasis, and associated expectations, given to it. Were this not so, then those who claimed they'd been called to celibacy by the Lord himself would have remained true to their vows *for life* – as many in monastic orders have done. Mick Haines, however, married in 2021, just a couple of years after he'd relinquished leadership of the doomed JFC.[a] Numerous other one-time celibates have gone on to marry, including Piers Denholm-Young, the brother who rapturously extolled celibacy as "priceless" and "pure" in one of the above quotations from SC's book. These rejections of celibacy speak volumes about many of the other "fabulous" claims made concerning the freedom and contentment which celibates had supposedly found. It can hardly be denied that, *at the time*, many brothers and sisters were sincerely enthused and motivated by the call of being undistractedly devoted to Jesus Christ for the remainder of their lives. But for most it was a tough call, and one which could only ultimately be verified by the test of time; a test which has shone a revelatory light for many on the authenticity of the celibate state.

Without wishing to deny the personal sincerity and conviction of those who believed themselves to have received the gift of celibacy, I would also suggest there were actually some distinctly prosaic reasons why certain brothers and sisters declared themselves celibate; reasons which they probably couldn't admit to themselves, let alone others. For some, the choice was probably related to how remote they felt the prospect of getting married was, especially at certain times when marriage was being discouraged. There was the period, for example, when Noel was urging us all to join in the battle to take the central ground and, until it had been won, forget about marriage. There were some, too, brothers and sisters alike, who were realistic enough to accept they were quite likely low down the league table of marital eligibility within the Community itself. The emotional pain of having intense hope for a relationship leading to marriage yet knowing this might never happen was all too real. One way to rid oneself of such pain was to declare yourself celibate: at least you then knew where you stood and weren't so burdened by the agony of having potentially unfulfillable dreams. There was also the benefit of knowing that, once such a celibate decision had been made, your spiritual status within the Community would immediately be increased quite significantly. Indeed, there were inevitably some who chose celibacy purely from motives – probably self-denied – of ego and advancement: much the same as wanting to get on in the world; and chosen by just the same kind of people who one would mark down as being keen to get ahead in general.

Another less-than-holy attraction of the celibate state for a brother was the opportunity it gave to share company with certain sisters without receiving the censure he otherwise would have done. It was generally supposed there was a significantly reduced danger of an avowed celibate brother becoming over-friendly with a sister in a romantic or sexualized way. That may well have

---

[a] In making this observation, my intention isn't to be critical of Mick himself – a brother whom I was very fond of. I'm delighted that Mick has fallen in love and been able to marry, and I wish him and his wife, Carol, every happiness.

often been true, but I'm aware of instances when it most certainly wasn't. Who would have imagined, for instance, that a leading celibate such as Mark Strong – the brother who got down on his knees and begged me not to get married – would have breached his vows by becoming romantically attached to a sister with whom he'd spent a lot of time, supposedly "shepherding" her – and without having raised any eyebrows whilst doing so?

As I've already mentioned, the sisters were the ones most affected by the Community's courtship procedures. Despite the unrealistic and unfair reassurances Noel had recklessly given at Ashburnham in 1977, the prospect of a sister being "left on the shelf" was very real; and all the more so – dare I say? – for those who were less attractive. In such circumstances, the lure of declared celibacy must have been a powerful one; and, at the risk of sounding immensely unkind, there wasn't too much surprise about the decision certain sisters made: they would quite likely have remained single by default if not by choice.

PART FIVE

Preparation for battle

One of the saddest things about our attempts to keep the kingdom secrets discussed in previous chapters under wraps was the impact it had on our moral compasses. We came to accept there wasn't anything wrong with being misleading and only economically truthful – or even telling outright fibs – if it was "for the sake of the kingdom"; so much so, in fact, that we must have very nearly stopped distinguishing truth from falsehood. Recognizing what was happening led me to believe that I too had become what I would go on to call a "moral robot". Once I'd finally managed to leave, I experienced an overwhelming sense of freedom at being able once again to follow the dictates of my own conscience. There will be much more to discuss and explain concerning such matters as we progress to the epoch when the Jesus Fellowship largely transmogrified to become the Jesus Army (JA), and then the Modern Jesus Army (mJA). Firstly, though, I shall resume my personal story just a few months after I'd flown out to Israel.

By way of commentary, I ought to explain that I've included some anecdotes in the next few chapters – as I did in earlier ones – purely because I believe those reading this book may well find them interesting or amusing. As such, I hope they will lighten the weight of the main subject matter. But many of these short stories – such as the one which touches on the subject of AIDS – are there as a prelude to what is yet to come. *All this will become clear before too long.*

CHAPTER TWENTY-ONE: Lasting love

It was the young boy with the red and white keffiyeh flung jauntily over his head, the one leading *my* camel, who first noticed the tell-tale marks in the sand. (How was it that I could never get *my* keffiyeh to stay on my head in quite the same way?) He gave a shrill warning-cry and, immediately, several of the Bedouin began waving sticks and running about frenetically in pursuit of some unknown quarry. They were very excited; far too excited to worry about poor *me* left clutching onto the camel's back, desperately hoping it would remain calm amidst all the shrieks and frantic movement. From the corner of my eye, I then caught sight of something slither across the sand with extraordinary speed into the cover of a nearby clump of dried-up bush. Instantly, the Bedouin began thrashing the bush with mighty blows of their sticks. On this occasion even an animal so evasive as a sidewinder wasn't able to escape their attack. Once satisfied there was no life left in the snake, one of the men got hold of its mutilated carcass and waved it triumphantly in the air. The once-deadly creature was then hurled away to decompose under the glare of the blistering sun. The Bedouin could now be certain this was another enemy which couldn't steal into their camp under the cover of darkness to deliver its deadly venom.

We were deep in the heart of the Sinai desert. Overnight, in the way we had done all week, we'd slept out under the stars. Surrounding us when we woke in the morning were literally dozens of camels that had appeared, seemingly, from nowhere. Groups of robed Bedouin men were stood around waving their arms with frustration and arguing with one another in spirited language. Each of them, together with their own dromedary, had turned up in the hope of earning some money by taking part in the desert expedition planned for the day. But there were simply far too many of them, and the complex, impassioned arguments concerning who should and who shouldn't be employed were only capable of being settled by the intervention and arbitration of their tribal leader. By the time I'd eaten breakfast with the others (avocado pear, tomato, dried bread and chocolate spread), many of the camels had been led away by their forlorn owners, leaving only half-a-dozen or so at our camp.

Our guide, Horah, a lecturer from the Hebrew University in Jerusalem, had led regular field trips into the Sinai peninsula over previous years and was well-known to the Bedouin. She was one of the few Israeli civilians with sufficient local knowledge about the area to guide a vehicle through such a remote, inhospitable wilderness. The sight of her open-backed lorry appearing once again in the distance meant another opportunity for these nomads to solicit the medical supplies which she always brought with her, and also another opportunity to earn "hard cash": money which could then be used to buy food or cigarettes when they visited centres of civilization.

On this particular day, the twenty-strong group of us – who'd virtually lived in the back of Horah's truck since entering the desert – were going to split two ways. Most were going to make the climb to St. Catherine's monastery at the top of Mount Sinai itself. But some, including me, were going to spend the day roaming the desert with the Bedouin and their camels; going to places only they knew how to get to and eating the food they would prepare for us over an open fire. To have been on this adventure was literally the opportunity of a lifetime, especially because it was the last time Horah would be able to lead such an excursion through the Sinai peninsula before it was handed back to Egyptian rule.

Me with Camels in the Sinai

I'd spent the day before we set off from Jerusalem wandering around the streets of Jerusalem's Old City with Jeanne, a nurse from London who was there on holiday. We'd met one another at a Christian prayer meeting in the Roman Catholic hospice of Ecce Homo ("behold the man"), which was situated just to one side of the Via Dolorosa (the way of the Cross). She'd seemed pretty casual towards me at first, although when we met on a second occasion – a celebratory "Feast of Tabernacles" parade through the streets of New Jerusalem – I had great hope that romance might be just a short way off. I cannot deny, having been so frustrated in love and now in my mid-twenties, I was longing to find someone who could at last reciprocate my deep longing for a close, enduring, loving relationship.

We'd begun our day together by exploring "Hezekiah's tunnel", an ancient passageway hewn through solid rock nearly three thousand years ago to bring water in times of siege to the pool of Siloam. One of the remarkable things about the tunnel is how it was cut from the two separate entrances – just like the Channel tunnel – twisting and turning with the natural contours of the rock formation. Where the two ends met can be clearly identified: an offset in the line of the rock walls which shows that Hezekiah's engineers had been accurate to within four or five inches. Absolutely amazing! Although it must surely be one of the truly indisputable biblical landmarks, Hezekiah's tunnel isn't part of the normal tourist trail. Apart from anything else, you have to plod through cavernous conditions, often stooping down and sometimes knee deep in water. What's more, you also have to know where to locate the Arab caretaker; the exchange of *baksheesh* – gratuity – being the recognized protocol for procuring his agreement to come and unlock the entrance gate.

After we'd successfully navigated the tunnel, we spent the rest of the day roaming here and there, chatting non-stop, bartering for trinkets in the souk, drinking long, thirst-quenching drinks of freshly squeezed carrot juice, and finding out as much about one another as could possibly be squeezed into the comparatively short time we had. With afternoon beginning to draw all too quickly towards evening, I kept trying to find enough courage to take hold of Jeanne's hand to confirm this was more than casual friendship. It had been so many years since I'd held a girl's hand, though, that I was, somehow, just far too unsure of myself. I'd almost resigned myself, therefore, to seeing the day pass by without the assurance of reciprocated fondness given by joined hands when we decided to go into a rather dinghy café in the souk for a drink.

'*Come on, John,*' I admonished myself, feeling the rhythm of my heart thumping away inside my rib cage. '*It's now or never. If you don't ask, you'll never know, will you?*'

'*I really don't know how to go about this kind of thing, Jeanne,*' I began, with embarrassing diffidence and ridiculous shyness. '*I mean, you might have a boyfriend back in England or something for all I know, and I don't want to make it awkward for you. But, well, I'd like to hold your hand if that's alright!*'

She looked at me sympathetically but quietly, as if she too was struggling to find the right words. I feared being turned down. A few seconds later she herself had taken hold of *my* hand and we sat together silently drinking our Cokes. When we said goodbye at the end of the day, we did so with a kiss.

For all my fascination with the landscape and culture I'd encountered during our expedition to the Sinai desert, I couldn't wait to get back to Christ Church Hospice and see if Jeanne had already sent any correspondence after her return home, cock-a-hoop when I found she'd written me a long letter while staying in Tel Aviv on the night before she flew from Ben Gurion. Its content left me with no doubt whatsoever "this" was for real. Over the next few months, while I lived with my parents and earned myself a small wage helping out around the hospice, we grew to learn about and love one another through page after page of correspondence. I think I shall always be thankful for such an innocent, rewarding, tender way for a romance to be born and blossom; I'm not sure I could have coped, at the time, with anything that would have required more sophisticated courtship skills.

As the Christmas of 1982 drew closer, my rehabilitation was gathering pace; but it was also proving very hard to discard deeply held convictions and attitudes without much soul-searching. I remained fearful of angering God by discarding the good as well as the bad, throwing out the baby with the bathwater; and there was much about the Fellowship's lifestyle which I still firmly believed was worth clinging onto. I remember sitting at the piano in the hospice church playing John Denver's "Annie's Song" and feeling slightly guilty for doing so. It was a piece of music I'd always loved, but it was still "worldly music". Liz, one of the hospice staff, came and sat down in the pews to listen. After I'd finished the song, I called over to her:

'*You'll have to forgive me! I know it's not a very **spiritual** piece of music.*'

'*Well cleaning your teeth isn't very spiritual either, deary,*' she replied in her wonderfully refreshing, no-nonsense manner, '*but I bet you do it anyway!*'

It was off-the-cuff remarks like this which helped puncture the self-righteous intensity and absurdity of the dogma I'd internalized. And slowly but surely I came to trust and respect the new friends I was making, even though, for years, I'd been taught to regard their Christian lifestyle as seriously deficient for want of true commitment to the way of the Cross, to the way of community.

After some three months of readjustment, my scruples about celebrating Christmas were fairly easy to cope with: all I had to do was to avoid the excess and enjoy the rest. There was much about the festival which was easy to enjoy; not least the giving of gifts. I'd carefully saved up most of the small wage I earned, and this was an opportunity to use it. I had a lot of fun in the souk, haggling with the Arab traders to buy various items at the cheapest deal I could strike. One gift was of particular importance as it was earmarked for Geoff, a young American who'd frequently come to the hospice for help of one kind or another.

Almost from the very first time I'd met him it was perfectly obvious that he was rather strange and eccentric; but I didn't have cause to suspect anything other than overt religious fanaticism and complete lack of sensitivity – quite common amongst the Americans who'd heard God's call to leave their families behind and relocate to Jerusalem, the city of David. All he'd wanted to do when he came to the hospice was sit around in the sunshine, open his big black Bible, and argue about the meaning of controversial passages. I'd often sat with him, patiently trying to understand what was going on his mind and get to know a bit more about him. *Exactly* why he'd come to be in Jerusalem, I had no idea; except that he was another of those many extremists who'd been enticed by the alluring spiritual nectar of the city and flocked there like bees round a honey pot.

The most I ever managed to get out of Geoff concerning how he supported himself was that his father "wired" him an allowance from the States. Whatever size this allowance may have been, he certainly wasn't using it wisely: he spent less and less looking after himself with each week that passed. While his clothes became increasingly shabby, the army-style holdall he always carried with him became ever fuller with expensive, hard-backed books. His behaviour also became insidiously aggressive. He stopped so much talking to people as shouting at them; and he often stormed away in a furious rage when contradicted or confronted.

During the last few weeks of the year, I caught daily sightings of him as he walked forlornly around the streets with his enormous bag. His book collection was now so voluminous that he struggled to lift the holdall off the ground once he'd put it down to rest. I knew how desperately he needed help. But not the help which I could give: Geoff needed medical help. If I had a prayer for him, therefore, it was that he'd let me take him to see a doctor. One sunny afternoon, having noticed him sat on a grass verge which fell away from the city wall to the west of the Jaffa Gate, I went over and sat down next to him. But even before I could say a word, he shot to his feet and began to shout:

'This man wants to kill me! He is from the Devil! He is filled with evil spirits!'

'Get away from me!' he screamed. *'Don't touch me! You have the mark of the beast on your forehead and I command you to go!* **In the name of the Lord, I command you to leave!'**

With his oily, unbrushed black hair and long scraggy beard he must have looked a peculiar sight to the other people sat around enjoying the sunshine. His searing denunciation concluded, he snatched at the handle of his bag, lugged it over his shoulders, and stormed away. I was left sitting there quite shell-shocked. Everyone was looking at me, presumably wondering what this was all about.

'Surely they must understand he's mad?' I anxiously thought. So I looked around me and shrugged my shoulders as if to say: *'Well don't look at me like that! I don't know how to make sense of it any more than **you** do.'* Then I got up and walked slowly away.

A few days later we had one of those torrential downpours to which Jerusalem is subject in the winter months. Geoff appeared in the hospice compound asking to talk with me. I was called from the office and saw him standing there soaked to the skin like a miserable drowning rodent, water running down from his bedraggled hair over his face. He asked, with no accompanying display of aggression, if I would give him some money so he could get something to eat. Thanking God beneath my breath for this opportunity to help, I took him straight off to a nearby café – it seemed a better idea than actually giving him cash. While we were eating, I tried to encourage him to let me take him to see a doctor. He refused point blank.

Christmas day came. I went to church in the morning and planned to go for a walkabout afterwards to find Geoff and give him his special gift. This proved unnecessary because when I came out of church he was there waiting for me, on a bench in the courtyard. I ran quickly up to my room and came back down with a large box which I'd filled with nuts, chocolate, Turkish delight, baklava, halvah, and all kinds of normal and exotic fruit. His eyes lit up with delight and, for the first time, he seemed at a loss to know what to say.

'Go on, take it,' I said, nearly having to force it into his hands. 'I just wish you'd let me get medical help for you. But don't worry about that just now... Happy Christmas!'

I'd booked a flight back to London for early in the new year. My plan was to have a three-week break and spend as much time with Jeanne as possible. The anticipatory excitement I felt was tempered only by my concern for Geoff. There was no one else I knew of whom he seemed to trust or who would keep company with him – which was hardly surprising considering the nuisance he'd made of himself. *What would become of him during the three weeks while I was away?* He'd grown so thin that I suspected he was nearly on the point of starvation; and yet somehow he was managing to cram even more books into his bag. Something about his deranged mind kept compelling him to buy books instead of food. I knew for sure that he'd been afflicted with some kind of psychotic religious mania.

With just two days left to go before my flight, Geoff again turned up at Christ Church begging me to help him get something to eat.

'Look, Geoff,' I said. 'I'm only going to get you a meal if you agree to let me find a doctor for you.'

'I don't need a doctor,' he said, quite aggressively. 'There's nothing wrong with me!'

'In which case, Geoff,' I replied with finality, 'there's not going to be any meal.'

I waited for the outburst from his venomous tongue, but he just glared at me and turned to walk away. Later that day, in the early evening, he was back at Christ Church with the same request. Again, I stuck to my ground:

'Let me get you medical help, Geoff, and you'll get a meal.'

He stood silently; a few tears came to his eyes.

'*Will you, please?*' he sobbed. '*Oh my God! Will you, please?*' And then he broke down in floods of tears on my shoulder.

It was only when I then went to the hospice phone that I discovered how little I knew about the Israeli medical system. I had *no* idea whatsoever where I could take Geoff to at that late hour of the day, or whether there even *were* A&E facilities like the ones back home. The job of locating an appropriate treatment centre was made all the more difficult by my inability to speak modern Hebrew, and those people who answered my phone calls didn't understand much English. The otherwise simple task of saying '*I have a friend who needs psychiatric help – can you tell me where I should take him to, please?*' became a huge communication problem in these circumstances.

I was eventually given the address of somewhere to try on the outskirts of the city, so I hired a taxi to take us there. It was a small, modern building, with nothing identifiable to confirm whether or not it was the right place to be – no signs saying "hospital" nor anything else in English for that matter. Furthermore, being late in the evening there were few people about: it wasn't, for example, like the casualty department of a large hospital. I felt totally alien and useless in this environment, especially so after we'd registered and then had to sit for what seemed like hours before anyone came to see us – giving me good cause to suppose we'd simply been forgotten. To crown it all; when a medic eventually came he spoke very little English, and there was nothing about Geoff's behaviour as he sat there which immediately signified anything wrong with him. I was going to have to rely heavily on sign language and the evidence of the bag. Amazingly, the man seemed to understand what I was trying to tell him. He instructed Geoff to open the bag and was then able to appreciate more about the problem. After he'd concluded a very brief and stunted interview with the subdued young man, he disappeared off elsewhere. We then had to endure another long wait before someone else returned to tell me, in broken English, that they would be admitting Geoff – so I could leave him there and go home. He also asked me to report all this to the American consulate. With huge relief, and extremely glad that I could now fly to London without this care hanging on my shoulders, I called another taxi and went home.

I went to the American Embassy the next day and was surprised to learn that the consulate official – who'd already been briefed by staff from the clinic I'd been to – had known of Geoff and his problems for several weeks. Geoff's father himself, worried about his son, had apparently been in regular communication with the consulate to try and make arrangements for repatriation. No one, however, had been empowered to take further action without Geoff's consent unless he were committed for psychiatric care – and that itself couldn't have been enforced unless he'd either been convicted of a crime or some member of the public had brought a complaint against him. I was then told that by having requested medical treatment for him, I had, effectively, made such a complaint. Already, therefore, arrangements were being made to reunite him with his family in the States.

During my months in Jerusalem I'd been literally inundated with letters from the Fellowship brothers and sisters, many of them begging me to return as soon as possible. It was perfectly clear that they'd not been told the truth about the arrangement I'd made with Noel. Using the office typewriter I sent a formal letter requesting him to stop misleading everyone. I reasserted the arrangement we'd made during our lengthy talks and made it absolutely clear I wouldn't be returning to resume membership. But I also reaffirmed my willingness to return after eight months so we could discuss ways in which our future "fellowship" might be possible. I told him to ensure this was properly explained to everyone else. Having sent the letter, I felt it must have sounded exceptionally blunt: uncharacteristically so, I hoped. Hot on its heels, therefore, I sent another handwritten one which emphasized how much I hated having to be so assertive and to-the-point, and how I'd never wanted, if at all possible, for there to be unkind words exchanged on account of my leaving. I reaffirmed my love and respect for so many of the brothers and sisters, and I expressed the wish to retain these friendships even though I would no longer be a community member.

The four months I'd spent in Israel had deepened my love for the country. But I don't think I could ever have settled as a long-term expatriate: I missed the familiarity of good old England too much.

CHAPTER TWENTY-TWO: South London life

I proposed to Jeanne whilst I was back in London and was thankfully accepted. She belonged to a flourishing evangelical church in South London – St. Mark's, Kennington, just across the road from the Oval cricket ground. We were married there in the autumn. Not that the road to the aisle had been altogether sugar-sweet and silver-lined: anything so straightforward was highly improbable if past experience can ever be taken as an indicator of what lies ahead. The problems, such as they were, were largely the result of my inability to let go of the indoctrination I'd received over the previous years. This resulted in my expectation that Jeanne would show me the same kind – or *very nearly* the same kind – of submissive obedience practised at Bugbrooke.

I was also frightened by the thought of being sucked into an avaricious whirlpool of worldly materialism and vanity, and this led me into conflict with Jeanne's parents over the wedding arrangements. They'd wanted to give their only child the best wedding possible, and they saw my stubborn refusal to countenance anything "fancy" as rather unkind, awkward, independent, and even somewhat arrogant – which, I regret, it probably was. I hadn't, however, behaved like this in an entirely thoughtless way; it was just that I'd felt compelled to stand firm, still convinced I had to pursue the simplest of lifestyles in order to please God.

For all my strange ways and ideas, for all the quirky dross which I carried out of the Community with me, for all the high-handed impositions I made upon both her and her family, Jeanne obviously felt that our relationship was worth it all; and without surrender of her own right to have a viewpoint she did everything she could to understand what was going on in my head and make allowances for me. She was unable, however, to restrict herself to just wearing long flowing frocks; it was *me* who had to accept that there was nothing wrong with a Christian woman wearing jeans as part of her normal way of dressing. Even so, she *was* gracious enough to stop wearing red toenail varnish, which, ridiculous though it may now sound, would have been just about more than I could cope with.

We memorized our wedding vows and made them, without any prompting from the vicar, as we stood facing one another. My experiences at Bugbrooke had taught me that I never again wanted to bind myself to an institution demanding wholehearted commitment – even that of marriage – without having made a full and honest appraisal of whether I had enough resources to complete building the metaphoric tower. I didn't, therefore, want to make my wedding vows purely on the basis of the love I felt at the time; I wanted to feel as certain as possible that I was strong enough to remain fully committed to our marriage even when the amorous aspects of our relationship should start to wane, which I'd come to believe would happen in most long-term unions. I haven't always been the best husband I could have been, the emotional tide of our love has known both ebb and flow, we have argued as all couples do, and when the balance of my mind was deranged – which is where my story began – I came close to betrayal through wishing myself dead.

The Happily Married Couple

It wasn't long after I'd returned to London that I eventually received a reply to the typed letter I'd sent to Noel from Jerusalem. This was the reply which I've quoted from in the first chapter of this book, the one which was signed by Noel himself but had been prepared, so it said, in consultation with other senior elders. This was the letter which had accused me of pride and deceit, and, more importantly, of having *sinned against the brotherhood.* It was the letter which had urged me to *repent of my pride and sin and return to the fold of the Community or else the judgement of Matthew 18 vv.15-17 will apply.* I replied straight away, making it quite plain – once again – that there could *never* be any question of me returning to Bugbrooke as a community member. Noel already knew this perfectly well, of course, and it was there for the written record in the letters I'd sent from Jerusalem.

Following receipt of my letter, my excommunication was ratified and the flock was instructed to have nothing more to do with me; neither to talk with me on the phone nor write to me, even in response to letters which former friends might receive from me. I was to be regarded as one under the judgement of God. Even dear old Betty, who had been something of a mother to me within the Community, became subject to these dictates. She *did* come to the phone when I rang and asked to speak with her, but then she briefly explained how she couldn't disobey the instructions she'd been given and wouldn't be able to speak with me again. Her tears were quite plain as she asked me sincerely for forgiveness. This, together with some much blunter rejections from those who'd been my closest friends, was painful; but I knew I couldn't allow myself to dwell on what had happened or I would never be able to truly start again. The saddest aspect of all this, I think, was the statement it made about the love and friendship by which, five years previously, I'd been so overwhelmed. *What kind of friendship is it that's based not on your loyalty to one another but to a "system"? What kind of friendship is it when your friend will "lay down their life for you" one day but then, the next, will scorn and reject you because they've discovered your allegiance to the corporate entity isn't pure?*

Those within the Community were only doing as instructed, of course, and the pressure to comply was enormous – nigh on irresistible. But no one can hide themselves behind the cloak of corporate responsibility for ever. All corporate action comprises the aggregated action of individuals, and somehow, sometime, everyone must answer for themselves. For *me*, I have no wish ever again to be told by a spiritual overlord how I should behave towards those people whom I regard as my friends. If they do me – or anyone else – wrong, then it's a matter to be sorted out between the pair of us within the parameters of our friendship; it's *not* a matter on which I will be dictated to by a third party.

Given the attitude towards contraception which I'd inherited from the Community (not to be used!), it wasn't really surprising that in August 1983 our first child, Rebekah, was born at Queen Charlottes's Hospital – where Jeanne had trained as a midwife – after scarcely ten months of marriage. It had been a long and difficult labour, and Jeanne had only narrowly missed needing to have a forceps delivery: the baby turned over from her transverse presentation just as the anaesthetist was about to plunge the epidural needle into Jeanne's lower back – and then everything happened amazingly quickly.

After baby Rebekah had been taken to the nursery, I sat quietly with Jeanne – who kept drifting in and out of an exhausted sleep. I wouldn't wish to belittle the intensity of my feelings by trying to describe them. There had been times when I'd despaired of ever becoming a father, but now my dream had come true. And here I was sitting with the woman who was at the heart of it all. I was alarmed, though, at the amount of blood I could see beneath her on the bed and suspected it not to be normal – inexperienced as I was in making assessments of this kind. So I left her alone to find the sister and express my concern. When she too had seen for herself the extent of the haemorrhaging, the senior registrar was immediately called. After an examination, his immediate concern was to arrange for an urgent blood transfusion.

'You must understand,' he explained, 'that the blood hasn't been screened.'

We knew he was referring to AIDS, an illness that had just begun coming to public attention. But the effects of the serious haemorrhage were potentially fatal if immediate action weren't taken. We therefore had to weigh up the balance of probabilities instinctively: a remote, unknown, uncertain risk against an immediate, obvious, visible, near-certain one. The only real choice available to us was Hobson's. Jeanne was given four pints of blood in total and, as the level of her haemoglobin rose and the colour returned to her face, we knew that all would be well with the three of us. The long-term risk of the transfusion was soon forgotten as we got on with the process of building our home and our family.

Simeon came next, fifteen months later, and *his* birth was even more fraught with complication – what is it about midwives? He was finally delivered by an emergency caesarean section. Given the effect of childbirth on Jeanne's body, given the clear compatibility of our bodily union, and given the time I'd now had to discuss, reflect on, and reject the dogma of *fornication for procreation only*, the decision we both came to about using rhythm-method contraception – for the time being anyway – wasn't a hard one.

CHAPTER TWENTY-THREE: Speaking out

One of the challenges which presented itself after I left the Fellowship – and which has given me enduring problems throughout the years since then – was what I was going to do to earn a living. My studies at Warwick had ended abruptly and I didn't have the necessary qualification to pursue a career in teaching: the career for which I'd come to believe I was best suited. The immediate problem I faced was quite simply one of needing to earn enough money to live on. The "relief of need" payments which the Fellowship claimed would be made available to those who left hadn't been offered to me, even though I'd handed over all of my university grant payments and all of the money I'd earned by working on the farm since the summer of 1979. No one had even contacted me concerning the small *capital payment* I'd made into the Jesus Fellowship Community Trust: a sum which ought to have been refunded but never was.

In different circumstances I might have considered reapplying to teacher-training college, but I needed – or rather wanted – to have a regular income as soon as possible so that I could get married and, so I hoped, begin a family. In Jane Austen's novels, the gallant male suitors are often required to wait until they have "established" themselves before marriage can be considered, a requirement that sometimes took quite a number of years. Hardly anyone feels the need to behave with such self-restraint and circumspection any longer, do they? I certainly didn't. Even so, I sometimes feel just a wee bit disappointed in myself that I didn't take a longer-term view of my situation. But I was impatient to "get on with my life" as I saw it back then; and I felt I'd already served sufficient time as a nuptial probationer. Whilst applying for jobs which I felt to be somewhere in line with my academic qualifications, I kept myself financially afloat with a series of casual jobs: minicab driving, market trading, and then window cleaning. As might be expected, each of these episodes is underpinned with a plethora of explanations and anecdotes. I shall restrict myself to just one of these, and this simply so I can also include an amusing aside.

When a new friend, Dave, was preparing to move to Brighton with his family, he somehow managed to strong-arm me into buying the small window-cleaning business that he'd been building up over a number of years. It was hard work, often cold, and sometimes dangerous as I literally hopped from one window ledge to another on the frontage of the large, three-storey town houses in the more salubrious parts of Kennington. But I applied myself to the task with the virtue for which I'd become known – diligence. In fact I even began to get some lucrative contracts in Chelsea, one of them being at a house belonging to the Rymans – the family who owned the hugely successful stationery chain.

The house in question should more accurately be described a mansion. On one occasion while I was cleaning the windows inside, I noticed

– looking out – that a chauffeur-driven Rolls Royce had pulled up close to the front door. The activity going on round about me within the household led me to conclude that young master Ryman, who kept coming and going with different items of luggage, was on the point of being taken back to boarding school. As he came past me in the hallway, I stopped what I was doing to have a chat:

'Looks to me as if you're about to go off back to school,' I volunteered.

'Yah. I am!'

'Where d'you go to?'

'Eton!'

'Oh! That's interesting! I went there as well, you know.'

The expression on his face was the perfect picture of being taken aback.

'Which house were you in?' he asked.

'RDB – Bob Baird's.'

'Crikey,' he said with astonishment – and possibly disbelief – *'I've never met a window cleaner who went to Eton before.'*

No, I don't suppose he had. Has there *ever* been another apart from myself?

'Ah!' I sighed, *'It's a long story; a long story.'*

My year-long career carrying around a bucket of warm soapy water and a scrimmy came to an end when I began taking on what can loosely be called "home-improvement work" for various members of St. Mark's church's large congregation. As has so often been the case with me, one thing led to another and I soon became competent at most kinds of decorating, tiling and joinery. Having carefully studied DIY manuals and pestered various tradesperson-friends with questions, I set about deploying my novice-grade electrical and plumbing knowledge whilst renovating our small, newly-acquired 2-up-2-down; and I fairly quickly became proficient enough to tackle jobs such as rewiring and kitchen/bathroom-fitting for remuneration: formal plumbing and electrical qualifications weren't compulsory back then.

In addition to my home-improvement work, I was also employed on a part-time basis by our church at Kennington. Luis Palau, an Argentinian evangelist in the mould of Billy Graham, hit town in 1984 with his "Mission to London". St. Mark's anticipated the arrival of new converts, and it also wanted to ensure everyone in the church was able to participate in the mission as fully as possible. The church was in a healthy financial position from its generous congregational tithes and donations, so the vicar and leadership team were able to offer a salaried position to someone they believed had the flare and organizational ability to ensure the mission objectives were met. Step forward yours truly! I was given the title of "evangelism secretary" and wholeheartedly enjoyed sharing in the excitement many experienced through our involvement with Luis Palau's crusade. When it was all over,

I was asked to stay on in post and take lead of the many different ways in which St. Mark's sought to fulfil its duty of being "a light to the world"; a responsibility that had very practical social-care dimensions as well as spiritual ones.

When, several months after Jeanne and I had tied the knot, I answered the phone in the little flat we were then renting, the very last person I would have expected to hear at the other end was Noel Stanton. His voice was in distinct "purring" mode rather than a "roaring" one.

'Hiya, bro, how ya doin? he began. 'I guess you maybe hadn't expected to be hearing from me.'

No! I Certainly hadn't!

He went on to tell me how he thought it would be appropriate to lift my excommunication now that I'd entered into wedlock – and would I like to come and meet some of my old friends as a step in the direction of "restoring fellowship"?

'On your bike, mate! You haven't even said sorry for the way you've treated me,' would have been a perfectly reasonable reply. And yet I couldn't resist taking advantage of my first chance in well over a year to see the likes of Shaun, Graeme, Betty – and even Nigel; so I accepted his offer. By now, however, I really should have known better, should have let my instincts warn me that something sneaky was going on – even if I didn't know what it was. Why should Noel have just rung me out of the blue given all that had taken place? And what earthly or heavenly difference had my marriage made? How could it have cancelled out all those sins against the Fellowship which Noel had explicitly accused me of and were the reason for my exclusion? My excommunication, so he'd claimed, came about as a result of consultation with a group of elders representing the Fellowship. 'How could it have been negated without a similar consultation?' I wondered.

I arranged to take Jeanne with me on a day-visit a few weeks later. And what a strange day it proved to be. Noel himself, although friendly enough, had very little to say to me; others didn't seem to know how to treat me. Shaun, who'd been detailed to "look after me" for the day, explicitly asked when I'd allow the Lord to deal with my "hard heart" so that I might be restored to the brotherhood. I felt certain, though, that at least Graeme would be his normal friendly self towards me – when I eventually got to see him. I kept reminding Shaun that I'd like to go to Cornhill Manor – where Graeme lived – before time ran out on us, and I was told it was all in hand. Finally, when it was very nearly too late anyway, I was told that "the brethren" – whoever they may have been – didn't think it would be a good idea for me to meet Graeme: he'd find it all too difficult; it wouldn't be "helpful". It was all beginning to sound very familiar! And where was Nigel I wondered?

'We've been having a lot of problems with Nigel,' one of the farm brothers explained, 'and now he's gone and split, leaving us with real operational problems.' he lamented. 'What's more, he's been spreading all kinds of malicious stories. Noel's really upset about it all.'

I bet he was! I should have put two and two together there and then. I should have realized that Noel, in his cack-handed way, had been trying to sweeten me so that when the inevitable happened, when Nigel and I ended up getting together, I would maybe not be such a kindred spirit with him as I otherwise might be. Noel hadn't, however, been able to roll back time and change the underlying attitudes towards me within the Community that he himself had brought about. Given the uncertain and ambivalent way Jeanne and I were treated, I felt even more distanced than before – if such a thing were possible.

Nigel somehow managed to track me down at my new address not many weeks later. Unsurprisingly, we spent the best part of the day together catching up on all the news about the Fellowship, and I learnt how his own departure had been just as messy and hurtful as my own. To say that he'd been treated badly would be the most gracious way in which I could summarize his story – far stronger words would actually be more appropriate. For years, Noel had treated Nigel as something of a confidante; now, apparently, he'd discarded him as a vindictive rebel.

Ever since leaving for Jerusalem, I'd believed it important to be circumspect in what I said to other people about the Fellowship. This wasn't *only* because I wished them no harm; it was also because I wanted to somehow prove that, contrary to the popular belief of many members, those of us rebels who'd split didn't necessarily end up becoming "all bitter and twisted". But all these self-imposed strictures, as I was now coming to realize, were still on *their* terms. I was still playing by *their* rules. What finally tipped the balance, I think, was hearing about an article which the minister of a church in Dunstable, Stanley Jebb, had written about the Fellowship in "Renewal" magazine – a respected mouthpiece and sounding board for the Charismatic movement in general. The article was written, so I understand, at the behest of Michael Harper – one of the most respected and well-known luminaries of the house-church movement. Michael had been invited to visit the Community during a reaching-out exercise Noel had initiated. It was following this visit that Michael asked Stanley Jebb to write an article. SC has referred to the article in his book and has this to say about it:

"Stanley Jebb attributed our comparative success to strength of leadership and careful shepherding, to the application of the Scriptures, to holiness and to covenant loyalty. The criticism, he reckoned, stemmed mainly from gossip and ignorance of the real facts.

'The church is orthodox in doctrine. Being different is not the same as being heretical. . .' he wrote.

He saw the danger of the Jesus Fellowship becoming isolationist. But he said there was also the danger of:

'having our way of life challenged, our horizons widened, and our understanding of Scripture tested if much contact is made with the Bugbrooke Fellowship. Some are not willing for this, so they stay away.'"[47]

Stanley Jebb's article infuriated me! He'd been lured into the same trap as Lewis Misselbrook before him. Both had presumed themselves able to write about the Fellowship on the basis of comparatively short visits and meetings with Noel. I was especially incensed by Mr. Jebb's inference that criticism of the Fellowship came from gossip and ignorance. His comments in general were well-intentioned, possibly, but arrogant. I wondered whether either of these men, whilst they themselves were sat at home in their comfort zone writing about what was or wasn't correct (and through a very narrow line of sight), had seriously thought about how the "ordinary" people within the Fellowship – the very real living souls – were being treated or mistreated. *Had they taken time to consider how what they'd written might affect the welfare of those who were agonising about what was happening to them in consequence of their Jesus Fellowship membership?*

Because I'd become utterly fed up with the extent to which the spiritual games being played affected other people's lives, I broke free from thinking that I needed to keep schtum and decided instead to do everything I possibly could to let the wider church and the world know what the Community was *really* like – as only an *ex-insider* could. *Let them call me a Judas; I no longer cared.* I had plenty of things I was all too keen to get off my chest. I'd seen too many of the manipulative techniques used to persuade other Christian observers that black was white, that the New Creation Christian Community was totally different to the damning picture of it painted by its critics. The so-called "openness" which had been utilized to self-publicize the Community provided the outside world with no more an accurate picture than the Queen's garden parties provide of the private life within Buckingham Palace. I found myself compelled, for the sake of truth and those left behind, to disclose everything I knew about life as a member of this cult. So I bought myself a little portable typewriter and set about writing a report which was largely based on the diary I'd kept while doing research at Warwick University. My manuscript, "The Church Community at Bugbrooke", ended up filling just over ninety pages of A4. An architect friend from church, who knew what I was doing and supported me throughout, volunteered the use of his office photocopier. Many days were then spent tediously copying the report, page by page, until I had about a dozen copies. These were distributed to the various church leaders whom I'd selected from the many more I would have liked to send it to had resources permitted. I'm no longer sure who the chosen ones were, but they certainly included leading figures in the Baptist Union and the Evangelical Alliance. I didn't know, of course, about the impact it was going to have, nor that it was the beginning of a long confrontation with the Jesus Fellowship Church which would wend and weave its way through my adult life.

CHAPTER TWENTY-FOUR: Engaging the media

Nigel and I became the best of friends after that first visit he'd made to our London flat. Our friendship was built on far more than our common experiences of the Community – and leaving it. We were both adjusting to the freedom of "life in the world" and discovered mutual interests in philosophy, literature and social observation. We found ourselves able to chat together for hours about all kinds of esoteric nonsense without getting bored, and most of all we found a mutual respect that had been markedly absent during our Community days. Although he lived in Leicester, Nigel often drove down to visit us at weekends; and all the more frequently after he struck up a relationship with Maggie, another member of the St. Mark's church family.

Noel, we discovered, had treated us both with remarkably similar methods of duplicity, and he'd then gone on to try and prevent us getting together as "a common enemy". His plan had backfired spectacularly, especially so after we agreed together that we should approach the Northampton Chronicle and Echo with our respective stories. Alex, the reporter assigned by the editorial team to meet with us, was a wonderfully lugubrious man with a droopy, walrus-like moustache and a disposition that made it hard not to think of him as being the macintosh-wearing caricature of a hack from the local rag. In actual fact he was energetically conscientious and wasted little time in beginning preparations for what he would call a "special report"; one which would run every day for a full week. We couldn't have wanted anything better. This meant that several articles would be published each day and would cover different topics in some depth: seriously rather than scurrilously – just as we'd hoped. It meant, of course, that Alex would be asking the Fellowship leaders to offer their own version of events too; but we were quite happy to have an opportunity to speak what we knew to be true, openly and honestly, and then let those reading the articles decide for themselves what they could or couldn't trust. Alex seemed to "get" the issues from the off and made his intent to report truthfully perfectly clear – he was going to check everything out for himself rather than regurgitate our own take on everything.

Alex's "Special Report" ran for five days from Monday 8th. October to Friday 12th. October 1984, and it included thirteen articles in total. The headlines for some of these were:

"A CLASS SYSTEM WITH A DIFFERENCE";
"SPREADING THE WORD AND THE EMPIRE";
"NO TELLY, NO RADIO, NO DRINK, NO SPORT";
"ALL OR NOTHING – THAT'S THE MESSAGE";
"FROM BANK CLERK TO FOLLOWERS FIGUREHEAD"; and
"OUTSIDE FAMILIES COME SECOND SAY EX-MEMBERS".

Nigel and I were each featured in articles which covered the essence of what we'd told Alex about our own experiences. He ran mine under the headline, "I BECAME A MORAL ROBOT". Revisiting it after all this time has left me feeling subdued and reflective, especially after reading Dave Hawker's responses as the Fellowship's PR man. Dave, whom I've kept in contact with ever since he left, has since told me that he himself became aware of having been brainwashed after he'd read my own comments on the subject within my report on the Church-Community. The tone of Alex's special report is well reflected in what he wrote about me:

"On the fateful day a man finally broke his ties with the Jesus Fellowship, one elder forcibly tried to prevent him closing his car door and driving away into the outside world. *'It was as if he were trying to prevent a burglar driving off with the loot,'* said the man. The reason for the action by the elder was that the man had carried out sociological research on the community and he wanted to take his confidential notes with him. *'I felt I was the only person entitled to possess the information and I was determined to take what was, after all, my own property,'* he added.

The breakaway by the man, now 27, and happily married, signalled the end of a remarkable period in his young life and the beginning of a new era for him. A life that had seemed full of promise when he won a scholarship to Eton; a life that went sour when he turned to drugs and 'dropped out'; a life that brought him into contact with the Jesus People where he rose to become a Household Elder; a life of love for another community member; and a life when he finally realised he had become what he called a 'moral robot'.

His story, told in quiet, reserved tones, sitting in the lounge of the London inner city house where he now lives, is a chilling tale, that begins at the firmly established school of Eton. *'I loved my first years there but somewhere along the line, the rot set in,'* he said. The rot was him flirting with the use of the drug LSD – *'a devastating nightmare from which I feared there would be no recovery'*. In the end, he had to leave Eton, and after specialist treatment, found a job in the Civil Service, returned to a College of Further Education, worked in a Home and Garden Centre and then accepted the opportunity to begin a social science course at the University of Kent based in Canterbury. While at the university, he became actively involved with the Christian Union where he met a young girl who was the first to tell him about the Jesus Fellowship. *'I was determined to go and find out the truth for myself and in my first visit I was very impressed by the industry and simplicity of lifestyle which the members displayed,'* he said. In fact, he stayed over the weekend and said: *'I returned to Canterbury assured that I had just spent a couple of days with a sincere company of believers.'*

Community members encouraged him to return and he did so in the summer of 1977 when he asked two important questions: *'If I join the* community will I be allowed to continue my university course – and, will I be allowed to get married?' He said: 'I was assured I would be allowed to continue my university course and was also told that if it seemed right for me to get married at some future point then no-one would object.' He added: 'After several weeks of formal residence within the community I was baptised by full immersion in water. I was also aware that at 20 years of age I was making a pledge of community membership which was lifelong.'

But the storm clouds were soon to gather over the man's involvement with the community. An elder was appointed to oversee him and 'I had to seek permission for almost every move I made.' Senior elder Mr. David Hawker commented: 'It sounds from this as if he was not free to make his own decisions. This is, of course, untrue. Elders in the church give advice and guidance, but do not forcibly impose their will on anyone.'

One problem was the man's course at University. 'When I returned to the community after my first week back at university, the Elder was adamant that I would need to leave. He was even unhappy about me returning in the same car as the woman [Debbie from Canterbury] to wind things up and instructed me to travel by train. I was very confused and eventually a more senior Elder intervened,' said the man.

In his third year at Canterbury, he started to fall in love with a young woman he had helped lead into the community. He was 22 at the time and confided his feelings to Elders. By the summer of 1980, he was still in love and talked with the girl's Elder about his feelings for her. 'He told me that I should leave it for a year and if I still felt the same way, then he would consider the initiation of courtship,' said the man.

And by the winter months of the same year the man began to have doubts about his life in the community. He said: 'I was aware that I had somehow been persuaded to take on board actions and attitudes which were totally against my innermost convictions as a person and as a Christian. For instance, I had become suspicious of other Christians – an attitude which, if not positively encouraged in the community, is implicit in so much of its teaching. In fact, I realised what a moral robot I had become.'

Mr. Hawker commented: 'If the man's attitude towards the other Christians was wrong, he should answer to his own conscience and not blame the community.'

Despite his misgivings, the man was appointed a junior Elder in January, 1981 and for a time the suspicions about community life disappeared. But within a couple of months they had resurfaced with his love for his fellow community member at the heart of the problem. In March, he asked the young woman's Elder if the time was ripe to begin a relationship with her *'as at the end of the year I would be 25 and had waited reasonably patiently for two-and-a-half years already,'* he said.

A month later her Elder said he felt confident a relationship should begin but within a few days he changed his mind. *'I felt like a helpless rag doll being torn in two directions,'* he said. It was at this stage that the man claims Mr. Stanton intervened. *'The cowardly way in which the whole affair had been handled left me with numb realisation that I no longer had any basis on which I could trust the leadership,'* said the man.

Mr. Hawker said: *'It is sad that the man is now expressing apparent bitterness over this affair. Mistakes may well have been made, but there was never any malice intended. In fact he would have married eventually. As it was, he took matters into his own hands and left.'*

The man got over the heartache – but began to look at his involvement with the community more closely. On September 31, he took a British Airways flight to Tel Aviv – *'a flight to freedom,'* he said. But Mr. Hawker emphasised that the Fellowship paid his fare for the flight in full.

While he was away, he wrote to Mr. Stanton making it clear that he had no intention of returning as a committed community member, but 'pleaded' not to be regarded as an enemy. In January, 1982, he returned to Stockton House in Warwickshire to collect his personal belongings, a scene which ended in near farce with an Elder hanging on to his car door as he drove off.

Mr. Hawker commented: *'It should be noted that, in spite of now being in a position of Christian leadership, the man has, over the past 18 months, rejected repeated attempts at reconciliation with the Jesus Fellowship. We find it strange that a Christian man should choose to attack his fellow Christians in this way and refuse to respect Church confidences. Jesus taught forgiveness, and we have no wish to retaliate in a similar way.'"*

Alex's special report had been, I felt, painstakingly compiled, comprehensive, and also even-handed. He had honourably covered all of the issues which Nigel and I had asked him to albeit that many of the punches were pulled, or rather parried, by quite a number of instances where Dave had been allowed to have the last word – the one, of course, which would remain in the reader's mind. His decision to afford so much space for the elders' riposte story may well have been journalistically correct; but, at least for me, it made for very hard reading. Unlike the other articles in which Dave's responses were included, the elders' story was entirely one-sided; nor had it been made available for comment from Nigel or me. This came as something of a disappointment, especially as it was published as a finale. Maybe Alex had been pressurized into presenting his special report in the way he did, either from his own editorial team or from the Fellowship. I simply didn't know, so I had to just hope that those reading "OUR STORY – BY THE ELDERS" would remember what they'd also read on the previous days. By way of completeness, then, this is what the readers had in front of them (with certain omissions purely in the interests of brevity):

"To round off our series, senior elder Mr. David Hawker, Mr. Noel Stanton and other leading elders have contributed this article...

Christianity has always been a radical and at times controversial religion. Jesus was so controversial he was crucified. The early Church was violently persecuted under the Roman Empire. And many Christian groups through the centuries have suffered in similar ways. So we are not surprised when, as 'Jesus People', we also are regarded as controversial, even in 'Christian' Britain. We hope it is because we have chosen to be radical in following Christ.

Some people are supportive and understanding, others are openly hostile. But most are simply curious, and perhaps a little suspicious of this unusual group of people who have a different lifestyle from their own. Although to the outsider we may seem mysterious, most of us are quite ordinary people with ordinary jobs, simply seeking to follow Christ in today's society. We are grateful therefore for this opportunity to share something of our beliefs and lifestyles. ...

... Community living did not start until about five years later. A book by an Anglican clergyman, the Rev. Michael Harper, prompted us to read again the description of the early church in the New Testament where we found that 'those who believed were of one heart and soul, and no one said that any of the things he possessed was his own, but they had everything in common.' (Acts 4:32) We prayed over what we read, and realised that God was calling us to follow their example. Pooling our resources and establishing community sharing was a challenging experience as we sought to apply New Testament truths in a 20th Century setting. We made mistakes and learned from them as we went along. ...

... We have survived, but it has not always been plain sailing. Some have left over the years, although few have seemed as disillusioned as those whose stories appeared in the Chronicle and Echo this week. Most leave simply because they feel unable to sustain the inward commitment needed for life in Christian community. Some remain members of our Church. Many who have left continue to be our friends. Is it really so hard to leave the Community once you have joined? Not really, although it is not something to be done lightly any more that you would join lightly. We have entered a serious commitment which we would normally hope to be lifelong, as in a religious order, and we are fully aware of what is expected through that commitment. The close friendships formed in Community are often painful to break, and these things naturally cause a certain amount of pressure upon a person to stay. But if someone expresses a settled intention to leave they can do so, and are normally given financial assistance as well. ...

... There are all kinds of people in the Church. Many of us were ordinary people who responded to the call of God to live as Christians in the world, but others were in particular need. Over the years we have seen God work in powerful ways in people's lives. Nothing brings us greater joy than seeing drug addicts and alcoholics released from their addiction, the sick restored to mental and physical health, and people finding healing from the traumas of marriage and family break-ups. Our gospel meetings are often full of people giving testimony to what God has done in their life: there seems to be a new story of God's saving work almost every day. ...

... But what about this famous 'business empire'? Are we really out to make so much money as we can? Certainly we need to make a profit, as with all businesses. But that is not the main aim. Some find it strange that Christians should be involved in business, although there is nothing wrong with honourable trade. Through the centuries Christians have run businesses. Our main purpose is to provide work for community members; and there are other benefits as well. Our businesses are flexible enough to release people for other Christian service when required; they help build a sound economic base for our outreach work; and they provide a service to the public. Farm work can fulfil a therapeutic need for those who are as yet unable to hold down a normal job. ...

Perhaps the most consistent criticism we face is that individual freedom is restricted in community. We see it as releasing the individual to find a new freedom in service to God and his fellow men. The commitment is entered into voluntarily with full knowledge of the lifestyle and responsibility involved. There is a probationary period of up to 18 months for new members. Each member agrees to submit his life to the disciplines and loyalties of the community. It is a little similar to the vows taken by members of religious orders. Of course we are not entirely free just to 'do our own thing' – selfish independence is replaced by interdependence. It is the same for all, including leaders.

We know we are not perfect, and we are still learning. Inevitably we have made mistakes over the years and, if we have hurt anyone we regret it. No malice is intended. We ourselves have been hurt at times, but have learned not to retaliate. We are willing to ask forgiveness where needed, and to seek reconciliation with any whom we may have offended.

The community welcomes visitors, both to its public meetings and to its houses. You won't be 'brainwashed'. No one will stand in front of the door to stop you from leaving. But we hope you will be challenged and inspired by seeing a group of people who, despite their many failings, have decided to devote their lives to follow Jesus Christ."

My feelings about this article were that, had I been reading it as a non-partisan local, I would probably have had sympathy with most of the explanations given. Rather than just bite my tongue, therefore (as I often had), I decided one last attempt was needed to defy the cynical cloak of concealment used by the Fellowship's leaders to confusticate the truth with what appeared to be plausible and conciliatory statements. Out came my letter-writing pen, and what it produced was published by the Chronicle and Echo in the letters page on October 25th. under the title, WHY I AM SO DEEPLY WORRIED:

"As an ex-member and junior elder of the Bugbrooke community (who featured in the recent series of articles by your reporter), I would like to point out that the comments from the Community's public relations officer, Mr. David Hawker, carry very little credibility.

Let me defend this statement by reference to some words from a popular Community hymn, authored from within the Jesus Fellowship and sung at their meetings. In the recent series Mr. Hawker claimed, 'if a person expresses a settled intention to leave nothing is put in the way to stop them.' Does Mr. Hawker regard the fear and guilt which the Community imposes on such people as "nothing"? I quote from hymn No. 486 (Jesus Fellowship song book) which is aimed at people who are intending to leave:

'Not with his Brethren would he stand.
His blood was now on his own hands;
He trampled on the son of god,
And thus profaned the covenant blood.'

I am deeply worried that impressionable people in your neighbourhood will be hoodwinked by the pious claims of the Bugbrooke Community in the same way that I was for many years. Oh yes, for some the first impression of the Community will be of an honest, warm, sincere company of believers. But oh, what a different story is revealed behind the closed doors of Community membership.

Mr. Hawker claims that only those who are 'selfishly independent' will suffer any restriction of freedom. I ask if it is 'selfishly independent' to want to sleep in the same bed as your wife? I think not, and yet many

Community couples are put under intense pressure to sleep apart in single beds. Is it selfishly independent to support a recognised charity (e.g. Christian Aid) from one's own earnings? I think not, and yet Community members are not allowed to do so.

Many people who join the Community in good faith but later wish to leave are prevented from doing so; not by locked doors and fears of financial hardship but by the indoctrination of the Community's lifestyle and teaching.

I beg you with my whole heart to print this letter in full and help spare some souls from the emotional and spiritual agony which I and many others have experienced through our membership of the Bugbrooke Community."

Passionate words, because passion was the sharpest tool I had available. Learning to reign it in over the years hasn't, alas, been altogether successful.

CHAPTER TWENTY-FIVE: Jesus Cult

The option to quietly and gracefully leave my experiences of the Jesus Fellowship behind me would have proved problematic even if it had been what I'd wanted. Old friends from inside, now on the outside, seemed to turn up on a fairly regular basis; so I was kept well-briefed on latest developments. But one person who came knocking at our door in 1985 was previously unknown to me, and it would have been all too easy to feel rather unsettled by him – even a little scared, maybe – if the judgement made from initial appearances had prevailed. There was something distinctly gothic about Pete Eveleigh – as I remember him – with his leather jacket, black clothes, and decorative accoutrements. Pete came to me with his story of three years spent in the Fellowship which had led him to consider it a cult. Like many, his departure had been an intensely difficult one. For all the goodwill I felt towards him, I couldn't somehow get the full measure of him or dispel the unease he left me with. Even so, we continued to meet up occasionally, and I gradually thawed towards him as I grew to understand the depth that lay beneath his unconventional and rather awkward outward persona. More than that, I came to value and respect the evaluations he made about what was happening within the Fellowship.

Through Pete in particular I got to hear all about the razzmatazz involved in the Fellowship's new style of street evangelism: exuberant outdoor singing and worship using guitars, banjos, trumpets and bongos; free "street papers"; stickers; banners; and the adoption of blue, gold, white and red as themed colours to visibly announce that the "Jesus People" were in town. Perhaps the most striking indicator of their arrival was the newly acquired coach which had been resprayed in their distinctive colours and elongated, copyrighted, red-cross logos. Named as "Crusader", it had been fitted out with a kitchen, tables and comfy seats; a base where the street evangelists could welcome those they'd met with refreshments and talk to them about Jesus and the kingdom of God. I also got to hear about the evangelistic outreach in Milton Keynes, and "Anchorage" – the new house, home and hub which had been established in Birmingham.

Pete showed me copies of the new "Lifenews" paper featuring stories of miraculous healings and astonishing conversions amongst those from the wilder side of life. SC tells us the Fellowship had even begun singing popular evangelical choruses from the "Mission Praise" hymnbook, one which was used in many of the "renewed" congregations up and down the land... its content would largely have been rejected as wishy-washy and compromised not many years previously. It *seemed* the Fellowship had loosened up and rediscovered some of the spontaneity and joy which had characterized those earlier days of outreach on the streets of Northampton: *this is where I came in* SC wrote, referring back to how things were well over a decade ago. But both Pete and I saw it all from a rather different perspective. I felt sure that nothing much had *really* changed, that the razzmatazz was only a cosmetic rebranding to achieve the same ends, that the focus remained on taking people from one kingdom to another – to Noel Stanton's one if I was going to stop, as he'd often urged, being mealy-mouthed. When Pete told me about the target that had been set for 200 Christian converts and how they were to be integrated into the kingdom at Bugbrooke, I knew I should hold firm to my convictions. He shared with me a confidential document distributed to leaders prior to the 1984 outreach campaign. In it, Noel told them to expect 200 people to be taken "into covenant" and gave the following instruction:

"When new friends are saved, urge them on to Baptism in the Spirit and Baptism in Water. They will then receive the Right Hand of Covenant and become Covenant Members. AIM FOR THIS TO BE COMPLETED WITHIN THREE MONTHS OF FIRST CONTACT WITH THEM."

I have sometimes been slated for referring to the Fellowship's outreach ventures as being "recruitment drives". In light of the above, what other description would be better? And what, too, about the professed probationary-period which claimed to safeguard people against pressure to become members? I desperately wanted to draw wider attention to such issues, but I was unsure about how far I was prepared to go in order to do so.

When Pete came to me with the idea of creating our own spoof copy of the pamphlets which were being circulated under the "Jesus People" moniker, I was initially very wary; all the more so after he suggested it should be headed as "Jesus Cult" and use a similar red-cross logo to the one which the Fellowship had adopted. I had, so I felt, avoided gratuitous provocation in the opposition I'd shown to date: Mr. Reasonable and Mr. Truthful were the titles I'd wanted to be known by. Further still, denoting the Fellowship in print as unambiguously being a cult would surely lead to a litigious response, wouldn't it? I had, by now, more or less secured my acceptance to be trained by the Anglican church as a priest, and I wasn't at all sure I could cope with any more boat-rocking on the path ahead. I now had the chance to pursue what I believed to be a genuine vocation and start a period of family and career stability that had so far eluded me. Pete had other ideas for me. He was persistent and persuasive and, one way or another, determined to go ahead.

The first thing I needed to get clear in my head was the certainty with which I could claim the Jesus Fellowship to be a cult – a claim which I could defend in court if need be. So back to the books. Different texts had slightly different definitions of a cult, but there were six key features on which all the texts seemed to be agreed. These were:

1. **A charismatic, authoritarian leader.** Religious cults always have a leader – normally alive but sometimes dead – who is venerated as being infallible, or very nearly infallible, in his prophetic interpretation of God's wishes and commands. The leader typically exercises a control which cannot be challenged: his word is final.
2. **Isolationism.** Cult members are encouraged to break contact with family and friends outside the group. They are taught that their allegiance should be towards the cult as their new, or real, family. Within the cult they find a new identity.
3. **Undisputable ideology.** Cult members are encouraged to renounce independent thinking relating to the organization's ideology. Criticism of this ideology is discouraged or even punished.
4. **Exclusivism.** Cults often claim the superiority of their lifestyle over other religious organizations. Members are taught to regard other religious people as inferior in some way to themselves because their devotion is less pure. Often, the cult claims esoteric knowledge which is only accessible to the initiated.
5. **Control.** Cult members are required to submit to the complete control of the group's leaders. Disobedience is regarded as sinful, and those who leave are labelled as being backsliders or even traitors.
6. **Fear of leaving.** Cult members are told that they will be punished by God if they leave. Members who do so are often shunned by their former friends.

Sometimes, for whatever reason, it's very hard to accept the truth even when it's staring you in the face. But set against the above criteria, I reassured myself that no one could deny the Jesus Fellowship was a cult, could they? Even if they did accept the cult verdict, however, the question remained about whether it was a "good" or "bad" cult. *'Was it possible,'* I'd often asked myself as a member, *'that a cult could nonetheless be a bona fide Christian church in receipt of God's blessing – i.e. a "good" cult?'* Despite having being equivocal about the answer for a very long time, I'd long since decided that the Fellowship had taken up a location on the dark side. Satisfied, then, that I could convincingly justify my claim about the Fellowship being a cult, it then became make-your-mind-up time. *Would I stick my neck out and support Pete's idea of producing a pamphlet or wouldn't I?* I knew he was headstrong and, in my opinion back then, still somewhat... rough-hewn, maybe? I also knew that the pamphlet would look very different if its design were to be entirely my own. *Was I, therefore, prepared to own the full weight of any criticism that might come of it?* I think I made the right choice. Somehow, I thought, we've got to make significantly sized waves if we're going to rock the Bugbrooke boat – and we *need* to rock it if we're going to be of any help to those we've left behind and those who might be thinking about membership. Pete, I decided, was going to get my unequivocal support. We put our heads together and decided the subjects we were going to tackle and who would write them. Once written, Pete took on the role of editor-publisher and came up with a professional-looking spoof of the Jesus People pamphlets then being distributed voluminously. The banner headline of our pamphlet, mimicking the one from the Jesus People, read "JESUS CULT: THE REV STANTON'S KINGDOM".

Distribution was left in Pete's capable hands, and so far as I was concerned there was nothing more to do. Until, that is, the vicar of our church, Nicholas Rivett-Carnac, asked to have a word with me in his office at the church. Nicholas, a wonderful man and also a baronet (though he rarely used his title of "Sir"), had received complaints from *someone* in the Fellowship about the pamphlet – had it been Noel or Dave, possibly? Nicholas and a small group from his church had visited the Community during 1981, and I'd actually been one of those who'd helped show them around. He had returned with a deeply favourable impression – I'd made sure of that, of course – which he still, I thought, clung to, even it had become somewhat tarnished. He'd been told some not-at-all-very-pleasant things about me by whomever he'd spoken with, and he now wanted to talk with me about it all. Nicholas would never have told me what I should or shouldn't do, and I feel sure nothing would have deterred him from being his own man so far as forming opinions about others was concerned. And yet my memory of our meeting is that it had been a rather strained and difficult one. It seemed he was irritated with me about the pamphlet, although he didn't explicitly say so. I remained convinced, however, that I'd acted in good faith and had done the right thing.

There were some other completely unanticipated consequences that came from the pamphlet's distribution. One of these was being contacted by a lady called Hazel Adams who lived on a neighbouring farm to New Creation. She was, so I learned, something of a pain in the flesh for Noel, and she has earned herself a mention in SC's book as the *local woman who was particularly virulent.* If indeed she was virulent in her opposition, and I'm sure she was, then her only motivation had been a genuine and disinterested concern about the way she felt young people were being treated. The time she spent liaising with parents and writing letters to one and all made her a genuine local hero in *my* book after I'd got to know her, and it still makes me sad to think that such a gentle and dedicated lady could have been vilified by the Fellowship in the way she was. Long gone now, may you rest in peace, Hazel.

Through Hazel – though I no longer have any distinct recall exactly how – I got involved in a London-based group who wanted to create a formal alliance to support those who'd been involved with cults. A certain Lord Rodney, whose daughter, Anne, had been involved with the Moonies, arranged some kind of inaugural meeting in the House of Lords, with Lord Denning – the incorrigibly mischievous former Master of the Rolls – invited as a speaker. This national treasure, a fearless-and-without-favour mercurial judge who had been wonted to deliver rulings on points of law which were often controversial but always wise, no longer looked majestic as he stood in front of us disrobed and without either wig or ermine. And when he began to speak with a broad local dialect that made him sound – to my own ear – like a close relative of Pam Eyres, it was a little hard to believe he'd once been the second most senior judge of the land. As such, it was a wee bit difficult, at least initially, to take him seriously; and yet his understanding of cults proved to be profound – especially concerning the Scientologists.

Also at the meeting was a certain psychiatrist called Elizabeth Tylden. Gobsmacked is an entirely appropriate word to describe how I felt when I realized who she was. This was the same "Betty" who'd so kindly and helpfully treated me after my LSD exploits. We had a wonderful and very happy reunion. This group of people gathered together in one of the House of Lords' committee rooms went on to form the core of what became known as "Cultists Anonymous", and I feel sure Pete was heavily involved in those early days. He was definitely responsible for "the Prayerforce Fellowship" which was connected in some way and was the named publisher of our pamphlet.

When Pete approached me to publish a second edition of the pamphlet, I found myself in two minds once again. Reports had filtered back to me about complaints being made to various Christian bodies such as the Evangelical Alliance, whose head office was only just down the road from our church. Brenda, a good friend, was PA to Clive Calver, the general secretary; and it was through her that I got to hear about what was happening. I admit to having begun feeling quite concerned about where all this was leading to, and I still wasn't convinced I could fully endorse the style in which Pete wrote his articles. Yet I continued believing I should support him: he was brave, energetic and perfectly well-motivated. So I agreed to write some more articles; but I didn't allow my name to be used as co-producer of the entire pamphlet, just as author of the actual content. Pete was happy with this and a second pamphlet came off the press. Given that we funded it all ourselves, the production run didn't amount to more than a few hundred. Once again, Pete took responsibility for distribution. Soon after, he moved to Bristol to begin a teacher-training course. We sadly ended up losing contact with one another for many years as so often happens when geographically separated.

The next I really heard about the pamphlets was when I read about them in SC's book many many years' later: I didn't get to read "Fire in Our Hearts" *in full* until 2015, or possibly even a bit after that. Knowing the effect much of it would have on me, I literally couldn't bring myself to invest the necessary emotional energy. But having done so, it seemed to me that the pamphlets' most profound impact was actually on the Fellowship itself, a completely unintended consequence of having produced them. Here's what SC has written:

"JESUS CULT — REV STANTON'S KINGDOM. That was us — according to a pamphlet that started to have a wide private circulation! This virulent little job carried allegations of heavy shepherding, deprived kids, infallible authority, legalism, empire building, world-hatred, recruitment and even forced labour. The authors twisted the truth until it was barely recognisable, and Noel in particular came under vicious personal attack.

Sadly, there was a ready market for sensational rumours, half-truths, and lies. What gave this pamphlet more credibility was that it was written by two ex-members, supposedly with 'inside knowledge'. But as Stanley Jebb had pointed out in Renewal, few churches would want to be judged by those who left them. The views of these brothers were particularly distorted. One elder who had left us received a copy and tore it up in disgust. Then he pieced it together and passed it on to us!

A group was formed to 'pray' against us, and they motivated a smear campaign. The 'Jesus Cult' pamphlet was distributed to ministers, relatives, new converts and the press. The Jesus Fellowship was discussed in churches, on radio, and even in Woman magazine! Letters flew around, and the media were fed with titbits. The effect was poisonous, and suspicion spread like cancer.

A Christian church had been reviled, and the name of Jesus dishonoured. New friends and converts stumbled as critics sought to turn away those whom we had led to Christ. We expected opposition, but this was shameful."[48]

Did our wee little pamphlet really have the profound and widespread effect which SC claims? If so, then we'd achieved far far more than I'd ever realized and I can much better understand why the Fellowship had made complaints about it. I'd often wondered what they were getting so upset about: it had felt like an elephant taking fright at the gnawing of a mouse. I fully accept that the title of the pamphlet was provocative, but less so when taken in its context as a spoof of a Jesus People pamphlet. What I'm unable to accept is the claim SC has made that its content was distorted. Take, for example, his claim that we'd written about "empire building" and "forced labour". He's referring to the content of my article about "Kingdom Riches". This is what I wrote:

"As British subjects we are all children of a 'materialistic society'. Noel Stanton preaches against the evils of wealth and materialism in no uncertain terms. He admonishes his listeners to separate themselves from the greed and injustice of a corrupt society and become members of a Community lifestyle of 'sharing and simplicity'. Such is the wonderful dream which is bound to stir the passion of those who want to fight for a better world.

CHAPTER TWENTY-FIVE

HOWEVER

In 1984 the assets of the Community holdings and business stood at a MINIMUM of between 3 and 4 million pounds. The figure increases continually as the cult's 5 or 6 businesses bring in a handsome profit and Community members donate all income, property, businesses and possessions to the Community Trust. The cult's hypocrisy is further underlined by the following points.

1. Full-time workers in Community businesses are paid only part-time wages (the rest of the working week is classified as voluntary labour) thereby minimising wage levels and income-tax payments. Meanwhile local businesses suffer because having to pay their employees a living wage means that they cannot compete. Noel Stanton simply does not care.

2. Unemployed people in the Community are required, as a condition of residence, to do labour for the Community's enterprises. Meanwhile they continue to draw D.H.S.S. payments which are immediately given into the Community.

3. The Community businesses are ruthlessly profit oriented. This is so to the extent that these 'simple religious people' employ factory-farming techniques and the cattle are injected with artificial hormones to increase productivity.

4. The Community businesses compromise their own principles for profit's sake. They sell health remedies (in their health food shops) which they admit are of questionable value. They sell sweets which members (children especially) may not indulge in, root beer and herbal cigarettes which members must not buy, and the latest in 'Worldly' clothes – against which Noel Stanton preaches."

The only sentence which I feel, with hindsight, was badly worded and ought to have been rewritten is the one about the residential condition for those who were unemployed. That they needed to "do labour for the Community businesses" could have, as SC suggests, been taken to mean "forced labour". But it wasn't entirely misleading given that work on the farm or elsewhere was a requisite residential condition for those without an income from employment. I should, however, have simply written that the unemployed needed to "work" – not "do labour" – within the businesses. My choice of words was an extremely clumsy one and I can't help but think I'd actually written, "to *provide* labour for Community businesses". If so, then "provide" was omitted when the article was prepared for print. But who knows? Quite independently of me, Pete also wrote about the "forced labour" in a different article:

"All unemployed members must do 'voluntary' farm labour. It is a condition of residence that all members 'voluntarily' give their entire income, capital and property to the community. In most instances all holidays must be spent working in the community."

What about the "deprived kids" SC mentions? There wasn't an article dealing with the subject of children's upbringing, as such, but I referred to it in the article I wrote about "Families and Marriage":

"Family life is not what the Community would have the outside world believe. Children within the Community are virtually prohibited from forming close friendships with children outside the fellowship. They are kept away from many social activities at school such as extra-curricular sport and drama. They are indoctrinated from the tenderest years and live under the expectation that if, by the age of 18, they have not accepted the Community's lifestyle, they will have to leave their homes and parents. One Baptised 17-year-old, who has been brought up in the Community, expressed a fear of leaving: 'I cannot leave because I'm afraid of what would happen if I died in the process.' She later said, 'I know that if I left my family and friends would turn against me.'"

I stand by every word of the article. If it can be inferred from it there were "deprived kids", then the Fellowship should have addressed such deprivation. And did we accuse the Fellowship of "legalism". Yes, we did – but with good reason. Here's what Pete had to say in his article, *"Thou shalt not"*:

"The Jesus People claim that they 'live by grace; not by law'. And yet they daily live according to an un-written legalistic code. So intense is the pressure to conform that a fellowship member will be made to feel guilty of sin even after watching T.V. or eating a Mars. Told that he cannot trust his own conscience (his conscience having been shaped by a corrupt world) he allows the community leadership to dictate the course of his life. A member will not ask himself whether or not he feels something is right or wrong but whether or not it is 'acceptable' in the Community.

Unless there is some valid reason for being absent all adults and children must attend all church meetings of which there are a minimum of 4 per week lasting between 2-4 hrs.

No: cinema, T.V., radio, secular music, secular books and magazines, games and sports, alcohol and tobacco, sugar in drinks, coffee, Gospel music and literature (like Buzz magazine), Christian teaching tapes, Bible study courses, attending rallies, conferences and other churches, social activities and concerts (except for proselytising), boy/girl relationships (beyond restricted casual friendships) and normal patterns of courtship amongst adults, choosing and buying clothes, dieting, make-up, pets, contraception and double beds for marrieds, toys (except home-made), 'pretend' in children's play, etc etc etc."

Pete wasn't one for holding back! Yet when I've reread what he wrote I can't find anything which is in any way untruthful. As for – finally – the "vicious personal attack" which Noel came under, here's what we jointly wrote in an article entitled, "the prophet":

"Mr Noel Stanton, who is not in fact a bona-fide Rev/Pastor (as recognised by the Baptist Union), sees himself as a prophet bringing salvation to the church and country. He views himself as a latter-day Wesley. The position of founder and prophet of the NCCC affords Stanton, a bachelor in his late fifties, several exclusive privileges as well as exemption from some Community Disciplines.

'He is a law unto himself.' He is not, in practice, subject to any control from amongst Community members and no Church Authorities outside 'Bugbrooke' have any jurisdiction over his leadership. The more mundane pastoral duties having been delegated to elders, he spends much of his time directing the fellowship's businesses, for which he is well experienced.

It is not our desire to spark a witch-hunt, but we must stress that Stanton's 'public face' is often entirely different from the one behind closed doors. Senior leaders have observed that he is very insecure and jealous of power, which 'when threatened causes the reaction of a spoilt child – temper tantrums, deceitful scheming and abuse.' He is very camera and press shy.

Since, on one occasion in a fit of temper, he called his most likely successor 'a madman', it seems likely that Stanton will retain leadership until his death."

If this was "a vicious personal attack", then it was certainly unintentional: there were far stronger words that *could* have been chosen. It may not have been a *comprehensive* review about Noel and his ministry, but it was never intended to be. It was a statement concerning his authoritarian exercise of power and the description of a hat which was a well-fitting one for him to wear. Throughout both pamphlets we bent over backwards to ensure the content was truthful, so there were no half-truths let alone lies or even exaggerations – whatever else there may have been.

CHAPTER TWENTY-SIX: Exclusion

Production of the Jesus Cult pamphlets must have caused far greater consternation for Noel than I could ever have realized until comparatively recently. Enlightenment came, once again, from reading SC's book:

"In 1986 we were embarking on a two year programme of 'explosive pioneering' all over England, evangelising and planting 'church households'. Noel had his hands full and Dave had the unenviable task of heading up a PR battle, answering the press and shuttling between leaders. Eventually we asked the Evangelical Alliance to stand with us publicly.

The Jesus Fellowship had joined the EA after Gilbert Kirby's visit in 1982. They regarded us as a controversial but doctrinally orthodox church. Not everyone agreed with us and some regarded 'community' as near heretical. Nonetheless they knew we were true evangelicals and the Alliance had welcomed us.

The EA suggested a meeting with our attackers, but we felt that unless they desired reconciliation, a meeting would achieve nothing. We were keen, though, to meet with responsible leaders and answer their questions. Dave corresponded with Clive Calver, the General Secretary of the Evangelical Alliance. In January 1986 Clive proposed a meeting of three of our leaders with some of the EA executive, and with leaders representing our opponents, to investigate 'the accusations made against the Fellowship . . . that these matters might be properly resolved'."[49]

The background to the EA's involvement, especially in the context of the Jesus Cult pamphlet, came as a surprise to me when I read about it; but it was certainly true that Clive – through his PA, Brenda – had asked if he could talk with me about the Fellowship in general. And SC's account helped me better understand what had prompted my vicar, Nicholas, to have asked for a meeting with me – the one I've already written about in the previous chapter. All those wheels-within-wheels and secretive machinations that turn and grind away when schemers deviously try to get their own way can be tortuously difficult to identify and understand until someone, maybe, throws a switch that lights up and illuminates everything. In the matter of how the Fellowship had tried to diminish the impact of the "Jesus Cult" pamphlet, it was SC who threw the illuminative switch for me. Clive Claver, it seems, had urged Noel and Dave to meet with Pete and I – their "attackers" – face to face. Unwilling to do so, and behind my back, it would appear they contacted Nicholas to ask if he would represent me – as my "responsible leader" – at a proposed meeting with the EA. No wonder the poor man was so nonplussed by it all! The cloak-and-daggers aspect of what was happening would have been way too much for him: a more transparent and open person than the late Reverend Sir. Nicholas Thomas Rivett-Carnac is hard to imagine. He would no doubt have pledged not to disclose the details of what had been asked of him, but I've little doubt he would have also refused, point blank, to have any further role in all these underhand shenanigans.

To the very best of my memory, the issue of the pamphlets didn't feature when Clive Calver and I eventually met at the EA headquarters. Most of our time was taken up discussing issues that I'd brought to light in my typewritten report, which had evidently ended up in his hands. I remember feeling chuffed that someone such as Clive had read through it all, which I doubt many had – and I'd often wondered if all the time and effort I'd put into producing it had been worthwhile. Clive explained that the EA had received a number of complaints about the Fellowship which were being looked into. In consequence, he asked my permission to have the report copied and circulated amongst members of the EA board. I willingly agreed.

A while later, Brenda told me about the meeting which had been arranged between the EA leadership board and two or three Fellowship leaders, including – so I understood – Noel Stanton. She asked if I would attend the meeting so that board members could question me before they met with the Fellowship representatives. I didn't have a proper understanding of what all this was *really* about at the time, and I feared it could well go badly for me. Ridiculously anxious as I was in everyday life about all kinds of imagined harm lying in wait to damage me and my family, this wasn't an invitation I welcomed in the least. But to have declined would have been negligent and cowardly: it would have meant abandoning the promise I'd made myself to do everything I could by way of helping all my friends back in the Fellowship.

My attendance at the meeting had a sort of conspiratorial edge to it. I was told that after I'd "done my own bit" I would be taken out the back door so that I wouldn't come face to face with "the others". It wouldn't have been a problem for me, personally, to have met them, so I wonder if Noel & co. had maybe said they wouldn't come if John Everett was involved? If so, were the EA themselves being a bit slippery? Tut-tut if they were! There were about a dozen board members sat around the table in the meeting room, which left me feeling a bit like the young, nervous schoolboy who'd faced all those intimidating schoolmasters across the huge table at Hertford County Hall when being interviewed for a scholarship place at public school. By the end of my session with the EA board it felt as if I'd been given a proper grilling, as if it was *me* who needed to justify and defend himself. Michael Barlow, a bear of man in many senses, was particularly probing:

'*You seem,*' he said, '*to be criticising the Fellowship on account of the profit which their businesses make.*'

He then looked around the table at the other board members:

'I'd be rubbing my hands with glee,' he said, *'if one of my own businesses was doing so well. Is it such a sin to be wealthy?'*

A few of the others round the table appeared to be nodding in agreement.

I replied with something to the effect of needing to understand the Fellowship's wealth in the context of their claims to poverty and simplicity, which, on reflection, wasn't the main point. What I should really have done is explained about the *means* of wealth creation: robbing the world and so forth. I think it was Clive who came to my rescue and answered Michael far more effectively than I'd done. All in all, I didn't feel as if I'd acquitted myself very well; not my finest hour as the saying goes. It led to one of the many times I questioned myself about whether all this "speaking out" about the Fellowship was something I'd got myself into "far too deep".

I heard from Brenda about the EA decision to revoke the Jesus Fellowship's membership with something close to astonishment – but deep relief. Although far removed from what I'd set out to achieve, it was also way beyond what I could have ever *hoped* for. But remembering the bile which I'd heard Noel spew out concerning the wishy-washy evangelicalism represented by many of the EA members, I didn't suppose it would have caused him too much loss of sleep. I still hadn't, perhaps, fully got the measure of the man. I hadn't appreciated just how deeply he craved veneration as the leader of a transformative Christian movement. It would seem that the EA's decision had been received with more discontent than I could have reckoned on. Over to SC again:

"We arrived in London eager to clear our name, but the EA had been receiving complaining letters and phone calls and feelings were running high. Churches, it was rumoured, had even threatened to leave the Alliance if we remained. The EA were under pressure.

We had innocently expected the accusations to be dealt with, the vendetta exposed and our integrity upheld, but the matter of the accusations was dealt with quite briefly. However, a different issue of poor relationships with local churches was raised. The EA felt compelled to suggest that we resign on this issue...

The Council sent Noel a letter assuring him that the question was not one of orthodoxy but of whether continued membership of the EA was desirable. On other matters they 'had no wish to sit in judgement'. It seemed as if they were washing their hands of us. A saddened Noel wrote back:

'Is it not surprising that a saga, which began with our advising the EA of a defamatory pamphlet and requesting their support, should end with the EA virtually dismissing us? ...

The EA has found this church an embarrassment because of opposition we are attracting in our stand for scriptural holiness ... The issues were:
1. Are the critics using lies, distortions, and unbalanced comment, and should they be reproved?
2. Is this smear campaign in the Spirit of Christ?'
Our appeal for support had been rejected. It felt like being handed over to our 'crucifiers'. Once again we experienced pain and humiliation. But the path of suffering would lead on to fruitfulness."[50]

This really was strong stuff! I was glad to have read about the Fellowship's explicit wish for me to be "reproved" – and their attempts to effect such a reproval – many years *after* this little storm in a teacup had erupted. I'd suspected that Noel and Dave had been pressing for me to be publicly discredited, and that gave me considerable anxiety in itself. *'Would this in any way affect my acceptance as an Anglican ordinand?'* I wondered. The tough skin which some may have assumed I wore simply wasn't there, as my future suicidal condition and mental illness would demonstrate all too clearly.

At roughly the same time as the EA inquiry there were further ripple effects spreading out from the distribution of my photocopied report. I was invited to a meeting with the Rev Bernard Green, general secretary of the Baptist Union of Great Britain. Unlike the meeting I had with the EA board, this meeting was one-to-one and extremely friendly. We talked for about an hour, and he told me that my report had provided the Union with the necessary corroborative information it needed – and wanted – in order to sever ties with the Jesus Fellowship Their dismissal was reported in the Methodist Recorder on November 27th. 1986:

"The council of the Baptist Union of Great Britain and Ireland has expelled from the Union the Jesus Fellowship Church (Baptist) at Bugbrooke.

The council's general secretary, the Rev Bernard Green, said the council wish to make it clear the Jesus Fellowship was free to act as they believed God was leading them. 'Our decision does not imply judgement of their standing before God.' He said the decision was made because developments in church government and authority and the change from a local church to a form of nation-wide organisation made it impossible for the Union to recognise the Fellowship as a local Baptist church.

Mr Green said the Fellowship's membership had been almost entirely nominal for many years, as illustrated by their lack of involvement in denominational life and their unilateral programme of recruitment and extension in the close vicinity of other Baptist churches without consultation. There was also the issue of adverse publicity for many years.

Mr Green stressed the Union's decision was not made with any anti-charismatic or anti-house church motives."

This time, the Fellowship were unable to soften the expulsion with the defence used concerning their EA dismissal; that the severance resulted from their resignation: they'd jumped, not been pushed. The fact they would have been pushed if they hadn't jumped was conveniently forgotten about. Unable to claim a similar leap away from the Baptist Union, Noel decided to portray it as something inevitable when a revitalized, Spirit-filled church came up against a traditional – and presumably spiritually defunct – organization such as the Baptist Union. The "official" response was quoted in the Northants Chronicle and Echo thus:

"This [expulsion] was not unexpected, because the church does not fit into the normal Baptist pattern. The Jesus Fellowship sees this [expulsion] as a victory for tradition over a living, radical expression of Christian faith."[51]

I wasn't aware at the time just how much my little jihad against the Fellowship had cost me. Although, on reflection, there must have been occasions when I engaged fully with my fight, most of the time it felt as if I'd actually been more intensely focussed on our family life and securing its future, which included the renovation of a dilapidated and ramshackle little end-of-terrace two-up-two-down that we'd miraculously – so we thought – managed to buy. I'd given up my search for graduate-grade employment after deciding to take the Anglican cloth as a priest, so the juxtaposition of self-employed home-improvement work alongside employment as an "evangelism secretary" at St. Mark's Church carried on right up until September 1986. The selection process to become an ordinand was a long drawn-out one which involved various demanding assessments designed to "test one's calling": to verify, so far as such a thing is possible, that my perceived vocation was a valid one. Nor were those responsible for selection in any hurry to get me trained up: generally speaking, the Church of England preferred its ordinands to be at least thirty – and therefore sufficiently experienced in life – before being thrown into the spiritual fray. In consequence, and after everyone involved had satisfied themselves that my calling was indeed a valid one, I had to wait until 1986 – the year when I turned thirty – before we could all move up to Durham, the city where I'd been offered a place on the theological training course at St. John's College, University of Durham. If I were to be entirely honest, then I think I would have to say that Jeanne and I made our choice as much because of how we instantly fell in love with the city itself as anything else. In doing so, we pre-empted Bill Bryson's similar falling-in-love-with-Durham experience by at least ten years.

Continuing down the road of honesty, I ought also to add that even though Cranmer Hall – a theological annex of St. John's College – had a well-established evangelical foundation, it also happily tolerated a *wide* spectrum of "churchmanship" – and I'd grown oh-so-weary of keeping pace with young, tunnel-visioned, enthusiastic champions of the faith who surged forward together, always looking for revival, always believing it to be their mission to save the world, and always rather critical – silently if not vocally – of those like myself who just wanted to sit down and rest a while, uncertain if the crowd with whom we were running was headed in the right direction.

If I'd said to Jeanne I wanted to establish a chaplaincy for astronauts in orbit, I think that she would have tried hard to make whatever adjustments to our lifestyle such a move would have entailed with enthusiasm. And if questioned about it, I think she would have said that so long as we were together as a family she would have followed me anywhere. This being so (but still having done my best to ensure we were "in this together", my best to ensure that the necessary decisions had been properly discussed between us), she gave her unstinted support to my sacerdotal ambitions. It was Jeanne who spent several days in Durham looking around for a suitable house to rent.

With all the arrangements made, we were due to move from London in September. In order to build our home and our life together, the previous five years had been hard graft; but we'd won through. Our house had been modernized, we'd been able to afford a comparatively new estate-car, we had all the furnishings and household equipment we needed (even though the living-room chairs weren't Parker Knoll), we had two lovely children (who'd done the decent thing in learning how to use potties and sleep through the night), we had one another of course, and we had an exciting future as a family ahead of us. *The meaning of all this after my unsettled years was immense.*

Before we could get away from London, however, there were to be a couple of incidents which would remind me, lest I should ever forget, how closely misfortune lurks – hiding herself in the shadows to trap the proud and unsuspecting. One of these took place when I was returning home from an evening meeting at St. Mark's. Walking along a small backstreet leading to our house (which I'd used hundreds of times previously), I heard the sound of running footsteps behind me. In the very same instant an urgent thought flashed through my head:

'This could be a really nasty place should anyone choose to attack me: no one else around, dark, and far enough away from the main road for shouts not to be heard.'

Then, for the second time in my life, I found myself looking down the steel blade of a knife, this one far longer than the first – more like a kitchen knife. It was being menacingly brandished by a young man who'd run past to get in front of me.

'Cash!' he said. *'Give me your cash!'*

His large eyes looked glaringly pronounced under the reflected haze of distant streetlights: they spoke of desperation and violence. Another youth had drawn alongside me; and I could feel the point of a second knife – held by a third assailant – in the small of my back. I was trapped. Bitterly afraid of what would follow, the situation had a petrifying unreality to it; all the more so because I knew I had no cash with me. As I stood there open-mouthed and speechless, the youth in front yelled at me again:

'Cash! Cash! Give it!'

'I haven't got any cash!' I replied pitifully. 'All I've got is credit cards! You can have those – there in my wallet in my back pocket.'

I was thrust against a nearby wall as hands groped all over me in an angry search until they'd managed to extract the wallet from the trouser pocket hidden under my duffle coat.

'Move!' one of them instructed. 'Walk! Don't turn round!'

It was an effort to do so; I felt stuck to the spot, shaking with fear.

'Maybe they'll stab me from behind when I begin to walk away,' I thought.

I just wasn't prepared, just couldn't believe it was happening. It was all so unreal, so sudden, so overwhelming. It had the same stupefying, freezing effect as the horror of a nightmare. Surely it couldn't really be happening? – and yet I knew it was.

'Just walk that way!' one of them said as he pushed me forward.

I then managed to set off, slowly and carefully. Once the distance between us was sufficient, I instinctively turned to see if I could catch sight of them running off. I saw them turning right into Fentiman Road, and they saw me looking back towards them. I took to my heals and ran for home as fast as I could. A few moments later I'd reached our front door. But I then had to fumble around for my keys before I could let myself in and close it safely behind me.

My wallet was returned to me the next day by someone who'd seen it being thrown into the rubbish shoot of his tenement block by three youths who lived on the floor above him. He'd recovered the wallet and obtained my phone number from the information inside. For all that he was prepared to tell the police what he'd seen, it wasn't considered strong enough evidence for them to make a search of the flat in question. My attackers were never caught.

Two weeks after my experience, a close friend was mugged in what must have been a very similar incident – maybe by the same gang. Paul was a solicitor who specialized in legal aid work on behalf of local young offenders. Knowing him as I did (we'd spent hours together musing over past experiences and discussing shared dreams), I suspect he may well have tried to reason with his assailants. I can just imagine him having provoked a frenzy of anger with his insisting to them that Jesus loves you.

When Robert, his neighbour, came to answer the entrance-system bell-call to their small block of flats, there was Paul – collapsed on the step and bleeding profusely. Clutching his wound, he spoke his last words:

'*Oh, dear Jesus, help me!*'

He died in the ambulance on his way to hospital. Had he lived, he would have been the first visitor from London to our new home in the North: the plans had already been made.

In many ways, London had been very kind to us; but we weren't too sorry to wave goodbye to the Mugger's Mile – as it had become known – when we drove away. Jeanne and the children were in our car and I was behind the wheel of a hire van. We'd arranged for a reliable couple of friends from St. Mark's to take on the tenancy of our little house during the forthcoming year and, with no reason to be unduly anxious, were looking forward to the quieter life awaiting us in the beauty of the Durham countryside. We drove through the night, arriving at the sleepy village of Ushaw Moor just after dawn had begun to cast her light through any gaps in the closed curtains all around.

CHAPTER TWENTY-SEVEN: Wishing myself dead

During 1987 whilst I was enjoying a romp through Durham's corridors of academia, the Jesus Army (JA) – the newly named outreach arm of the Fellowship – was marching through the streets of Northampton, Coventry, Birmingham, London, and many other towns and cities. There was an all-out drive to ensure the army was visible at the forefront of the country's Christian evangelism. Noel had become determined that people would sit up and notice his troops, not ridicule them. Becoming daredevils for Christ and warriors for Jesus, engaging in jubilant praise, rescuing society's dropouts and its scorned – all these, and more besides, were ways in which the JA sought to create a highly visible and street-orientated profile. Members were encouraged to take inspiration from general Booth's Salvation Army vision and the all-or-nothing zeal of its early pioneers. The concept of armies and battles started to become enmeshed in the very warp and woof of the Fellowship structure. The most noticeable feature of this, of course, was the combat-style JA uniform which Noel introduced; apparently he thought the jackets looked "manly". I imagine many of the sisters must have been thankful they were only required to wear green skirts and cross-emblazoned T-shirts. There was much more besides: badges, arm bands, khaki shirts, flags and banners, all featuring the JA colours – green, red, white, black and gold. A brightly painted coach was fitted out to be an evangelistic hub, and a march was held in Northampton during April to officially launch the Jesus Army as the evangelistic face of the Jesus Fellowship.

The Fellowship's numbers began to increase significantly as the street warriors ensured the name of Jesus rang out to the accompaniment of jubilant shouting and music. Targets were set for dynamic growth, not just in converts but in all areas of the Fellowship's membership structure; the number of celibates and elders for example. But many of those who were "saved" through the JA's outreach continued to remain on the periphery of the Fellowship itself, and this became a cause of concern for some of the Community stalwarts. They were also worried that amidst all the energetic activity an erosion was taking place of covenanted commitment to Zion in the form of community brotherhood and holiness. As ever, there was a lot more going on *within* the Fellowship than may have been supposed from their outward-looking presentation.

Important note: Given that the visual face of the JFC was to become increasingly identified with the Jesus Army, to the point where the movement became generally known by this name, most of my references to the JFC will now be under the abbreviated title of "the JA". I will, however, continue to use "the Fellowship", "the Community" and other titles where appropriate.

CHAPTER TWENTY-SEVEN

Jesus Army Double-Decker [a]

I knew little, if anything, about the JA activities whilst fully immersed in my theological studies and training at Durham. By the summer of 1987 I'd finished my first academic year and was doing just fine, thank you. Our rented house in Ushaw Moor had a beautiful vale, the Deerness Valley, just down the road from where we lived. A disused railway which followed the valley, now restored as country trail, was perfect for the runs I'd started taking for exercise and so-called pleasure. One gorgeous summer evening I got back from my run and threw myself down on my bed. *'Heady days,'* I said to myself, *'heady days.'*

The summer vacation, however, wasn't quite so heady. Our house in London was on the market, and for various logistical reasons I thought it was imperative to get it sold before the new term started in September – not least because it would have been left empty, and Kennington-Stockwell wasn't exactly the safest of places in the city. The exchange of contracts kept getting delayed and further delayed, whilst I became worried and more worried. I didn't handle it very well at all, and my anxiety began to affect my mental health. Thankfully – "praise the Lord" as I used to say – the situation suddenly and unexpectedly resolved itself with breakneck speed and the deal was finalized. We moved into a three-bedroom detached house in another ex pit-village close

---

[a] Jesus Army bus parked at Charing Cross in 2006. Photo loaded to Flickr by Nick Jeffrey: https://www.flickr.com/photos/nickjeffery/116013155/

to Ushaw Moor, one which we'd been able to buy from the proceeds of the sale of our London house without a mortgage and with quite a bit left over. All looked rosy enough. But I remained aware of being highly strung, carrying around with me a kind of premonition that something bad was going to happen. This was nonsense. Nothing *need* to have happened, and it wouldn't have done if I'd not been so sensitive and insecure.

Later on in the term I succumbed to a viral inflammatory fever. I ran a temperature of 103 degrees or more and was bedridden for the best part of a week. It gradually began to subside but left me feeling well and truly battered. Standing on the bathroom scales informed me that I'd lost nearly half-a-stone: I felt weak and feeble – a downright wreck. Several days later and I'd not perked up at all. And then it hit me! It was, genuinely, "just like that"; just like a sudden devastating revelation. *I've got AIDS, haven't I? That explains why I've become so feeble.* The blood given in the transfusion Jeanne had needed after Rebekah's birth, so I supposed, must have been infected. *They **did** warn us that it wasn't screened, didn't they? I've obviously caught the HIV virus from Jeanne and have now contracted AIDS.* And this was God's judgement, I told myself, for having sinned against the Jesus Fellowship, the chosen people of Zion whom he guarded jealously. Perfect! A perfectly honed, inescapable punishment delivered by an avenging God.

For a while I lay there very nearly frozen with fear. The immediate resolution to my bewitchment might have been to metaphorically throw myself into God's arms in repentance for my wickedness and plead for his mercy. But the God I'd known as a father, and the Jesus I'd known to walk with me as a friend, had forsaken me: I was on my own. I tried to think it all through, to identify any lies I may have told or any malice I'd shown; but it was all to no avail. There was nothing for which I could feel any genuine sorrow; nothing I could find to repent of. All I could feel was total numbness. This, I told myself, must be what was meant when – as I'd heard Noel preach about so often – enemies of Christ were "given over by God to a hard heart". I had sinned against the Holy Spirit and the opportunity for enlightenment would never be mine again: it was all exactly how Noel had predicted it would be in that dreadful letter I'd received. I could recall what had been written vividly, how Noel had quoted biblical verses such as ones from the book of Titus at me:

"Reject a divisive man after the first and second admonition, knowing that such a man is warped and sinning, being self-condemned." (Titus. Chapter 3, V10)

Yes! Self-condemned! That's exactly what I was. The final stage of the judgement written about in Matthew 18 had been pronounced and I'd been cast out of communion with God's church to be treated as a heathen. In short, I was beyond God's grace. Those diabolical words of judgement from one of the apostle Peter's biblical letters now begun to take a grip of me and I seemed utterly powerless to shake them off:

"For it is *impossible* for those who were once enlightened, and have tasted the Heavenly gift, and have become partakers of the Holy Spirit, and have tasted the good word of God and the powers of the age to come, if they fall away, to renew them again to repentance, since they crucify again for themselves the Son of God and put him to an open shame...

It would have been better for them if they had not known the way of righteousness than, having known it, to have turned from the holy commandment delivered to them. But it has happened to them according to the true proverb: 'A dog returns to his own vomit, and a sow, having washed, to her wallowing in the mire'."

I carried all of this around with me over the following days as my body gradually began to strengthen after the fever. My disconsolate countenance, however, told the true story. I visited our local GP surgery as soon as I could to have an HIV blood test – as did Jeanne. Both our results were returned negative and that should have been the end of the matter. But all I did was transfer my anxiety onto abnormalities I thought I'd discovered within my body, such as a bony-type lump in my neck: this, I convinced myself, shouldn't be there and was probably cancerous. Slowly but surely I was becoming mentally ill.

I held out for several weeks before my eventual collapse. I'd got to the point where the mantra of being a *sow wallowing in the mire* took total control of all my waking thoughts; every other thought had to be painfully processed and squeezed in alongside the mantra. "Resistance is futile" couldn't have been a more apt statement. *How could I hope to fight against an almighty God?* I could feel myself being sucked into a downward-spiralling vortex in which I was trapped just as certainly as if I'd fallen into a black hole: there was to be no escape. My overwhelming emotion was that of cold fear. Naturally, suicidal thoughts began to crowd me; yet I feared the afterlife of damnation more than I feared the current one, so I became torn this way and that.

The day came when I found myself in Durham's County Hospital, asleep under the influence of powerful sedation. The detailed process of how I got there can be passed over, save to say that my so-called "voluntary" admission had been the consequence of an instruction from my GP to willingly accept hospitalization as an alternative to being sectioned. Put another way, I'd jumped as an alternative to being pushed: God's mocking way of showing me, probably, how Noel must have felt after the Fellowship was forced to accept exclusion from the EA. Huh! Once I awoke from the initial heavy sedation, the panic I'd previously succumbed to immediately gripped me once again: suicidal thoughts now romped freely throughout my head; all I needed to do was work out "how". A consultant was called and she told the nurses to give me a hefty 100 mg dose of a major tranquilizer called Chlorpromazine. I was then moved to a side room of my own and placed under twenty-four-hour-a-day "suicide watch". This meant I had someone with me at every moment, whatever I did and wherever I went. The only place I was allowed to be alone was inside the loo cubicle. It was little better than being straightjacketed, compelled to endure the torments in my head through the physical restrictions placed on me. The tranquilizer doses were increased to the highest possible levels – 150 mg four times a day – and eventually subdued me so much that it might have appeared I was actually beginning to calm down. In reality, I was little more than the walking lobotomized zombie depicted by Jack Nicholson in "One Flew Over The Cuckoo's Nest". The suicidal urges, however, hadn't been similarly subdued; they remained very much alive.

If only I could bring it all to end, my family could then begin to rebuild their lives free from the curse which I carried with me.

'Don't jump! Think of your family!' By Christ, I wished that thinking of my family would have put it all into perspective and exorcized the madness.

I had a plan though!

Having been taken off suicide "constant observation", I slipped out of the building after breakfast one Sunday morning and, in the small shop under the railway arches, bought a newspaper. If questioned on my return, I could produce it to use as an excuse for why I'd left the building without permission – permission which wouldn't have been given had I asked for it. Next, at the chemist, I bought a large bottle of Paracetamol which I then slipped into the inner pocket of my coat.

Back to the ward, and back to my room – unnoticed and unquestioned. Good! Write a short note to Jeanne. What shall I say? How will she understand? No need to say to too much; I've already said it all. She won't be surprised. Just tell her how much I love her and the children. Tell her how this is the best thing for all of us. Now, open the bottle. Start taking the pills.

One, two, three...

...four, five, six, seven, eight...

My hope of finding a means of escape was not, however, going to be so easily rewarded with success. *How could I have ever thought it would be?* One of the side effects of my high-dosage medication was a continuously parched-dry mouth: I had to chain-suck boiled sweets just to create enough saliva to keep my mouth moist and stop my tongue sticking to my palette. This meant that every painful attempt to swallow each large tablet of Paracetamol needed the help of several mouthfuls of water. It would have proved physically impossible to drink enough liquid to consume the fifty or sixty tablets I'd planned to take – not to mention the suspicion I would have aroused amongst the nursing staff as I trudged to-and-fro between the kitchen and my room to refill the water jug. I aborted my attempt after the eighth tablet.

Despite plenty of suicidal thoughts, there were to be no further genuine attempts. The plain truth is that I just didn't have the courage. I kept thinking to myself, '*what if I end up in Hades itself? What if death leads to something which is far worse than what I'm going through at the moment?*' I wanted to die. Yes I did; with the *whole* of my heart. But because I already had some insight into the concept of everlasting torment, I didn't dare risk trading one Gehenna for an even worse one!

I should like to be able to say that even while I walked through this forlorn valley I was still lifted in spirit by Luton Town's impressive run in the League Cup, which this season would, at last, take them to Wembley and glory. Through compulsive habit, I did, of course, follow their progress, but it was without much care or enthusiasm: nothing but nothing seemed worthwhile any longer. Set against the enormity of the darkness that encircled me, everything else had no meaning.

I survived my internment in "the County" by accommodating myself to the rhythm of the hospital's daily routine, learning to live from one set point in the day to another: from lunch at one o'clock to dinner at six o'clock; from one drug-round at two o'clock to the next at seven o'clock. When Jeanne came for her evening visit, I knew that I'd more or less got through another day. I also knew that in her company I would be allowed to leave the building. Every night we went for a walk through the town: up the steep path by the river and alongside the floodlit castle, over Palace Green with the huge pinnacles of the magnificent Cathedral to our right, and back through the cobbled marketplace in the direction of the hospital.

Many ordinand friends from Cranmer Hall also came to visit me. Some of them were more welcome than others: the *most* welcome being those who were patient enough to play chess with me. Even though I was far too distracted to ever mount any serious challenge to my opponents and always lost, I nevertheless found I could muster just sufficient engagement with the game to allow a very slight quietening of the accusing voices in my head – which were relegated to a position of less urgency but never forgotten. I hope that the other visitors – those who came with advice to give, to pray with me, or wanting *me* to talk with them about "how I felt" – weren't actually treated rudely; but they seldom came back a second time once they'd encountered my dull, discourteous muteness.

After nearly two months of imprisonment as a psychiatric patient, it would have been totally wrong to suppose I was recovering from my illness: the continuous battle with tormenting thoughts carried on relentlessly. But I *had* managed to settle into a more stable, mechanical rhythm of daily life, and I *was* being allowed to leave the hospital for extended visits home. My final discharge came sooner than expected, however, when – at one my regular consulting sessions – I found myself talking to a different doctor. It transpired that the previous one had only been acting as a locum to cover for staff shortages occasioned by illness. Nobody had ever felt it necessary to explain this to *me*. They probably felt it would have been of no concern given the intensity of my "psychotic breakdown" – as it was described. The new doctor – Mrs. Tarry, the "regular" consultant – had a totally different attitude to her hireling predecessor and was immediately prepared to review my situation, as reflected by the question she put to me after only a very brief interview.

'*What do* **you** *think the next stage of your treatment should be, John?*' she asked, with transparent empathy and kindness – which I'm afraid was altogether lacking in she who had previously set herself up over me.

'*I'd like to be discharged,*' I replied, without a moment's hesitation.

Later that *same* afternoon I was collecting together my effects, including my priceless collection of music cassettes (which had in some small way helped me through the blackest moments), and waiting for Jeanne to arrive in the car to take me home. I had so many pills-and-things which had been sent down for me from the hospital pharmacy that I needed a small carrier bag to carry them all. Strangely, my prescribed medication included several tubes of sunblock cream: notwithstanding overcast, wintry conditions, I was actually getting sunburnt from the walks I'd begun to take outside the hospital. It was an alert junior doctor who'd noticed my acute photosensitivity, another side-effect of the near-ridiculous drug cocktail I was being treated with.

It's of no great consequence to relate, in detail, what took place over the next nine or ten months. Every day was a repetition of the same kind of mental agony already described. And despite all the good intentions of the many people who came to visit me, I got *no* better. If anything, my mental state deteriorated further. I only ever found what may described as "some kind of peace" when yet another day had been ticked off and Jeanne was holding me tightly as we sat on the settee together just before bedtime. I subjected myself to every kind of mental scrutiny imaginable, confessing to Jeanne and seeking forgiveness for just about every blighted deed and thought I could dredge up from my memory, but always with no abatement to the fear of that which I believed to be responsible for all this – God's anger and punishment.

In my deluded desperation, I even phoned Noel to tell him about my plight and confess it was the consequence of the way I'd treated the Fellowship. He was polite enough in what he said; and he went so far as to tell me he didn't think I should see myself as someone who was beyond God's grace. On the other hand, he clearly didn't want anything more than a very short conversation and seemed reluctant to give any advice which would help me break through the cloud of depression and despair. Nor did he call me back at any point to ask the question: *'how ya doin, bro?'*

Nigel travelled up from Peterborough to visit me one day whilst I was still in hospital. Sensing the helplessness of my condition, he was one of the few with the sensitivity to offer his *company* as the most valuable gift he had. Forget about me having tried to make any kind of fraternal response to my visitors, it was just about as much as I was able to do to *cope* with most them. In all honesty, I only wanted the company of those very few people whom I trusted implicitly – which included Nigel. I'm afraid there must have been many who thought me to be either a lost cause or exceedingly impolite. What can I say?... *'I'm truly sorry!'*

Before he left, Nigel said to me:

'John, you must know that nothing like this goes on for ever.'

I wished he hadn't said it. So many prayers had been offered up for me and so many words of spiritual counsel had been given, but *no one* had yet offered me a key which could even be inserted into my prison-door's lock, let alone open it. *Every* morning, the very first thing which came to my mind when I woke up was the mocking certainty of God's punishment on me; and it remained there with me for the duration of the day. I'd convinced myself that because it was God himself who was punishing me it would surely go on for ever, and ever, and ever, and ever...

All the same, there was something about what Nigel had said – and coming from the person it did – which stuck in my mind. So even though for a while it only helped to compound my despondency with its damning promise of unachievable hope, yet still I couldn't forget it... *nothing like this goes on for ever.*

England failed dismally in the European championships held that summer, and the Olympic athletes did little to raise national spirits. But Luton Town FC – *my* Luton Town FC – beat the mighty Arsenal in the League Cup final at Wembley. I managed to concentrate long enough to watch the whole match on the TV and even came close to holding my breath when the Arsenal were awarded a penalty in the latter stages of the match, already 2-1 in the lead. Our reserve goalkeeper, Andy Dibble, made a glorious save. Stirred by the injustice of the penalty decision (and the justice of the save), Luton went on to get two late goals to clinch the match.

How I wish I could have been in my right mind so that I could have shared in the full joy of the occasion: back then, our finest hour!

If I were to say that rock-bottom came in late summer, it wouldn't actually be true: every day was a new rock-bottom. But there was definitely one particular evening when my head span with such dazed, drugged bewilderment that when I closed my sleepy eyes I honestly believed the end of my mortal road had come. When the final last breath failed to come, however, and my eyes reopened, I had to then fight back tears of anguished exhaustion: *'how much more can a human soul take?'* I asked myself for the thousandth time. And thinking thoughts of my little children playing outside in the road earlier that day with such blissful abandon, I implored of God, pounding as it were on his door, to show me how to get through this nightmare – if not for *my* sake, then for *theirs!*

There is something about autumn which, even though it heralds the onset of winter darkness, has always inspired in me a quiet kind of reassurance. The long, heady days of summer are replaced by the more subdued, less-demanding colours of greyer skies. It's as if nature is beckoning us to take our foot off the throttle, to cut back, to draw in, to be gentle with ourselves; for the time of expansion and blossoming and bursting-forth has passed for yet another year.

I distinctly remember being strangely comforted by wearing a scarf to fend off the chill as I set out on my habitual evening walk to the nearby beck. Nearing the stream, I felt the cool breeze of the autumn evening on my face; and in its gentle caress it seemed to me that the hand of providence had brushed my skin with reassurance of love. The moment soon passed, but I couldn't deny what I'd felt. Miraculously, all kinds of other thoughts began to take shape as I walked apprehensively along the Deerness-valley track. They were thoughts I'd long since given up hope of ever entertaining again; ones which suggested I *could* feel good about myself, that I *wasn't* wicked through and through. They gave me hope that, if I could but keep it in my sight, there was, after all, a way through the awful sunless valley which I hadn't been able to escape from.

The beginning of the end had indeed begun. The clouds had parted and a small chink of blue sky had appeared with all its wonderful promise of reprise. A small – very small – message of hope, carried on the wind of an autumn evening, had whispered quietly into my ear. I don't know from where it came or how it had been summoned because I'd passionately implored it many many times before to come to me. But all of a sudden, amazingly, *just like that* – just as unexpectedly as it had all begun – I felt myself up for the fight again. Not that I was hyperphysically cured spontaneously or that my psychotic symptoms disappeared with painless ease and swiftness. But there I was, believing and hoping that at last I'd begun to find a path through the swamp.

In the next few days I found myself able to actively mount a mental counter-offensive against the mind-set which, having claimed squatters rights and settled in, had been inhabiting my head with all the swagger and assurance of a tenant who believed himself to be beyond forceful or legal eviction for far too long. I found myself attacking and rejecting the damning thoughts which continued presenting themselves to me. And even when I grew weary of doing so and felt in danger of yielding to their persuasive strength – and that it was useless to offer resistance – I still somehow managed to keep denying them; still managed to talk to myself in the language of reassurance. It all sounds so easy now as I look back; and I can't deny that the improvement, once begun, definitely progressed with almost breathtaking rapidity. But those first few days of recovery weren't as easy as I perhaps make them seem in my attempt to find words to describe the way it all happened. In fact, I remember all too well the resurgent panic I had to contend with as the fight seemed to be slipping away from me and the voices in my head mocked me for being so stupid as to think they could be evicted.

My recovery was further aided by the coincidental out-patient appointment which my psychiatric consultant made for me with another physician. The consultation with Dr. Munroe proved invaluable. Apart from giving me the benefit of his plain, refreshingly straightforward counsel, he also readily agreed to let me have a prolonged course of diazepam (Valium) – which he recognized as being helpful in treating my fear of experiencing LSD-style hallucinatory flashbacks on top of everything else. The dosage of the major tranquillizer was reduced, and the antidepressant which I'd been put on – medication I'd always disliked and felt to be an irritant, not a help – was changed for another; one that he felt would be more sympathetic. With my newly discovered mental tools and the altered medication my insanity soon began to yield in a way which was noticeable to others. Laughter was one of the first strangers to be shown hospitality again. And as I began to find myself actually enjoying people, and enjoying "doing things" again, the pace of the recovery gathered unstoppable momentum.

The storm had been too powerful to fight. My biggest mistake, probably, was trying to offer up resistance to its fury rather than running for shelter and weathering it out in the harbour. There is a time to tough it out and another to take refuge. Even so, I doubt whether in those days I had the self-knowledge or navigational skills to find a welcoming port. So perhaps I had no alternative but to drift helplessly on a restless sea, battered by a storm which had been gathering itself together for a long long time and couldn't have been diffused without unleashing its thunder and fury. But the isobars had, at last, definitely begun to widen and the storm had all but expended itself. Now was the time to seize the opportunity and set about repairing the damage which had been inflicted.

Looking back through four decades I can now say with some assurance:

'Thank you, Nigel, you were absolutely right when you said that "nothing like this goes on for ever."'

All things must pass!

1989 to 2023

PART SIX

The fight goes on

My rescue from the clutches of insanity might well have been a good place to finish: it's a fully rounded story in its own right. But the Jesus Fellowship and Jesus Army were very much alive in 1988 and stood on the threshold of significant change and growth. There was much swordplay between us yet to be engaged in, so I shall carry on right through to the very end.

CHAPTER TWENTY-EIGHT: Onwards

In the wake of mental illness, my faith in God had been shaken like never before; nothing had escaped the interrogative searchlights of my restless mind, and no sacred truths remained which couldn't be challenged during my struggle to work out what was left of my Christian beliefs. Against this backdrop, resuming my theological training wasn't something I wanted; and nor was it a viable option: all parties to the matter agreed that I should take a prolonged sabbatical and revisit the issue of what-to-do after a year or so. As a family, we retained close ties with our adopted church in Durham, St. Nicks; and I once again started doing home-improvement work to begin earning an income for us. Word of mouth reports that I was once more "on the tools" somehow filtered their way back down to London, which resulted in several invites from friends-of-friends to travel down and be paid for various decorating, plumbing and electrical jobs. At the inflated London rates of £8 an hour for this kind of work, these were opportunities I couldn't shun; so I packed my bags and made quite a number of trips "down souf" during 1989 and 1990.

During this restorative time I gave the JA very little thought. The phone call I'd made to Noel during my illness had been nothing more than an act of desperation, one that had originated from a willingness to do *anything* I could think of that might lead to some light shining in the dark wilderness of my mind. I wished I hadn't rung, but at least Noel's polite indifference reminded me how callous he could be. Thereafter, I assumed the phone conversation we'd had would most likely be my last direct involvement with the Fellowship. I hadn't, of course, anticipated a very different phone call I'd receive sometime early on in 1990. *How could I possible have done so?* How could I have known that my old roommate at the farm, Roger, would effectively elope from the Community together with – and this is what, to begin with, made it almost unbelievable – my ex would-be love, Angie? *The old rogue* was an expression I kept repeating to myself whilst I tried to absorb what Roger had told me over the phone: *the old rogue, indeed.* Eight years had gone by since I'd left, and I was now married with two children. No reason at all, therefore, why Roger shouldn't have set his sights and heart on Angie, nor any why she shouldn't have likewise responded to the charms of a tall, intelligent and very manly man such as Roger. *But to have eloped together!* That must have taken some doing and, so far as I was aware, must have been a first. How on earth had they managed to become so close that they could have discussed and planned it all? I was truly thrilled for them both, but achingly curious to find out the full story. Their leaving together was a significant enough event within the Community for SC to have mentioned it. Referring to a perceived drop in the standards of discipleship within certain households, he wrote:

"Some celibates began to question their lifelong vows; a few brothers were losing their way by getting too involved with sisters. The London household was badly hit when their main celibate brother and a leading sister whom he pastored suddenly left together."[52]

It was whilst I was working on a job in London, sometime early in 1990, that Angie, Roger and I met up for a meal in a Leicester Square restaurant. I got to hear how Angie had been on the point of calling me several times in the past, and how she'd once dialled our home number but then lost her nerve when she heard my voice answering the call. During our two hours together they told me a good deal about recent developments; especially those concerning the new London household and the JA's street-evangelism in Leicester Square – just a few yards away from where we were now eating together. I also got to hear about exploits on my own doorstep: the visits to Newcastle by a "church-planting team" under Pete Mattacola's leadership.

Enthused by our get-together, I began to consider resuming my efforts to spread awareness about the Fellowship. Angie and Roger had made it abundantly clear that, at root, everything was much the same. But with this new outward-facing appearance displayed by the *Jesus People, Loving People* image, it had become even harder for many to understand what lay beneath the surface. The exact sequence of events during the following years – the nineties and noughties – has now become rather blurred; but I've still retained enough mental time-markers of sufficient clarity to feel certain I won't be *too* far off the mark with the chronology as I write about what-happened-next. With a fair degree of confidence, therefore, I can recall my reading of a "flyer" invite to a nearby JA meeting – in Gateshead – as being the prompt which set me on the warpath once again. I'd made the firm decision not to continue with my theological studies and felt myself sufficiently grounded in my recovery and lifestyle to stick my head above the parapet once more.

Jeanne and I agreed together that, in response to the JA invite, we should get some of our *own* flyers printed: A5-sized ones with a few bullet points to warn those attending the Gateshead meeting about what they might be getting themselves involved with – nothing too detailed or provocative; just a warning. We weren't sure, though, about the best way to distribute them. Probably best, we reckoned, if I didn't go to the meeting myself as I might not yet have been able to cope with any flack that came my way. Best to be on the safe side. So Jeanne went, together with our very good friend – the irrepressible and garrulous extrovert Susan East, godmother to our newly born son, Benjamin. They waited until just before the meeting started before placing a flyer underneath the windscreen wipers of every vehicle in the car park. Then, they went inside and meekly sat listening to Pete Mattacola's exhortations to renounce the world and march with the Jesus Army as a warrior-member of God's kingdom.

Jeanne and Sue were swiftly identified as the most likely suspects to have distributed the flyers, so they were duly charged – after the meeting – with being an associate of a certain John Everett and having aided and abetted him in his pamphleteering crime. They neither confirmed nor denied having been connected with the misdemeanour; nor did either of them own up to being my associate. Not known for having much by way of submissive simplicity or sisterly self-effacement about her, Sue would have forcibly held her ground in any discussion which followed. Jeanne, far shyer and less self-assured, would have quietly explained her disagreement with what she'd heard in the meeting. I was enormously proud of them both.

Before Jeanne and Sue had returned from Gateshead for a campaign debrief, I took a phone call from a lady who'd been at the meeting: I'd put my name and phone number on the flyer in case anyone should wish to contact me for further information or help. This particular outspoken lady most certainly didn't want either of these. She wished to tell me, in rather direct and colourful language, about the close association she knew me to have with Satan and my consequent need for urgent repentance. There was no persuading her otherwise, so we had to end the phone call with my suggestion of agreement to differ; an offer which I don't think she accepted.

I knew very little about the large meetings now taking place on an annual basis at the Wembley Conference Centre except that they were part of a campaign to launch the JA into a new position of mainstream acceptance. Nothing anyone had been able to tell me softened my conviction that it was yet another event which should be treated with great caution. To that end, I prepared another batch of flyers for distribution which detailed certain issues I thought attendees at the event should be aware of. Primarily, these were key features that I believed identified the mother church, the JFC, as being a cult, together with a few lifestyle concerns such as the promotion of celibacy and the treatment of women.

Together with a new friend, Maddy – who'd previously rubbed shoulders closely with the JA – I drove to London so we could distribute the pamphlets during the 1991 Wembley day. Not wanting there to be any "agro" before we'd had a chance to target as many attendees as possible, we sat on wall outside the main entrance – along with quite a few others – and tried to remain as inconspicuous as possible until the doors opened and those in the long queue began to go in. We were desperately hoping, of course, that we wouldn't be spotted by anyone who knew us, and I personally found my heart began to literally pound away within. Possibly sensing that I didn't look comfortable, a sister came and sat next to me with the gentle offer to take a sweet from the proffered paper bag. I declined the offer and looked down at my feet, hopefully conveying the message that I didn't want to talk. After a painful wait which had felt far too long, the queue started to move.

'Let's go', I said, turning to Maddy.

267

We both began handing out our pamphlets to anyone who would take one: at first, there were many – we'd managed to retain the necessary element of surprise. I still recognized many of the JA members within the queue from "the old days", and other members were easily identifiable in their colourful jackets and dress. In amongst them, rather lost amongst the vivid mass, were those in civvies: a marked minority. These were the ones whom we were most keen to target even though we offered our handouts to all. We didn't have very long, sadly, before the pamphlets were being refused. Word must have fairly soon got back to the high command about an enemy incursion, and a red alert was issued. With the army now in full defensive mode, a few brothers were detailed to keep an eye on us and warn everyone not to take what we were offering – but we carried on regardless.

As I continued progressing along the queue, I noticed a couple called Ron and Maggie; a lovely pair who'd stood out visually when I knew them at Bugbrooke: together, they looked much like one's imagined image of the stereotypical hippy couple. I'd spoken with them in the minibus back to Daventry on my very first visit to the Fellowship. Maggie, a petite and pretty sister with long curly brown hair, had told me how difficult she'd found it having to give up wearing Laura Ashley dresses. I didn't like to confess at the time that I didn't know what a Laura Ashley dress looked like, or even what one was. Ron, her 1970's Glen Frey (*The Eagles*) lookalike husband, spoke with a soft, grizzled, laid-back voice like someone who'd just taken a few satisfying inhalations from a hand-rolled cannabis cigarette. They'd both split the Community some time well before I did, and I'd heard others talking about them in a way that led me to think they'd become openly antagonistic. It seemed – from their very presence at the event – they must have been reunited with the Fellowship at some point. I greeted them both as old friends whom I was most surprised – but genuinely glad – to see. Sadly, the affirmation of friendship wasn't returned. Instead, Ron looked at me suspiciously and growled out something about his disgust with what he'd heard about my opposition to God's people. It hurt immensely.

Maddy and I had become separated by the time I reached the end of the queue, so I walked back towards the main concourse to try and find her. Whilst doing so, I was collared by a brother whom I'd lived with at Harvest House in Warwickshire – it's probably best if I don't reveal his identity. Having cautioned me for being a servant of the Devil, he followed it up with an instruction that brokered no misunderstanding:

'*I rebuke you in the name of the Lord and command you to stop what you're doing!'*

He then repeated his injunction, possibly twice. Given how loudly he'd spoken, quite a few eyes were turned. The incident had the makings of becoming a damaging one for the JA's image, not to mention an uncomfortable one for *me*. Thankfully, a brother whom we had all called "Marky Sparky" intervened by issuing my assailant with a cease-and-desist order and asked him to move on, which he did. Marky, whom I had worked with at the farm, had been given his moniker on account of his prowess as a vehicle electrician, but he was quite remarkably talented in all kinds of ways: the only person I'd ever met – or would ever meet – who could strip down a gearbox into its component parts and rebuild it. Very insecure when he first arrived at the farm, he was forever saying sorry for this, that and everything. This aside, he'd been the kind of person who somehow made you feel good just by being with him. And he was his old friendly self with me there at Wembley. After he'd offered what amounted to an apology for what had just happened, we chatted together for quite a while. I found him far more self-assured; and all the better for so being. He told me he'd replaced Nigel as a farm manager, and I gathered that his status within the Community had grown considerably. The full significance of our chat, however, wouldn't become apparent to me until a few years later.

Once reunited with Maddy, I was thankfully reassured that she'd not herself had any problems. But like me, she'd now hit a brick wall so far as pamphlet distribution was concerned; so we took an extended break until the evening session. Had I anticipated what was likely to happen when we returned, I wouldn't have suggested to Maddy that we do so. Almost as soon as we'd begun handing out our pamphlets to the evening attendees, we were intercepted by security men from the conference centre. Following complaints they'd received, we were told we weren't welcome on the centre's property. This included the main concourse and – apparently – the footpath running alongside where people queued. We were therefore essentially restricted to the main-road pavement outside the centre's frontage. Very few people arrived from this direction we soon discovered, so it was pretty pointless staying there. Not yet completely beaten, we waited in a car park to one side of the centre where we could wave the pamphlets at the infrequent latecomers, urging them to cross the road and take one. But I don't remember any of them doing so.

As we were about to leave, a long-time elder called Bob came over to talk with me. Even though he was perfectly open about his disapproval of me, his demeanour and tone of voice were those of a friend. He wanted to reason with me, not attack me. We ended up going to sit in the front of a Fellowship car where we discussed everything heart-to-heart in one of the sincerest conversations I'd had with *anyone* in a position of authority from the Fellowship. We parted amicably, even though he'd not managed to regain my heart in the way he'd hoped to. Or was that what he'd *actually* wanted? *Had he just claimed that this had been his intent so he could get to hear what I actually thought about everything?* I've no way of knowing. But I wasn't nearly as surprised as I otherwise might have been when, not more than a year or so later, I heard that he and his family had left the Community to resettle in their homeland, New Zealand. If our presence at Wembley hadn't achieved much else (although I think it probably did), then having had the chance to help Bob see a little more clearly through the mist was more than worthwhile in itself. Good on you and yours, Bob. And thank you so much, Maddy, wherever you are now. Your encouragement and support made all the difference!

During the late eighties and nineties I only knew as much about the Fellowship as I'd heard from those who left – as well as what I'd seen and experienced at the Wembley event, of course. All this was enough to convince me that people were still being moved around Noel's spiritual chessboard as little better than pawns to accomplish his masterplan of revival, one that sprang from his vision of building God's kingdom with himself as the prophetic figurehead. The fact remained that people, *real living people* – a tautological truism, I know – were being damaged and even crushed in the wake of it all... how am I to sufficiently emphasise people's humanity and worth without feeling compelled to use a truism, and a diacope one to boot? Individuals themselves were only important insofar as they fitted into the current shape of Noel's vision. Outside of this, they became of little worth. Inevitably, therefore, people in general became divided into two camps: those for and those against. Unfortunately, the same kind of thing happens, to a greater or lesser extent, in all kinds of movements and institutions; political, social, religious and environmental: those willing to toe the party line and those unwilling; those who support and are therefore accepted, and those who don't and are therefore rejected. (Think about Angela Rayner and her dismissal of great swathes of those labelled as "Tory Scum".) If you fitted obediently into the structure of the Jesus Fellowship and flowed along with it – even as someone with deep problems who might be struggling to keep up – then you found yourself accepted with deep, brotherly love. If you showed support for the Jesus Fellowship, even as an outsider, then you were considered to be one of their "righteous friends" – Christian or non-Christian. If you criticized the Jesus Fellowship as a member or someone still loosely attached; if you refused or found yourself unable to accept the current direction or vision; then you found yourself isolated and uncared for. If, as an outsider or ex-member, you spoke out against or hindered the Jesus Fellowship in some way, then you found yourself demonized for taking sides with the Devil himself.

I still remembered, all too vividly, those occasions when we were compelled – yes! *compelled* – to ensure we rid ourselves of *any* criticism towards the Fellowship, however small, and confirm, possibly under examination, that we'd done so. *What did those church leaders who were lending their voice and support to the Fellowship's Wembley celebrations make of that? Did they know? Did they care? Or did they think that, under the new guise of "the Jesus Army", things had changed within the Fellowship?* If anything, I felt it more important than ever to stick to my guns and try to make my voice heard. This wasn't, however, going to be an out-and-out vendetta: I had a family to support, children to nurture and enjoy, a wife to love, bills to pay, friends to be friends with, Luton Town to support, and my love of running to pursue as a sport: the

1992 Great North Run was to be the first of the twenty consecutive ones I would race in, alongside many other half and full marathons. Opposition to the Jesus Fellowship would have to fit in with all the other things going on in my life, not *become* my life.

The latter chapters of "Fire in Our Hearts" – which I've only read recently – tell us about Jesus Fellowship and Jesus Army developments between 1988 and 1996 that have left me with nothing other than disbelief, bewilderment, and a hard-to-shake-off visceral sorrow. Had I read these chapters before the closure of the JFC, I'm not sure how I would have dealt with the powerful, eviscerating emotions they generated. The overwhelming impression I'm left with is one of constant flux as Noel endeavoured to retain the vision of sacrificial community brotherhood alongside a no-holds-barred evangelistic thrust which would ride the wave of national revival and secure acceptance for the Jesus Army as a radical, pioneering champion of the true faith; not forgetting, of course, who its commander-in-chief might be. If I were to say that by hook or by crook Noel was determined his name should be recorded in the history books alongside the revivalist greats such as Charles Spurgeon, George Whitfield and John Wesley, then I would possibly be going too far. But I challenge anyone to read the latter parts of SC's book and not find in them astonishing twists, turns and cycles of development that can only be explained by looking at what was happening with Noel himself and his deep-rooted anxiety for recognition. This anxiety saw him reaching out to secure the maximum benefit possible from alignment with what he himself identified to be movements of the Holy Spirit in other places, at home and abroad. When Noel moved to the left, so did the rest of the church; and likewise when he moved to the right. Everyone was expected to follow the path which Noel himself mapped out for them. That Simon himself had significant problems trying to make sense of the directional changes required by Noel's seemingly contrary and contradictory visions – and then adapt to them – is written in bold print between many of the lines. Keeping track of right and wrong is a real challenge when yesterday's wrongs become today's rights – and vice versa. Yesterday, Noel was lampooning the worldliness of theatrical performance and rock-band-style music used by other Christians to promote faith and worship the Lord; today, guided by the Holy Spirit, Noel announces a new vision to harness a vast range of modern technology as a means not only of worship but also of reaching out to rescue the downtrodden and lost. Born from "today's" vision was the 1992 multi-media theatrical spectacle of "Jesus Live" which was used by the JA as the centrepiece at Wembley – and also at other celebrations and campaigns across the country.

1988 seems to have been a year when change was very noticeable in the air. Keen to demonstrate they *really were* as accepting of fellow Christians as they now claimed to be, Jesus Army "soldiers" took part in the nationally organized "March for Jesus". In preparation they started learning Graham

Kendrick songs – a radical change indeed! – and using a rock-band style music group to lead in worship, much the same as many other fellowships had been doing for years. Even more of a volte-face, possibly, was how Noel started visiting other fellowships to meet with their leaders and demonstrate – ostensibly – his receptivity and openness. SC tells us, however, about the scepticism which Noel retained concerning the more-extreme manifestations of the Holy Spirit that had originated in some American churches and were now gaining widespread acceptance in many of our own UK Charismatic ones. It wasn't just Noel, though, if we take SC at his word the scepticism was shared by others:

"We continued to hear interesting things of the ministry of John Wimber and Reinhard Bonnke, but were reserved about the spectacular: what some called being 'slain in the Spirit', and so on. It was intriguing, 'But,' we asked, 'does it build the church?'"[53]

When SC speaks about "we", who exactly is he referring to? We as a church, presumably. But does a church really hear something as a unity and speak with one voice, or do the individuals who comprise it have their own attitudes and views concerning matters non-critical to the essential aspects of creed and orthodoxy? I would argue that it *should* be the latter, but I suspect that SC's "we" belongs to the collective voice of the Fellowship as spoken by their main man. Either way, the reserved attitude that they ("we") held concerning the phenomenon of being "slain in the Spirit" was to come under challenge.

Following his visit to a conference in Birmingham, where many were being slain in the Spirit and physically falling over under pastor Bonnke's ministry, Noel came to believe that this was indeed a phenomenon – a spiritual blessing – which came from the Holy Spirit. Fallings-over began immediately once Noel himself became a portal for introducing the spiritual blessing to the Fellowship – and many other "wonders" followed on. Brothers and sisters alike began to find themselves in receipt of heavenly visions and intoxicated with laughter. Some became insensible for hours as the Holy Spirit immobilized them in overwhelming rapture. Most of the elders were also "slain" at their very next meeting, many of them rolling about on the floor in fits of laughter – or twitching and groaning as if taken hold of by a seizure. Any remaining sceptics, such as SC himself, were also eventually struck by the Spirit as the experience took hold of the whole Fellowship. It reminded those who'd been there nearly twenty years' ago of what happened when the Spirit had first taken hold of Bugbrooke: miraculous healings started to take place once again together with other extraordinary happenings that could only be understood as themselves being miraculous. 1988 had become the year when a new anointing swept through and revitalized the Fellowship.

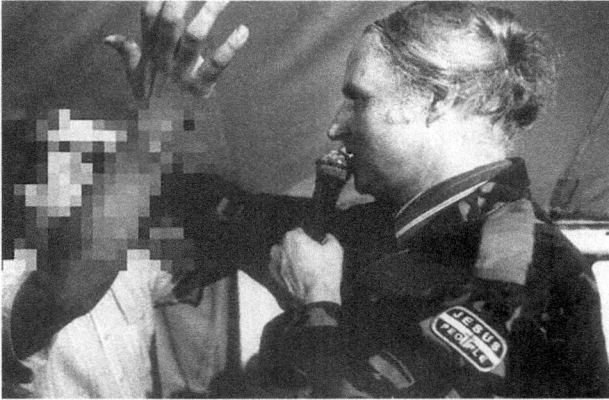

Noel Ministering in the Spirit

The energy of this anointing carried through into 1989 when a new liberty in praise erupted. Celebratory events across the country were garnished with streamers, balloons, air-horns, and party-poppers. Exchanging a party-popping mood for a damping party-pooping one, I feel it important to emphasize that such joyfully exuberant activity – whatever one's personal take on it might be – all originated from *one* man having decided that *this* was the way forward – under guidance from the Almighty, he would no doubt have insisted. Noel led, others followed. *Where was the "we" which SC has written about? Why was it always the case that Noel had to decide something was OK before it became OK – and then mandatory?* The new direction now being taken had not emerged organically from within; there wasn't any "we" about it. The Fellowship members had previously been in thrall to Noel's prophetic ministry; now they were in thrall to his whimsy as well.

A little further back in this chapter I wrote: *if you criticized the Jesus Fellowship as a member or someone still loosely attached; if you refused or found yourself unable to accept the current direction or vision; then you found yourself isolated and uncared for.* SC himself has acknowledged this to have been true, even if only indirectly. Not only has he written about Noel being "resistant to criticism", but he has also explicitly confirmed that there were those in the Fellowship who were unable to accept the changes he'd championed:

"When Noel was sufficiently convinced, he could enthusiastically preach what he had once had little time for. Some couldn't take that. They saw the way we were now going as a sell-out, the end of what we'd fought and sacrificed for. They lost confidence in the prophetic direction and became cynical."[54]

Mark Strong, my very good friend from times past (even though he'd turned against me over the issue of my marriage), was one of these cynics:

"Mark wasn't keen on the Jesus Army image, nor was he impressed with all the changes that had come from hob-knobbing with other charismatics. Shoutings and shakings, dancing and drama were, in his eyes, so many fireworks that distracted us from our true calling.

Most of us were happy with the new direction, but those who resisted it increasingly lost their bearings. Some of them gravitated towards Mark, who became more and more bogged down with their problems. The new anointings came as a divide.

The cloud moved on, and those who did not move with it found themselves struggling."[55]

Those who resisted lost their bearings! Those who didn't move on found themselves struggling! The Jesus Fellowship had taken a new direction, maybe, but nothing had changed with respect to the fundamental truth that Noel remained in total control of it all. Those who disagreed with his vision – even though he could change it whenever he saw fit – were deemed, at best, to be out of step with and resistant to the leadings of the Holy Spirit; at worst, they were deemed to have sided with the Enemy.

Mark had once worn the mantle of being the Fellowship's leading celibate brother, someone whose authority and wisdom were revered by many. And if anyone had Noel's ear and was able to influence him, Mark was that brother. But even Mark became sidelined when he no longer danced to the piper's tune. And that's exactly what I mean when I write about individuals having been pawns in the grand masterplan. Once your usefulness to the plan had faded, so did your worth as an individual: you became expendable. Which is exactly what ultimately happened to Mark. Like Dave Resolute before him (Dave, if you recall, was the former PR spokesman), he became totally disillusioned with everything, renounced his celibate status and left.

Mark and Dave had been brothers whose opinions and reservations should surely have been listened to. They were mature, intelligent, influential men of extremely good standing who had been in the Fellowship since the early 70s. They deserved to have been heard: they too had waited on the voice of the Lord for guidance; they too had only wished to see the Fellowship strengthened with God's blessing, not weakened. But no! The prophetic vision which Noel was currently propagating needed to be followed with no dissent: it brokered no challenge. There wasn't even room to try and accommodate those who'd previously shown uncompromising loyalty and had given their all for Zion. Even the bonds of brotherly love weren't enough to allow room for reconsideration.

What mattered most? Pressing ahead with Noel's masterplan regardless, or trying to work out how it might be possible to avoid losing brothers who weren't just valuable but also dearly loved by many? Pressing ahead, of course! Seen through the eyes of an army on the march, those brothers who couldn't keep up or wanted to reconsider the direction would struggle and lose their bearings. Best, therefore, to let them fall away and not allow them to halt the army's progress. The Fellowship's loss of Mark was, however, my gain. I was able to resume my close friendship with him even though he chose to settle in North Wales, a good four- or five-hour drive from Durham. The irony of it all, at least in Mark's case, was that it wouldn't be too long after he'd left before Noel himself decided that an emphasis on restoring the "purity of Zion" was needed – as we shall soon see.

Another aspect of the Fellowship's thrust for wider acceptance within evangelical Charismatic circles, according to SC's account of it, was the public admission that mistakes had unfortunately been made. The nature of these mistakes wasn't specified explicitly, but we're told that remorse and sorrow were shown for having caused unnecessary wounds to some when the sword of God's word had been brandished too fiercely. When reading about this wave of contrition over past mistakes, I've found myself wondering if I was included amongst those whom they – Noel? – were admitting to have wronged. If so, I didn't get to hear about it from anyone. But surely I *must* have been a beneficiary of the embracing forgiveness SC tells us now started flowing out to those who had "written or spoken against us". Fine words and fine sentiments. *But what did this mean in practice? If I was included amongst those being forgiven (and why shouldn't I have been?), did this mean I wouldn't face hostility, for example, when I came across JA members in the future? Why was it, then, that I continued to be reviled despite all the regret over past mistakes and consequential absolution the Fellowship was claiming to have dispensed by the bucketload?* The truth is that I only ever came to know about the alleged forgiveness being shown when I read of it in SC's book. Prior to that, nothing! To my mind, forgiveness means very little if its recipient isn't made aware of it in some way. Wearing my cynicism quite openly on my sleeve, I don't know of anything to change my conviction that the public expressions of "mistakes made", and the declarations of "forgiveness given", are best explained by the Fellowship's wish to be seen in a softer and more inclusive light by the wider church.

It was inevitable, I think, that the time came – sooner rather than later – when Noel began to take stock of the effect which the Jesus Army campaigning was having on the very core of the Jesus Fellowship: the communal lifestyle of the New Creation Community Church – the jewel at the centre of Mother Zion. Sharing all things in common within the structure of a holy brotherhood needed jealous guardianship. With many more people joining the Fellowship within one of the newer, looser categories of membership – the reward of having broadened out to reach out – the need of ensuring a corresponding growth in the size and strength of God's kingdom, as represented by the NCCC, stood in some danger of neglect; especially when it was sensed that too much exposure to the world was resulting in an encroachment of its values into the fabric of the kingdom lifestyle. SC put what happened like this:

"Opening ourselves to the mainstream had threatened to blunt our prophetic edge. Easier paths were on offer. That was why we had once stood apart. The city needed to stay firmly on the hill, undiluted, undiminished and uncompromised if ever she was to meet the desperate need for God's alternative."[56]

As the emphasis on "holy brotherhood" was brought back into sharp focus, SC tells us that it became a time of *tearing and repairing*. Noel reminded everyone that the Fellowship would dig its own grave if it didn't constantly pursue the prophetic vision which God had communicated through his preaching and ministry. Noel stood there as a watchman over Fellowship standards: he'd done so before and would do so many times again. SC has summed this up neatly in his observation that *"as long as Noel was around sinners would definitely not be at ease in Zion."* I've spoken with those who have shaken their shoulders as if drenched by freezing water when they've described these periods of "tightening up". *'Brrrrr'*, they've said with a cold shudder, *'I remember those times all too well.'* We may assume that Noel didn't hold back when delivering the requisite correction, something which SC acknowledges by telling us that:

"the anointing had come in wild and was renewing her [Zion] ... 1990, had been a painful turning point."[57]

With households (e.g. London, Hastings, Sheffield) and church-planting campaigns (e.g. Manchester and Newcastle) that were becoming ever more geographically detached from Northamptonshire, Noel had recognized three issues: the danger of standards being diluted, the status of his vision for radical brotherhood being diminished, and the creep of worldliness advancing. It was concerns such as these that led him to issue the precepts I've referred to right back in the "antescript-postscript" section at the beginning of this book. The rationale behind the precepts is explicitly acknowledged in the preamble which went with them:

"As a people of "New Creation" committed to developing a kingdom of God culture, we have taken a stand against the spirit of the world in many aspects of our life together. This is particularly true of our community houses, where over the years we have established a number of "precepts" to guide our practice and act as benchmarks for our radical commitment. It does seem that in recent years some of our distinctiveness from the culture of the world around us has been lost. We are therefore listing below a number of precepts covering what seem to have become "grey areas" in our community life. Please consider before God whether they highlight a loss of radicality in your community house life, and if so take appropriate action."

These precepts had been explicit enough to cause considerable concern in future years when the spotlight – including one from a police investigation – began to shine on dark corners previously hidden from public sight. In consequence, all members were encouraged to get rid of any printed copies in their possession. Thankfully, a good number of them have survived the Fellowship's damage-limitation efforts; and one of them has eventually found its way to me. I hope its content is sufficient to convince those who otherwise may have struggled to believe the extent of control exercised over Community members – especially Noel's hand in it all – and the deceitful way in which this control was often denied.

CHAPTER TWENTY-NINE: "Dial Midnight" and other TV programmes

During the early nineties my name often came up when TV-programme researchers were looking for someone to talk about their experiences of the Jesus Army. This led to four occasions when I took part in the filming of TV shows or documentaries, three of them national and one regional. Each of them was quite different in its format, but all of them were exciting breaks – if only very brief ones – from what sometimes felt like the daily grind of being at work. Apart from anything else I had some expenses-paid trips to London and elsewhere, which included hotel accommodation and meals – an entirely new experience and therefore quite a thrill. I could easily have got used to all this as a way of life and would be lying if I said I hadn't enjoyed facing the cameras. But none of it was sought out; each invite came totally out of the blue as a complete surprise.

The first occasion came when Nigel and I were both invited to take part in a live discussion being held on Midlands TV. Shamefully, I remember more about the meal we had with the production team the evening before than I do about the debate itself. Lor! Reviewing our contribution on a video replay, I took note of how well Nigel had acquitted himself by addressing the camera with a confident posture and providing clearly spoken, intelligent comments. By contrast, my own posture on the shared sofa looked slovenly and my voice, always quite mild, sounded rather feeble. Hardly surprising, then, that I seem to have blanked out any detail of the debate itself.

My appearance on the then-popular Kilroy Show in 1993 didn't amount to much at all; yet it was a quite revelatory experience in itself to meet the famous man and get a genuinely informative exposure to all that goes on in a TV studio during the live transmission of a show like this one. Coming in the wake of the "Wako massacre", when a suicidal conflagration followed the siege of a "Branch Davidian" cult HQ by US federal troops, Robert Kilroy-Silk led a wide-ranging debate about the nature of cults. The Jesus Army, suggested by some to be a British version of such a cult, didn't end up being discussed; my only contribution was the short reply I gave to a question from another member of the audience.

Documentary stardom followed – or at least *should* have done – after I'd been filmed on the university campus at Canterbury; a location chosen by the director because of my previous association with it. Once again, sadly, my memories about the documentary's content are sketchy; nor do I even remember its name or which channel it was shown on. My most vivid recollection is the one of having had to wait outside the student union building for well over an hour before the film crew turned up. This was the pre-mobile-phone era, so I had no way of knowing – beyond the power of trust – whether anyone would eventually arrive, or even whether I was in the right place: it was the kind of thing I might well have got wrong. But the crew *did* arrive eventually, although the evening was well progressed by the time the filming was finished. I remember being asked to walk away towards the university library in the final shot of my contribution. Wearing denim, and walking westerly, I was depicted in this scene rather like a cowboy in an old Western walking off towards the sunset.

"Dial Midnight" – a long-running, rather wacky Saturday-night London Weekend TV show, written and presented by Anastasia Cooke, Samantha Norman, and James Whale – was, without a shadow of doubt, the one which I enjoyed the most – for many reasons. An Irish folk-rock band called "the Saw Doctors" put in a foot-stomping live performance right alongside where I was sat. I'd never even heard of them before but straight away set about acquainting myself with their music on my return to Durham. They became, in fact, the first band I ever took my youngest son, Benjamin, to see – at the Manchester Apollo – when he couldn't have been much older than eight or nine. Jeanne, having taken to their music as enthusiastically as I'd done, came with me to half-a-dozen or so Saw Doctors' gigs over the next few decades; and it somehow feels as if we've grown old alongside them: their songs have been part of our musical background.

But I hadn't gone to the studio to discover the Saw Doctors, of course. Anastasia, one of the presenters, had been in contact with me over several weeks whilst researching material about the Jesus Army, which was to be featured during the show – and she also invited me to take part in it. Ian Haworth from the Cult Information Centre was another on the guest list: I'd spoken and corresponded with Ian previously but had never actually met him. I wasn't initially told that a small gang of JA members would be there in the audience as I think Anastasia was concerned I might not agree to take part. She needn't have worried: the prospect of coming face to face with some former friends was of no concern to me whatsoever; quite the opposite, it was something I would look forward to. But nor did she tell me that the JA didn't know about *my* being there, which I thought was unnecessarily sneaky after I'd found out.

The centrepiece of the Dial Midnight studio was a bright-red sofa covered in cone-shaped spikes. That anyone would be able to sit on it didn't seem physically possible; yet those invited to do so plonked themselves down with apparent disregard for the protrusions… it would have been fun to have had a try for myself. Anastasia and Samantha sat to one side, with John Perceptive (JP) from the JA to their left and Ian Haworth to their right. About a dozen or so foot-soldiers of the JA, male and female, were given a place to sit on the floor of the studio. Distinctive in their colourful army attire, they nonetheless looked like a rather forbidding and cheerless corps with dour, sombre expressions and a distinct impression of being there under duress. Another entourage – to be featured first – were some flamboyantly gregarious gay men dressed as nuns, complete with habits and wimples, who called themselves "the Sisters of Perpetual Indulgence". These sisters were presented from the floor of the studio by the facially hirsute James Whale and were immediately followed by the Saw Doctors, who sang "The Music I Love" as their first number. I took to the band almost immediately, which meant a relaxing three or four minutes before "our" turn came round.

In chapter twenty I've already included a transcript of the initial exchanges between Anastasia and JP. I would like to rerun part of this in the light of the "Community Precepts" which I didn't have access to at *that* point of writing this book (see "Community Precepts – an 'antescript' postscript" before chapter one).

Having received a flat rebuttal of the initial allegations which she'd asked JP to address, Anastasia – somewhat aghast – narrowed down her question:

*'What? Is there **any** truth in this? About the socializing... are members in the Community not allowed to socialize with people outside of it?'*

To which JP replied:

'No! That's not true. Obviously, our emphasis on Christian community is on being together, attempting to serve Jesus, to serve God. But of course lots of people have friends outside; people have jobs outside.'

We **now** need to compare JP's reply with a couple of the explicit Community precepts concerning outside activities, relationships and friendships:

"We neither hold nor attend parties, barbeques, buffets etc. except for evangelistic purposes."

And,

"We mix with the people of the world only to befriend and win them for Christ."

In other words, JA members were categorically NOT allowed to "socialize" with people outside the Community; they were NOT allowed to mix with them on a casual, social basis. *What could be clearer?*

JP's response to Anastasia needs to be called out correctly for the lie it was. It was only one amongst the many he came out with during his defensive and evasive responses to questions from both Anastasia and Ian Haworth – someone who, for my money, was right on the button in the contributions he made.

The questions which Anastasia asked of me weren't ones which I'd been able to prepare for. Nor had I anticipated them in the exact format she presented them. I needed to think very quickly on my feet – or, more correctly, from where I was sat in the audience. Watching a video replay a few days later, I was relieved and reassured to find I'd given clear and concise answers that were not only relevant but also free from deviation, repetition or hesitation. For once I felt I'd probably done as well as I was capable of and didn't feel like reaching for the remote to switch off the TV. I was able to explain – quite articulately, so

I thought – about the issues which led me to believe the Fellowship was a cult; my personal experience of being brainwashed; how "the man at the very top" had been responsible for preventing me beginning a romantic relationship; and the ways in which Noel regarded himself as being a prophet.

Soon after my slot, Anastasia asked a lady sat next to me – someone I didn't know – to talk about what happened to her family after her son had joined ranks with the JA. From the off it was clear she was someone determined to make the most of the opportunity to air her grievances on live TV; neither Anastasia nor JP had much success in stemming her flow. She passionately explained how her son had been pressurized – so she claimed – into being baptised after only ten days of involvement and how he'd changed almost overnight into a "raving religious fanatic" (her own words). It became apparent that she and her husband had already become a thorn in the Fellowship leaders' flesh with forthright expressions of opposition to their control over her son. Alarmingly, we then heard about threatening anonymous letters which the couple had received; letters which told them about the judgement to come if they didn't stop interfering in their son's involvement with the Fellowship. We even heard about a bomb hoax which had been inflicted on them.

JP kept trying to interrupt and explain his position with regards to these threats. But the lady wasn't for turning at that point. She kept waving one of the anonymous letters in the air whilst insisting that it couldn't have been written by anyone who didn't know about her son from *within* the JA. Eventually, JP was able to offer his response. The smoothly restrained and subdued tone which he'd hitherto spoken with was now gone: he spoke with visible animation and clarity. The Fellowship itself, he explained, had had nothing whatsoever to do with these threats. He urged the lady, as he'd apparently often done previously, to report the receipt of anonymous letters to the police; and he gave a cast-iron assurance that the Fellowship would cooperate fully with any investigation that followed. For once, I found myself very nearly wanting to applaud and shout, *'hear hear!'*

On the other hand, of course, this lady and her husband – sat next to her – were evidently in considerable distress. *They* weren't to have known with certainty, as I did, that writing anonymous letters would *not* have been sanctioned by the JA's leadership. Having refused to accept the sound advice JP had evidently been giving them, these aggrieved parents had then embroiled themselves in a vendetta which was easy for the Fellowship to label as misconceived – which indeed it was. The lady's TV rant was unhelpful, from my perspective, because it had associated the Fellowship with behaviour from which it was easily able to distance and disassociate itself. Moreover, the advice given by JP meant that the Fellowship appeared to be being reasonable; the upset parent unreasonable. For reasons such as these – in addition to the voice of my own conscience – I was determined to ensure my own opposition to the Fellowship avoided anything which was malicious, hyped-up, or based on falsehood – including so-called false truths.

After the show, all those who'd contributed were invited to an upstairs' lounge bar so we could wind down and mingle together. Taken somewhat off guard, I was surprised to discover that, in addition to JP, the invitation had been extended to *all* of those JA members who'd been present – some of whom I knew quite well. The polite chat I had with JP was more or less just that: polite and reasonably friendly. Not so some of the other ones I had. Most memorable was the dressing-down I received from a brother whose name is best withheld.

'*You're a slimy toerag,*' he told me. And then, unable to find a better way to express his contempt, he gestured to spit at me – without, thankfully, the release of any spittle. He didn't have any need to explain that he'd not strictly speaking been spitting at *me*, but rather at my master, Beelzebub himself, whose demonic agents were attacking the Fellowship *through* me. I was reminded of the reports which had filtered back to me of the "holy curses" issued over me when Fellowship members had been urged to pray against me in person. *'What was that all about?'* I'd wondered. *'From where had Noel derived the biblical justification for using incantations which were more commonly associated with the occult?'* It's strange, I thought, what a difference the prefix "holy" can make; it can almost make *anything* sound acceptable. *Holy curses, indeed!* At least I'd had the sense not to be upset by what I'd heard; I recognized how futile such curses were. Nor was I particularly fazed by the taunts I'd just been given in the lounge bar: by now I'd managed to grow a thick-enough skin to protect myself against such attacks, and so I didn't feel any sense of personal injury. *But how did this tally with "the rekindled willingness to forgive those who spoke or wrote against the Fellowship" that I would later get to read about in "Fire in Our Hearts"?* Perhaps it was something that had been easier for them to promotionally boast about rather than actually put into meaningful practice.

The nineties marched inexorably onwards, as years are wont to do, and the JA marched forward with them: the Jesus Army was rebranded as the "Modern Jesus Army", replete with modernized "space jackets" and other aspects of uniform; another double-decker was added to the fleet of buses; communication technology was increasingly harnessed for outreach; and a colourful, professionally designed, award-winning website was launched. Printing and distribution of street-papers and other literature continued to increase; the "Multiply Christian Network" – launched to unite regional bases of the JA with other like-minded local fellowships – continued to grow and even include members domiciled abroad; the "Jesus Praise Band", performing at Spinney Hall in Northampton on Sunday evenings, became increasingly polished and started to incorporate UV lamps, strobes and "intelligent" lighting within its worship; church-planting activities led to new households being established, such as "Abundant Grace" in Brighton; and another converted coach became the tour bus for the "UK Ignition Gospel Roadshow" on its three-year nationwide tour. Under the project banner of "UK People, We Love

You!", the roadshow used a softer approach than the Jesus Army's military-style one. In alignment with a perceived resurgence amongst the young to be unified with the mystical elements of "the natural", *One World* and *Butterfly* stickers were given out to emphasize the strength of Jesus's love towards the Earth and its inhabitants. With Christian revival erupting in various places visited by "UK Ignition", those involved went along expediently with the flow as they watched people's lives being taken over by God's love. SC tell us:

"We now baptised anyone, anywhere, who had faith in Jesus. Covenant membership was our strong heart, but anyone who loved us belonged. We were inclusive."[58]

Modern Jesus Army Bus in Oxford[a]

This demonstration of inclusivity towards the newly converted ran alongside the extended arm of fellowship towards other local Christian groups – as enshrined in the objectives of the Multiply Christian Network. It was enough to convince the Evangelical Alliance leaders that the Fellowship had demonstrated sufficient alliance with others to enable acceptance of their 1999

---

[a] https://oxford-chiltern-bus-page.co.uk/150908-Editorial%20and%20Features.htm: Photo of Leyland Olympian bus by Gavin Francis

application for readmission. This was also the year when a former cinema in Northampton was bought for conversion into the first of the "Jesus Centres" – multi-purpose buildings to be used not only for worship gatherings but also as local-outreach bases and drop-in centres for homeless and others in deep, personal need. Each of these centres took the name of "the Bridge".

Jesus Centre Northampton[a]

Amidst all the energy and activity of the nineties, about which I received regular reports from those who'd split, the issues which most concerned me about the Fellowship hadn't gone away. They were far less visible, without doubt, yet I remained convinced – sometimes, it felt, against the flow of revised, wider evangelical opinion – that Noel Stanton's ultimate control, and therefore his ultimate influence, hadn't been reduced. And nor had he shown what I considered to be any genuine contrition for the harm he'd caused. Whilst this remained the case, my conviction remained intact that were I to return – purely hypothetical, of course – I would find little had changed at the very heart of everything. Reading SC's book, I can trace Noel's hand in the repeated cyclical efforts which were made to ensure the central vision of Zion wasn't diluted by the outward-facing activities. Consider this in reference to outreach within the hometown of Northampton:

"We were talking war here. It was useless trying to capture enemy territory if our own ground was vulnerable and insecure. As Ed Silvoso pointed out, Hezekiah first cleansed the temple before he was able to convert the city. Our community households needed cleansing and reviving. The spirit of radical

---

[a] https://structurae.net/en/structures/northampton-jesus-centre

pioneering had been our genius over the years. This had to be recaptured. If residential community was to be a minority portion in the church, it must be the white-hot centre, unadulterated and undiluted. Retaking the central ground was first priority."[59]

Following my series of TV contributions, I made no further contribution to any form of opposition to the Fellowship for quite some time. Apart from anything else, these were critical years in our family life; years when our two eldest children attended secondary school and when we moved into a larger house – in Durham City itself – which gave us much-needed extra space and was considerably closer to where both Jeanne and I worked. But somehow, completely unsolicited, the legacy of the Fellowship never seemed far away; and not just because I occasionally bumped into Pete Mattacola's team of church-planting pioneers as they demonstrably introduced their presence in Newcastle's pedestrianized city centre. Not too long after I'd met up in Wales with Mark Strong and his wife, Julie (who, as a then single sister, had also left the Fellowship with him), news came of Graeme Merciful's departure: Graeme and I had been almost inseparable for several years. Given the distance from his new home in Milton Keynes to mine in Durham, it took a long while before the opportunity came for us to have a face-to-face reunion – but it had been well worth the wait when it came.

Next to leave was Marky Sparky: ace gearbox mechanic; my defender from defamation at the JA Wembley meeting; and general all-round prodigy. He sort of landed on me in Durham like a flaming astral fireball, though I'm not entirely sure whether it was an illuminative one sent from paradise to light my way or a destructive one sent from a far-darker place to burn and torch all those who crossed its path. Mark's story of leaving the farm had all the familiar elements which my own and Nigel's had. Having fled to Germany, where he lived and worked for a year or so (and where he learnt to speak the language more or less fluently), he'd come to Durham in a somewhat desperate state, not least financially, hoping I might be able to help him. He found himself in luck: I could. I was able to settle him in a nearby semi-stately home, Flass Hall, which I looked after in my sideline role as estate manager and factotum for its wealthy owner, Prof. Robin Medforth-Mills – who worked abroad with UNICEF. I put Mark to work helping with some of the renovations which were in progress. My main job was now at Durham University, where I was the buildings' manager for one of the colleges; so I was also able to wangle a job for Mark on a few of the summer building projects which were threatening to overwhelm us.

Naturally, I got to hear from my old friend a lot about what had been happening both within the Fellowship and specifically at New Creation Farm. In fact, he even persuaded me to revisit the farm with him on our way back from a visit to Luton, assuring me that Dave "Forthright" – a brother we'd both been close to and who was now working as one of the farm managers – would be glad to see us. To a point, yes he was. The three of us walked through the orchards and had a lively discussion together: one which was made possible, I think, by the fraternity we shared as those who had each fallen from grace in one way or another. Out of respect for Dave, I need to draw a veil over the detail concerning his own non-venial peccadillo.

Flass Hall's owner, Robin, took an almost instant liking for Mark when he came back from Iraq on one of his regular visits; so he invited him to extend his tenure at the hall in order to supervise the building of a triple-doored, stone garage – with loft and office space – adjacent to the main building. Mark proved himself nothing less than remarkable. Whilst I stood watching him survey the garage site through a theodolite, I wondered if there was *anything* to which he couldn't turn his hand. Maybe mastering the technology of jet engines might have stretched him too far – but you never knew with Mark. The garage rose majestically under his guidance and physical involvement; although yours truly had a small part to play as well. I particularly remember helping Mark to lug some massive coping stones up a ladder and onto the garage roof in defiance of all proper safety considerations and in freezing cold weather – and this when I should really have been tucked up in bed to nurse a nasty attack of man flu.

But there was also a dark side to Mark which I hadn't previously known about. It started coming to my attention when I heard reports of his driving Robin's Rolls-Royce Silver Shadow around Esh Winning village late at night, windows open and stereo turned up full blast – and I was also told he'd been heavily inebriated at the time. Unverified hearsay, true enough, yet the list of his misdemeanours ramped up remorselessly – as did his temper and irresponsibility. Regretfully, his behaviour became increasingly erratic to the point where I needed to "let him go" – as they say. It was an immensely painful time for both of us. I last heard direct reports about Mark from another rather eccentric but much-loved ex-brother – a certain, near-legendary Andie Duthie, the same brother whom I'd overheard on my first visit to New Creation Hall explaining he was "purging the bed of the elders". Andy told me he'd seen him walking around Northampton dressed in a flamboyant white suit and sporting an ivory-topped black cane as if he thought himself a latter-day Oscar Wilde. That was Mark to a tee! I once heard Pete Townsend from *The Who* rock band say of their drummer, the late Keith Moon, that he was an incredibly difficult person to live with but even more difficult to live without. There was definitely something of the achingly-adorable-yet-destructive Keith-Moon spirit about Mark. He could drive you to utter despair and yet you couldn't but help yourself loving him. Reading between the lines of certain social media postings, I'm fairly confident that Mark has gone on to lead a far more settled and successful life since those tumultuous times of yesteryear.

Apart from a letter I wrote to Mr. J. Dickie, Leader of Northampton Town Council, explaining my objection to the JFC's building and usage proposals for the old Canon cinema as a Jesus Centre, I think that we've brought the 20th. millennium to a close so far as any first-hand account of involvement with the Fellowship is concerned. I'd needed some persuasion from certain others to write the letter, anticipating its futility, and there was nothing whatsoever about the Fellowship which now featured on my personal agenda for the new millennium. I'd taken a new position as Services and Facilities manager at Van Mildert, one of the larger university colleges, and my main concern had become to get us over the midnight threshold without the Millennium Bug closing down our computer services, especially those which controlled the heating systems.

As a very brief endnote to the chapter, I should mention that the decade about to vanish had started witnessing reports – either by word of mouth or in print – of abuse, adultery, and even isolated instances of bestiality within the JFC. The report reproduced below from the Northampton Chronicle and Echo on April 22nd. 1997 is one example:

JESUS ARMY BANNED KIDS HAVING TOYS, GAMES OR SWEETS

"A woman and her family lived with the Jesus Fellowship for almost two decades. This month, she was in court in London to see a church member convicted of two counts of indecent assault against her, a story the Chronicle and Echo featured first. Now she tells her incredible story to Hilary Scott.

The woman seems far more mature than her 19 years. Until recently, the teenager lived in a world where women are still considered servants to their male counterparts. She was born into the controversial Jesus Fellowship Church based in Bugbrooke, the fourth in a family of six children who were to grow up in the sect.

'I think I always questioned what was going on there, even when I was very small.' She said.

'I was a very noisy child and that was frowned upon by the male leaders of the church. Children were not allowed to be children and they weren't allowed toys or games, or to watch television. We were denied a childhood. But we were allowed to go to normal schools, and I went to Bugbrooke primary. That's when I started to realise the kids from the church were different.'

'Once when I was about seven years old we were on the Jesus Army bus which stopped at a service station. This little old lady came up and said what beautiful children we were, and gave us all a Mars bar. We hadn't had chocolate before and all got on the bus clutching our Mars bars with pride. Then the leader took them all off us and threw them out of the window, saying they were the devil's food. We were terrified and didn't know what we had

done wrong.'

'Women within the church don't complain either, because they are too frightened. If you question the church at all you are told you are speaking with the Devil's tongue, and that God will disapprove. Religion, as they use it, is a powerful threat.'

The Jesus Fellowship, also known as the Jesus Army, was started by former Bugbrooke Baptist minister Noel Stanton. The church has become notorious for its military-style evangelism, with members wearing combat-gear targeting former criminals and down and outs.

The Woman said: *'The success of the Jesus Army is that it involves vulnerable people who want someone to listen to them and care for them. Those people are in every walk of life, not just on the streets. And the Jesus Army seems to care. It's not until you are in that you realise how difficult it is to leave. It convinces its members it is the only thing that matters. They use the Bible to convince people that they are right, and that everyone outside the church is wrong.'*

On April 4, a jury at Isleworth Crown Court found a church member guilty of indecent assault on the woman. She said the abuse started when she was 13 after the family had moved to a spin-off commune in Acton, London.

'I was working by the time I was 16 in an old people's home, and I had to hand over my wage packet or Giro cheque to the church each week. I wasn't allowed to keep anything personal. After three years of misery I started to keep back some of my wages, and opened a secret bank account. When I had enough money I left. My older brothers and sisters had already left by this stage and the leaders told me I would be dammed if I joined them. It was constant mental abuse, making you think you were wrong and they were right.'

The woman said her decision to speak out against the fellowship was to warn others about the consequences, not as an act of revenge. *'I don't hate the Jesus Army, I pity them,'* she said."

Reading accounts such as this prompted me to write a manuscript which would incorporate my own experiences within the JFC. Its wider theme was to be an autobiographical explanation of events that led me to Bugbrooke's door and how I ended up facing down suicidal urges in a mental hospital. I took a six-month sabbatical from my university employment to write the manuscript and called the completed draft "Looking for Freedom – Fighting Madness". My serious attempts to find a publisher only initially led to the receipt of several rejection slips – letters which authors dread so much. The chapters concerning the JFC would later be incorporated within the JEANNI website I created; and further down the road I found myself on the verge of having them serialized in a popular Sunday magazine. The opportunity slipped away, however, because I was unable to summon up the wherewithal to make the necessary editorial alterations required: ten years or so had passed since I completed my first draft and I no longer had sufficient conviction about the relevance of what I'd written.

CHAPTER THIRTY: JEANNI website

The Millennium Bug failed to have any real impact; but would that have still been the case had so much effort not been expended on precautionary IT measures? Who knows? Certainly not me! I was just glad that the heating controls at Van Mildert college continued to operate as normal.

Throughout 2000 and 2001 I had no agenda whatsoever in relation to opposing and exposing what was happening within the JA. Every so often I took a look at their website; but truth be told, I was often baffled by it: I just couldn't seem to get my head around how to reconcile the revivalist excitement that leapt out at me from nearly every page – alongside self-congratulatory claims to be champions of the Christian church's mission amongst the poor, homeless and marginalized – with the authoritarian insistence on building God's kingdom and being a people set apart which I remained convinced was at the heart of it all. It riled me to think about the false impression being so powerfully communicated whilst not knowing how, or having the ability, to do anything about it. Still, there were some lighter moments to amuse me during my browsing. I became intrigued by the avatar which had been integrated into the website, something I hadn't previously come across. "She" was there as a kind of counsellor or advisor in matters spiritual, so I put her to the test. Sadly, I cannot remember the *exact* form of the words I used, but one of my conversations with her ran something like this:

Me: *What does God think about the Jesus Fellowship Church?*
Avatar: *The Jesus Fellowship Church is being blessed by God.*

So far so good. But I decided to press her a bit more closely.

Me: *Why exactly do you say that the Jesus Fellowship Church is being blessed by God?*
Avatar: *Because that's what John Campbell programmed me to say.*

Her reply, hand on my heart, was exactly as I've written it. In many ways it couldn't have been a better metaphor for the disquiet I was feeling: the need to reveal the truth concealed behind the website's glossy veneer.

2002 came around and the dynamics of our family life had begun to change appreciably. Our eldest, Rebekah, had graduated from the Northern Ballet School in Manchester and had now begun the first of the many voyages she would complete as a cruise-ship dancer. Simeon, second eldest, was in his A-level year and we'd begun to see less and less of him in our day-to-day lives. Benjamin, our baby then and forever (sorry, sonshine!), no longer needed walking to and from his primary school every day and was already asserting his independence as a secondary-school rebel-in-the-making.

Hounded by certain well-known proverbial sayings such *as all it takes for evil to prosper is for good men to remain silent* and *better to light a candle than curse the darkness,* I felt the time had come for me to stop yielding to the enervating and stifling conviction of not being able to do anything and start being bold enough, yet again, to make a mark. I still nursed some kind of self-reproach which often taunted me with its question, *if* **you** *don't do something with what you know, then who will?* I had a duty to do something – that's what it was; a duty – which was no less imperative than the compassionate one I'd have if I saw Noel Stanton himself lying injured by the roadside. It may sound very noble, but it wasn't: it was no more than what I knew I *had* to do.

It didn't take long to decide that a website was needed.

'But hold on a moment,' I reasoned with myself, *'surely there must already be other websites which counteract John Campbell's JA one,'*

Extensive searching informed me that there was only *one* other: www. jesusarmywatch.org – the Jesus Army Watch. The site initially seemed to be something of an enigma as I couldn't really fathom out its purpose. It was packed with factual information about the JFC's structure and businesses, together with a comprehensive archive of press clippings dating right back to 1970. A huge amount of work had gone into the compilation of everything. But why? And who was behind it? The overall feel of the site seemed to suggest something like: *we've got our eyes on you, Jesus Army, and we're going to keep you under the spotlight,* which was much needed and immensely helpful. But what I had in mind to create was more along the lines of what a Facebook group would become; a sort of internet meeting place where information could be shared and people could network together and discuss the latest developments. The Jesus Watch website already had a "news" page; but it wasn't conversational or word-of-mouth news, it was all taken from newspaper reports.

Satisfied that I wouldn't just be replicating what was already available, I set to. I needed to start from base-zero of knowing absolutely nothing about either the construction or the hosting of a website. The very first thing I needed, of course, was a title suitable to yield an acronym: and thus was the Jesus Army News Networking and Information site born – JEANNI. The similarity of JEANNI with my wife's name, Jeanne, was as coincidental as the one linking her name with the little cabin boat – "Bonny Jean" – which we rescued from virtual abandonment a few years ago. Next up came the writing of content, mainly completed on a Microsoft Word Webpage template. It worked, as I was to discover, by translating the text and page layout into Microsoft's own bastardized version of readable code. At the time, all I cared about was whether or not it would produce an accessible website.

When it felt like I was getting near to completion, I got in touch with the "Jesus Army Watch" webmaster, Mike Aldrich, to let him know what was afoot.

He responded swiftly and eagerly to my email request for a chat. More than that! He already knew of me from features in his news archive – which included the Jesus Cult pamphlets – and was keen to know what I thought about *his* site. If I say that Mike proved to be just a "regular" kind of guy, then it wouldn't do him justice. He was – and still is, of course – so much more than regular: an intelligent, highly-motivated and extraordinarily capable person. My ascription of "regularity" related to his religiosity. He'd never been part of the Jesus Army, nor anything similar: in fact there didn't seem to be anything about Mike which could have linked him with extremism of any description. It's possible that his collection of pub gaming-machines – which I got to see when I visited him at his home – might have been a sign of a certain eccentricity; but isn't our society just crying out for such good, old-fashioned, harmless eccentrics these days, don't you think? Mike explained that, as a Northampton local, he'd been intrigued by the Jesus Army and had decided to create a website which did exactly what it said on the tin: watch them – watch them very carefully and cautiously.

With Mike on board and the content of the site complete, I began trying to figure out the mechanics of actually getting it all "up there onto the Web" using a File Transfer Protocol programme. After several failed attempts came the elation of seeing my handiwork right there in front of me, "live" on my laptop screen: not exactly how I'd planned it to look, but not unrecognizable either. I went ahead with an "official" launch on March 3rd. 2002. It befitted, I thought, a press release; one which I duly wrote and sent out.

Some of the first reactions I had to the website were from those who'd spotted just how dreadful the coding language was. Inevitably, this also meant that the layout of each page was very erratic and prone to considerable change depending on which browser was being used – Firefox; Netscape, Internet Explorer etc. My learning curve was to be a steep one, but one which I knew I needed to clamber up quickly. To do so, I bought some HTML textbooks and began to immerse myself in them. Slowly, with each new iteration, the quality of the site began to improve; but when I hit a brick wall – as I often did – and nothing worked in the way I wanted it to, I knew that I could ask for Mike's help: something he offered very graciously and patiently. It was Mike who put me onto a wonderful web editor, Evrsoft 1st. Page, which I still use; and Mike, too, who introduced me to the wonders of CSS, a web design feature that I used for JEANNI – several years into its life – after I'd splashed out on yet another textbook and done my best to absorb its content.

The paragraph above is a condensation of what happened over quite a number of years. In the first few months of the website's internet tenure, however, it attracted far more "hits" than I'd expected given its near invisibility on most search engines. Even after several months it didn't appear in the top ten pages of a Google search using the most likely key words; and yet the JA's "www.jesus.org" website consistently hogged the top three or four entries on page one. *'How so?'* I often used to wonder. It would be several years before I acquired sufficient knowledge about using SEO – Search Engine Optimization – to begin making any impact on JEANNI's ranking. During those first few years many of my web pages didn't even have a proper title in the coding header for goodness sake. What hope did I have? My main concern had been just to be "out there" as a resource for those who needed help or further information, so I naively assumed that such people would somehow discover JEANNI.org after a bit of searching around. And to a certain extent they somehow did. Initially, the undeniablity of the website being so poorly created and displayed didn't present itself to me as too much of an issue.

It didn't take very long for me to realize that the most obvious benefit of the site would be the opportunity it gave for people to contact me via email with either their questions or to share their experiences. But before I share some of these email exchanges, perhaps I should share the content of a few pages from the website as it was early on. I'm doing so from a sense of honesty and comprehensive transparency, and definitely not from any sense of their merit. When I look back on what I wrote, and the style in which I wrote it, my knees want to crumble with embarrassment. But there it is for better or worse: this was the best attempt I could muster to light a candle in the darkness. The content of one of my earliest "Home" pages – my saved files only go back to the beginning of 2004 – read like this (structure, grammar, punctuation, spelling mistakes as they were):

jeanni stands for **J**esus **A**rmy **N**ews **N**etworking and **I**nformation.
Why has jeanni been set up?

1. To provide a site where people can share their stories, keep in contact with one another, and seek help and advice. **I hope to concentrate on this aspect of jeanni in the coming weeks and months.** Please click on the **Networking** tag in the left hand menu bar.

2. I think that the Jesus Army needs to remain under the investigative spotlight because we are dealing with the lives of REAL people. And, just as with many other radical societies, individuals can all too easily become pawns in someone else's game of chess – shunted about from here to there as necessary and all-too-easily sacrificed in the cause of the greater scheme! Please click on the **News** and/or **Information** tag in the left hand menu bar.

3. The Jesus Army seems to have convinced many other Christian organisations and churches that they have reformed those practices which had previously resulted in their exclusion and isolation. If other people are convinced, then I'm not! I hear all kinds of stories (many of them first-hand) which make me extremely worried about the way Jesus Army members are treated. Please click on the **News** and/or **Information** tag in the left hand menu bar.

Different people will visit these pages for different reasons:

If you are closely associated with the Jesus Army and are having misgivings about the organisation, then I suspect your misgivings will only be strengthened by what you discover here. No apologies about that. Take courage! Follow your convictions!

If you have a loved one in the Jesus Army, you may well feel anxious about their involvement. Please get in contact with me (Click here) and I'll do all I can to help you.

If you are simply curious, or are visiting for some other reason, then I hope what you read gets those old grey cells working. Whether you agree with me or not, I would love to hear from you.

I'm not afraid of criticism or dialogue, so tell me what you think: (Click here)

So there we are. Please be kind to me by remembering that it really was the best I could do at the time: I was working alone and didn't have anyone to help who could have reigned in my verbosity and intense intensity or cut down the conversational content – nor warn me about what a fool I might be making of myself in the eyes of some.

PART SEVEN
Other voices

Looking back through my archived records of the correspondence that came through JEANNI, I've needed to relive, once again, all those stupefying emotions of disbelief, outrage and sheer frustration at the likelihood of being able to make any impression on the duplicitous frontage of the JA. Many were being damaged in just the same way they had been ten, twenty, maybe even thirty years ago. As I reread my correspondence, I couldn't escape feeling that I was right back there in the thick of everything, kicking against the pricks to make myself heard. Strangely, on the evening after I'd completed my review, I came across a passage in "Our Mutual Friend" – which I'd started to reread – that struck me as being superbly pertinent. Referring to that "something" about Mr. Boffin's secretary which he carried with him, an undefinable visceral something which hung over him like a "nameless cloud", Dickens observes that this something was somehow ever-present and would never leave:

"It has been written of men who have undergone a cruel captivity, or who have passed through a terrible strait, or who in self-preservation have killed a defenceless fellow-creature, that the record thereof has never faded from their countenance until they died." (p239)

There will be many, like myself, for whom the shadow-record of the harm we've received through our membership of the Jesus Fellowship will always be there, no matter how well-recovered we are. Whilst rereading my old correspondence, this shadow-record has manifested itself in those dark memories of believing myself to be in battle against an oppressively powerful opponent who could disguise itself as an angel of light whilst treating its subjects with disdain and cruelty as the need arose. The shadow has frequently brought me low, not least on the present occasion. Some will feel equally sad when they themselves read extracts from my JEANNI correspondence. For now, then, I shall largely let some of my email friends tell their own story. Where necessary, identities have been changed or scrambled; but in many cases it's been possible to retain genuine names. Amongst the many emails received, I've selected several – spread out across the decade – which help to reinforce different aspects of the Fellowship that I've written about. They aren't, therefore, entirely representative of the range of views from opposed to supportive. The mail I received from the supportive cohort was small in comparison with those opposed, with some writers expressing their displeasure toward me in quite fruity language. Even so, I will include a few of these to offer a balance of sorts.

CHAPTER THIRTY-ONE: From the mouths of others

In the quotations to follow I have done my best to reproduce the text exactly as it was sent to me, including all typos, spelling mistakes and grammatical structure. I have, however, in the interests of brevity and readability, made certain redactions and minor changes as required.

Also, a number of names have been changed to protect identity and safeguard confidentiality and privacy.

Heidi – *"I was brainwashed".* In September 2002, Heidi wrote:

"Dear john.

As an ex-member of the jesus army, I have full praise for your efforts in making this site and hope you stick at it. A site such as this is good news for me and many others who have been or thinking of becoming a member of the j.a. The jesus army IS a dangerous cult, it uses subtle (and sometimes not so subtle) methods to first entice new members and then do everything possible to make sure they stay. I myself was BRAINWASHED for two years, and only through some inner strenth managed to break free from the web.

I wish you all the best with your site, you can never blaspheme against that evil organisation enough. good luck"

Teresa – *"Are men taught to mistreat women?"* Teresa emailed me in March 2003:

"I have never been involved in the Jesus Army as I knew it was a cult all along, having originated from the Bugbrooke Fellowship. The latter has been depicted as a kind of cult by Buzz Magazine and the former was a subject of debate on OEFII on BBC2 around 1989/90.

However I have come across men who have been involved with the Jesus Army and I've been mistreated by them. … Are men taught by the JA to mistreat women or are those type of men deliberately recruited by them and their misanthropist ideas confirmed. Which comes first the chicken or the egg? For years I blamed myself for what had happened and thought that I was to blame; I was too sexy, I was not 'giving' enough, I was too fun loving, I was too bossy, etc. Because of this I blamed myself for 'leading men on' in other walks of life and became paranoid. I've been afraid of starting a relationship in case I get mistreated again.

Now I realise I'm not to blame for 'making my brother stumble'. I had to have a female support worker from a local Mind association come and visit me when I made a complaint about another Mind user sexually harassing me at a music group. She tried to convince me that it was not my fault and I agree with her now as he was sexually harassing everyone else. I also now believe that when somebody criticises me or behaves badly towards me it says something about them more than it does about me.

I've been looking at anti-cult websites, particularly Rick Ross's website, and finding about mind control in cults. A lot of 'straight' churches are exhibiting some degree of mind control on some if not all of their members. Brainwashing people to go against the norms of the society they live in and expecting total commitment from them to me is mind control.

Going back to the Jesus Army, I think that they deliberately recruit violent types (ex-prisoners and alcoholics) in order to exert control over members who dissent and even passers-by who dare to criticise them blatantly. As for asking for different levels of commitment from members, this is just a way of ensnaring them gradually. As one group of people are only asked to give a basic level of commitment, then this is being used by the Jesus Army as some form of public relations to show the public that recruits don't have to be totally isolated. That is their 'public face'. I've also seen elements of the Jesus Army in some fundamentalist churches... It's very hard for some people to see the Jesus Army as a cult when how they behave is really an exaggeration of what goes on in certain fundamentalist churches. But that doesn't make it right."

Rebecca – *"Noel was very rude about other churches."* Rebecca wrote me a very long message in September 2004 and we continued to correspond for a while afterwards. I've needed to make alterations to most names and places to respect certain people's identities:

"Hello John,

I arrived home this morning after spending the weekend at [Zion House]. I'd been invited there by James who is my neice's husband's brother. Darius, my husband, died four years ago, and since then one by one the children have left home. My youngest daughter was married three weeks ago, and Paul, one of James's relatives, was at the wedding. Paul had often encouraged me to contact James so I thought I would as I wanted to look at community based living. I knew absolutely nothing of the Jesus Army. Paul gave me James's mobile (company one) number and the house number.

In the meantime Paul phoned James warning him I'd be ringing. By the time I spoke to James, he'd already cleared the way for me to visit Zion House. He told the community members I was Aunty Becks. True, because this is who I'm referred as in Paul's household. I went this weekend, arriving on the Friday evening, ready for the 'off' to Northampton celebrations and all that which took in Saturday, Sunday and Monday. There was a look of shock and horror on the face of Jenny who let me on Friday evening. I'm 56, trendy and still have blonde hair, and am considered very attractive (people usually think I'm at least ten years younger) so the Aunty they were expecting was probably in their minds, quite old, dowdy and with grey hair (or a blue rinse).

I was ushered into the kitchen whilst someone went to fetch James, they told him HIS Aunt had arrived. I had to explain to them that I was not his aunt but his sister-in-law's aunt. James gave me a hug, made me some tea and we went to sit in the lounge. I had gone there with an open mind, totally unbiased, but had prayed that the Lord would reveal anything to me that He wanted me to see. James and I were able to talk relatively privately for the remainder of that evening in the lounge (door open), but if I'd known then what I knew by the end of the weekend, I never would have asked him some of the questions that I asked at that time, and which may have been overheard. Paul had told me at various times that James had been thinking of leaving the community, and I asked him this, in all innocence. When I did, he squirmed uncomfortably, and I could not figure out why, but he said that he had no intention of leaving. He seemed pretty nervous.

Next day, Saturday we went to Northampton and to the marquee. Not one of the worship songs were about the Lord, and His goodness and actually praising Him for who He is. They were all about 'me' and what I should be. Then Noel Stanton spoke. When I'd heard Noel's name mentioned before, I thought Paul referred to Noel Richards! Not a hope! I had a shock when I heard NS speak. I thought he was horrible. He was very rude about other churches, and complained that people were leaving the community houses, and called them traitors and Judases. I thought 'so what' people do leave churches and move on and go to other churches but that does not make them traitors.

... Throughout the weekend, the Lord showed me different things which shocked me. At one point, Noel told everyone that when we read 'Israel' in the New Testament, we're to replace it with the word church. I spontaneously turned to James and said, "that's not right," and he gave an embarrassed smile. On the way back to the bus i said to James – "so you go to Israel every Sunday then, do you?" He roared with laughter – which was my intention.

Five men are being 'trained' to take over from Noel who will eventually step down. They are horrible. one of them gave a word of knowledge – "there is a brother here who is contemplating celibacy. However, you keep getting text messages from your girl friend. So get up here now and take your celibacy oath'' – It was not given kindly but barked out very abrasively.

Noel had had a word for people in the meeting, that there were sinners and people with filthy minds there, and as he was saying this some young men walked out. Noel said we must pray a disaster on their lives, so that something very nasty would happen to them to bring them into the Kingdom. I thought he meant the kingdom of Heaven, but disagreed with that kind of praying too, but later realised he meant his own little kingdom.

I quickly discovered that celibacy is revered as the highest form of service to the Lord. It was talked about and discussed a great deal. I was shocked to discover they had a service akin to a marriage service where men and women take the celibacy vow. I mentioned this to Jenny who was sitting next to me. I told her that I was celibate, that i chose to be until and if I remarry. She then told me I wasn't celibate and that i was single. I disagreed with her, and she made me feel very dirty. As we left that meeting, I mentioned this to James who said there were degrees of celibacy. I said you were either celibate, or not, and that it wasn't necessary for the world and his wife to know. I also told him I felt that many of the married couples felt very inferior. I also felt that many of the married couples were having problems with their lovemaking.

... I was able to spend almost an hour alone with James in the kitchen talking through things very late on Sunday night. We went through some of the scriptures together regarding marriage and celibacy and he asked me what I thought of the community. I said that I would not consider joining theirs because I disagreed with their theology on quite a few things. I did not tell him that I would not touch it with a barge pole because of the whole system operating under spiritual bondage and control. I also asked James if he got 'pocket money'? He laughed when I asked him this, but I was actually very serious. It did not take me long to work out that there must be a lot of money sloshing around somewhere, and why was it not spent on upgrading the houses? Also why wasn't their diet improved, and why could not the women wear make-up and be allowed to wear brighter, cheerier clothes ... I noticed all of the other women wore dowdy long skirts and frumpy jumpers, all of their clothes were high necked. I also asked about the sleeping arrangements, and there was not one double bed in sight, and the married's beds were single and on opposite sides of their rooms! James also said that in order to protect one's dignity, curtains were hung on the outside of every room.

I'm sorry this is so long, but I am very concerned for James. I have wept so much for him since I returned home. Paul is very concerned for James and we all realise that James needs to know there are people who do love him and there are several people who would give him a home."

Becky – *"I do not think the church is financially corrupt ... basically it's sneaky!"*
This from Becky in October 2004:

"dear john

I have read your website and appreciated it very much .

Been a member of this so – called church for eight years. I was 'saved' into a pentecostal church from a druggie/ political type scene . It was my husband who was then attracted to and wished to join the J.A and, having heard loads of crap about women submitting to their husbands I joined the church (wow what a prat!!) I have always managed to avoid the community thing, although we have had two brief sojourns into the common purse, which I quickly backed away from – too little control oneself and too much control in the hands of religious loons!

We are now in the situation of leaving our home with our 4 kids as it is a church housing association property and I no longer wish to go along with all their bullshit . This is a big problem, not only because we live in Brighton on the south coast, where homes are hard to come by, but also because my husband is still an 'elder' in the church . Obviously he is not a full elder only an acting one as he is not in the c.p and therefore dosn't quite make the grade !!!

I ask myself often how I got myself in this mess (a spiritual Laurel and Hardy thing?) but I need to think these through methodically, as I need to clear my head so I won't bother you with them.

... Noel was ministering at the last celibates meeting that the church would no longer bless the weddings of those who had broken vows of celibacy – this is the churchs response, no attempt at self examination etc simply the old 'must not abandon the vision given by God and weaken Zion His prophetic people'

There is also a lot of sickness around – an unusually large number of people suffering from m.e and related illnesses. (also anorexia amongst sisters). When I have pointed out to people that whole households seem to be suffering from exhaution, it is simply taken as undermining etc. The 'word' given is that God is always giving life in his spirit and so we should always be up for it. This is always qualified by someone saying "but it is o.k to be tierd" – the implication and the reality is the opposite . This kind of double speak happens with loads of issues.

The point you make about finances is an important one. I do not think the church is financially corrupt, however by paying people the minimum wage knowing this will be made up by the state is undrehand and ethically wrong and

I think has a knock on effect in the way things are done – basically it is sneaky!!

On a happier note the church is in a big mess, whatever image they present, and has not got enough people with the ability to carry it forward. I assume you know that Mick Temp has been chosen to lead the church when Noel goes. A lot of people take heart from this, that he is a gentle person etc. This is true, but he preaches the same stuff!! At the last weekend he had every one on their knees pledging to sacrifice more to make the church grow. Peolpe are running on empty as it is and new people who do come usually leave pretty quick as they are put under so much pressure to perform.

I am one angry person and a bit messed up but at the moment I am trying to see the funny side as I have to sort our lives out. I am worried abuot my husbands mental health though and this is another reason to be as calm and rational as possible .

One more thing – many people who spent time in community talk of the special bond etc. I spent ten years squatting, living with lots of folk and the same thing existed there. That doesn't go down well with community members if I mention it to them.

> bless you and I hope this makes sense
> becky"

CHAPTER THIRTY-TWO: Another sad Community death

Gail – *"Recently, a young man [a brother] died from 'dehydration' in his sleep. I am desperate to get my sister out of there."* In 2006, a worried Gail had this to tell me:

"Hello John,

Thank you for this great resource. I spoke to Ian Howarth today at the Cult Information Centre (he says hello). I have been reluctant to contact you in case it put my sister in danger but Ian reassured me that you were genuine and suggested I make contact. I am very concerned about my sister who is involved with this group for 3 years now. She lives in community in Daventry. She is still in touch with some family members (although she and I have had words about the group) however I do not think she would refuse contact with me. Recently a young man, in the house next to hers, died from 'dehydration' in his sleep after driving a lorry for many hours. My sister recounted this story to another sister as if it were a totally natural thing to happen! I am desperate to find a way to get her out of there. I have done a lot of research on the internet and I am personally satisfied that this group are a danger to her. I would appreciate any advice and would be happy to contribute towards the running costs of the site as without people like you we would be in an even more desperate state.

Thanks, Gail."

I'd made myself a promise to reply to everyone who wrote; so this was my one to Gail:

"Hi Gail,

I read what you had to say about your sister with a great deal of sadness, especially the robotic way in which she spoke about the young man's death. This is by no means the first time that someone has died in rather strange circumstances. In fact there has been a whole catalogue of them over the years. A friend of mine, who also runs a Jesus Army information website, has provided a list of all these deaths. If you click here I have inserted a link which will take you to the relevant web pages: or you can click on the following http://www.jesusarmywatch.org.uk/scrapbook/death.htm

I deeply regret to tell you that there's very little that I can recommend to do by way of helping people to leave the JA. Once they have become part of the whole system then they are well and truly locked in until they themselves decide that the time has come to leave; and, believe me, this can happen to the most ardent JA member, even after many many years of membership. Often, they will then tell you how unhappy they had been all those years but had remained loyal to the group primarily because of the friendships they had within the Fellowship and also the indoctrination that was continually being reinforced.

It sounds as if you are doing all the right things, the most important of which is to reassure your sister that you will always be there to help her if she ever wants help from you. One of the most difficult things for people who are struggling with the decision of whether to leave or not is the problem of where they are going to go to and what are they going to do financially. Just to know that there is someone who is willing to help them in the short term is an immense reassurance! But as well as assuring your sister of your support and love, it is also a good idea to let her know about your negative feelings concerning the Jesus Army. She may not be very keen to listen to you, and may well argue back, but be firm and stand your ground. So long as you do so in a way that is gentle and understanding, you will be planting seeds of doubt in her mind that may well take root and flourish in the fullness of time. It is important, however, that she doesn't come to see you as an enemy of the Jesus Army, so there is a delicate balance to strike here: how to strike that balance, I shall have to leave up to you and your own knowledge of the relationship you have with your sister.

Once again, many thanks for writing to me. I hope I will hear from you again soon. Until then, I wish you all the very very best."

DJDicka – *"Many thought he [the dead man] was worked to the ground. My friend returned home suffering deep trauma."* Paul – aka "DJDicka" – was someone else who referred to the unexpected death of a young man living in a Community household. He wrote to me following my response to the posting he'd made on JEANNI's guestbook page. It makes for hard reading, but it's worth the effort:

"Hi john

Thanks for your reply its nice to hear from the first person who understands what i went through in leaving the ja as you say i think its changed a bit from when u were there and that was even confirmed (to there distaste) by older ja members but its still the same principal

When i left i had them on the phone when are you coming back ect!! although i was shocked that they wanted me because of things i did when i was there such as getting a job in the cofee shop in the new jesus centre and when evangelised to people who were homeless i actually told some of them that coming to live in comunity wasnt there best option!

I think alot of people in the ja are suffering with depression and mental ilness i got a feeling that some of them actually felt a great sence of bitterness as to the fact that they had given up there chance at life and actually got mad with me because i wasnt willing to do that but still remained amongst comunity!! Unbeknown to them id actually had a chat with the house hold leader and put him straight on my future plans. Me and my best friend originally went there me for a better life and him because he was sufffering his dads death and how they soon split us up as my best friend discovered a dead man in the room next door!! he had recently joined the ja from our home town and to the belief of many they had worked him into the ground! and he died soon after (pressure was being put onto him to get a fully paid job so he was over compensating with trying to help!. My friend returned home suffering deep trauma and when i returned from work i wasnt told that he had seen the body and they said hed just gone home!!! so i never returned to comfort him

When i left i had a strong urge to do something like you do with your web site and to warn people but i had a fear in my heart and was actually warned when i was there that id be going up against god in doing so! its passed now though."

Leon Bush – died 24ᵗʰ. July 2006

Mike Aldrich did some of his amazing ferreting about on the Internet for me and passed on all he'd been able to find out concerning the death which has been referred to in the previous emails. I don't believe that anyone will be adversely affected by the disclosure of information some twenty-two years after Leon first wrote to Mike, and eighteen after his death; so over to Mike:

"From what i was told and could find out, he died overnight on the eve of 24 july 2006 (i think). I believe his name was Leon, as over the following weeks i came across mention of a book of remembrance being collated within the fellowship for Leon's parents. I've just checked electoral roll records, and found a Leon J Bush, amongst the fellowship registered at both farms throughout the period 2002 -2006 – then no local electoral roll record the following year... so i'm deducing that that is likely to be him. I haven't found any details of a postmortem or inquest occurring though, and came across nothing in the press around the time.

... Oh, something just clicked !!! – i thought that name rang a bell, – have just searched my email archive, and found the following email from a leon bush, which i received on 1/1/03, it appeared to have been stuck/ restricted by the TBS merchants email server for nearly two months. I wrote to him on the yahoo email address later that day, but didn't receive any further contact from him – this was quite a few years earlier on, though. (Unusual yes, but everything seems to be with my infrequent contacts with members of the fellowship).

email below from Leon copied in confidence:

Date: Tue, 05 Nov 2002 14:48:30 +0000
From: Leon Bush <Leon.Bush@tbsmerchants.co.uk>
Organization: Towcester Building Supplies
To: Feedback@jesusarmywatch.org.uk
Subject: hmmmmmm

Hmmmmmmm! got some great stuff you should know – only if this is private … contact me at stagezoom2002@'yahoo.co.uk and we shall chat about what you want to know and I'll tell ya."

Mike's capabilities as an internet ferret seemed to have no limits. Astonishing! But why did he go to such lengths? I can offer no explanation other than the need he felt to establish the truth. I think he felt that if he used his IT skills to help ensure "the truth will out", then the truths he'd discovered would tell their own story.

Rob – *"All things in common? Equality? Not in the JA!"* In July 2006 I had an unusual email insofar as it came from someone who was still a member of the JA – Robert Cook (aka Robert Resourceful):

"Hello, John.
        Sorry, I've not had the time or opportunity to get back to you yet. There are some things now that I would air.
        When I first met this church, in 1992ish, I had seen something that I wanted. Something different, vibrant and new. I suppose you had the same experience and feelings. But now I've been a member for some 4 years now, things are somewhat different from when I met the church.
        It seems the longer you are in, and the more you get involved with, there are many issues that spring up that have not been sorted or have been ignored by certain leaders. When they begin to involve you, you are the one who has to deal with the problem, not them.
        Family contact, whilst not rejected, is somewhat looked down upon. After all, you have a new family. All true and biblical. As we are told in the bible, we are to 'hate' (love less), our natural family, and look to our new family more. *Why is it then that some household leaders tolerate disloyalty and wrong among their own family, whilst seeking to control a stranger's life down to the letter.* It is quite sickening sometimes.

306

We are called to be poor and have all things in common. This is the lifestyle that drew me to the church. I like it, even though it scares me at times. However, what is practiced at times is the complete opposite. Leaders use their position and authority to get what they want, 'and stuff the rest of you'.

All things in common? Equality? Not in the JA. As a leader told me recently, that is not what it's all about. If I want that kind of life, I am to find another church.

I feel quite edgy at the moment, but be assured, I want to continue dialogue. I must read again your book, also 'Fire in Our Hearts' and see what the reality of it all is.

Thanks for your help. I hope I'm not a hinderance to you."

Rob ended up leaving the Community and returning to his hometown of Dundee. Without work, however, and without having had any financial help from the Fellowship, he turned to me. I made a day-trip to bonny Scotland with sufficient funds to tide him over a wee while, and thereafter we became close friends: Jeanne and I have enjoyed having him stay with us on numerous occasions since we first met.

Sometime around 2007 I started latching onto the way in which an increasingly popular and rapidly expanding Facebook could be used for the kind of group networking that I'd hoped for from JEANNI but had never managed to create: thus was born "the JA Blues" Facebook group. This, too, never really took off in the way which some more recent groups such as "the Survivors Association" one has – "Freedom and Truth". It *did* serve a limited purpose, and a time came when there were a dozen or so members. Some of them told me how much they valued being part of this group and I shall add some of the postings towards the end of this chapter. The group also led to a renewed correspondence with Pete Eveleigh, who was himself an avid poster on various forums as he strove to spread awareness about the JA. I ended up needing to defend him on several occasions after his plain-speaking posts provoked an angry response from other contributors who felt he'd bullied or insulted them with his direct language. I had Pete's ear and he was willing – sometimes a bit reluctantly – to hear me out and accept his need for restraint. Our exchanges were occasionally nothing less than blunt. For my part, I believe I stood by him as a brother through the nastiness of some scrapes he got himself into; and I did so out of appreciation for the braveness he showed in putting his money where his mouth was and speaking out without fear or favour.

Noel Stanton died in 2009. I will give an account of my reaction to his death in the penultimate chapter of this book. Meanwhile, back to the emails:

Jade – "*Two leaders were sexually abusive to me.*" When Jade wrote to me in 2010, it was very very hard to fully accept that the allegations of sexual abuse which were starting to filter through could possibly be true. But they were!

"Hello John

Hope all is well with you and that your father is getting better from his stroke.

I read your article about Celibacy and relationships in the Jesus Army and can confirm and relate it to what I have seen and heard when I attended the church, Jesus Centre and community house this year and last year.

When Noel Stanton died I think a guy called Mick Haines took over his job. When I started going to the Jesus Army worship meetings I was appointed a sister called Jane ... I was appointed a Shepherd called [name redacted] who's job it was to prepare me for my baptism.

I have had some strange encounters with some of the Jesus Army members that live in community and members of the church in ******** when I have see them in the town centre of ********. Some of them just stare at me but do not say hello even if I say hello and some pretend that nothing happened and invite me to come back to church even though they know why I don't want to go back. Some of the leaders and managers threatened me when I have spoken openly about what happened when they confronted me in the street. Two leaders were sexually abusive to me. One said he could rape me then he knew I would be his when he saw me in a car park and another asked me to go with him to have sex. Another wanted me to go off with him and marry him that night and come and live in community. I find their behaviour very disturbing. I find it incredible that even though they banned me from the Jesus Centre because I spoke about the abuse in the first year I attended which was last year, and then [name redacted] banned me the second year via a text when they believed someone else's lies, that they would carrying on being abusive when they see me even though I am no longer part of their church.

I try to forgive them like it says in the bible and not to harbour bad feelings but I believe more and more now that the Jesus Army is a sinister cult.

I think you did a marvelous job with your book and the JA blues and that it will help many people be strong when Jesus Army members are trying to make them question themselves about what really happened to cover up there own bad behaviour. I know we are all capable of sins but I feel that people have a right to know when an organization is deceiving people and trying to coerce people into giving up all they own to become part of a household where they are dictated to and controlled and work for nothing and have very little say about their own life's."

I also think it is marvelous that you have got on with your life and are dedicated to making the planet a better place through green energy. Good luck with your wind power.

Thank you John."

Jade's account of sexual abuse surprised and shocked me. From then on, however, I received an increasing number of reports from different sources about abuses which people had suffered, sexual and physical. I think I almost didn't want to believe them because of the potential sadness involved. In spite of everything about the Fellowship which I objected to so vehemently, I thought the leaders would have pulled out all the stops to prevent such abuse once any incident of acknowledged significance had come to light. Equally, of course, I had no reason to suppose that my correspondents were being untruthful; so I began to feel that in many ways I no longer properly understood what was going on and increasingly began to feel way out of my depth.

'Should I just throw the towel in?' I began to wonder. *'What, in the light of these alarming developments, had I achieved or could I achieve?*

We now know that various sexual and physical abuses most certainly happened, and some of them were extremely serious. We also know that some of these abuses were effectively covered up for a considerable time. The long and short of it all is that hubris had entered the soul of the Fellowship, just as it always does when megalomaniacal aspirations of glory are allowed to go unchecked. Noel Stanton's delusional drive to extend God's kingdom by "spreading out" across the land meant, ultimately, he lost control in key areas; especially those pertaining to safeguarding of the vulnerable. I shall return to this!

I decided to plod on with the website, keeping it updated as best I could and making sure I replied to those who wrote to me. There can be little doubt, though, that I was running out of steam and inspiration: it all became little more than "keeping the show on the road".

Scott – *"The JA Covenant is a total perversion of God's character and grace."* In 2011 I had an erudite, theologically intense email from Scott (and if the theological matter is all a bit too much and you decide to skip it, please don't miss out on the last few paragraphs):

"John

I will get in touch soon. First of all – I'm going to put something together and send it to you. Since leaving JA, God has been so good to me and my family. We've come into a rich revelation and understanding of His grace.

His grace is best understood in a biblical understanding of Covenant and in particular the 3 core covenants of the bible: The Abrahamic Covenant, The Mosiac Covenant and the New Covenant in Christ. Most of the church is not covenant minded – partly down to western mindsets. But God clearly relates through covenant to people and Covenant is at the very essence of His being. For instance God made Covenant with men in the Mosiac Covenant and there was blessings and curses for obedience / disobedience. But the New Covenant is not God making Covenant with us. It is God the Father making Covenant with God the Son, who lived as a man – a perfect man.

The Jesus Army Covenant is deeply herectical and is a classic 'Galatian Error'. It's a total perversion of God's character and grace. The New testament also reveals that the Holy Spirit is not empowering the Old Covenant Law, even though it originated with God, but the Spirit now exclusivley empowers the New Covenant alone. The NT reveals that any system of relating to God outside of the freedom of the Grace New Covenant is actually empowered by demons, which is why Paul writing to the Galatians said 'Who has bewitched you'. The word bewitched in Greek = occultic power.

I've just wrote of the top of my head – but I'm going to put some more thought to it and write to the Evangelical Alliance. In recent years – the JA has introduced more hellish control freak covenants (community vow) and I'm not sure if the EA knows. I'm not wanting to go to Tabloids, but I think it's proper to go to EA. JA also updated Zion's Aims and precepts calling it the Community Charter. Wish I still had a copy. But the EA ought to ask them to look at it.

Regards
Scott"

Dave – *"it is my belief that Noel Stanton was latently homosexual."* By 2011 the flow of emails landing in my JEANNI inbox had slowed to little more than a trickle; but it remained a *steady* trickle, and the emails' content continued telling me either about the current damage being caused or about the pain some still carried even after many years had elapsed. Dave's email was a case in point:

"Hi, Hope you're keeping well and would like to commend you for your in depth and correct analysis of The Jesus Army! I had a short involvement with this 'church' many years ago and it is my belief that Noel Stanton, late titan of the group was latently homosexual, which I have no problem with, but espousing celibacy and being ensconsed at the farm with lots of young blokes to be 'affectionate' with, albeit in a supposedly brotherly way and his victorian attitudes towards women and his closeted disdain for women makes one rather curious, I think the celibacy was his smokescreen invention which he sought to foister upon others, your observations on his control of the physical relations between married couples were also highly disturbing and I think a product of his well-entrenched sexual frustration! I think he hated women and just wanted to be surrounding with young blokes and wanted to keep them away from women and inflict his other dogmas upon them, I would value your thoughts on my theory, thanks for your time and attention, best wishes from Dave in Banbury Oxfordshire."

My reply:

"Dear Dave,

I would love to give more time to reply than I am able to. . .life in the 'Everett' household continues apace (in spite of the frequent, abrupt admonitions I get from JA stalwarts to 'get a life'). My JA website is only really a 'static' one. I update it in minor ways every now and then, but I simply don't have the time to keep abreast of all the latest developments in order to give it true authenticity (I used to check the company/trust accounts every year but am no longer able to do so). I still know people, however, who have close connections with the JA, and my opinion is that the 'root' of the organisation remains the same as ever it was. In some ways this is even more dangerous than it used to be, because there is now a superficial appearance of 'laissez-faire' (easy come-easy go).

I think your analysis of the late Noel Stanton is spot on, and extremely well-articulated. Did you ever get to read the chapters of the book I wrote which are available on the website? In one of them, I describe the time I went into his room and he was lying on his bed (in his underclothes) with his arm around a young 'brother' - who was fully clothed I ought to add. I don't actually believe he ever abused anyone sexually, but you are right to identify the whole scenario as suggestive of suppressed homosexuality.

Due to my involvement with the JA, I came to regard homosexuality as 'sinful'. It took me many years to shed this conception. Happily, I no longer see it like this. It's a subject, however, that I cannot summarise in just a few lines; but I now have no prejudice against homosexuals. In fact people like Peter Tatchell are amongst those whom I consider to be 'modern heroes'. And yet I despise Noel Stanton's latent homosexuality and the way he used it to repress other people and their own sexual inclinations. He is responsible for a huge amount of guilt, which I personally believe has possibly been responsible for some of the suicides/'open verdict' deaths which have occurred within the JA.

311

I would love to correspond more on the issue, but you will need to be patient with me – please – if there is some delay between email exchanges (especially over the next few months.)

Very best!
John"

My final email correspondence – which was with someone called Lisa – was in 2013. So far as the website was concerned, its time had come and gone: I would soon take it off the Worldwide Web. Lisa wrote:

"Hello John,

I've been looking at your website with interest and yes I used to go to one of the houses in the Jesus Army for a time. I even took covenant too but left as I got fed up with being treated as a second class person even though I was a woman. Anyway I was involved in New Creation Hall with Ian Willing and Linda as his co-worker in charge. I was there when the house at Sheffied was starting up and we used to go there on friday night for evangelism and so forth ... I didn't live in community yet but they kept trying to talk me into giving everything up so I could live there but something always seemed to stop me doing this and now I know why.

I used to really fear Rufus Frampton so much, yes I know he was a softie with some but when you get told that I shouldn't speak to him as he's such a big man in the church then you have the fear put upon you as you very well know. I used to end up in the quiet room so many times as I wouldn't conform to their ideals of a woman should be within the church and I wouldn't be treated like a slave but some of the stuff still gets to you doesn't it and when you see things in other churches being done in the same way it brings back some of the bad stuff you would rather forget.

I suppose it goes with time but you never seem to trust anyone anymore, I don't know if you have found that too. I suppose everyone who has had dealings with the Jesus Army, even if it was short or long gets affected in one way or another.

... I can remember what happened a few years ago when someone took someone to court about sexual abuse that happened and I can remember her dad was one of the sheperds in new creation hall at the time and I'm trying to think of his name but its gone at the moment lol.

Anyway good luck with the site, and hugs to you.

Lisa"

As an initial, brief reply I wrote:

"Hi Lisa!

Thank you for your lovely email. . .I read it with great interest. As ever, with those who have been significantly involved with the JA and then left, I found reading what you had to say tinged with much sadness. I'm very glad to hear, though, that it now belongs to the past. I think the parents of the girl who was abused were [names redacted] - but I too might be getting mixed up.

Please bear with me a little while longer and I'll write to you 'properly' just as soon I can. . .I promise I won't forget. Meanwhile, thanks again for writing!"

To this, Lisa wrote back:

"Hey John,

Just received your email while I was just checking and yes your right it was [names redacted]. I used to be nervous of them but their kids were great lol. They used to have one of the flats about the house, oh how the memories come back once you have a name to a face lol. Thanks for that one lol.

my Phone number is ***** and I'm in most evenings so give me a bell sometime and I will try and remember some of the other stuff too and also some of the antics I got upto as well when I used to clash with Ian Willing.

I did, by accident meet up with the church a couple of years ago when they were at the Sheffield meeting, yes it was a shock when I saw them, Ian knew it was a waste of time trying to say anything and he was his usual self trying to be the big man in front of others but I just told him where he stood and he knew not to try and push me as I said what I thought and always did. See I've been one of those rebels too, anyway its great to hear from you so keep in touch

hugs

lisa"

Joy – *"[The JA] helps all persons, all faiths, all sexuality, all nations."* Before bringing this chapter to a close, I've not forgotten about including a couple of the emails which were supportive of the Jesus Fellowship. This one came from Joy.

"I find your site very good and interesting, having lived in Brightfire Birmingham for a year (over 10 years ago) and now as a friend of Jesus Army. I see your points as to the old JA, but like many church starting out, they where finding there feet.

313

Like the Salvation Army who themselves have rules, both couldn't do what they do. There Centres couldn't operate:
They help people find places to live,
Breakfast in the morning,
Activities clubs, hill walking, (a local Church offers there van), painting, cooking etc
Other churches in the area, volunteer there time, money and support.
Go to a drop-in, they get there clothes washed, phone calls, advice (money, benefits,etc). They point to other churches to go to (yes, not all members do?) They help other churches in Africa and alike. (people go out to talk and build buildings)

Helping all person, all faiths, all sexuality, all nations. There no requirements to be a JA person or to become a member. Yes, once you would like to be a member, you know the requirements of the church. All churches have some rules, my old Church had rules and asked people to leave or change. But, my old church has not once feed the poor or anything near JA activities. They had there calling and so has the JA. We can not do it all, we can only play our part, in person and church.

What you say about JA, would be the same with other churches. I could tell you stories about my past church, which turned me off Christianity for a time. Pastors affairs, church male member in ladies clothing, accountant sent to prison. I went back to visit 2 years ago, they gone from 600 to 50 people, 4 members I knew and they didn't ask me back to dinner. With the JA as many people leave as join, but maybe that's a good thing, some of the JA ideals go with the person.

I didn't wanted to live in community, the one year experience shown me that but back then community was membership. Now, more JA live outside community than in, JA is community, community is JA."

Paul – *"It's so so sad the way you put down this amazing church and the great people involved."* Finally, then, I shall let Paul have his say. I didn't get more than three or four emails which were as unkind as his was, and it was probably the most vindictive of the lot. Please read it with the pity it deserves:

"Its so so sad the way you put down this amazing chuch and the great people involved. I would of been dead along time ago if it wasnt for the Jesus Army. Its so unfair how you just broadcast the few negatives an not the thousands of positive. You sound like a demon driven busy body. Grow up an get a life will you. Please just do something else with your life, why dont you try and help the homeless and poor instead of critising those who do like a

314

bitter side line critic. Its so weird how uve let this un holy compulsion ruin your life. If your not careful it could also ruin your eternal. Nobody is listening to you except your self centred ego. So sad. If your that concerned about vunerable people why dont you use your time helping them instead of trying to put down those who are trying their best to love and except them. Sure some ppl in the church have made mistakes but why put the basket in the bin because of a few rotten eggs. Look at all the mistakes uve made in your life. Would you like it if I broadcast on the internet all the porn uve looked at. Dont say you haven't. Take that log out of your own eye mate before you point out the speck in others."

CHAPTER THIRTY-THREE: Rachel's story

The most rewarding and beneficial outcome of JEANNI, I think, was probably the friendships that grew from email correspondence. With some, I ended up chatting about all kinds of things, as friends do, totally unrelated to the JA. With Sabine, a German woman who had lost a daughter to the Fellowship, I had in-depth political discussions that were often tinged with refreshing humour: we carried on writing to one another over the course of several years. One of the first of such friendships was the one I made with "Rachel" (an alias), a young lady who'd been treated abysmally during her membership and who remained forever scared that her ex-shepherd would somehow catch up with her. Once a mutual trust had been established, Rachel agreed to share her story with me in writing. Finding she didn't know how to go about doing so, she asked me to send her some questions which could guide and prompt her. With the demise of the JFC I now feel able to share some extracts from her replies whilst protecting her identity. But looking through what Rachel wrote has reminded me that I haven't yet mentioned "Caring Brothers and Sisters". Everyone in the Fellowship was meant to have someone else, a peer, who would be – or who would *try* to be – your closest friend and confidante. "Caring Brothers and Sisters", therefore, weren't so much appointed as acknowledged. In my early days of membership, for example, Shaun and I had formed an instinctive friendship. As the more established Community brother within our friendship, he soon became recognized as my Caring Brother – there to turn to when I felt myself in need of a listening ear. These relationships didn't always run smoothly, as Rachel herself will explain:

"**John**: How did you first meet up with the JA? What did you think about them initially? Did you have ANY doubts or reservations?

Rachel: I met the Jesus Army shortly after returning from a holiday camp. I was messed up. By then my mother had left home (she had just packed her bags and left us all, including my 9 year old brother) Although back in touch with her, life as you can imagine was more messy than ever. I was having a fling with my friend's common law husband and things were messy there and I was sleeping on a floor in a shared house.

One day walking through my local park I spotted the 'GOLDEN MARQUEE'. I felt there was something not right about them but I could not put my finger on it. All I know was there was this married couple (who became my Shepherd and Caring Sister) and they showed me scripture about how as Christians we left our parents and God gave us knew ones. At last a family – they even encouraged me to call them mom and dad – a thing I stopped after a short while because I did not feel comfortable with it. I remember distinctly in the early days my caring sister telling me that no other church but them could ever understand me and other churches would always make me feel rejected. A few times I tried to stop going to the Community House I was part of, but my caring sister would keep coming to see me. On one occasion when I refused to answer the door to her she sat on the door step for ½ hour until I eventually let her in. I did not see this as harassment – I saw it as her showing me how much she loved me. Not long after I was invited to stay for the weekend – after this I went home about twice for short periods before I moved in permanently. A week before my baptism I did have doubts, but felt that this was the devil attacking me. I think, like they do now, if I had a choice of not taking Covenant at that stage I would not have done so, as it was in those days you got baptised in Chapel by Noel on the Saturday and on a Sunday morning at Ben Hall you took Covenant.

John: When did you join, and when did you leave?
Rachel: I joined in 1986, 'spilt off' twice (see below) and left in 1999.

John: Where did you live in the Community?
Rachel: The [House of Peace]. I moved in 1986 and moved out about 12 months later – I left by doing a runner (asking to leave was not an option). I went to stay with my mom – talk about frying pan to fire – I could not cope, mom was permanently drunk and as cruel and malicious as ever. Every week, my caring sister came to see me, every week told me how much I was loved and missed and eventually I moved back... I worked in a community business and this lasted 6 months – I could not cope with community I again walked out. I stayed with my mom for a while and then my caring sister inherited a flat off her father which they rented to me for a very low rent – I never left the church – it was as though I could not cope without them. I did everything for the rest of my years in the JA bar live at the community house.

John: How did life as a 'sister' change while you were a member? When I met some JA folk in Newcastle a while ago, I noticed that quite a few of the sisters now had shorter hair. Was this just part of the whole process of presenting the JA as being much more 'in tune' with attitudes of the wider Church? Or was there some genuine attempt to let sisters express their own individuality and taste?
Rachel: When I met them, I always wore trousers. Shortly after I stopped wearing jeans – I'd been given gifts of shapeless pinafore dress, long floaty skirts, T shirts that covered everything. I grew my perm and colouring out of my hair and let it grow long – this was very much in line with the biblical basis of the church and its vision for women. My jewellery went, I stopped

wearing makeup and basically did everything I could to not be 'noticed' when in company so as not to be like Eve and stumble the brothers. Years later I had my hair cut. The church wanted to come back in to the Evangelical Alliance – it put on a public face and only the people like myself with the real vision for Zion kept the values. Hair was allowed to be cut (but most of us who had been around for a long time would always make sure we had the covering of our shepherd before we did this). The sisters living in community still could not visit a hairdresser, they had to allow one of the other sister's (usually unqualified) cut their hair. To an extent sisters could express themselves more – in the last five years there have been more people choosing to live out of community and have therefore been able to choose their own clothes and their own hairstyles – those living in are still trapped very much in the 60's style of dress and hair – clothes for them are chosen by the brothers at the FDC.

John: How did people in the *Community* (especially the leadership) GENUINELY regard people from other churches? Did you regard the Jesus Fellowship as being 'better' than other churches?

Rachel: I was always led to believe that going to any other church was choosing to walk a lower way with God, a way that God did not want and a way that God would certainly never approve of – in the last few years I was there I longed to leave but knew it was sinful to want to walk a lower way so stayed and become very miserable and low.

An example I have is we had a new sister join us, and at one agape meal in 'sharings' she said she had got talking to someone from the local Baptist church and would be visiting them the following Sunday. Straight after 'sharings' her shepherd was having a 'talk' to her – needless to say she never visited the other church. The general view of the JA is that they are a better church, they claim to be more caring, more loving and more understanding. Yes at the beginning and around new people they are! But once you have joined them they are controlling and manipulative. And if you question this they turn it back on you as though you are in the wrong and you end up being the one 'repenting' or being 'delivered' from your rebellion demons.

John: Did you regard the leadership of the JA as always being totally open and honest? If not, can you give some examples of when they were deceitful?

Rachel: The leadership I knew had two faces – the public/new members face and the face that only you saw. For the first year or few months they were caring and always there for you, and then when they got you they would treat you like dirt. For the last two years I was around, my Shepherd would only acknowledge or speak to me when there was a visitor or someone else in the room. The rest of time he ignored me – this crushed me as it made me constantly feel I was in trouble, like he was punishing me for something I had done – but I did not know what I had done. An Elder at one of the nearby community houses had the Church Video player (strictly for evangelism and baptism teaching videos) in his bedroom and on a Friday evening would go to the local Blockbusters to rent a 'worldly' video for him and his family to watch. When questioned by his sheep, the elder 'over' him would rebuke them and say they were speaking out of turn.

John: Although not everyone lived in community, was pressure put on people to become part of the Community?

Rachel: In the early days, yes, since rejoining the evangelic alliance, no – although the vision of the JA when I left was still very much *'come out from among them'* and community was 'where it was at'. You were certainly much more esteemed if you lived in community. I felt under pressure to move back in. And ironically enough when I left I was making plans to return to community – thinking this would stop me feeling so unhappy and stop me wanting to leave the church.

John: What were the high points of life in the JA?

Rachel: I am sure there must have been some – but I cannot remember any.

John: What were the low points of life in the JA?

Rachel: When friends left and I was not allowed to stay in contact with them because they were anti the church. On and off throughout the time in the JA I suffered depression, this got worse and I started to self harm myself. I was put on to medication (Prozac for three years) by the doctor and saw a Community Psychiatric Nurse (CPN) each week. After each session with my CPN I would have to spend an hour with my caring sister (this was given to me by what is called a discipline – which means someone tells you to do something to help you grow in the lord!) and would have tell her everything I had said to the CPN – this was so she could pray for me.

My lowest point was about 3 years before I left. I had been feeling very down and depressed for a while. Every time I saw my caring sister I tried to tell her how I felt, but could not put into words the sense of desperation I felt. One Saturday night after the house meeting we were in the kitchen. There were people milling around and she snapped. She started to slap my face, first one side, then the other, then back to the other side. I do not know how long this lasted, but it went on for a while. I was aware that everyone left the kitchen and shut the door – even though they were aware of what was going on. All the time she was hitting me she was shouting at the top of her voice, shouting out things I had shared with her in confidence over the years. This hurt more than the slaps – it was a betrayal. I had trusted her with my deepest fears, thoughts and shames and she had in that one night destroyed any trust I had left. Eventually she stopped and I turned to leave the kitchen, but I realised my glasses were on the floor the other side of the kitchen (I had not felt then come off – and this shows the force with which I was being hit). As I got my glasses I looked at her and she had such a look of shock and horror on her face I actually for a moment felt sorry for her! She came over and said something like I could not just leave we had to get reconciled. I was not going to argue with her – I was frightened she would flip again!! So I let her hug me. I remember as she was hugging me something inside went bang and I started to scream hysterically – no one came into the room to see what was going on, and when she apologised I actually said something like *'its ok I probably deserved it'*! I went home that night, I was in shock, I could not stop being sick. To this day I regret not leaving the church that night, but I felt that if I did not go back everyone would think that I was to blame for what had happened ! The next day I saw her daughter who came over, hugged me and said *'welcome to the family – she's treating you like one of her kids now'*!

No one in the House of Peace ever mentioned what had gone on that night, not even my Shepherd! It was as though it had never happened – yet I was not the first person she had assaulted. Two months ago I finally talked to some prayer counsellors (who have been helping me get over the spiritual abuse I have suffered at the JA) about that night. For the first time ever I realised what she had done was wrong, and I had not deserved it. I have forgiven her and finally found healing for the memories that night left me.

John: How much pressure was put on you to take a vow of celibacy?

Rachel: None on me personally – from day one I made it clear that I would not even attend a celibacy meeting. Although most sermons would bring up the fact that staying single and choosing to take a vow of celibacy was the highest possible way to walk with God and it was implied that God valued single people more than married people. I was encouraged to attend a celibacy meeting in the early days but I never in the 13 years I was there attended.

John: What did you feel the general attitude was towards people who split?

Rachel: People who split were looked on as traitors. There was always a sharing by their shepherd about how this person had done this or that, but how we should trust and pray for them to return. You were not openly encouraged to contact the person who split off, only a select few were encouraged to stay in touch and win them back.

John: What led you to split?

Rachel: It was not one thing but loads. I suppose over the years I had seen 'cracks in the walls' yet had chosen to 'paper over them'. Why did they not as Christians recognise Easter? Why not celebrate Christmas? Why was it that in all of their big meetings there was never a call to salvation or the need for salvation, only emotionalism, talking of abuse and homelessness and rejection. And also, when I first joined the church a girl I become friendly with from Daventry had spilt of and went to the newspapers and was on the news about what had happened to her. When I questioned this I was given a very plausible explanation. She contacted me and met me outside work with some people from the 'Cult Information Centre'. As a result, this was the first time I split off. But as things were so rotten at home with mom and I could not go to another church because I had been told *'only we can understand you'* I could not manage without the JA. When I left for a second time I moved out but continued attending meetings/house of peace 7 days a week.

I guess after the assault on me by my caring sister, things never were the same. I was constantly in fear of her, and she had a stronger hold on me – she knew I was scared of her. After a deliverance ministry once (which would involve people shouting), a brother even thumped me in the stomach as he wanted to make the demon to come out even though there was nothing to be delivered of (he got a reaction alright – but I do not think it was a demon reacting it was a natural reaction to being thumped!!!) A friend summed up the deliverance ministry lovely – she said after a while she got so fed up of them praying and shouting *'get out'* that she pretended to cough as she knew this would make them think she was delivered and make them stop!

The final week a few things happened. On the Sunday my caring sister had a real go at me at the end of the meeting for failing to go to the house meeting the night before. She said they had all felt 'bereft' – they knew I was ill, I was suffering from bronchitis! On Tuesday agape-meal night (I was still ill but did not dare miss the agape meal) one of things my shepherd shared was that it was wrong for a sister to cut a brother's hair – I remember sitting there thinking what a load of rubbish. He then added, *'and if you are reacting against what I am saying then it is the demonic and wrong'* – I knew then that things were not normal or right and my reaction was not demonic because he was talking a load of rubbish!

On the Saturday night I attended the house meeting. Before the meeting my caring sister took me into the study. She was quoting the prayer Paul prayed from the book of Acts and was generally having a go at me for not wanting to be with my brethren, was saying how I been part of the church for many years and was needed to be an example to the others of commitment. I went home that night and told her I would not be back until I had decided one way or another what I wanted to do – this could not go on any more.

John: Please can you tell me a bit about how you actually managed to leave – and what you felt like 'inside'?

Rachel: For the first week I was away I prayed and asked God to show me what to do – God was a stranger, all those years I had been encouraged to have a relationship with my shepherd, my caring sister, my brethren – community and church life was too busy for a personal relationship with God! After that week I started to think about the way I had felt for the last few months, the way my caring sister was treating me and starting to question inside whether or not this was right. Eventually I telephoned a local church and was put on to the minister's wife. I told her about the way my caring sister was telling me off every time I missed a meeting and how she was always criticising everything I did and I asked if this was right. She confirmed what I already knew – it was not right. That was the Saturday. I prayed and knew in my heart of hearts I would never return. On the Monday night I telephoned my caring sister and told her I was leaving the church. She asked me why and I said something like I no longer shared their vision and that I felt it was God's Will for me to leave. At this she exploded, she started to rant and rave down the telephone, and the one thing she did say which I still struggle with occasionally was *'it is never God's Will to break your covenant'*. She may as well have condemned me to Hell with those words. I put the phone down on her. It was November 1999.

Since leaving it was as though I had never existed – only my discipler was in touch, visiting me and phoning me on a weekly basis, constantly 'encouraging' me to stop running away, to come back and get reconciled etc – I lost touch with her when I moved house and changed my telephone number and 'forgot' to pass the new details on! I had sent a letter to the leaders of the house, formally renouncing my covenant and membership with the church.

When I left I did not know what I liked to wear any more. I remember sitting in my new church one Sunday in a skirt which showed my knees. I felt very uncomfortable and started to pull my skirt over my knees. The thought then struck me that if the sight of my knees was going to stumble a brother then it was he who had the problem and not me!

On leaving the church I knew that if I did not find another church I would end up not coping and going back to them. I did not want this to happen so I immediately set about finding a new church. After a few, shall we say interesting, visits to other churches I ended up at the local Pentecostal Church. After the service the Pastor came to speak to me. I immediately told him I had broken a covenant (I was so scared he was going to make me go back!) He knew of the JA – he had 'lost' a friend to them and was very sympathetic and understanding. He introduced me to two other people in the church who are now my closest friends. One had been part of the Church of Christ and the other part of the Yahweh Fellowship – both 'cults'. The friend from the Yahweh Fellowship has an almost identical story to mine. I stayed at the church until October 2001, but unfortunately because of my hang ups with leadership, male authority etc I could not cope at church. Things to do with the JA were constantly coming up and so I left. It was no one's fault – I guess I had gone as far as I could go at that church. I felt that I would never be able to trust or go into another church.

In November last year, by chance I got put in touch with two Christian women who have a prayer counselling ministry. I have visited them twice a month since. One of them is a pastor of a church – God has used the very symbol of what has damaged me to bring his healing and love to me. It has not been easy. At times I have felt I would never be free of my past and I would also be in the mess I was in. Nothing is impossible with God. One of the biggest steps was renouncing the covenants I made in the JA one by one and finding Gods healing.

As wounds have been healed, people forgiven and memories shared I have found a desire to build a personal relationship with God. In May this year I stated attending the local Salvation Army. Never before have I met such a bunch of people to who are so genuine and honest and caring – but who are into building the kingdom of God."

PART EIGHT

The end days

I shall make various references in this closing section to a group of people who have called themselves "survivors". These survivors had a hugely significant role to play in ensuring that the JFC accepted the gravity of its abuses and "systemic failings", and they stood guard over the drawn-out legal processes involved with establishing an accessible and robust redress scheme. At the centre of it all was a group who became the "Jesus Fellowship Survivors Association", and they were behind the influential "Freedom and Truth" Facebook group. Others, too, played their part – and I shall mention a few of them. I only know many of these survivors by name, but I swell with pride when I reflect on what they have collectively achieved. In addition to those whom I will be writing about, the survivors' roll call of honour includes— but is by no means limited to—the following:

Nina Tobin
Mellow Baku
Naomi Brown
Erin Woodger
Becky Ayres
John Bavester
Karen Wesley
Sally Hirst
Vicki Miles
Lemuel Freezer
Esther Sooriah

CHAPTER THIRTY-FOUR: Facing personal defeat

The work I put into keeping the website relevant and engaging often left me feeling I was doing little more than trying to clear snow whilst it was still snowing. Especially futile, I felt, were the challenges I presented to Christian leaders who might be visiting JEANNI. Nothing I ever read or heard gave me reason to think that any of these leaders had either read or responded to my appeals. Here are some extracts from the challenges as they appeared in 2006:

Challenge to Church Leaders

"Where is the man or woman amongst you who is going to make their voice heard and start seriously challenging the faith and lifestyle promoted by the Jesus Army? When is the conspiracy of silence going to be broken?

Some of you instinctively feel, 'who am I to criticize?' Some of you long to see a restoration in the fortunes of the Christian Church and believe that the reason for its decline must be to do with its having compromised and strayed from the path of righteousness. You are all too well aware of the dominant individualistic, materialistic culture which seems to prevail as much within the Church as it does elsewhere, and it makes you feel second best when you compare and contrast yourselves with the 'all or nothing' commitment of the Jesus Army members.

... In recent years, various well-known leaders in the evangelical, Charismatic sectors of the Church have spoken in defence of the Jesus Army and have endorsed their status as *'pioneers who will inevitably attract opposition on account of their radical agenda'*. The launch of the Multiply Christian Network and the associated readmittance to the Evangelical Alliance has also helped draw the sting from the isolationist criticism they so much wanted to shake off. Inevitably, there are some of you who, like sheep, are just going along with what influential Christian leaders are saying.

... Openness to different ways of doing things is to be applauded. Inclusion rather than exclusion can often promote change. Tolerance is a strength. But who exactly is calling the tune? Don't you see that your complicity has played straight into the hands of the Jesus Army and that you've actually betrayed the many vulnerable people belonging to the JA who wanted to hear your voice. Things would be different if they could hear a strong, clear message of opposition from people in the Church. In its absence, they have no way of knowing what to think or do other than what they are being told by those closest to them – their friends and leaders in the Jesus Army – and all those Christian leaders who are saying, *'the Jesus Army is ok! We're all on the same side!'*

... Would YOU join the Jesus Army? Do YOU believe that the type of Christian lifestyle promoted by the Jesus Army is the way forward?? If not, then I beg you to make your voice heard so that other people can benefit from your wisdom – the light that is currently hid beneath the bushel!"

I also presented challenges to members of the JA themselves:

Challenge to JA members [extracts]

"If you have a definite (or nagging) feeling that there is something fundamentally wrong with the ideology and lifestyle of the Jesus Army, then I would urge you to do something about it!! In my experience, there are at least three extremely important obstacles to action.

1. The fear of being disloyal to all the wonderful people who have become your friends within the Jesus Army.
2. The fear of being disobedient to God. You feel, no doubt, that it is God himself who is behind the Jesus Army and therefore, by definition, your own involvement with it; and for all kinds of reasons (fear, humility, compliance, indoctrination, zeal . . .) you don't want to go against His will.
3. The hope that things will change! You are not a quitter, and you think (hope) that those aspects of the Jesus Army which distress you will sooner or later be made good.

Be ruthlessly honest with yourself, even if it hurts and makes you afraid of what lies ahead! Do you honestly and truly believe that the Jesus Army lifestyle is right? Do you honestly and truly believe that this is what the Christian lifestyle, or life in general for that matter, is meant to be like? Do you honestly believe that your estrangement from the rest of the world is God's intent? And what (remember, be honest with yourself), is your GENUINE impression of Noel Stanton, and other high-ranking leaders (Mick Temperate? John Campbell?). It can be very very hard, and it can mean the breakdown of everything you've believed in so strongly. But if your answer to these questions is the one which I suspect it will be, then you have no moral choice other than to do something about the situation you're in.

So be bold and cut yourself loose. Ignore the torments from within your own head and from elsewhere, they will soon subside. Take your place in the mainstream of society again. Oh yes! There's a lot of corruption, selfishness, dishonesty (you name it!) all around. But there's also a lot of goodness to be found, if only you have the eyes to see it. The world is there for the brave to live in and, if necessary, to change!"

When, several years after it had been released, I eventually watched the documentary that Leon Regan had made about the JA's "Battle Centre" in London, I knew it was time to once again blow on my little candle flame to make it shine at least as brightly as possible even though I was under no illusion concerning how dim it was in the big scheme. I captured some still images from the TV screen on my digital camera and used these as inserts between the page text. I began my commentary on the film like this:

"The Battle Centre documentary was first shown on national TV in 2001. It traces several months in the life of one of the Jesus Army homes in London – Battle Centre. Four characters feature strongly in the narrative: Steve, the house Elder; Billy, described as the house 'father figure'; Alec, a twenty/thirty(ish) Scottish JA rookie; and Keith, a seventeen-year-old runaway. I knew the house Elder – Steve – from way back when. We called him Steve Capable in those days – 'Capes' for short.

Quite a number of people who saw the documentary before I did told me that it hardly portrayed the JA in a very favourable light: not least because Keith, the 17-year-old, is quite literally dumped on the streets and told he can't return to Battle Centre as a resident; Alec gets fed up with the feelings of imprisonment he experiences in the house and leaves; and Billy, who for years has denied his HIV-positive status, develops full-blown AIDS and dies.

On the face of it, then, Leo Regan, the investigative film maker, appeared to have done a good job by 'infiltrating' the JA to create another documentary for the 'True Stories' series *(and he therefore deserves tribute for having produced a quite fascinating and incisive film!).*

But even though many negative features were exposed and shrewd observations made, the film gave the viewer plenty of scope to believe that this was all part and parcel of the Jesus Army's radical lifestyle: the unfortunate consequence of their commitment to roll up their sleeves and dirty their hands in service of the many hurting people whom they were trying to help. The hypocritical, dissembling, manipulative aspects of their lifestyle were not really brought to light; I found myself wanting to shout at the TV screen. In truth, those aspects were there for all to see; but I wonder how many people were able to see them? We were introduced to the Jesus Army with shots of Steve weeping for all those hurting people out there on the streets of London. Genuine tears? Genuine pain? Probably, yes! Genuine, that is, insofar as they represented deeply felt emotion; but disingenuous so far as the way many of the hurting people were treated after becoming involved with the JA."

... and I carried on like this:

"Please spare me all the sanctimonious cant about the way you care for the poor and needy if what you really mean is that, in keeping with the Calvinistic dogma of your leader, you want to save all those lost people out there in the Kingdom of the World and bring them into the Kingdom of the Elect, the Kingdom of the Saved. Speak it the way it is, then at least I could maybe find it within me to respect you."

... and to wrap it all up:

"The documentary finishes with an eulogy to Billy, who dies from AIDS during filming: a poignant event saturated with sadness. Was I the only one who was angry that, for so long, his illness went undiagnosed? Angry that leading members of Battle Centre had believed this patently ill, withered man was suffering from **depression**? Please will someone explain to me why it was that he was not urged to seek treatment months before he eventually did?

To my mind, Billy's treatment within Battle Centre was another indictment on the way in which individual dignity and integrity is subordinated to fit in with the Jesus Army's grand spiritual interpretation about the nature of this world and its inhabitants. **There is enormous scope for great psychological and emotional damage when individuals derive their identity from their membership of a society that substitutes the way things really are for a vision of what they believe they should be: it exerts extreme pressure on people to deny the truth about themselves and conform to an identity that is fashioned by the society's beliefs – and the more radical those beliefs, the greater the potential for harm.**"

Had the success of JEANNI been measured in direct relation to the effort I put into it then it would certainly have made a much greater impact than it did: "I left it all out there" as commentators now say to describe a team's efforts during a sporting event: often used, for example, after Luton Town have lost another match in the final moments after yet another heroic performance. I wrote numerous articles and features which I either incorporated into the site or made available for download. The chapters of the book I'd written, "Looking for Freedom; Fighting Madness", relating to "the Bugbrooke Years" were also made accessible. Aware how much it was costing me – and not *just* financially – I decided it wouldn't be at all improper if I charged a small fee for some of the downloads. I was only likely to get back a token amount, so I reasoned, and would only be able to do so if I could direct more traffic to the site. I started an account with Google, therefore, which promised greater search engine success when key words were selected. Top of my search list were the two words, "Jesus Army". But it only took a few days before Google told me that

I couldn't use this juxtaposition of Jesus and Army: someone had notified them of their being copyrighted. I wonder who? So *that* plan became dead in the water before it had even started to float. From then on the website's days were numbered.

I'm fairly certain that it was nothing more than a coincidence, but the "JEANNI years" (circa 2003 to 2013) were ones which presented me with what seemed like more than my fair share of personal challenges. The beginning of the century found me struggling with what all those around me identified as being a mid-life crisis. I'm sure they were right. It was like a new wave of adolescent ambition enticing me to let my wild side have some freedom, especially when I realized that there were attractive women who still found *me* to be so: I wasn't too old yet! And when over-inebriated – which was becoming more and more often – my moral direction easily lost its bearings. "Bravely" putting my own chance of imagined happiness before that of all others (as modern attitudes often suggest we should), I became entangled in two relationships whose initial promise quickly turned to dust. One of these relationships became what many would call an affair – "it's complicated", as it always is – which resulted in Jeanne and I technically separating as a married couple for six months or so; yet we continued to cohabit for quite a while: a strange and miserable time. I hadn't been *totally* to blame, however, so we *both* had to dig as deep as we could to find the mutual forgiveness required to heal the wounds. Both of us now regularly express our eternal gratitude to one another that we managed to do so; and also to whomsoever or whatsoever had reached out a helping hand to get us there.

That I still wasn't yet tamed as a fifty-something-year-old was plain to see. But, no, I didn't become an irresponsible middle-aged hellraiser. I remained as hard working and diligent as ever; still someone who fulfilled the public-school maxim of working hard and playing hard. Together, Jeanne and I led fulsome, rewarding lives in which we created memories we shall return to time and time again and which will continue to sustain us in old age. These included those that were formed from having contributed to the establishment of our children's settled adult lives and sharing in the happiness of their own long-term relationships and marriages. Being thankful for having come into possession of such life-affirming memories doesn't mean we would wish to airbrush out the heartaches and struggles that were also part of the whole story, nor wish to suggest they aren't capable of being challenged by the unhappy ones we've also inherited along the parenting road – and will continue doing so as we never-endingly traipse and trail along it.

My work at Durham University changed completely after I was recruited to take charge of a new hospitality-and-conference computer-based booking system being introduced. Once more into the unknown! I'd been chosen for my perceived talent rather than any relevant experience in such a role. This meant having to familiarize myself from scratch with an IT system – Kinetics Solutions – being used for the very first time; another of those instances when it seemed I was having to restart my career all over again and learn new skills far more quickly than I would have liked. Not for me, it seemed, a job where I could roll into work and more or less get through what needed doing with my eyes shut.

After two years of what had effectively become a nine-to-five job I'd had enough of its demands: overworked and underpaid – same old story. Set alongside the position's cons were some significant pros, including job security, membership of generous pension scheme, and the prospect of an imminent promotion – with more to come. But none of these allurements could prevent me feeling that I'd be somehow selling myself out if I carried on. I had an over-optimistic, Wilkins Micawber-like conviction that "something would come up", that everything would turn out alright if did what I thought was *right* rather than play safe for the sake of holding onto security. Some – many, perhaps – would have considered me to be a bit perverse and incorrigibly obstinate, but I had a deeply ingrained, fatalistic kind of confidence that the right course of action to take in any given scenario was always the one which, having given the matter honest consideration, I genuinely *thought* to be right. You can call it all kinds of things – such as "following my feelings rather than my head" if you like – but it was a trait which I'd had since childhood and had never been able to fully shake off. My Eton housemaster, Bob Baird, recognized and amusingly commented on it in one of his termly reports all those years ago in the summer of 1973:

"John has almost limitless self-confidence, and in general he is quite certain that if the world was not made the way he thinks it should have been this is entirely due to an oversight on the part of the Almighty who will see to it that no harm comes from John assuming that white is really black."

Engrained in my psyche was an aversion to becoming complacently settled in a mundane routine. Argent, the legendary 70s rock band, had included *it's never too late to work nine to five* in the lyric of what was perhaps their most famous hit, "God gave rock and roll to us". The impressionable teenage-me interpreted the lyric like this: *working the same hours day after day in a job that does little more than pay the bills is something that should only be done as a last resort.* Even in my fifties I still believed I didn't *need* to do a job that was unsatisfying; I felt sure there was something *better* I could do, though I didn't really know what "better" meant in the context. *Something would come up* if I was true to myself and quit; of that I felt very nearly sure. But I still needed a little helping-hand of a push. This came when I had what was to be an irreconcilable falling-out with one of my managers (I had two bosses). Nervously, yet satisfyingly, I told her I was leaving. Within no more than two weeks, my other manager generously offered me the opportunity to continue providing the staff training I'd been doing for her, but this time in a freelance capacity – and with an hourly remuneration that sounded implausibly high at the time.

My restlessness also led to my becoming involved with Greenpeace – this from an urge to do something worthwhile in a wider environmental context. I bought into the Greenpeace message with passion, but not quite with the near born-again zeal of some. As I became increasingly involved in their campaigns I recognized worrying signs of "groupthink" and "environmental elitism": perhaps my cult background had at least taught me some useful life lessons. Whilst protecting myself against those cult-like aspects of Greenpeace which worried me, I nonetheless met some outrageously brave, knowledgeable and inspirational people. I learnt from them much of what I now know about the threat we all face from continued fossil-fuel exploration and extraction – but that's another matter altogether and one which I've tackled in my book about fuel-thirsty vehicles, "SUV Madness". I also became enmeshed in an offshoot of Greenpeace called "yes2wind", an onshore-wind campaign which I worked for as its "environmental director" for a good number of years: another change of direction which, for better or worse, has characterized my jagged career.

Following a triple-heart-bypass operation in 2011 and subsequent stroke, my stepfather – who was also now suffering with Parkinson's disease – was extremely lucky to survive. From thereon he was seriously diminished in both his physical and mental capabilities. This meant I needed to spend an increasing amount of time travelling up and down the A1M between Luton and Durham to care for *both* my parents: my mother, herself in decline with what would prove to be a terminal illness, didn't drive and they lived in an isolated village with no post office, no shop, no surgery, no nothing. With such a long distance between us, caring for my parents became an enervating responsibility which steadily began to levy its toll on my *own* physical and mental wellbeing. But perhaps the most serious health aspect of what I've called "the JEANNI years" was the depression which periodically threatened to strangulate me. Ever since doing time in a mental hospital back in 1988, Churchill's "black dog" had continued tormenting me with its occasional aggressive snarl and bark. Sometimes, when its attack was serious enough, I was also visited by an incapacitating fear that control of my mind would once again be surrendered to the dark torment of yesteryear. These black episodes weren't in any way the norm for me: they came and went, sometimes very quickly, sometimes not-so-quickly. They were only ever prolonged enough for me to shut down completely and take a few weeks off work on maybe three occasions. Their root, I think, lay in a very generalized disapproval of myself and a proneness to excessive anxiety – sometimes verging on an obsessive one – that this, that or the other was going end up badly for me and the family.

I was first treated with codeine after experiencing persistent neck pain. The doctor who prescribed it was quite laid-back about letting me take quite large dosages and assured me – so I remember – that it was non-addictive. Having no idea to begin with that it was an opioid, I simply enjoyed the drugged-up feeling it gave me without undue concern. I also discovered it had an almost-miraculous ability to defend me against the threat of depression: all in all it gave me a serene feeling of wellbeing and confidence, a boost I came to rely on. Without being aware of any obvious downside to the way in which codeine affected me, I carried on requesting repeat prescriptions long after my neck pain had been alleviated through physiotherapy sessions. It doesn't take any great powers to work out what happened, nor any need for me to relate the whole story. It's enough for me to own up to having become a codeine addict pretty quickly: an addiction which I nurtured right up until 2014.

That wasn't all. Another habit I'd developed after my hospitalization in 1988 was drinking alcohol – mainly beer – most evenings. In fact I credited alcohol with having assisted my recovery by providing a readily accessible pick-me-up when the fight against mental illness appeared to be drifting away from me. Once habituated to alcohol again in my post-Bugbrooke life, I also rediscovered the pleasure of occasional excessive drinking. In other words I got well and truly stiff on certain social occasions – which probably came around far more often than I liked, or like, to admit. Aware of government safe-drinking guidelines, however, I managed to keep a lid of sorts on my drinking habits right through until, I guess, sometime around 2010. But the writing was well and truly on the wall well before then. Taking codeine alongside drinking alcohol gave a sufficiently strong mood lift to facilitate overindulgence in another of my addictions: work. The opioid provided a powerful stimulus to counterbalance the soporific effect of alcohol, meaning I was both happy and able to keep going far longer than my brain or body would otherwise have allowed. Gradually becoming dependent on the sense of wellbeing derived from taking an ever-greater strength and quantity of my alcohol-codeine cocktail eventually pushed me over the one-way Rubicon line which demarcates alcoholics and addicts from the rest. Because for most of the time I continued functioning pretty much normally, it makes it a lot easier for me to say I developed a serious alcohol and codeine problem than it is for me to admit I became either an alcoholic or an addict – in fact I was both. In 2014 the local health authority funded a three-week sojourn for me in a local rehab clinic, and I emerged from the other side as a free man. I have had, it must be said, a serious relapse since then which needed further treatment, but I'm writing this story as someone "in recovery" who can tick off his sobriety across a sufficient number of years to suggest that those ahead will also be sober ones. Without apportioning blame, the link between my personal struggles and my experiences as a member of the Jesus Fellowship will be clearly traceable for most, even if the strict chain of medical causality is rather tenuous.

Having covered my dealings with the Fellowship during the JEANNI years, together with the associated account of my personal experiences, the "story side" of my war with the JA is near its end. All that will remain is for me to address a few outstanding issues concerning the Fellowship – notably those of abuse and safeguarding – and deliver my final assessment of Noel Stanton.

It seems entirely appropriate to conclude this chapter with the valedictory statement I posted on JEANNI prior to its closure in 2013:

"This site has been in operation for longer than I can remember – fifteen years, maybe? *[I think I must have meant to say ten years]* I have done my very best during this time to provide information which I believe to have been truthful about developments within the Jesus Army. I am unaware of anything I have written that has been improper. As a direct consequence of the website, I have formed many meaningful and valued friendships with people who have written to me. Thank you!

I no longer feel, however, that I am the right person to host a website such as the one that JEANNI was. This is not due to any change of heart but the need to openly accept that I don't have (i) the requisite up-to-date knowledge, (ii) the time or ability to acquire the requisite knowledge, or (iii) the time to respond to enquiries which are made.

Much of this is related to my increased need to care for elderly parents who live at almost the opposite end of the country to myself.

Having weighed all this up, I feel the right time has come for the JEANNI website to retire. I will leave this single page and message for the next couple of months and will then remove the site completely.

I have acted towards the JA in the way I believed to be right, even if there are those who themselves believed me wrong to do so. At times, it has been very hard to maintain this position when I have been acutely aware of my own vulnerability and weakness. If I confess that it is something of a relief to 'stand down', I am not revoking the position I have taken: a position that I needed to take in order to be true to myself and to others.

That said, it gives me nothing but pleasure to wish each and every one who reads this well, irrespective of your affiliation.

I send you all my kindest regards!"

CHAPTER THIRTY-FIVE: Operation Lifeboat and safeguarding

Operation Lifeboat was the name given to a police investigation that followed on from numerous allegations of sexual and physical abuse within the Jesus Fellowship. I had absolutely no involvement in the investigation even though one of those who'd agitated for it, Jim Clark, had done his best to persuade me that I should. Jim had grown up in the Community and, in his exuberantly unique style, had become quite a force to be reckoned with. From about 2012 onwards I'd begun to hear more and more about actual violence and sexual assault within some of the Community households, but I couldn't properly tie it in with everything which had gone before: I remained convinced that the Fellowship's eldership would have neither condoned abuse nor tolerated it. *So what was going on?* The only thing which made any sense of it all was that the Fellowship itself had broken down in some serious way; yet I had no evidence this had happened.

With hindsight it's clear that a collective hubris within the leadership had prevented their acceptance of what was happening virtually underneath their own noses. Noel's determination to ensure that his creation, his church, should be the one which would lead the way to a glorious national revival – with the Zion community at its centre – had opened the floodgate to numerical growth that couldn't be properly ordered and contained within the existing structures. In short, things had begun to run beyond the leadership's control; and pride stopped the truth being acknowledged and acted upon.

I had had some kind of suspicion in 2010 that the anticipated introduction of stricter safeguarding regulations for children and vulnerable people would threaten the structure of Community households. Unless they fell in line with the requirements of the "Vetting and Barring" scheme, I recognized that there would be trouble ahead. And if they *did* fall in line with them, I couldn't see how the Community at the centre of it all could carry on in its existing format. The very last report I wrote to be featured on JEANNI related to this matter. This is an edited version of it *(with most grammar, punctuation and spelling mistakes retained)*:

"Abuse within the Jesus Army

Child Abuse and the Vetting and Barring scheme

For all its absurdities, the Vetting and Barring scheme has the potential to ensure that sexual abuse within the Jesus Army is never again allowed to stain the lives of those who innocently felt such things belonged to an entirely different world.

In May this year, the Northampton Chronicle and Echo reported the story of a paedophile who, as a JA member and employee, indecently and sexually assaulted boys who lived within the community. He was found guilty at Northampton Crown Court of the offences. The man, James Gardner, had a string of previous convictions and yet the JA were apparently unaware of them – despite the opportunities he had for contact with children and vulnerable adults. And although the offences took place in the late 1990s, it emerged during Garner's trial that CRB checks have not been made on those who 'work' with children within the JA.

Judge Wide QC warned that children living within the Jesus Fellowship were 'plainly at risk of abuse'. His comments came as no surprise to those of us who have, for many years, tried to highlight the dangers inherent in the lifestyle of the JA, where not only do those with criminal records have close contact with children and vulnerable adults on a regular basis, they actually live together under the same roof.

The Jesus Army Lifestyle and its dangers

The ideological appeal of what the JA represents, and the genuine sense that many experience of belonging to a loving society, means that the very mention of words such as abuse — spiritual, psychological or physical — is dismissed by some of the brothers and sisters, and especially the elders, to be no more than the language of persecution from those who are opposed to their lifestyle. Or else they feel that it was something that *may* have previously happened but has now been sorted out. Take the thrashing of children with wooden rods as a case in point. Noel Stanton used to often rant about the need for physical discipline: the danger of 'sparing the rod and spoiling the child'. Wooden canes were kept in hidden but well-known locations in every community household – often above the toilet or bathroom door architrave. The sound of a young child screaming in pain as his father beat him mercilessly is one which still haunts my memory. But it wasn't just parents who used the rod: there were many un-related brothers and sisters who were entitled to use this corrective facility when necessary.

Following the sect's dismissal from the Evangelical Alliance of Great Britain in 1986, it appears that that this was one of the practices that was quietly 'sorted out' whilst they tried to gain readmission. Too late, though, for those poor children who had been psychologically scarred for life. Too late for the psychological damage done to those of us who witnessed what was going on and were unable to do anything about it! Nor, given the living arrangements within the NCCC and the damaged people who live there, should it be any surprise that sexual abuse took place. I happen to have been a near-victim myself. I remember only too clearly the day when a brother told me that he had woken up in the night and realised that another brother, Scott, had his hand underneath the bed cover and was masturbating him. Come daylight, he wondered whether it had all perhaps been a dream. Incredulous that this could have *really* happened, I assured him that a dream was the most likely explanation. *And that's what I myself believed!* Until, that is, I was disturbed one night soon after by the feeling of a hand on my body. Awakened in a flash, I managed to apprehend Scott before he'd made his escape. Being something of a softly spoken young man with lovely curly brown hair and gentle facial features, it wasn't the only time I'd attracted unwanted homosexual attention. I was over eighteen at the time; but there were often brothers in the household who were minors. And there was nearly *always* someone living in each of our various households who would have been defined within the vetting and barring scheme as being a 'vulnerable adult'.

I don't think that what happened had any lasting impact on me. I can't say the same for Mike (the brother assaulted by Scott), nor for those victims whom I don't know about. Pity the young man who wrote to me recently and told me stories of being dragged upstairs by his ears – by one of the so-called leaders – and made to parade the streets in Jesus Army clothing and suffer the taunts of his school friends in order to teach him how to identify with the suffering of Christ. Worse still, he too was 'touched' in the nighttime by someone who had been brought into the house as a result of the JA evangelistic outreach. His whole family were JA members; and when he told his father about what had happened, he was simply told that he needed to forgive the abuser.

Spare a thought, too, for the sexually abused pin-down child survivor who tells the story of being paired off with a homosexual man in order to help him overcome his 'problem'.

'I found out that I had been virtually put up for auction by JA elders – a homosexual man told me that he had been encouraged to have a relationship with me, to try to wean him off being gay! I was so hurt by the way I was treated, I knew nothing about this until this man told me, and I had trusted and liked some of these elders, I had thought of them as my spiritual brothers. I was outraged that my Christian family should treat me in such a disrespectful way.'

The vivid accounts which people give of what has happened to them whilst being members of the JA are too detailed, too similar, and too poignant to disregard. The most recent account I have of life as a community member within the JA comes from a young woman, Naomi, who left a year or so ago. She talks about being made to feel like a celebrity when she first moved in and how she felt that the loneliness of being a single parent would be consigned to the past. With the passage of time, however, she became aware of more and more rules that she was expected to comply with. Some of them were trivial, such as not being allowed to buy coffee from a vending machine; others, such as the prohibition on reading any secular books, were far more demanding.

Naomi writes of how she came to live in fear of inadvertently breaking yet another rule and the reprimand that would follow from the household elder when she did:

'More and more new rules and regulations emerged, and the first time I heard of them was when I broke them.'

One day, a document was put on the household notice board that she describes as having *'scared the living daylights out of me.'* It was called the New Creation Christian Community Charter and was a 'breathtaking' ten-page document of dos and don'ts – the later being far longer than the first. Naomi was shocked to realize that she was breaking about 70% of the rules. She dreaded having to have a 'performance review' that would then be posted on the board for all to see. Worse still was the fact that she was hardly getting any time alone with her young boy. At the end of her day's work she was expected to perform domestic household duties and then, on most evenings, attend a worship meeting that went on until ten; either that or engage in some other ministry such as helping out at one of Jesus Centres or street evangelism. She became desperately worried that her son was being neglected; even more worried as she thought about what lay ahead for both of them as a requirement of living within a New Creation Christian Community household.

'You were expected to share your room with any guest of the same sex. I have always been a light sleeper and if I had to sleep in the same room with anyone who snores, I wouldn't be able to sleep a wink. I could see just how I could get more tired than I already was.

My son would be moving into the brothers' quarters when he reached 13, and in the same way he would be expected to share his room with any male guests. I shuddered to think of this! I knew nothing about the men who came to stay in the house for holidays or for weekends, and there was no guarantee that none of them had unhealthy interests. Even if my son wasn't sharing a room with a total stranger, there were no locks in any of the doors. I just didn't feel safe there anymore.'

The Jesus Army and Slovakian Gypsies

With a healthy income from the businesses, and the donation of capital and income from many hundreds, the JA is in a good position to attract people with its offer of shelter, work, and enough fraternal love to strengthen the most fragile of egos. If it's not possible to place someone within one of the House of Goodness businesses, then the sect will use its resources, human and material, to help the unemployed find work elsewhere. It's a package that had great appeal to a group of Romanies from a resettlement village in Slovakia.

As a follow up to her award-winning film, 'Gypsy Tears', Austrian film maker Zuzana Brejcha spent over a year making a documentary about what happened to a group of Slovakian Gypsies who had been recruited to become part of the Jesus Army movement in Sheffield. The resulting film might just as well be called 'Gypsy Tears – part two'. Despite enough journeys between Slovakia and Sheffield to make Lewis Hamilton's carbon footprint appear insignificant, the vast majority of Gypsy converts ultimately returned to their home village in Slovakia with the feeling that they'd been cheated by the JA.

What happened to them followed a pattern that has become extremely familiar to those of us who have been observers over many years. It all starts off as very nearly too good to be true: a real-life fairy tale. That's certainly how many of the Romanies saw it. Coming from a background of desperate poverty and welfare dependency, where the monthly welfare payment was almost immediately handed over to usurers, this was Shangri-La indeed. The menfolk were thrilled to have jobs, be it as delivery drivers or cleaners.

It was only when the reality of what belonging to the JA really meant, and what the JA really wanted, that the rot began to set in. What was being demanded of them was nothing short of a complete and radical change of lifestyle: a lifestyle that would have overturned centuries of Romany culture. The sense of frustration, sorrow and anger as the Romanies started coming to grips with their sense of imprisonment is all too clear in the film. Some of the men began returning to their old ways of doing things. When a couple of them lost their jobs as cleaners, they took their revenge on the boss with their fists. Zuzana told me about an incident which more or less summed everything up, for her and myself alike.

A young, pregnant Romany woman, Sophia, hadn't been eating very well and the family were worried about her. Her mother had been cooking schnitzels and there was great delight when Sophia was the first to help herself and start munching. Her husband, a young JA member who had embarked on the relationship with Sophia against the traditional approval of the family, tried to take the schnitzel away from her, complaining that it wasn't good food to eat. When Zuzana tried to intervene, she was told that if Sophia wanted to be part of the JA then she had to do as she was told: **she had to 'adjust and follow'.**

The bitterly sad ending to the film featured one of key characters, Joseph, reminiscing on where it had all gone wrong. Lying on his bed, this tough Romany man was close to tears. His verdict?

'They fooled us!'

The same theme ran through a documentary made by Leo Regan about eight or nine years ago for the 'True Stories' series on Channel Four. It features the London Jesus Centre, otherwise known as 'Battle Centre'. If ever there was a clearly documented example of the living arrangements which afford opportunity for close contact with children and vulnerable adults, then this is it. Indeed, one of the central characters is a young boy called Keith, who becomes a member of the Battle Centre household before he has turned eighteen. And it clearly illustrates the way in which young men like Keith are targeted by the JA, not least when you see one of the elders, Steve, talking about how his heart bleeds for all the *'broken, hurting, people out there on the streets of London.'* When, however, everything turns sour and Keith is unable to conform with the Jesus Army lifestyle, he is ceremoniously dumped back onto the same streets – at which point Steve-the-elder explains that he cannot take responsibility for everyone who they invite back to Battle Centre, nor can he take the weight of the world on his shoulder.

In actual fact, I would suggest that under the terms of vetting and barring scheme, along with many others in the Jesus Army, Steve is designated as being a 'Regulated Activity Provider'. As such, he has legal duties to observe. This includes the need to inform the Independent Safeguarding Authority of anyone whom he has any reason to suspect might pose a threat to children or vulnerable adults. *If he's unwilling to take the weight of the world on his shoulders, then he must at least take the weight of the law on them.*

Protection of children and vulnerable adults

So what exactly is 'regulated activity'? Quite simply, it's any activity undertaken, either professionally or voluntarily, that involves working closely with children or vulnerable adults on a regular basis. It's time to mention the Jesus Army Charitable Trust. This is the trust that has been set up to fund the 'charitable' activities of the sect. The objectives of the trust are clearly set out in its financial statements, as are the means of fulfilling them:

The objectives of the charity are to assist people in need or suffering hardship because of their social and economic circumstances, to advance the

Christian religion through the provision of places of worship and to provide facilities for recreation in the interests of social welfare.

The current strategy for meeting these objects is operating Jesus Centres providing care, worship and social facilities in major towns and cities around the United Kingdom.

It's perfectly clear that those responsible for the running of the Jesus Centres, and, I would suggest, any Community household that has children and vulnerable adults living in it, are providers of regulated activity. Explicitly: if the Jesus Centres are providing assistance to people who are *in need or suffering hardship because of their social and economic circumstances,* then they are providing assistance to vulnerable adults. Likewise, any sect member, or visitor, who engages with children in a context of *instruction, supervision or care* is engaging in regulated activity.

Although the fine detail of the vetting and barring scheme is quite complex, the basic situation insofar as it applies to regulated activity is quite straightforward. Those organisations which provide regulated activity (e.g. schools, Sunday schools, Scouts and the JA) have a legal – let alone moral – duty to establish a procedure of due diligence to ensure that their staff, members and volunteers pose no threat. This involves processes such as obtaining CRB (Criminal Records Bureau) checks and enquiring into people's background. Anyone who is subsequently suspected to pose a threat to children or vulnerable adults must be referred to the ISA. **If any JA member who is engaged in delivering the objectives of the Jesus Army Charitable Trust's hasn't been suitably screened, then those who are responsible for providing the regulated activity will be committing a serious criminal offence.**

One ex-JA member has often asked me how it can be possible that a convicted sex offender is allowed to live and work within one of the Jesus Centres. Unless this man has been referred to the ISA and given clearance, then my answer is that he is doing so in flagrant violation of the law. Unless the relevant authorities take action, then there will be many who remain at risk."

There's one great big lump in my throat when I read back what I wrote. Heaven only knows I wasn't trying to help the JA get its act together and ensure its survival; but had the eldership seriously considered what I'd written and acted on it, then they might have curtailed the worst of what was about to happen. How ironic, then, that John Campbell treated me in the way he did when I visited New Creation Farm in 2011. I wrote an article about the visit for JEANNI:

"Working on a yes2wind project near the DIRFT (Daventry International Rail and Freight Terminal) area in Northampton, I found myself with a morning to spare before the exhibition I was attending opened at 3 pm. On an impulse which was mainly driven by nostalgia, I decided to go and visit the leader who has taken over from Noel Stanton – Mick Haines.

I drove up the drive to New Creation Farm with great trepidation. Having followed signs to 'reception', I asked the pretty young girl who greeted me if Mick was around... naively, I had assumed he would have moved into the farmhouse where Noel used to live. When told he wasn't available, I asked to talk with my old friend Dave Elder. The young lady rang Dave on the phone and addressed him as 'dad' – I nearly fell over with surprise! We arranged to meet for lunch. Meanwhile, I went to visit his wife, Pat – also an old friend – in the farmhouse.

It was a real joy to see Pat, and, forgetting protocol, I gave her a big hug. We sat and had a very amicable talk about the woes of bringing up children, which was interrupted occasionally by Pat's need to respond to text messages. Innocent as ever, I had no idea what was in store. I asked Pat if we could look around the farmyard: the place where I rebuilt my first ever tractor engine and which, for all the pain, I remembered with great affection.

The old pig-farrowing shed, which we went into, had now been turned into a retail outlet for what I believe is called 'Good Timber'. There were exquisite, hand-crafted, ornamental items and furniture on display and I would love to have bought something had I been able to afford to do so. As Pat and I came out of the building we nearly collided with John Campbell (aka John Perceptive – JP – the Jesus Army PR supremo), who had come looking for me. The jungle drums – or modern-day text equivalents – had obviously quickly been sounded.

Initial polite greetings soon turned into a direct question about what I was doing. I hadn't prepared myself for a meeting with JP, so I simply explained that I was reliving a little bit of nostalgia and having a look around the farmyard. I should, perhaps, have also explained that I'd come to talk with Mick Haines (Mick 'Temperate' as he's known). More quickly than normal politeness would expect, John was asking challenging questions about my opposition to the JA. To this, I had to hold my hands up and say that nothing had changed... I was as opposed to the JA, in principle, as I ever had been. JP then began to tell me, put simply, how unwelcome I was. Poor Pat had become more or less mute. I explained that I'd arranged to have lunch with Dave, but this was instantly dismissed by JP as being inappropriate without any willingness for reconciliation on my behalf.

After I'd replied by making it perfectly clear once again that my attitude toward the Fellowship hadn't changed in any way whatsoever, I knew our encounter was on the threshold of becoming heated and sour; so I also explained, as I had done to Pat, that I hadn't come to get involved in any argumentative disagreement. I went further, in fact, and explained that I was so keen not to be drawn into saying anything argumentative that it would be best if I just left there and then rather than be drawn into unintended unpleasantries. JP agreed with me.

I thanked Pat for her kindness in showing me around and asked her to pass on my apologies to Dave. Closely shadowed by JP, I walked back to my car (a hired Vauxhall Insignia, which looks flash but is horrible to drive) and drove off. JP held up his hand to wave but I refused to reciprocate."

CHAPTER THIRTY-SIX: Disclosure and defeat for the JA

Once the new post-Stanton senior Fellowship leaders had finally accepted the elephant in the room, i.e. the seriousness of the abuse which had been committed, a "disclosure" period was initiated. This involved asking members to provide the leaders – confidentially – with information about any abuse they had themselves experienced or knew about. The disclosures – which the leaders intended investigating and, where required, responding to and acting on – were logged within the Fellowship's IT systems. Various computers containing these disclosures were subsequently taken away by the police in the course of their ongoing investigations into sexual abuse.

The full account of all that happened between 2015 and 2019 – when a statement was issued announcing the closure of the Jesus Fellowship Church – belongs to others, especially those who formed the nucleus of what became known as "The Jesus Fellowship Survivors Association". Legal pressure procured by these stalwarts of justice, some of whom grew up in the Community, has been successful in holding leaders of the Fellowship to account and instigating a "redress scheme" to offer apologies and compensation to all those damaged by their Fellowship involvement, especially those who lived within the Community.

In order to bring us to the point of closure, both my own and that of the JFC, I hope to provide a sketched coverage of the disclosure period through the following news reports and correspondence.

Website: ITV News
Date: 20/08/2015
Link: http://www.itv.com/news/anglia/update/2015-08-20/police-investigating-sexual-and-physical-abuse-arrest-jesus-army-members/

"Members of the evangelical Christian group, Jesus Army, have been arrested by police investigating historic sexual and physical abuse. The group, also known as Jesus Fellowship, is based in a former cinema in Northampton and works with homeless and vulnerable people. The arrests followed referrals from the church itself and centre on incidents alleged to have happened between the late 1970s and late 1990s.

Mick Haines, Jesus Army National Team Leader
'In 2013 the Jesus Fellowship initiated a process of inviting disclosures of any past abuse which might have occurred in the church, or during its activities, ever since the church was founded in the seventies. This is a similar process to that undertaken by the Methodist Church, the results of which were published recently. We believe that openness and transparency is very important.The welfare of children and young people is

of paramount importance, so the Church has also commissioned an audit of its current Safeguarding procedures and practice which is being conducted by an outside, independent agency.'

The Church has other centres in Coventry, London and Sheffield and plans to open one in Birmingham later this year. Northamptonshire Police confirmed the investigation is underway into people who were members of Jesus Fellowship and others who, 'frequented their premises on an ad-hoc basis'."

Website: Northampton Chronicle and Echo
Date: 27/08/2015
Link: http://www.northamptonchron.co.uk/news/police-renew-appeal-for-potential-victims-to-come-forward-in-jesus-fellowship-abuse-investigation-1-6927674

"Northamptonshire Police has renewed its appeal for potential victims to come forward in its investigation into alleged historic sexual and physical abuse at the Jesus Fellowship. Last week, the Chronicle & Echo revealed that Northamptonshire Police had arrested a number of people following a series of historical complaints of physical and sexual abuse from various individuals, many of whom were referred directly to police by the current leadership of the Jesus Fellowship (formerly Jesus Army). Some of those arrested were members of the Northamptonshire-based religious group, while others frequented their premises on an ad-hoc basis.

All of the complaints being investigated by detectives refer to alleged incidents dating from the late 1970s through to the late 1990s.

Northamptonshire Police is working closely with the Jesus Fellowship leadership as well as partner agencies to investigate the allegations.

Assistant Chief Constable Ivan Balhatchet said: *'I would like to reassure the public and any other potential victims yet to come forward that we take all these allegations very seriously and they will be investigated with the utmost sensitivity. We would always encourage victims and witnesses of sexual offences recent or historic to report these to Northamptonshire Police.'"*

Further light was shed on the disclosure process when I got to hear that a doctor in the Community had approached Noel sometime in the noughties to suggest that abuse within the Fellowship should be investigated internally and then, if necessary, referred to the appropriate authorities. He was concerned, apparently, that the issue would come back to bite the Fellowship if it wasn't handled correctly. How easy it would have been for Noel to heed such well-meant advice and instigate measures to ensure that past misdemeanours were brought to light and systems established to prevent reoccurrences. I feel confident the public response to such openness would have been positive, with few standing in judgement over the Fellowship for the exposed and condemned violations of individual members. But no! Of course not! I initially imagined that he refused to act on the proposal due his concern that it would provoke further persecution: it was more important to safeguard the Fellowship's reputation than it was to safeguard the vulnerable. I now understand there were quite likely to have been other reasons as well. *What if any internal investigations should result in Noel himself being accused of abuse – as they were almost certain to?* His obstinate rebuttal of the investigation proposal meant more people ended up becoming victims whilst he himself went to the grave with his reputation seemly untarnished by being accused of committing abuse or proven to have done so.

In 2013, as we now know, the group of senior leaders then known as "the Covering Authority" – which included the new senior pastor, Mick Haines – decided that a disclosure process was definitely required. Reports given me suggest that this resulted from a request issued by the Fellowship's insurers; a precautionary measure to serve as a defence against future liability. Jim Clark, the ferociously tenacious anti-JA warrior whom I've previously mentioned in connection with "Operation Lifeboat", had sunk his teeth into the Fellowship concerning abuse accusations and was determined to ensure the police investigations exposed those who were guilty and brought them to book. He fitted perfectly into the category of those who can be described as "once met, never forgotten": Jim was a veritable bulldog, in physical stature as well as in character – and I expect he still is, of course. Jim had his own inimitable take on the events I've described, explained here in an extract from one of his Facebook postings:

"... the next day I received a call from DC Dave Calvert (one of the investigation team). Dave talked to me for about an hour and told me the following: Last year 2014 the leaders of the Jesus Army had come to them saying they had carried out an internal investigation where they had asked current members to name individuals that have either been offenders in handing out abuse or victims of abuse and these would be dealt with. Quick question to everyone, why are the JA taking this action and why now??? (I'll answer this in a while)

The file the leaders passed to Northamptonshire Police included 130 names, some offenders some victims and I don't know the split, however what I do know is the Police had spoken to nearly all and they said only around 10 in number wanted to move it forward to Court. What the Police were totally unaware of was that mine and many of you reading this were making further claims against the current Leadership team which the likes of John Campbell, Kelly, Mick Haines, Huw, Steve Calam etc. had failed to disclose to the Police. So back to the question?

I heard from the Police that the JA carried out this survey/investigation because they wanted to show that they had dealt with issues in the past and that now Stanton was dead they had changed as a group and were honest and open and transparent to the outside world, with a hope they can finally dust of the accusations they are a cult. I have now heard of this investigation from various sources all good ones and the latest was that Pete Walsma (former GP) had gone to Stanton in earlier years and said 'look bro, we need to deal with these issues and work on a plan of reconciliation and to also cover ourselves' Stanton being the megalomaniac that he was refused this and removed Pete from main leadership, however when Stanton died Pete raised the issue again and upon advice from their Insurance company they were told to carry out this investigation in the hope they could mitigate against any potential damage claims in the future."

Jim was on a mission and couldn't be held back, even if anyone had thought it possible to try. I certainly didn't. I'd spent an evening with him in London when he took me to see the JA houses and places where they evangelized. He was outlandishly forthright, but I knew beyond doubt that his motives were as honest as those of anyone else involved in the struggle to expose the JA. I'd therefore like to include a few more quotes from his posting, ones which give some further background to what, unknown to many, was "bubbling under":

"... Throughout our lives as kids growing up in that place we suffered great hardships and were taunted by the outside world, some greater than others I know but the fact remains we are and were all victims. One of the fundamental things that I learnt and I am sure you will all agree with me was that despite being called 'Jesus Freak' or other more colorful language and despite being bullied at school because we we're different or spat at or had things thrown at us we all built up a huge amount of resilience and an ability to find something deep down which we know as inner strength. Us kids have something that lots of the 'worldly people' don't and that's a fight, a strength an ability to overcome and each time we get knocked down we get back up and fight again and again and that is because we have got the guts to say no matter what we fight, we don't run away and we deal with our problems. So I urge everyone reading this to one be inspired and two to get up on your feet and make a difference. This is the only time in all these years have we ever been in this position and in part the JA have shot themselves in the foot so let's stand together and in the word of the England Rugby world Cup winning team 'Stand strong and hit hard' ...

... For those of you who say it doesn't bother me anymore and I want to leave it in the past then I do respect that but if you are true then you will know if you don't face your fears and deal with the past then your future won't be happy. We've only one life to live, we aren't coming back to this place so why live in anger and hurt, lets together face our demons and together heal our pasts and together face a brighter day Thanks everyone I respect all of you and remember the best is yet to come!"

I have little doubt that the background pressure applied by Jim was hugely influential in creating the conditions where the Fellowship leaders faced up to the enormity of the abuse which had been perpetrated and the realization that it was wrong to continue functioning as a church – and nor was it possible. Shortly after making his Facebook posting, Jim sent me an email brimming with confidence that the JA apocalypse wasn't far off:

"John, I am sure you are aware that a campaign is well underway against the old enemy the 'Jesus Army' and whilst I appreciate you have been somewhat silent over this which I respect I am writing to appeal to you really just for some help. As you know we have never been in this position before and we have already taken so much ground but we need more and I for one would really appreciate your assistance.

... After speaking with several key people it is becoming clear that their was a very serious sexual threat coming out of the JA with Noel at the heart of it, can you help with anything based around this?

Also lawyers are working hard and trying to obtain evidence that would give them a clearer picture of the goings on and I wondered if you had information you might be able to give me on this such as any literature you kept or guidelines that surrounds how children should be raised.

Again, I appreciate you have fought this fight for many years and I can understand the frustration but I reiterate, we have never got this far before, we have never been in such an advanced position and your knowledge is just what we need at this crucial time. Again if you don't wish to be involved that is fine but if you could see that you would give me your file I'd be happy to sift it just to get the help we badly need.

If you wish to chat it over, it would be much appreciated."

With shame, I confess I didn't share Jim's confidence in where this was going to end. It had become virtually impossible for me to believe in the possibility of the Fellowship "going under". I remained convinced that their ability to survive under the camouflage of chameleon-like transformations would somehow enable them to carry on carrying-on well beyond my own lifetime. Even so, I wanted Jim to know I was fair and square behind and alongside him (in defiance of scientific possibility!); so I replied to that effect, assuring him that even though my "file" had become depleted of content over recent years I would be sure to share whatever information I had and would always be prepared to give written or verbal evidence about my own experiences.

Fast forwarding to April 2018. One of the ex-members I'd "met" through JEANNI and sporadically kept in touch with was a lovely lady called Patricia Lawrance. She'd previously been in Fellowship membership for nearly fourteen years. The email I received from her in 2018 came like the proverbial bolt from the blue:

"Dear John,

Hope I catch you on this e-mail address as it's such a long time since I've been in contact you may have changed it. I expect you have heard about the J.A. . . . . .'.the chickens are coming home to roost' as they say. All the senior elders have stood down. My heart really goes out to some of the people who have been taken up with it for many years giving their whole life to it; a bombs been dropped on it all. I pray that justice will be done. Do hope you are well; I expect your family are grown up now. . . . .time flies ! I am not so well now with many chronic physical problems.

With best wishes."

I *hadn't* heard anything about all this. Excitedly, I put some search words into Google Chrome on my laptop and was directed to the following:

Website: Northampton Chronicle and Echo
Date: 06/07/2017
Link: http://www.northamptonchron.co.uk/news/jesus-army-leaders-in-northamptonshire-step-down-after-complaints-over-handling-over-abuse-claims-1-8042088

"The leaders of a Northampton-based Christian organisation, once branded a 'cult', have stepped down while complaints into how historical abuse claims were handled are investigated. The Jesus Army (JA) has confirmed five 'apostolic' leaders of the sect, founded in Bugbrooke in 1969, will now be subject to an independent investigation.

Mick Haines, the senior pastor and de facto leader of the Jesus Army is among the men to have stepped down from 'pastoral duties', a spokesman told the Chron. The other four to face investigation are Mike Farrant, John Campbell, Ian Callard and Huw Lewis, the spokesman confirmed.

In 2013, the JA called on ex-members to come forward and reveal instances of past abuse, either sexual, physical, financial or spiritual. Following investigations by ex-members of the fellowship and the Chronicle & Echo, it is now known about 150 claims were made ...

... Spokesman Laurence Cooper, said in a statement: *'Questions have been raised about the handling of information by the senior leadership of the church, relating to past cases of abuse ... The five people you mention have agreed to step down immediately from pastoral duties and any leadership authority in the church while an independent investigation of the allegations is undertaken. They remain members of the church but they are not in a leadership position at this present time.'"*

My, oh my! I could hardly believe what I was reading! But my cynicism was now so deeply rooted that I remained convinced the "stepping down" of the so-called "apostolic five" would be no more than a cosmetic ploy of some kind. I couldn't make sense of it all except to think that sooner or later we'd find out how the Fellowship had managed to wriggle free from its present troubles. I said as much in my reply to Patricia:

"Hi Patricia!

Thanks for getting in touch once again! The business about the senior elders having stood down *had* gone under my radar somehow or another, although I've now read about it all online.

I've not really been very involved in any kind of opposition to the JA for the past five or six years because I felt I didn't have any more to offer of value after such a long time, and I was also aware that there is a new generation who are taking the Fellowship to task; many of them being children of those who were contemporaries of mine. They seem quite well organised as a group, and some of them are extremely angry (quite rightly of course). So I only get to hear bits and bobs every now and then; and I didn't know about the recent investigations that have led to these five elders stepping down.

I'm still quite suspicious about it all, however! In other words, I still don't trust them and would suspect that there is all kind of manoeuvring going on to try and limit whatever fallout there may be from the investigation into abuse. I very much doubt that there has been any fundamental change of heart in the ambitions which the leadership still have for the future of the Fellowship.

I shall be very very interested to see how it all turns out. But more than anything else, I'm just incredibly sad about it all. I've had to carry the 'fallout' of having been a community member throughout the whole of my adult life; and I still feel deeply scarred by it after all these years. No doubt there are others who will have suffered even more intensely. I cannot, I'm afraid, find it within me to forgive: the best I can hope for now is to forget as much as possible.

Sorry to hear about your own health issues, Patricia. I do so much hope that inner peace may be your companion in spite of the physical infirmity!!

With much love and every best wish!"

Patricia replied:

"Dear John,

So pleased I got through to you. Yes I can understand that you have done your bit in the past but it's so good that people like you are now being vindicated. I now go to a Baptist Chapel in Luton and when I first went there in about 2004 the Pastor in his preaching said that Jesus never hits his sheep on the head but leads them; it made me cry and sob as I thought of the 'heavy shepherding', as they call it, that I had been in."

In 2019 my cynicism was finally shown to be misconceived: the JFC *had* folded. I hardly, however, felt any emotion whatsoever when I read about it in an article which Mike Aldrich had recently included in the Jesus Army Watch website:

Website: Northampton Chronicle and Echo
Date: 28/05/2019
Link: https://www.northamptonchron.co.uk/news/crime/northampton-s-je-sus-army-votes-to-disband-in-wake-of-historic-abuse-claims-1-8942854

"Leaders of the Jesus Army – the Northampton-based religious sect variously described as a 'cult' since its launch 50 years ago – have voted to disband the church in the wake of an abuse scandal. The news comes five years since the launch of Operation Lifeboat, a police operation looking into historical sex abuse at the 1969-formed Baptist movement.

In 2017, The Chronicle & Echo revealed there had been some 150 reports made of either sexual physical, religious or financial abuse at the church and that at least 40 people were pursuing legal action against it. On Sunday, with the reputation of the Jesus Army 'badly damaged' and membership declining rapidly, its leadership voted to revoke the church's constitution.

In a statement released this morning, its spokesman Laurence Cooper, said:

'The NLT (National Leadership Team) and the members of the JFC (Jesus Fellowship Church) recognise that, over a sustained period of time, there have been faults and failures in the Church that have had a profound impact on many people's lives. We are deeply sorry for, and appalled by the abuse that has taken place within Jesus Fellowship Church and the New Creation Christian Community (NCCC) and offer our heartfelt sympathy and unreserved apology to all those affected. Children and vulnerable people were entitled to expect full protection from harm. We acknowledge the pain many of those people continue to feel. As things have become clearer to us, we are grieved and deeply troubled.'

... in 2017, the church's de-facto leader Mick Haines conceded that his predecessor Noel Stanton had a 'flawed character'. The Chron later revealed that many of the abuse claims related to Mr Stanton himself – who died in 2009.

... Following the disclosures process, the current National Leadership Team decided that they did not have the capacity or the desire to continue leading the JFC. Taking into account the scope of the problems they were facing, they did not believe anyone else could, or should, try and lead the organisation. The National Leadership Team, therefore, recommended to the members that the national JFC be dissolved – and that has now been approved by the members. The church has now formed a redress scheme for those affected by the abuse under the Jesus Fellowship Community Trust.

Mr Cooper continued:

'While the trustees have a legal obligation to provide for the welfare of current members of the Community Trust, they want to provide help and compensation for those who suffered abuse or poor treatment in the past. They are seeking to provide resources to help former and current members towards closure from the mistakes and painful experiences of the past.'"

I think the numbness I felt when I read this is possibly explained by my inability to process what had happened properly. This was a vindication of everything I'd been saying for nearly forty years (as Patricia Laurance had recognized), but all the lies told about me remained non-recanted and just as painful. I suddenly felt very small and alone – forgotten, maybe? I don't believe I'd ever wished or campaigned for the JFC to have been defeated in this kind of way. What I'd wanted most of all was for the glaring deficiencies to be acknowledged, addressed and then redressed in a very personal way. I wasn't convinced the total JFC closure I was reading about represented the best way of providing atonement for the widespread damage inflicted on so many. I'd always told myself that I'd never believe there had been any *real* change of heart until the day came when I'd been approached face-to-face and given a genuine, heartfelt apology for all I'd been put through. This was categorically not because of personal need but because I felt it was the only yardstick I could use to evaluate the level of genuine remorse. Nor did I experience any desire to celebrate. Margaret Thatcher's shrill exhortation to "rejoice", given after victory in the Falklands war was announced, had made me squirm and I'd never forgotten it. But how repellent, also, the jubilant mood of some – including certain friends from Greenpeace – after her death. *Ding, Dong the witch is dead* became the rather sick Wizard-of-Oz rallying call to celebrate and party following her demise. Like many, I personally hold Mrs. Thatcher to account for the introduction of a whole raft of policies which have had a ruinous effect on many, and I felt a huge sense of relief and thankfulness when she was finally ousted as prime minister. But she died a defeated, dejected, disparaged, sad old lady who was suffering with dementia and living a lonely life in her suite at the Savoy. *Fine for some,* was, I guess, the attitude of those who disliked such privilege and probably thought it unfair and undeserved. But even so, this was – in the name of all that is humane – no occasion for celebration. Likewise, I didn't feel the collapse and closure of the JFC was anything to cheer about given the legacy of hurt and pain which would remain for many. There's an extremely moving scene in the film, "Shadow Lands", where C. S. Lewis – played by Anthony Hopkins – is sat on the floor of a barren room with the bereaved son of his wife-of-convenience alongside him. Trying to find words of comfort, he then breaks down in tears whilst sobbing:

'*It's all just a mess; nothing but a wretched mess.'*

These words and the emotions they illustrate are an almost perfect reflection of how I felt when I read about the JFC's ruinous dissolution – maybe expressed with a little more colour:

'*It's all just a mess; nothing but a bloody mess!'*

CHAPTER THIRTY-SEVEN: Survivors

As time passed and my understanding of the JFC's disintegration deepened, I increasingly came to appreciate and admire the efforts being made to by a group of "survivors" who'd grown up in the Community to secure full redress for the abuses suffered by many. This was to include recognition of the widespread hurt and damage caused by the repressive proscriptions of women and the emotional or psychological damage inflicted by excessive control and bullying. The redress being sought wasn't restricted to financial compensation; it was also to include a full confession of the Fellowship's malpractice and the issue of meaningful apologies. Achievement of these goals, I fully accepted, would be something of immense import and couldn't be bettered. I joined the "Freedom and Truth" Facebook group and dipped into it every now and then to appraise myself of developments. I also sent a post in December 2019 offering my congratulations to the group for everything it was doing.

My visits to Facebook have only ever been infrequent ones, so I didn't see a message from my old New Creation Farm friend, Shaun, until May 2020. He'd sent it way back at the beginning of the year, so I guessed he probably thought I hadn't wanted to reply. His message, when I eventually read it, came as such a surprise that, truth be told, I didn't know whether I wanted to reply or not. I'd started getting a few friendship requests on Facebook from some old JFC buddies and remained highly suspicious and cautious: I wasn't about to get taken in by spurious friendship requests when my mistrust of everything connected with the JFC remained on high alert. No thank you! I wasn't ready to lower my guard against the Fellowship's deceptive charades without being far more certain of what exactly was happening. For all I knew, at the time, there could well be little pockets of Fellowship members who were still bound in a covenanted union that would enable them to carry on much as before but beneath the observational radar: there was little I would have put it past them doing. So I left Shaun's message a while and returned to it a few days later. This is what he'd written (exactly as it was):

"Hi John saw your comments on the freedom and truth group. Really good to read. I apologise for not understanding your position many years ago. My outlook has changed. Hope you are well. Your old friend Shaun."

Whilst rereading it, I found myself mellowing. During the forty years since leaving I'd grown a protective shell within which I no longer cared – genuinely didn't care in the least – what any of my erstwhile friends at Bugbrooke thought about me. I'd seen the look of disgust Shaun had given me on the "Dial Midnight" TV set and it had had little effect on me other than the creation of reciprocal contempt: I was perfectly well able to get on with my life in the face of his hostility. Now, however, I could sense something of a thaw taking place. As yet, it didn't amount to much; *but wasn't his message an apology of sorts? How genuine was it?* I very cautiously began to entertain the possibility that he'd genuinely severed his ties with the JFC and wanted to put things right with me. Even as I allowed myself to think like this, I began to feel the warmth from embers of friendship that had been relit within. I was beginning to melt – hence my reply:

"Hi Shaun! How lovely to hear from you. I must admit you're looking good from what I can see on Facebook; as handsome as ever! I'm sorry you've not had a reply. I only visit Facebook very occasionally and haven't done so this year before now. I had prostate cancer in 2019 and needed surgery. This left me with quite severe complications which are still ongoing, so I've been neglecting Facebook even more than I normally do. Also, I needed knee replacement surgery last October, and this too has left me with problems: I've been in severe pain and needing to use crutches. Thankfully, please God, I think I've begun to turn a corner. I'm certainly in a LOT less pain. Why don't you email me, please. I'm much better with emails and will gladly send what I think will be a 'proper' reply.

Please send my love to Rifka, and love to you too my dear old friend. John

I didn't have to wait long before receiving Shaun's email reply. As soon as it pinged into my inbox I began reading it:

"Hi Old friend

So good to hear back from you from my somewhat obscure facebook message . Really glad you eventually found it.

So here's a little update on our family life We now have 5 children Kean, Cara, Kristian,Nathan,Simeon. Also 5 grandchildren to Cara and Tim

We are still here in London 1 Emanuel Avenue Acton w36jg Just me and Rifka two sons Nathan and Simeon And Nathans partner Naomi also Jean Phillip a friend who lodges here . . ..

Its been great to have our own space as a family for the last few years .As you are aware all propertys are due to be sold so we dont yet know what we are going to do .Thats a bit of a worry but never mind . . ..

I should apologise to you for seeing you as an enemy of the state 'as taught in those days' – if you know what I mean, thats what it was like those many years ago. Please note you have always remained in my thoughts as one of the best friends I ever had. I need to state that I was so stupid. I always felt regretful and I lost such a good friend and thats a shame.

I ve been working self employed doing my own small buissness thing. I have a local client base which is good and my son Kristian works with me alot.its just a modest income but has kept us going

Please tell me a bit about your family, your current health situation, were do you now live etc . . .

Theres a lot of water under the bridge so hard to know were to start so just a bit at a time is probably best

Excuse my spelling the sun is in my eyes and my spell check is off.

Looking forward to hearing from you John take care for now"

I would have had to have a soul shrunken to the size and shape of a sun-baked, shrivelled prune not to have been moved by what I read. This was a full-bloodied apology which must have taken some courage to write. It wasn't an apology from the Fellowship, of course, but at last I began to believe that a corner had genuinely been turned: this wasn't cosmetic any longer, it was genuine. Most important of all, I'd regained a very dear friend and would enjoy the opportunity of us getting to know one another all over again. Confirmation that the light had clearly illuminated Shaun with a fresh understanding came in the next email I received from him. Here's an extract:

"Dear John

Thank you for your last email, wonderful to hear back from you. I'm glad you did take the position you did well done. I didnt understand it at the time, I think because I was losing a best friend, unfortunately I was the wrong side of the line. But that is now well in the past. I understand the toll those years took on you that's regrettable.

There is now no JF. . . That JF has been dissolved, many young people have left, many have joined other churchs, a few community houses are still functioning and a few local church groups kind of splinter groups from the J Fellowship have formed with new congregational names.

The reputation of the JF that it may have had "questionably" is well gone. Sadly, disclosures of all types of abuse have surfaced with police inquiries going on for the last several years, the Church is pretty much broken including many of its former members.

In brief many years ago I began to fear we were heading toward being a cult due to the leadership hierarchy, what I could see was alarming me, I shared my fears and concerns about this and in particular regarding Noel and the London leadership team of which I was one of course. I began to withdraw in ministry and leadership totally pulling back. I was aware that the future could bring up ugly things regarding the community, and it did."

In the autumn of 2020 I received email confirmation about the establishment of a redress scheme by the Jesus Fellowship Community Trust (JFCT), now operating solely as a residuary body to wind up the affairs of the Jesus Fellowship Church. I registered with the scheme and then more or less sat back to see what happened. The wheels of the winding-up process moved slowly – far too slowly in the opinion of some "survivors" who believed it to be heel-dragging. By now, however, I had full confidence that the redress promised by the JFCT would eventually materialize – these things take a long time, I was well aware of that.

In November 2021 a final closure statement was issued by the JFCT. It came with a warning to former members that some of its content could well prove to be distressing. And so it was. I read it all as if it had very nearly been a point-by-point summary of everything I'd been trying to expose throughout my whole adult life. Numbing, that's what it was. And almost beyond belief that the issues it addressed had taken so long to be accepted. *And what about all those Christian leaders who'd toadied up to Noel and dismissed the opposition of ex-members as little more than ignorance or sour grapes? How did **they** now feel?* They, too, had had their part in prolonging the agony of it all.

I've included a *full* copy of the statement as an appendix. Should you choose to read it in full, I think you'll agree that you already knew about it all from what you've so far read in this book. For now, here are the introductory pages:

"JFCT Closure Statement November 2021[a]

Introduction

The Trustees of the Jesus Fellowship Community Trust and I wish to state publicly that we are deeply sorry for, and appalled by the abuse that occurred in the Jesus Fellowship Church (JFC) and the residential New Creation Christian Community (NCCC). We offer an unreserved apology to all those affected.

For some time, the Trustees have been aware of the need to definitively explain and share information that relates to allegations of abuse in the Jesus Fellowship Church.

The purpose of this document is to set out the Trustees' understanding of certain aspects of the JFC's history, which is based upon the evidence we have seen and heard.

We believe this statement will provide meaningful recognition of harm, abuse and adverse experience suffered by individuals, and help those affected in their journey to find closure and new hope in their lives.

---

[a] published on Jesus.org.uk on 12 November, 2021 (https://jesus.org.uk/updates/closurestatement

The Trustees are also aware that this statement will hold significance for Trust members, other churches and faith groups, and the wider public.

The Jesus Fellowship Community Trust is committed to fair Redress and this statement sets out the Trustees' reasoning in the design of the scheme. It also provides draft details of the Jesus Fellowship Redress Scheme, including eligibility criteria and the scope of abuse and adverse experiences to be included. The final scope of Redress remains subject to ongoing legal and insurance consultation, plus current JFCT member feedback.

Please note that this statement is not the conclusion of an investigation, nor is it an exhaustive treatment of the history of the JFC. The Trustees believe further information may come to light through the Redress Scheme, and if so, this will be publicly reported on periodically.

Martin Desborough
Chair of Trustees
Jesus Fellowship Community Trust

Note: *Since December 2020, The Jesus Fellowship Community Trust has existed solely as a residuary body with one purpose – winding up the administrative affairs of the Jesus Fellowship Church. New trustees were brought in to oversee this work, which includes implementing the redress scheme, supporting survivors and former members, and ultimately closing the Trust.*

Background

In 2013, the Jesus Fellowship Church (JFC) invited people to make disclosures about their experiences of the organisation. Many came forward with harrowing accounts of non-recent bullying, financial, emotional, physical and sexual abuse.

This information was passed to the Police, who launched 'Operation Lifeboat' and investigated the allegations. A number of criminal prosecutions followed, and the Police expressed particular concern at the extent of male authority figures suspected or ultimately convicted of sexual abuse of both male and female children within family units.

The Churches Child Protection Advisory Service (CCPAS) was commissioned by the Jesus Fellowship in 2015, to undertake an independent review of safeguarding. As a result of the ongoing disclosures over a period of time, a number of senior leaders of JFC including Trustees, Directors and senior pastors or Church elders were suspended from duty.

CHAPTER THIRTY-SEVEN

In July 2017, several other senior leaders of JFC stood down.

A total of 82 allegations, including the failure to report abuse, interference with witnesses and mishandling of disclosures, were independently investigated by Vicki Lawson Brown, a Senior Practitioner with CMP Resolutions. The summary of her findings has been circulated to all participants in the investigation and the full report was passed onto the Police. To date, however, there have been no prosecutions by the CPS.

Following the disclosure process, the National Leadership Team decided it did not have the capacity or the desire to continue the JFC. Taking into account the scope of the problems they were facing, they did not believe anyone else could, or should, try to lead the organisation.

The National Leadership Team therefore recommended to the JFC members that the Church be dissolved, and on Sunday 26th May 2019, the members of the Jesus Fellowship Church voted to revoke its constitution. In 2020, the Police concluded 'Operation Lifeboat 2', that focused on failures to protect vulnerable people under the care and control of the Jesus Fellowship Church, including failures to report allegations of abuse. This included a review of the full independent investigation by CMP Resolutions and its findings, and police also conducted their own additional enquiries.

The Jesus Fellowship Community Trust (the 'Trust') was the part of the JFC jointly responsible for the residential community and ownership of the House of Goodness business group. The Trust has its own members, who were JFC members who fully participated in residential, community life. In December 2020, Trust members voted to close the Trust.

This statement is being made because the Trust is the organisation delivering a Redress Scheme, as part of the formal closure process agreed by its members."

CHAPTER THIRTY-EIGHT: The last word concerning Noel Stanton

The most distressing part of the JFCT closure statement related to Noel Stanton himself. For many, it would have made a far more harrowing read than it was for me: I already knew him to have been a deceitful bully whom I completely distrusted. For those who still hadn't managed to grasp the truth; those, for example, who still revered him as an anointed prophet of the Almighty, or at least someone whose heart had been in the right place, the statement would *not* have been a gentle let down:

"Noel Stanton

It is important to make specific reference to Noel Stanton as founder of the JFC. His character and influence directly shaped it in decisive ways, and he was critical to the growth and culture of the church, including its prevailing systemic failings.

As of August 2021, the Jesus Fellowship has received 22 allegations of abuse against Noel Stanton. This includes serious incidents of sexual, physical, financial and emotional abuse.

The Trustees believe it is likely Noel Stanton was at times the instigator of, or was at other times involved in, the abuse of both children and adults."

Noel Stanton Preaching

Whilst I was living at New Creation Farm there were times when Noel literally repelled me. I've already referred to his disparagement of middle-class characteristics. Surrounded by a coterie of young brothers at least half his age, he encouraged them to behave disrespectfully towards the sisters and with manners that many would have called loutish. He urged them, for instance, to display their rejection of middle-class politeness by belching fulsomely as and when their digestive system prompted them to do so. He led by example in this respect; something I found disgusting. Watching and hearing him perform – for theatrics it most certainly was – whilst he sat slovenly reclined in one of the farm's armchairs wasn't an edifying spectacle for *anyone*, let alone for someone like me who'd stubbornly – and shamefully, I presume – retained his bourgeoise sensibilities.

In chapel meetings, Noel often urged the brothers to become more "manly", especially when it came to asserting their authority over women. Married brothers, in particular, were admonished for failing to ensure their wives submissively complied with any instructions given them. It was one of the issues that frequently animated him to a tub-thumping fury. On one occasion, having completed his censorious diatribe, he came out with an unforgettable nugget of marital counsel: *'she's always wanted to have a tough guy as her husband, you know,'* he announced smugly to murmurs of appreciation from brothers and sisters alike. He was definitely one of those who would have approved of the advice that men should *treat 'em mean to keep 'em keen*.

Noel's temper was legendary; and he was actually quite lazy, seldom getting up before nine or even ten in the morning – when most of us farm brothers had already been at work for several hours. But there were also times when he displayed what I myself and most others believed to be genuine empathy, understanding and kindness: a benign avuncularity if you like. I well remember an occasion in chapel when he corrected himself for having used the wrong tone of voice:

'No', he said, gently, *'that came out as sounding harsh and it wasn't at all how I'd meant it to be.'*

He then repeated what he'd previously been saying but with an emphasis that made it sound far kinder. I warmed to him as much as I'd ever done in that moment, sensing a humility I was sure belonged to him but which he displayed far less often than I would have liked. Nor was it easy to forget the way he'd treated me with fatherly affection after my leg had been crushed by the David Brown tractor's lift arms. He wasn't able to be like that all the time, of course; I accepted that! As a pastor and prophet, and as leader of the Fellowship, he carried huge responsibility before God on his shoulders; so I made full allowance for his need to be resolute and strict, even demanding and bone-headed, in his determination to uphold righteousness. Many brothers spoke of a willingness to give their right arm on Noel's behalf: he commanded immense loyalty on account of both his leadership and his stature as a man.

On the other hand, he all-too-often revealed his insecurity through defensive behaviour, verbal abuse, and dismissive rejection of other people's viewpoints. This made him notably volatile and you never really knew which Noel it was you'd be dealing with. I often thought he'd be far better off spending more time in the company of other men his own age; others who would hopefully pierce his pomposity and refuse to accept his rather juvenile tantrums. I told him as such during the week we spent having long conversations when I was on the point of leaving; and I also made it clear that I thought some of the relationships he shared with other young brothers were completely inappropriate. He scoffed at my suggestion and accused me of being unsupportive and critical of his role at the farm. In fact, he was only stating what was undeniably true.

Noel seemed completely unable to laugh at himself, as on the occasions already recounted when Graeme Merciful light-heartedly teased him and he responded with a poker face. If only he could have seen the funny side of Graeme's impromptu and clever wit! I received the same rebuffs to my own attempts at humour, none more memorable than the time when I made a "cooling-fan" joke which was met with a withering look of reproach. At Noel's behest, a huge overhead fan had been installed in Bugbrooke chapel to circulate air and help us all stay awake. Alongside his frequent demands to open all the windows, he often stomped his foot and bellowed for the fan to be turned on or sped up. I would dare to suggest that – except for Noel, of course – the fan became an object of universal hatred, especially on account of its being called into service on freezing cold winter evenings when the windows were already fully open. It was just another of those things we got used to, and you had to remember to make sure you'd got yourself wrapped up as warmly as possible for cold-weather meetings in the chapel.

Noel and I had occasion to be making some kind of inspection of the newly built cattle shed at Shalom farmyard. One section of it had been filled with dozens of straw bales which had been soaked by the rain before we'd collected them in from the fields. As we got closer to them, a noticeable haze of steam became visible and it was evident that a considerable amount of heat was being generated from the decaying straw. Noel became worried that they might even spontaneously ignite.

'I wonder where we could get a big fan from to cool them down, bro?,' he asked me innocently. Although not normally someone capable of instantaneous repartee, on this occasion I was able to give a tongue-in-cheek response quick as a flash – and with some feeling:

'I know **exactly** where we could get such a fan from, bro!' I said, with a glint in my eye. A few seconds passed whilst the implication of what I'd said sunk in. Then Noel scowled at me:

'Have you got some kind of problem with our chapel fan, John Diligent?' he asked, using my "full" name. I didn't answer; there wasn't anything I could say. I was disappointed he hadn't appreciated my joke, which I thought had, for once, been quite funny.

The first I knew about anyone accusing Noel of sexual impropriety came from the following report in the Northants Chronicle and Echo:

CHAPTER THIRTY-EIGHT

Website: Northampton Chronicle and Echo
Date: 11/05/2017
Link: http://www.northamptonchron.co.uk/news/exclusive-sexual-and-financial-abuse-claims-made-against-founder-of-the-jesus-army-in-northampton-1-7956742

"The founder of the Jesus Army in Northampton, who was accused of running the organisation like a cult during his lifetime, may have abused some members 'sexually and financially', according to claims by his successor.

Former Bugbrooke pastor Noel Stanton formed the evangelist movement in 1969 and went on to set up New Creation Farm on the outskirts of Northampton, a segregated commune that eventually spawned a number of offshoots. He remained leader of the Jesus Army, also known as the Jesus Fellowship, until his death in 2009, when more than 2,000 people lined the streets of Northampton to pay tribute to the pastor. But we are today launching a call for a full public inquiry after it emerged his successor made a number of claims and admissions at the organisation's annual conference last month.

In a speech before hundreds of members, talking about 'radical transformation', current Jesus Fellowship leader Mick Haines said he had become aware of 'serious allegations' about Mr Stanton. He said:

'The apostolic group of the Jesus Fellowship church have in recent months, from December 2016, received new allegations from members of our church concerning Noel Stanton – senior pastor between 1957 and 2009. The allegations are of financial abuse of individuals and spiritual and sexual abuse. We are not in receipt of all the facts, but we are seeking to move forward in bringing in a new culture that is distinct from the past. We have taken these allegations very seriously. As presented, they indicate serious character faults.'

Mr Haines was named as Mr Stanton's successor before his death in 2009 and spoke at a thanksgiving ceremony for the former leader at the Jesus Centre, in Abington square, Northampton, in 2009.

'His heart was to the people of Northampton,' he told a packed hall eight years ago. *'This is a very significant day for the history of Northampton and the history of the Jesus Army.'"*

Mick Haines went on to describe how he had been filled with the Spirit under Noel's ministry and venerated his achievements. His conclusion, apparently, was that of Noel being a "flawed character". If *that* was Mick's verdict, then I didn't think the claims made against Noel would end up being substantiated – he clearly felt that there was sufficient wiggle-room left to carry on representing Noel as having been a great man, albeit a flawed one. Nor was I convinced myself about the credibility of these allegations, which hadn't as yet been proven. Whilst I'd come to my own conclusion that Noel had been a repressed, non-practicing closet homosexual, I'd always resolutely defended him against having behaved improperly.

As for what Mick had to say about "Noel's heart for the people of Northampton", it deserves to be called out for what it was: nothing more than a load of old tosh! Noel had no more of a heart for them than he did for the crowds who flocked to the nearby Silverstone racetrack: he cared for neither of these collectives in their own right, both of them belonging to the kingdom of the world. Possibly he may have cared for them as communities from which the lost could be found and removed, or as entities which could be robbed of their wealth; but nothing else. As I've explained, the very concept of caring about – "having a heart for" – the essential welfare of an urban community, or any kind of secular association, was total anathema to him: he would have berated it as a self-righteous waste of Christian endeavour. I hadn't really known what to think about Mick after he took the role of being the Fellowship's leader as I didn't really have any intelligence about him to make an assessment. I liked him well enough when we lived at Harvest House together and found him trustworthy; yet I took a very bleak view of *anyone* who could spout such misleading claptrap about Noel's "heart for people" knowing full well it was at the very best deceptive.

The first *specific* abuse-allegation against Noel that came to my attention was in an article posted on Facebook by a former member. He described himself as an "ex teenage-rebel" and wrote convincingly about his experiences in considerable depth. With regards to Noel, he had this to say:

"On the occasion in question I was sent to his private bedroom for a talk. The first important thing to understand in this, is that entry to that room was extremely rare for all but a very select few. I definitely wasn't part of the select few at that time! On entering the room we proceeded to have a conversation which was both flattering and full of praise. Stanton had taken the decision to discuss how I could play an important role within the church as a guiding light and example to the youth. Utilising, as he put it, my strong character, reputation, natural leadership and influence amongst the young to keep the youth involved and lead by the example of a "rebel for jesus".

On the face of it this appears to be very innocent, and in many ways an affirming, shepherding conversation; but takes on a very different texture when taken in the context of the visit as a whole. The almost secret visit to his private room, the level of flattery of a spiritual, personal and physical nature – coupled with a hand on the knee and an arm around the shoulder from a man in his late 50's who was fresh out of the bath and still wrapped in his towel – all made me extremely uncomfortable. This discomfort was further endorsed when I was invited to kneel with him by the side of his bed. An invite I hurriedly refused and on refusing left the room immediately. I believed at the time that I was in the early stages of a seduction routine and other testimonies I have become aware of in recent times plus the statement from Mick Haines, Stanton's successor about his "flawed character" leave me in no doubt whatsoever that this was the case. Nothing more was ever said by either the Stanton or the person who had sent me to his room and my blood still creeps to remember it."

Reading our ex-rebel's statement put me in mind of several incidents SC had written about in "Fire in Our Hearts" which described how Noel had shown preferential favour to several young tearaway brothers whom he'd treated as if they'd been his very own beloved prodigal sons: he tolerated and forgave their rebellious transgressions with a fatherly affection withheld from others whose behaviour was similarly defiant. Had Noel actually been grooming these favoured brothers, I wondered, and was the brother who believed himself to have been subjected to a seduction routine one of them? It wasn't until I'd read reports such as his that I began to accept the possibility of Noel having been the sexually abusive person we now believe he was. Until then, albeit that I'd concluded he must have been a repressed non-practicing homosexual, I'd resolutely defended him against suspicion of sexual impropriety.

When I heard from another ex-brother, whom I trusted implicitly, about how – as an adolescent – he'd been the victim of an attempted sexual assault from Noel, it was as if the proverbial scales finally fell from my eyes: Noel had all along been abusing his leadership position through the ability it gave him to secretly satisfy his sexual urges. "The bastard" was the only expression that I could immediately find to express how I felt. The truth was finally out so far as I was concerned and it enabled me to at last unravel some of those unsolved enigmas about Noel – and the Fellowship in general – that had previously eluded my full understanding.

This new light on everything, which many now accept as valid, begs the question of course concerning what the whole JFC experiment amounted to. There were hundreds of us who, for differing lengths of time, believed the Holy Spirit of the Almighty had breathed a powerful blessing on the Fellowship and bathed us in Christ's love – and I imagine there are those who will tenaciously cling to such a belief. *But how can such a thing be possible if there was darkness at the very centre of it all? How can a rotten tree bring forth good fruit?* It can't, is the simple answer; hence the ignominy of the Jesus Fellowship's eventual but inevitable collapse. For over forty years I've known that the Jesus Fellowship was phoney, if for no other reason than that its leader was a phoney. I hadn't, however, fully grasped the extent of Noel's duplicity in the way which I do now. It will be very hard, perhaps impossible or unthinkable, for some to accept such a verdict; and I'm not sure I see the purpose, or have the wish, to press any harder. By this stage of my book I'm more than happy to believe that I've presented enough material for everyone to think for themselves what they will.

One final series of questions: *Did Noel genuinely believe in everything he preached about? Did he genuinely believe he was being used by God to establish His kingdom and facilitate widespread revival? Were his failings those of the rest of us; those whose sights are set high but who are sometimes caught out and undone by our weaknesses?* Further back, I wrote that you often didn't know which Noel it was you were going to be dealing with; the implication being that there were two sides to him, a split personality – the syndrome many associate with the names of Jekyll and Hyde. Should we wish to accept Mick Haines's verdict that Noel was a "flawed character", then we can happily agree his split persona is the best way of explaining his behaviour: there were times when he regretfully adopted the character of the evil Mr. Hyde whilst his predominant identity was that of the benign and honest Dr. Jekyll. The explanation is a perfectly satisfactory one for those who wish to believe that Noel had been a worthy vessel to channel God's blessing.

But many probably haven't read the story of Dr. Jekyll and Mr. Hyde for themselves, as I hadn't until very recently. What R. L Stevenson's remarkable story makes perfectly plain is that the evil Mr. Hyde stood alone in his corporeal identity; complete in himself once freed from the restraint of his high-minded alter-ego. As such, he was by far the more powerful, complete and properly representative of the two, and it was *his* destructive and murderous actions which prevailed. Dr. Jekyll was the one who embodied both personalities, and it was *he* who yielded to the dark impulses of attaining a different body that permitted free reign to his compulsive urge for wickedness; and thus was born Mr. Hyde. Dr. Jekyll was feeble beneath the powerful shadow of Mr. Hyde, who knew of no such weakness. It would be foolish to go too far with this analogy: Stevenson's novel was only fictional, after all. But I believe it helps us understand how Noel most probably lived as a subject to lurid impulses he may have been ashamed of and wished to supress but was unable to. It was his "dark side" – if we can call it that – which called the shots and which he hid away beneath the concealing cloak of righteousness.

I can only go so far and remain willing to accept I might be wrong: there may well be other credible explanations for what happened within the JFC. As things stand, I have offered a theory which best fits the facts as I understand them. Leaving aside the need to take into consideration the more-recent accusations against Noel which have arisen from internal JFC disclosures, my readers will have discerned the suspicion and low opinion I already held of him as detailed throughout this book. I cannot recant. If I had to summarize my opinion towards both the JFC and Noel himself, then I don't think I can much improve on the letter I wrote to the Chronicle and Echo following his death in 2009.

"Dear Sir!

Your paper ran a story last week in which the death of Noel Stanton, leader of the Jesus Army (JA), was reported.

The comments from readers which have been appended to the online version of the story are characteristically eulogistic, although I note that at least one has been removed following complaints concerning its suitability. I would surmise it carried criticism of some kind!

I became a junior leader of the JA back in the eighties. Shortly after, digging deep into my fragile reserves of courage, I left. This was because I had come to the conclusion, partly as a result of my sociological research at Warwick University, that the sect had all the hallmarks of being a cult. I have done my very best ever since to draw attention to the harmful aspects of the sect. I prompted the Evangelical Alliance and the Baptist Union to investigate their suitability for affiliate membership, and both organisations agreed that their membership should be withdrawn (albeit that the Evangelical Alliance agreed to restore it many years later). I believe that, if nothing else, I have made it somewhat easier for others to follow in my footsteps and leave!

In order to provide a central point of contact, I launched a website called JEANNI (Jesus Army News, Networking and Information) earlier this decade. It has now been visited nearly 7,000 times. Through it, I have been contacted by many people whose lives have been traumatised by their membership of, or association with, the JA. I have spent literally hundreds of hours writing to, or visiting, people who have suffered genuine, sometimes severe, emotional and psychological distress. Nor have I any reason to disbelieve the allegations that involvement with the JA has been responsible for certain suicides.

Some people have described Noel Stanton as 'humble' and 'inspirational'. *They certainly aren't words which I would use!* It was Stanton who, in the early eighties, established a system of yearly appraisals for those who were 'covenanted' members of the sect's community. My abiding memory of him will be the occasion when I overheard another leader very nervously ask Stanton what the procedure would be for his own (Stanton's) yearly appraisal. To say that he flew into a rage would be the only way to describe his response; nor was this an isolated incident.

I myself, along with many others, shall remember him as a coercive bully boy!"

CHAPTER THIRTY-NINE: Redress and apology

Throughout several years from 2019 onwards the JFC assets and properties were offered for sale, with proceeds being held by the JFCT for future redress. In September 2022, the JFCT announced that the format of its Redress scheme had been completed and it would accept applications between 26th. September 2022 and December 31st. 2024. (Please refer to the Appendix for full information concerning the Redress scheme.)

Philippa Barnes, who featured in the article, *Alleged victim of historic abuse reveals traumatic childhood growing up in the Jesus Army,* which I quoted from earlier on, was a founder and key-contributor to the "Freedom and Truth" Facebook group which I'd come to admire so strongly. In September 2021 she sent me a Facebook message asking if I could contribute any material to support research for a documentary film about the JFC which was in the offing. With fingers tightly crossed for its return, I sent her my only remaining copy of "The Church Community at Bugbrooke" report together with videos of Zuzana Brejcha's "Gypsy Tears" films and anything else I had which I hoped might be of use. I'd very nearly forgotten all about having done so when I was contacted by Ellena Wood, a director with Big Sister Films, who asked if she could talk with me about my JFC experiences. Evidently, Philippa had passed on the package of information I'd sent her, and Ellena had been deeply impressed – so she told me – by what she'd read in my report. She also told me the stupendous news about her company producing two one-hour features for BBC2 dedicated entirely to the rise-and-fall Bugbrooke story. I was elated at the prospect of a serious, in-depth TV disclosure such as this. I met with Ellena and her right-on-the-ball researcher, Esme, at a canal-side trendy restaurant near Kings Cross on a wonderfully hot summer afternoon. They had both acquired a profound understanding of the Fellowship's structure and history, which enabled me to plunge straight in – as it were – to the nitty gritty of it all in answer to the questions put to me. We spoke together for several hours all told. Several months later they invited me to interviewed and filmed as a contributor to the documentary. This happened in November 2023 and was a mesmerising, fascinating, all-day event. I came away from it with my head buzzing as it hadn't done before in recent memory. When I last heard from Ellena in March 2024 she told me the film was in the final stages of editing and was nearly ready for a first review by the BBC.

I finally submitted the redress claim that I'd been preparing on and off for several months in December 2023 – far too close to the end-of-year deadline for comfort. In February 2024 I received a significant payment from what was called the "Community Adverse Experience" aspect of my claim. Of equal importance was the formal apology I received:

"Dear Mr John Howard Everett,

On behalf of the Jesus Fellowship Community Trust, we are deeply sorry for the experiences you suffered during your time in community and for the distress and harm that these have had on your life; it is matter of profound regret that they were able to happen at all, and in the very place where you should have felt safe from harm.

We recognise that no current actions can compensate for your relationship with others being controlled, and being prevented access to support outside the Community.

We are grateful to you for your courage in ensuring these aspects of the Jesus Fellowship's past have now been confronted. As you are aware, the Jesus Fellowship Church and Community has now closed down and thus can cause no further hurts.

It is with heartfelt regret that your experience of the Jesus Fellowship was not as it should have been and we genuinely hope that the future holds better things for you.

Signed by two of the JFCT trustees."

Many others will have received an identical apology, which gave no claim to being personally tailored. Even so, it was hard not to feel a wave of emotion on reading it and a sense it was something of immense significance. It certainly wasn't the apology I'd been looking for down the years as my surety of a change which was genuine rather than cosmetic. And I would also have liked it to have been signed by someone who I felt had had some direct responsibility for the hurt and damage caused to myself and many others. Yet I acknowledged it for what it was, and the wording was an expression of what I believed to be a profound humility and sincerity. This was as good as it's going to be, I told myself, and I was very thankful for it.

The very first deep friendship I had within the Community – the one with Shaun – has been renewed and is gradually being fully restored; so far as such a thing is possible, that is, when we live at very nearly opposite ends of the country. And I'm waiting with anticipatory excitement and impatience for the "Big Sister Films" documentary to be shown, when at long long last Noel Stanton and the JFC will be shown in their true colours – not just the flamboyant ones of the JA combat jackets and gaudy double-decker buses. All in all, if I don't find closure after all this then I maybe never will – and whose fault will that be, I wonder?

APPENDIX to War and Defeat

JFCT Closure Statement: November 2021[a]

Introduction & Background (See chapter 37)

Aims of the Jesus Fellowship

The Jesus Fellowship Church (JFC) was founded in 1969 by Noel Stanton (1926-2009). He had been a lay pastor at Bugbrooke Baptist Chapel (part of the Baptist Union) in Northampton since 1957, and appealed to a younger generation of worshippers through charismatic preaching. His congregation grew rapidly.

In 1974, the JFC residential Christian community was founded for the Church's growing membership. Initially, two small community houses were bought, followed by a large Anglican rectory in Bugbrooke, renamed 'New Creation Hall'. Several members of the JFC moved in and it became the first centre of a community lifestyle. By 1979, several other large houses in the surrounding area had been acquired, accommodating 452 residents. By 1987, there were 40 large households and smaller houses, with 798 residents (589 adults and 209 under-16s).

JFC Community life was shared; individual earnings and assets were placed in the 'Common Purse', a central household pot of money used to cover basic living expenses, with any surplus donated to the central Church. Households, usually comprising numerous family units, single people and individuals invited into community through the various JF evangelical outreach programmes, worked, ate, worshipped and shared dormitories together.

During its time the JFC was also known as the Jesus Army (JA), the Modern Jesus Army (MJA) and the Jesus people.

Some of the common aims of the Jesus Fellowship Church, over time, were stated as:

- Bringing the Christian gospel to the searchers in today's spiritual culture, to those trapped in social evils, and to victims of poverty and injustice.
- To go anywhere to help men and women in need through addiction, degradation or other unfortunate circumstances.
- To offer the saving life of Jesus to any person and help them in their need.
- To offer friendship, without discrimination and prejudice, and identify with all people groups, meeting them in UK cities and towns, and showing the love and life of Jesus.
- Respecting all religious faiths and support for all lawful authority, working with police, probation and social services.

---

[a] published on Jesus.org.uk on 12 November, 2021 (https://jesus.org.uk/updates/closure-statement/).

- Adopting charismatic worship and showing a living, rather than religious, Christianity.
- For members to enter into a covenant of loyalty to the cause, being available for any service, as they love the lost and build the church of Jesus Christ.
- To unite believers in holy, loving and just church communities, which show the end of social and racial divisions and demonstrate a new sharing lifestyle as the brotherhood of Jesus, shining as 'light to the world'.

Earlier in the life of JFC communities, members committed to live by strict precepts or common rules of behaviour. These included not partaking in secular television, music, books, leisure or entertainment activities, sports or hobbies, to live simply and modestly, and avoid cosmetics and jewellery. Members were to give all of their time, income and involvement to the work of the church and community life; for many, this was a freely chosen, radical expression of their faith.

In later years, whilst some of these precepts or rules no longer applied, the overall culture and behaviour of the church and community life continued to follow similar objectives.

The Trustees recognise that there is a broad spread of experiences of the JFC, and differing views of its history. The JFC also evolved in its approach, with various forms of teaching, community rules and aims or objectives.

Most members of the Trust wanted to follow a genuine Christian faith within the JFC, which for many included a wholehearted, well-intentioned attempt to live a radical, sharing Christian community life that included and provided support for the marginalised.

Allegations of Abuse

This statement does not seek to diminish the journeys of those who selflessly joined the church and served one another for the good of the wider public. However, the allegations made in recent years are extremely serious, and this statement focuses on acknowledging and affirming those who suffered harm and abuse.

Operation Lifeboat investigated the alleged incidents over many years, and police brought a number of successful criminal prosecutions as a result.

The JFC has received further disclosures and as of August 2021, the total stood at 291 allegations of harm and abuse. These were made against 125 individuals, at various levels of leadership and membership of the church. In addition to the known allegations of harm and abuse, the Trustees are aware of at least a further 265 individuals who have registered for Redress and have not yet made a disclosure.

Although the vast majority of incidents have been reported recently, the allegations themselves relate to incidents ranging from the 1970s right up to 2019. Most concern the period between the 1980s and 2000s, with the majority coinciding with the 'Jesus Army' years. See the Appendix at the end of this document for detailed tables setting out this information, including Operation Lifeboat.

Systemic Failings

The Trustees recognise the JFC had begun to make changes prior to its closure, but they believe there were systemic problems which had a profoundly negative impact on some people's lives, in some cases exposing members to harm or abuse.

Some of these issues are listed below. This is not an exhaustive list and emphasis has been placed on matters the Trustees view as particularly significant in relation to the Trust's closure and consideration of the Jesus Fellowship Redress Scheme.

Leadership Structure and Culture

The JFC had a hierarchical leadership structure. Significant decision-making was restricted to the founder, Noel Stanton, and the most senior leaders.

New members of the most senior leadership could only be appointed by the senior leaders themselves, and whilst candidates' suitability could be challenged by members, this was actively discouraged and opposed.

Allegations against the church demonstrate that those who challenged Noel Stanton were relegated, and members who disagreed with him or other leaders at various levels, were heavily criticised.

There is a particular emphasis among the allegations indicating the abuse of power by Noel Stanton, who adopted a domineering style that prevented him being held accountable by fellow senior leaders. For example, on numerous occasions it is alleged Noel Stanton took decisions on behalf of the JFC, against the wishes and advice of his most senior colleagues.

People who disagreed with Noel Stanton were characterised as rebellious and told they would be 'subject to the judgment of God'. It is alleged leaders of other JFC households and congregations also adopted this style of threatening teaching, which for many led to a climate of fear. These wider leaders were often never held to account or disciplined.

Whilst members sought in principle to share their belongings and finances in community life, decisions such as where people should live and what they might buy were routinely made or controlled by centralised leadership.

In practice, many members found that decisions made or access to funds were dependent on factors such as position in the hierarchy, personal relationships and gender. As a result, adults living in community houses became institutionalised. Their ability to make decisions in respect of their own lives was compromised, with choice and agency removed.

The Trustees believe that within this hierarchical structure, Noel Stanton and other JFC leaders were insufficiently accountable to the members of the Jesus Fellowship and the Trust.

Teaching on Forgiveness

JFC teaching and practice at one time included an incorrect emphasis in relation to 'forgiveness' and 'grace'. Forgiveness was taken to mean, in certain instances, that abusive people should remain in, or be returned to, leadership and positions of influence. This left the abusers in proximity to vulnerable people.

Due partly to the lack of accountability in the leadership structure and this misleading teaching of 'forgiveness' and 'grace', the Trustees believe there was a fundamental failure to keep members and children sufficiently safe from harm and abuse over the life of the Church.

Despite the more recent openness and co-operation with the Police and other authorities, including positive steps taken by JFC leaders to address safeguarding within JFC and changes to JFC doctrine, the Trustees fully recognise there were significant failures in the handling of abuse allegations and perpetrators by JFC leaders in the past.

Loyalty and Commitment

The teaching of the JFC emphasised commitment to the organisation, its aims and objectives. Over a significant period of time this was at the expense of valuing external family relationships and the work of other Christians and churches.

Onerous expectations were placed upon members, exceeding every other consideration. The JFC had a culture of constant busyness and activity, with the work of the church becoming dominant in a way that eroded family life, health and faith. For many, this was exhausting and holidays were banned or discouraged during the life of JFC.

All things were regarded as subservient to the 'cause' of the church. It is alleged that deviation from the commitment to the JFC called for rebuke, character assassination or ostracisation of many members.

For many, controlling behaviour overshadowed people's lives in the Trust. For example, there is no doubt individuals were afraid to leave New Creation Farm because they were told, explicitly or implicitly, that they would be 'damned by God' if they did so.

There was a distrust of other organisations and outside influences, and this was often explicitly taught in meetings. Until recently, external advice or support was not sought, and where this was given, it was not sufficiently heeded.

This was accompanied by a lack of transparency with external bodies and insufficient accountability to other Christian groups or networks.

A similar point has also been made by the Evangelical Alliance when it wrote to the JFCT in 2018, leading to the resignation of the JFC from the Alliance:

"We have note of the actions taken over the years to address the past and to support those who have been victims of abuse and recognise the enormous pressure this puts you under. It seems that, in spite of efforts and your direction of travel, the

past abuse and mode of leadership continues to impact both members and former members so deeply that a more radical approach is required if a healthy future is to be realised...

"We would suggest that the Jesus Fellowship needs to come under the oversight of a stream or established denomination which will give wise, ongoing oversight and accountability in the years to come. In effect, this represents a radical reshaping of the Jesus Fellowship and a recognition that without external, ongoing oversight, your past risks blighting your future..."

Until recently, other churches and Christians were unjustifiably criticised, and members were dissuaded from attending other churches. Senior JFC leaders would often speak against previous members, and lead current members in praying against – and cursing – those who had left.

The Trustees believe that there was a misplaced vigilance for disloyalty to the 'cause', stifling individual freedom of choice and self-expression.

Attitudes to Women

Women were not treated equally in the JFC. They were not listened to, and their views were not accorded as much significance as those of men. The intensity of this sexist culture in the JFC varied depending on locality, but it certainly pervaded the church until its closure.

There was an expectation that women would give up their aspirations and careers to serve the church and men, taking domestic roles in community houses, for example, or behind-the-scenes administrative duties. Women living in community were not expected to return to employment after having children. In some cases this constituted a suppression of their aspirations.

Women were denied a voice, and the opportunity to have a say in the direction of the JFC for much of its history. The church's structure was distorted by a lack of adequate female representation.

Whilst some women aligned with this practice and associated teaching and beliefs, many left the JFC because their aspirations were unsupported, or they were treated negatively or abusively.

Women were often blamed for the misdeeds of men, in particular where allegations of abuse were disclosed. Women, including victims of abuse by men were, for example, often characterised as 'jezebels', meaning to tempt and distract men.

The Trustees believe this systemic attitude to women was – and is – wrong, and that the alleged practices concerning women within the JFC produced a sexist and victim- blaming attitude.

Wellbeing of Children

For many people, being a child in the JFC community was at worst abusive, and at best lacking in full opportunities.

At times, the outreach efforts of the JFC towards the poor and the marginalised created situations where very troubled or distressed individuals, such as addicts, were wholly inappropriately mixed with children and other vulnerable individuals. Child safety and well-being was placed behind that of the person being helped.

This culture gave rise to children being exposed to abusive, frightening and/or destabilising influences from adults who presented a very serious risk to them. The allegations show this was often against the wishes of parents, but at other times parents encouraged this culture and the importance of the outreach work.

The Trustees believe the emphasis of outreach work over the safety and wellbeing of children was unacceptable.

Children were inappropriately and harshly disciplined by adults, including those who were not their parents. At times in JFC's history, this included corporal punishment ('rodding').

The Trustees recognise that this teaching and practice was wrong, with some victims living with lasting distress as a result. Such treatment is unlawful today.

The allegations confirm that the views of children were not taken sufficiently into consideration when decisions were made that affected their lives. Many people who had an adverse experience of the church were the children of parents who joined the JFC. These children feel they were forced on a journey they neither chose nor desired.

Many children were removed from their parents' household or influence in their teenage years and put under the responsibility of 'shepherds' or 'caring brothers/ sisters', at times against the wishes of parents.

In many cases, children in community lacked opportunities, choice, recreational activities and the chance to develop themselves. Parents often followed the teaching and culture of the church to deny toys and the celebration of events such as Christmas.

Under JFC community rules at times, partaking in sports, school trips and participating in school plays or other extra-curricular activities were forbidden. Instead, children were made to partake in onerous schedules of worship or serving community needs.

When children told their parents and the church that they were being bullied at school, they were encouraged to view this as welcome persecution. Their experience of bullying was not properly addressed, to their lasting detriment.

The Trustees believe that the well-being of children was not paramount in the practice of community living, leading to increased risk of abuse by members or visitors and lasting harm for those individuals affected.

Supervised Relationships and Celibacy

JFC teaching emphasised that church members should avoid flirting and over-familiarity. Relationships were to be conducted through a supervised 'relating process'.

There are examples where relationships or friendships were deliberately blocked or discouraged when they might otherwise have flourished. Equally, some relationships were engineered, encouraged, or even insisted upon.

Strong emphasis was placed on celibacy. This led in some cases to people making a celibacy vow without adequate counselling, preparation or maturity. Although the JFC's emphasis on celibacy created space for single people in the church, it also fostered the prevailing view marriage was second-rate.

The Trustees believe third parties interfered inappropriately with decisions that were matters of personal choice of individuals who may have wished to enter into a relationship or friendship with another person.

Suspicion of Education

Further education and training were treated with suspicion. Young people were dissuaded from attending University and other places of study.

There was great reluctance to train Church members, even in JFC businesses. Until comparatively recently, little emphasis was placed on developing people through training, education and self-improvement. These were often portrayed as the activities of self-centred, wrongly ambitious and independent people.

The Trustees believe this negative and misplaced attitude hindered people's growth and personal development. There was little acknowledgment of the fact training and development are important and necessary aspects of the modern workplace, and indeed of church life.

Noel Stanton

It is important to make specific reference to Noel Stanton as founder of the JFC. His character and influence directly shaped it in decisive ways, and he was critical to the growth and culture of the church, including its prevailing systemic failings.[1]

As of August 2021, the Jesus Fellowship has received 22 allegations of abuse against Noel Stanton. This includes serious incidents of sexual, physical, financial and emotional abuse.

The Trustees believe it is likely Noel Stanton was at times the instigator of, or was at other times involved in, the abuse of both children and adults.

(1) This paragraph was edited 16/02/2022 for accuracy

Jesus Fellowship Redress Scheme

Outline Scope of the Redress Scheme

The Jesus Fellowship Redress Scheme is being set up by the Jesus Fellowship Community Trust (JFCT) to enable fair Redress to be available to those who suffered sexual, physical, emotional abuse or adverse experiences whilst living within its Community.

Please note that this outline is a draft which remains subject to ongoing legal and insurance consultation plus feedback from current JFCT members.

The Scheme is intended to provide comprehensive Redress to Eligible Claimants. Eligible Claimants will be entitled to:

A written apology acknowledging what has happened to them, providing acceptance of responsibility and an assurance that lessons of the past have been learnt and shared with relevant authorities;

i. For sexual, physical or emotional abuse, an award of compensation for the harm they have suffered, aligned with common law compensation awards;
ii. For sexual, physical or emotional abuse, an invitation to meet with a Trustee of the JFCT closing team;
iii. A dedicated Support Fund for individual grants towards counselling, training or other support, where the criteria for a Community Adverse Experience is met;
iv. The return of Capital for previous members of the Jesus Fellowship Community Trust;
v. The Jesus Fellowship Community Trust will also seek to address claims relating to individual employment matters. Due to their nature, these matters will be investigated on a case-by case basis.

If, after addressing all of the above categories, sufficient funds remain, the Jesus Fellowship Community Trust may seek to extend the Redress Scheme scope to allow for discretionary compensation payments for those who have suffered Community Adverse Experiences.

Eligibility for Sexual, Physical or Emotional Abuse

The persons entitled to Redress under the Scheme are as follows;

Any person who can establish they are/were a member or probationary member of the Jesus Fellowship Church and/or Community and/or a child of a Family in the Jesus Fellowship Church and/or Community and;

There is evidence to show that on the balance of probabilities he/she suffered;

i. emotional abuse; and/or
ii. physical abuse; and/or
iii. sexual abuse; and/or
iv. psychiatric injury
AND
The abuse was committed, counselled or instructed by a person at that time engaged in the leadership, management, operation or supervision of the Church and/or Community and/or Community Home and/or Community School, whether as a Leader of the Church and/or Community or a person for whom the Trust would be vicariously liable;
OR
The abuse was committed by an individual invited to stay in a Communal Home by a member of the Church and/or Community in the circumstances where there was inadequate safeguarding measures in place.

Eligibility for Community Adverse Experiences

The persons who are entitled to a Support Fund grants plus any future discretionary compensation payments (if Trust funds are available following other categories), are any Eligible Claimant who;

i.   was a child resident in a Jesus Fellowship Community home for 3 months or more and who can establish on a balance of probabilities that they experienced Community Adverse Experience as defined below; or
ii.   was an adult resident in a Jesus Fellowship Community home and who are/were a member or probationary member of the Jesus Fellowship Community Trust, who can establish on a balance of probabilities that they experienced Community Adverse Experience as defined below.

Children in Community

For the purposes of this Scheme the following circumstances are considered Community Adverse Experiences for individuals who were children when they arrived in Community;

i.   Witnessing abuse of others (sexual, physical or emotional).
ii.   Removal as a child from parenting or domestic family unit.
iii. Lack of safeguarding, opportunity to access medical care, protection from harm that had been reported to an adult.
iv.   Unhealthy religious practice in childhood; exorcisms and/or extreme schedule of worship which caused harm.
v.   Being denied educational engagement or educational activities owing to influence or direction of Jesus Fellowship Leaders or persons for whom the Trust are vicariously liable.
vi.   Being denied social interaction (outside of Community & preventing male/female friendships in & outside Community) owing to influence or direction of Jesus Fellowship Leaders or persons for whom the Trust are vicariously liable.
vii. Child Labour in circumstances where there was alleged neglect or harm was caused.
viii. Having toys, games, childhood comforts removed.

Adults in Community

For the purpose of this Scheme the following circumstances are considered Community Adverse Experiences for individuals who were adults when they arrived in Community;

i.   Harmful treatment of Women as subordinates and/or Women suffering detriment and harm through being placed in positions of servitude.
ii.   Being forced to leave a positive/stay in an abusive relationship.
iii. Prevention of access to outside world (doctors, police, social services).
iv.   Failure of individuals in position of leadership to act positively to reports of abuse or harm.

Appendix to JFCT Closure Statement

The following tables set out the number of known incidents and when they occurred, together with details of police prosecutions and action.

As of August 2021, the total number of known disclosures stood at 291 allegations of harm and abuse. Of these, 181 incidents relate to Sexual, Physical or Emotional abuse.

In addition to the known allegations of harm and abuse, the Trustees are aware of at least a further 265 individuals who have registered for Redress and have not yet made a disclosure.

Years	Total Number of Incidents (where known)	% of Incidents
1970s	14	8%
1980s	49	27%
1990s	59	33%
2000s	28	15%
2010s	31	17%

% of incidents over time

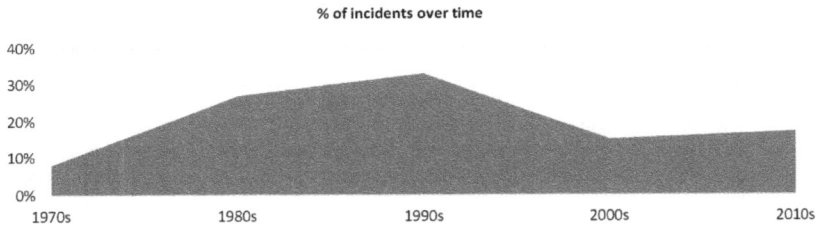

Within the total number of allegations, there are one hundred and thirty eight (138) allegations of Sexual Abuse.

Sexual Abuse Definition: Any act that involves forcing or enticing a child to take part in sexual activity for the sexual gratification of another person. Non-consensual sexual activity between adults.

Years (where known)	Number of Sexual Abuse Incidents	% of Incidents
1970s	7	7%
1980s	30	29%
1990s	41	40%
2000s	16	16%
2010s	9	9%

Within the total number of allegations, there are fifty-nine (59) allegations of Physical Abuse.
Physical Abuse Definition: Any act which caused physical harm to a child or adult.

Years	Number of Physical Abuse Incidents (where known)	% of Incidents
1970s	7	14%
1980s	17	34%
1990s	16	32%
2000s	6	12%
2010s	4	8%

Within the total number of allegations, there are thirty-seven (37) allegations of Emotional Abuse. Emotional Abuse Definition: Abusive conduct resulting in psychiatric damage.

Years	Number of Emotional Abuse Incidents (where known)	% of Incidents
1970s	0	0%
1980s	2	7%
1990s	2	7%
2000s	6	21%
2010s	18	64%

Criminal Proceedings

The Trustees are aware of at least 11 criminal matters that have resulted in convictions dating back to the 1990s.

During Operation Lifeboat, 11 suspects were arrested and seven suspects were interviewed without arrest. There were six convictions and one person was charged without conviction. The final number of referrals into Operation Lifeboat was 214.

The allegations received by Northamptonshire Police included:

- an alleged perpetrator put their hands down a child's trousers during a bike ride;
- a child was touched sexually while sitting on an alleged perpetrator's lap;
- a child was abused by a strange man while a religious gathering was held in the home;
- an alleged perpetrator put his hand up the skirt of a child;
- a child was anally raped; and
- a child was orally raped by an adult male.

IICSA Report

The Independent Inquiry into Child Sexual Abuse (IICSA) was set up in the wake of some serious high profile instances of non-recent child sexual abuse. Through investigations and public hearings it has examined what went wrong across a wide range of institutions including religious organisations.

The Jesus Fellowship Church was one of 38 religious organisations to be investigated. The inquiry included a statement given by Northamptonshire Police in regards to Operation Lifeboat as well as a statement from a member of the Jesus Fellowship Survivors Association.

The full report into Child Protection in religious organisations and settings can be found here: https://www.iicsa.org.uk/reports-recommendations/publications/investigation/cp- religious-organisations-settings

Index

End Notes

1 "Have You Eaten Grandma?" by Gyles Brandreth – 2018. Page 150
2 https://discovery.nationalarchives.gov.uk/details/r/e40b84b7-3706-4b2d-b0b4-6813ab15e3fa
3 "Fire in Our Hearts" by S Cooper and M Farrant – 1997. Page 32
4 Ibid., Page 32
5 Northampton Chronicle and Echo. June 19th 1972
6 "Fire in Our Hearts" by S Cooper and M Farrant – 1997. Page 109
7 Ibid., Page 110
8 Ibid., Page 120
9 Ibid., Page 109
10 Ibid., Page 94
11 Ibid., Pages 130 and 131
12 Northampton Evening Telegraph on June 29th:
13 Northampton Chronicle and Echo. December 17th. 1982
14 "Fire in Our Hearts" by S Cooper and M Farrant – 1997. Pages 178 and 179
15 News of the World. April 12th. 1981
16 Northampton Post. February 27th. 1982
17 "Fire in Our Hearts" by S Cooper and M Farrant – 1997. Page 180
18 Baptist Times.April 10th. 1980
19 "Fire in Our Hearts" by S Cooper and M Farrant – 1997. Page 183
20 Ibid., Page 169
21 Taken from "We Believe: An introduction to the faith and practice of the Jesus Fellowship". A Multiply publications booklet. 2000
22 "Fire in Our Hearts" by S Cooper and M Farrant – 1997. Pages 118 and 119
23 BBC News website: "programmes/working lunch/principles before profits" 17th. October 2002
24 25 leaflets in the Flame series were available for download from the Jesus Army website
25 From Flame Leaflet 5, Zion, City of God, published by the Jesus Fellowship
26 From Flame Leaflet 21, Wealth Creation, published by the Jesus Fellowship
27 Ibid.
28 £21,975,232
29 £5,565,526
30 Taken from page one of the Jesus Army Charitable Trust Financial Statements for the year ended 31/12/2005
31 Ibid.
32 £1,096,832
33 £4,900,484
34 Taken from page one of the Jesus Fellowship Life Trust Financial Statements for the year ended 31/12/2005
35 Ibid.
36 £522,624
37 From Flame Leaflet 5, "Zion, City of God", published by the Jesus Fellowship
38 "Fire in Our Hearts" by S Cooper and M Farrant – 1997. Page 364
39 National Statistics. Annual Survey of Hours and Earning
40 "Fire in Our Hearts" by S Cooper and M Farrant – 1997. Page 158
41 Ibid., Page 172
42 Ibid., Page 149
43 Ibid., Page 150
44 Ibid., Page 203

45   Ibid., Page 304
46   "Undivided" magazine. Edition 13. October 2000. A Multiply Christian Network
     Publication
47   Ibid., Page 175
48   Ibid., Page 226
49   Ibid., Pages 227 and 228
50   Ibid., Pages 228 and 229
51   Northampton Chronicle and Echo. 13th. November 1986
52   "Fire in Our Hearts" by S Cooper and M Farrant – 1997. Page 276
53   Ibid., Page 252
54   Ibid., Page 275
55   Ibid., Page 275
56   Ibid., Page 281
57   Ibid., Page 283
58   Ibid., Page 344
59   Ibid., Page 349

www.ingramcontent.com/pod-product-compliance
Lightning Source LLC
Chambersburg PA
CBHW020147090426
42734CB00008B/728